BECOMING MULTICULTURAL

BECOMING MULTICULTURAL
Immigration and the Politics of Membership in Canada and Germany

Triadafilos Triadafilopoulos

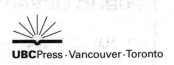

UBCPress · Vancouver · Toronto

20 19 18 17 16 15 14 13 12   5 4 3 2 1

Printed in Canada on FSC-certified ancient-forest-free paper
(100% post-consumer recycled) that is processed chlorine- and acid-free.

Library and Archives Canada Cataloguing in Publication

Triadafilopoulos, Triadafilos
    Becoming multicultural: immigration and the politics of membership in
Canada and Germany / Triadafilos Triadafilopoulos.

Includes bibliographical references and index.
Issued also in electronic formats.
ISBN 978-0-7748-1566-6

    1. Emigration and immigration – Government policy – Canada – History – 20th
century. 2. Emigration and immigration – Government policy – Germany – History
– 20th century. 3. Citizenship – Government policy – Canada – History – 20th
century. 4. Citizenship – Government policy – Germany – History – 20th century.
5. Multiculturalism – Canada – History – 20th century. 6. Multiculturalism –
Germany – History – 20th century. I. Title.

JV7225.T698 2012   325.7109'04   C2012-900549-5

Canadä

UBC Press gratefully acknowledges the financial support for our publishing program
of the Government of Canada (through the Canada Book Fund), the Canada Council
for the Arts, and the British Columbia Arts Council.

This book has been published with the help of a grant from the Canadian Federation
for the Humanities and Social Sciences, through the Aid to Scholarly Publications
Program, using funds provided by the Social Sciences and Humanities Research
Council of Canada.

UBC Press
The University of British Columbia
2029 West Mall
Vancouver, BC V6T 1Z2
www.ubcpress.ca

Contents

Acknowledgments

This book could not have been written without the support and generous assistance of a great many individuals and institutions. I am pleased to take this opportunity to express my sincere gratitude.

I thank Aristide Zolberg for being a tremendously valuable source of inspiration and knowledge, and a good friend whose warmth and generosity I treasure. I also thank Victoria Hattam, David Plotke, John Torpey, Adamantia Pollis, Patrick Hossay, Peter Benda, Fiona Adamson, Dagmar Soennecken, Willem Maas, Catherine Frost, Tobias Vogel, Barbara Syrrakos, Leah Bradshaw, Kevin Bruyneel, Joe Lowndes, Priscilla Yamin, and Andrej Zaslove for their important contributions to the development of this project in its early stages. Their skilful balancing of frank criticism and constructive advice and encouragement was essential to helping me sort out where I intended to go with the book.

Many more friends and colleagues also went well beyond the call of duty in providing support. Since arriving at the University of Toronto, I have been truly privileged to work with colleagues whose brilliance is matched by their generosity. I am particularly indebted to Joe Carens for his patience in providing equal combinations of wisdom and common sense. Thanks also to Randall Hansen, Jeffrey Kopstein, Linda White, Joe Wong, Lilach Gilady, Matthew Hoffmann, Wendy Wong, Nancy Kokaz, Christian Breunig, Grace Skogstad, Antoinette Handley, Audrey Macklin, Jeff Reitz, Donald Forbes, and Graham White for their criticism and suggestions. Karen Schönwälder,

James Ingram, Rainer Ohliger, Shaun Young, Myer Siemiatycki, Hesh Troper, and Anna Korteweg have been wonderful friends and critical readers whose solidarity I treasure.

I wish to acknowledge and express my gratitude for research support from the Social Sciences and Humanities Research Council of Canada, the European Union Center of New York, the German Academic Exchange Service (DAAD), and the University of Toronto's Connaught Foundation. I thank Rainer Münz, Ralf Ulrich, Antje Scheidler, Veysel Özcan, Stefan Alscher, Michael Wuttke, Dirk Zimmermann, Daniel Kovacs, Silvester Stahl, and Ingo Haar for their warm hospitality and friendship during my research stay in Berlin. I was fortunate to have had such wonderful hosts. Several other friends and colleagues in Berlin helped me with various scholarly and practical matters. I am particularly grateful to Kaoru Iriyama, Gustav and Ingrid Klipping, Peter Kraus, Silke Steinhilber, Susanne Schwalgin, Ulrich Preuß, Felicitas Hillmann, Matthias Tang, Hannes Heine, and Pertti Ahonen.

In Canada, John Widdes of Library and Archives Canada went out of his way to help me with my research and I thank him very much for his efforts on my behalf. I truly appreciate the late Tom Kent's willingness to discuss the origins of the points system with me: it was truly a privilege to confer with the principal architect of a structure I was so keen to understand. I also thank the many individuals in Germany who agreed to be interviewed for this book. Their insights and willingness to assist me in my research are truly appreciated.

I have been very fortunate to have worked with outstanding research assistants: Diana Aurisch, Salman Dostmohammad, Patricia Greve, Inder Marwah, Kelsey Norman, Natalie Conte, Sonja Friesel, Craig Smith, and Joerg Wittenbrinck. I thank them for going far beyond the call of duty and devoting so much care and attention to the book. It truly could not have been written without their help.

I have had the privilege of teaching and learning from excellent undergraduate students at the University of Toronto Scarborough and exceptional graduate students at the Department of Political Science and the School of Public Policy and Governance. I am particularly indebted to Deb Thompson, Jenn Wallner, and Rainer Thwaites for taking time from their busy schedules to read and comment on my work. It's good to see them all embark on successful academic careers. I am also indebted to the hardworking staff at the University of Toronto; their support has been absolutely essential and I thank them for their dedication. Thanks also to John Miron,

Ted Relph, Matt Hoffmann, David Cameron, and Mark Stabile for their excellent work as administrators.

Emily Andrew at UBC Press has become a good friend over the years that this book has been written. I truly appreciate her support, good humour, and always sage advice. She is a brilliant editor. Thanks also to the rest of the team at UBC Press, including but certainly not limited to Peter Milroy, Randy Schmidt, and Holly Keller.

My greatest debt is to my family. I humbly thank my mother, Panagiota Triadafilopoulos, for her many sacrifices. She works harder than anyone I know and loves more deeply too. I thank my brother John for his unflagging support, and my mother- and father-in-law, Metaxia and Nicholaos Koromilas.

I could not have completed this project without the love and support of my wife Mary, daughter Anastasia, and son Niko. Writing a book can be very difficult for loved ones: there are many missed occasions and far too many unreasonable demands. Mary, Stasia, and Niko accepted all of these impositions with love and understanding. I am very lucky to have them in my life.

My father, Anastasios Triadafilopoulos, died on October 25, 2009, after a long, courageous battle with cancer. He had a keen interest in my work and in this book in particular. I was lucky to spend some time with him discussing his immigration story, when his illness slowed him down enough to sit down and chat. What he shared with me during those occasions was gripping and put my work in a very different perspective. I am sorry I could not complete this book in time for him to read it. I dedicate it to his memory.

An earlier version of Chapter 2 appeared in the *Journal of Historical Sociology* 17, 4 (2004).

BECOMING MULTICULTURAL

1 Introduction

The division of the world into discrete, sovereign nation-states makes international migration a fundamentally political problem. Border crossing "is not merely movement in relation to environmental space, but a *process* whereby, in deviation from the universal norm in which the world is organized, individuals ... are transferred, temporarily or permanently, from the domain of one state to another" (emphasis added).[1] This change of domains on the part of migrants provokes receiving states to distinguish their status, rights, and membership prospects in relation to those of members of the established "national" society. This is true of all international migrants, be they carefully selected knowledge workers admitted with permanent resident status, temporary foreign workers whose stay and rights are bounded by strict contracts, or uninvited asylum seekers fleeing persecution. The rationale driving border crossing and distance travelled are of incidental importance; what matters conceptually "is the crossing of a border."[2]

This defining characteristic of international migration generates what I call the migration-membership dilemma. On the one hand, admitting migrants may help meet labour market requirements and serve related economic purposes or advance other ideological or political interests, as the acceptance of refugees often does. At the same time, the satisfaction of these objectives often provokes sharply negative reactions from actors with conflicting material interests and from those with a different set of normative priorities, such as the protection of national identity.[3] Efforts to address this clash of distinct interests and concerns drive the politics of membership. Immigration and citizenship policies not only determine whom states admit, on what grounds, to what ends, and in whose interests but also, in so doing, speak to more basic questions of identity: Who are we? Who do we wish to become? Does the admission of immigrants help us reach that goal? "And most fundamentally, which individuals constitute the 'we' who shall decide these questions?"[4]

This book explores Canada's and Germany's responses to the migration-membership dilemma in the twentieth century. My decision to compare Canada and Germany may strike some readers as puzzling. Canada and Germany have been assigned distinct statuses by students of immigration and citizenship politics. Canada is classified as a "classical immigration country" shaped by successive waves of migration, while Germany is cast as a prototypical "labour recruiting nation" grappling with the unfamiliar consequences of unwanted immigration.[5] As the "most-different-cases" approach to comparative research argues, however, these striking differences between Canada and Germany are what make them excellent cases for comparison.[6] Despite their differences, Canada's and Germany's responses to the migration-membership dilemma followed remarkably similar long-term trajectories. Both countries began the century by prohibiting the entry and incorporation of immigrants deemed undesirable because of their putative racial or ethno-national characteristics. Canada developed an array of policies and administrative practices that barred non-white migrants and upheld a vision of Canada as a "white man's country," while Germany combined a system of temporary foreign worker recruitment with a descent-based citizenship law that excluded "unwanted groups" and reinforced an ethno-cultural conception of German nationality.

Yet, by the end of the century, both Canada and Germany had developed into de facto multicultural societies as a result of liberalizing changes to their migration and citizenship policies. In Canada, the introduction of a universal admissions policy in 1967 and its entrenchment in the Immigration Act, 1976, shattered the foundations of "white Canada" and created the conditions for Canada's development into one of the most culturally diverse countries in the world. Whereas immigrants from "non-traditional" source regions, including Asia, the Caribbean, Latin America, and Africa, comprised only a tiny fraction of Canada's total immigration intake from 1946 to 1966, by 1977 they constituted over 50 percent of annual flows.[7] Today, "visible minorities" (the Canadian census term for "persons, other than

Aboriginal peoples, who are non-Caucasian in race or non-white in colour") make up half of Toronto's population and significant percentages in other large cities, such as Vancouver and Montreal.[8]

In Germany, failure to implement an effective mechanism for ensuring the "rotation" of temporary foreign workers in the 1960s and early-1970s led to mass immigration. On the eve of the "recruitment stop" of November 1973, Germany was host to some 2.6 million foreigners, including 605,000 Turks. But the 1973 recruitment stop did not put an end to immigration. Family reunification and refugee admissions pushed the total number of foreigners in Germany to 4.5 million, or 7.4 percent of the total population, by 1983, and the flow has continued since.[9] The presence of so many "foreigners" provoked intense debates over the appropriateness of Germany's restrictive citizenship law. Ultimately, the liberalization of naturalization policies in the early 1990s and the introduction of *jus soli* in 1999 granted former guest workers and their children greater access to German citizenship and, in so doing, transformed the boundaries of German nationhood.[10] This has led, in turn, to recent efforts to integrate Islam into Germany's elaborate system of church-state relations.[11] These developments speak to the profound changes postwar immigration has wrought in Germany.

The principal aim of this book is to explain how and why these consequential transformations in Canada's and Germany's membership regimes took place and, in so doing, to contribute to our understanding of the dynamics of membership politics and policy making in contemporary liberal-democratic countries. I explore three interrelated questions. First, I ask a question about long-term outcomes: Why did two countries so determined to limit cultural diversity through the first half of the twentieth century find themselves so thoroughly transformed by immigration at the beginning of the twenty-first? What explains the similarity in outcomes, especially given the striking differences between Canada and Germany in some respects? Second, I ask a question about timing and conflict. Although both countries ultimately changed their policies in fundamental ways, liberalizing change came relatively quickly and quietly in Canada and was slower, more contentious, and subject to compromise in Germany. What explains this difference? Was it due to the fact that Canada was a classical country of immigration and Germany was not? Or was it the result of other factors? Finally, I ask a question about the dynamics of the policy process. To what degree were the changes in Canadian and German policies the result of deliberate choices by policy makers, and to what extent were they the unintended outcome of other factors? Were policy dynamics similar in the two cases (like the fundamental transformations that took place in both) or different (like the differences in timing and conflict)?

In response to the first question, I argue that world-historical events and epoch-defining processes, including the Holocaust, decolonization, and the emergence of a global human rights culture, gave rise to a distinctive normative context in the post-Second World War period that discredited long-standing discriminatory policies. As self-declared liberal democracies, Canada and Germany found that their postwar commitments to human rights sat uneasily with their established immigration and citizenship policies – a point highlighted by domestic and international critics of racial and ethno-national discrimination. I argue that the similar transformation of membership policies in Canada and Germany was ultimately due to the preceding and profound underlying transformation of the normative context within which liberal states operated. Norms and corresponding ideas played a fundamental role in shaping answers to questions of membership.

With respect to explaining differences in the timing and degree of conflict accompanying policy change in Canada and Germany, I argue that two factors were of particular importance. On the one hand, I argue that differences in Canada's and Germany's respective traditions of nationhood and migration histories played a key role. This fits with arguments advanced by other scholars (and repeated with varying degrees of sophistication by politicians and members of the media and broader public).[12] On the other hand, I also argue that politics played a much more important role than many scholars have recognized and that variation in the political dynamics shaping membership debates in Canada and Germany were not simply the result of the underlying differences in conceptions of nationhood and migration but were also shaped in large part by differences in political institutions and corresponding political opportunities.[13] In short, if the similarity in long-term outcomes shows that norms and corresponding ideas matter, differences in the timing and degree of conflict show that politics also matters.

Finally, with respect to the question of policy dynamics, I argue that changes in the two cases followed a remarkably similar pattern despite the differences in timing and degree of conflict. This was not, however, because policy makers embraced the underlying shift in the normative context of liberal democracy. On the contrary, in both states policy makers initially resisted these ideological changes. Rather than comprehensively amending their policies to meet the expectations of a new normative context, policy makers made modest adjustments to established policy regimes in an effort to co-opt critics. Their central objective in both cases was the preservation of prevailing notions of membership. In both cases, this strategy backfired, as seemingly modest concessions aimed at mollifying critics and preserving the status quo encouraged further challenges, which, in turn, necessitated additional amendments. In time, once-coherent policy regimes devolved into confused and confusing patchworks that were of little use to officials charged with administering their country's membership policies. In both Canada and Germany, policy makers were compelled to reconsider their approaches to the migration-membership dilemma in a more fundamental way than they had intended, ultimately introducing changes that aligned their states' immigration and citizenship policies with the standards of the prevailing normative context.

The remainder of this chapter unpacks the arguments and resulting analytical framework sketched above. I begin by detailing my understanding of how global normative contexts intersect with and influence domestic politics. Next, I consider how to account for "variation *within* convergence" – that is, how to explain differences in the precise timing and nature of broadly similar outcomes.[14] Finally, I outline my conceptualization of the dynamics of norm-driven policy change.

The approach developed in this book is reflective of what Ira Katznelson dubs "configurative macro-analysis": Agents' actions are situated in distinctive world-historical periods and domestic political contexts to track "how structures constitute and cause identities and actions by tilting and organizing possibilities."[15] As the chapter summary that concludes this introduction suggests, meeting this end requires pivoting from theoretically informed comparisons of normatively distinct historical eras to tracing processes of policy change via detailed case studies. My methodological approach is in keeping with the complexity of the book's subject matter and the challenge of explaining processes as profound as those that so transformed Canada and Germany in the second half of the twentieth century.

Argument and Analytical Framework

Normative Contexts

States' responses to the migration-membership dilemma depend on a host of factors, including economic requirements, real and perceived demographic needs, and distinctive traditions of nationhood. Limiting our attention to these domestic variables, however, obscures more encompassing structures that influence outcomes across states. As Aristide Zolberg notes, domestic policy making "takes place within the context provided by changing conditions in the world at large. Hence ... analysis must take into account the configuration of international conditions that generates changing opportunities and challenges in relation to ... immigration."[16] Zolberg's efforts to explain the development of immigration policies in relation to changing "world systems" – shaped by the "dynamics of world capitalism, on the one hand, and the international state system, on the other" – represents one important effort along these lines.[17]

Scholars associated with the "Stanford School" of sociological institutionalism argue that global macrostructures extend beyond the interstate system and global economy to include a distinctive "global culture." This global culture is rational and modernizing, privileging certain modes of social organization and understandings of progress.[18] Among the most important attributes of world culture in the post-Second World War period are human rights; indeed, the Stanford School sociologists maintain that legitimate statehood is premised on states' acceptance of human rights.[19] Global culture is thus understood as an independent force shaping state development – ensuring that states otherwise separated by geography, history, and local cultures come to share strikingly similar institutions in core areas of social organization.

Alan Cairns' work on the transformation of indigenous peoples' politics in Canada provides a useful application of the Stanford School's approach. In *Citizens Plus*, Cairns argues that the dramatic contrast in historic assumptions governing Aboriginal/non-Aboriginal relations in Canada and contemporary paradigms – specifically the move from assimilationist models to models based on self-government – cannot be understood without recognizing the impact of changing global norms, in particular the demise of European colonialism:

> Put simply, if somewhat exaggeratedly, the world turned over in the decades following the Second World War ... The independence of dozens of former colonies in Africa and Asia eroded the close correlation between whiteness, or Europeanness, and imperial power that had long prevailed. In that former era, the message that tumbled across state borders in Canada and other Western countries made the subject, marginalized, and outsider status of Aboriginal peoples appear to be in the nature of things. Now, the nature of things outside our Canadian window is very different. A pale skin no longer carries with it an entitlement to rule over those whose skin is pigmented or whose cheekbones are differently shaped.[20]

Postnationalist theories of citizenship also emphasize the importance of global culture in explaining the extension of rights to non-citizens in the postwar period. Yasemin Soysal argues that postwar changes in the organization and ideologies of the global system "shifted the institutional and normative basis of citizenship to a transnational level ... extend[ing the] rights and privileges associated with it beyond national boundaries."[21] Similarly, Saskia Sassen contends: "the *legitimization process* of states under the rule of law calls for respect and enforcement of *international human rights codes*, regardless of the nationality and legal status of the individual" (emphasis added).[22]

Constructivists in the field of International Relations usefully note that the "power" of global norms varies across cases in relation to regime type.[23] According to Jeffrey Checkel, international norms are embraced more readily in cases in which they cohere with domestic norms – liberalizing norms will likely have greater purchase among liberal regimes.[24] Amy Gurowitz adds that states concerned with their standing internationally will also be more vulnerable to criticisms levelled by reformers.[25] Foreign policy interests, particularly regarding states' efforts to join or lead the "international community," influence the degree to which they acknowledge and incorporate global norms. Christian Joppke, formerly a staunch critic of postnationalist arguments,[26] now acknowledges that the "outlawing of race" following the Allies' victory over Nazi Germany prompted the emergence of a global human rights culture that made it difficult for liberal-democratic states to maintain discriminatory immigration policies.[27] Like Gurowitz, Joppke stresses the importance of foreign policy considerations in driving liberal states' embrace of non-discrimination in immigration policy after the Second World War.

My conceptualization of "normative contexts" builds on these insights. Normative contexts consist of complex configurations of global structures (e.g., the international state system), processes (e.g., colonialism, decolonization), and beliefs (e.g., scientific racism versus human rights) that encompass and shape domestic policy making, authorizing particular political identities, policies, and practices while discrediting others. The legitimacy of domestic institutions – understood broadly to include rules, practices, and policy frameworks – is based not only on their efficiency but also on their "fit" with the generic norms of appropriate behaviour that constitute international society.[28] These rules are subject to change: shifts in normative contexts throw policies enacted under previous contexts into doubt as the grounds of legitimacy underpinning them are challenged.[29] Normative contexts thus embody a particular era's moral foundations: states' decisions as to whom to admit into their national space and on what grounds have much to do with how their decision makers think about the morality of exclusion as measured against prevailing normative standards.

I distinguish between two periods with distinct normative contexts. The first period spans the turn of the twentieth century until the Second World War. The second emerges as a consequence of the war and related developments, including the Holocaust, decolonization, and the emergence of a global human rights culture. Both contexts had a profound effect on immigration and citizenship policies in Canada, Germany, and other immigrant-receiving countries. Solutions to the migration-membership dilemma devised at the turn of the twentieth century through the interwar period were influenced by prevailing attitudes towards racial and ethnic difference, nationalism, and state sovereignty, tending, on the whole, to legitimize discriminatory exclusions and the heavy-handed use of state power. Immigration selection was predicated on notions of racial suitability. Certain peoples were deemed incapable of contributing to the development of "civilized" nations.[30] Just as eugenics policies sought to limit the influence of "substandard" domestic groups and individuals through instruments such as sterilization, discriminatory immigration and citizenship policies and practices were devised with an eye to guarding the nation against foreign threats.[31] Prevailing views of state sovereignty also justified the indiscriminate use of coercion, exercised most decisively through the summary deportation of "unwanted aliens." In short, the illiberal worldviews and ideas that so marked the late nineteenth and early twentieth centuries informed and sanctioned states' illiberal responses to the migration-membership dilemma.

The discrediting of scientific racism, integral nationalism, and white supremacy as a consequence of the Second World War, the Holocaust, and decolonization established a starkly different logic of appropriateness for states claiming a liberal-democratic identity in the postwar period. The group-centred racism of the prewar period gave way to an individualist ethic, holding that all persons were endowed with fundamental rights regardless of their race, ethnicity, or nationality. This message was advanced through postwar social science, international organizations such as the United Nations, and the human rights statements and instruments that proliferated during this period. As a result, established policy regimes came under pressure as individual rights-based claims for equal treatment made by and on behalf of previously excluded groups clashed with the rights-denying policies and practices they informed. Canada's and Germany's identification as liberal-democratic countries that respected the rule of law and human rights made them especially vulnerable to charges of hypocrisy by domestic and international critics of their immigration and citizenship policies. This is not to say that racial discrimination disappeared after the Second World War; rather, the discrediting of racism and integral national-ism as legitimizing principles made discriminatory policies harder to de-fend and maintain in the face of normatively sanctioned criticism. In both Canada and Germany, governments' sensitivity to these views created the conditions for policy change.

Politics and Policy Change: Explaining Variation within Convergence

Although analogous forces drove changes in Canada's and Germany's im-migration and citizenship policies, the precise timing and nature of policy change in the two cases differed. Policy change in Canada was character-ized by what Hugh Heclo refers to as "puzzling" – processes of trial and error shaped by the pursuit of relatively well-defined goals on the part of relatively small and insulated groups of experts.[32] Conversely, liberalization in Germany was very much in line with "powering" in that change was more politicized, less coherent, and subject to delay and compromise.

Three factors shaped Canada's and Germany's respective paths towards reform. First, distinctive "traditions of nationhood" played a key role in steering actors' choices of issues and symbols, helping to determine which battles were fought, how broadly reformers' criticisms resonated, and what solutions emerged.[33] Canada's self-identification as a settler country meant that immigration itself was accepted (if at times grudgingly), and debate re-volved instead around the legitimacy of criteria used to regulate admissions and to grant immigrants access to citizenship via naturalization. Germany's quite different migration history meant that the very idea of Germany's be-ing an immigration country was hotly contested. In the absence of consen-sus on such a basic point, it was all the more difficult to rationally debate the incorporation of former guest workers and their children.

Second, formal political institutions such as electoral laws, party sys-tems, federalism, and judicial review shaped actors' political strategies, en-abling support for reform in some instances while creating opportunities for opposition in others.[34] A key difference in this regard lay in the manner in which institutions engendered political consensus in Canada while prompting its erosion in Germany. In Canada, "one party government in a parliamentary system ... tended to reinforce the effects of executive policy-making by dramatically curtailing avenues for challenging ... policies."[35] The dominance of the federal Cabinet in the sphere of immigration policy during the period under consideration allowed for an insulated form of policy making that engendered experimentation, elite learning, and the relatively rapid implementation of new policies.

In contrast, the combination of frequent electoral cycles and multiple veto points in Germany provided opponents of liberalization opportunities that were unavailable to their counterparts in Canada.[36] We should not imagine that differences in conceptions of nationhood and experiences of migration made it impossible for political actors in Germany to consider any fundamental change in membership policy. On the contrary, Germany's unwillingness to expel workers who had been explicitly admitted on the understanding that their stay would be temporary, and its acceptance of ongoing family reunification for immigrants in Germany after the 1973 recruitment stop, show that the new postwar normative context was already setting important limits to the power of traditional understandings of German nationhood and policies towards migrants. Indeed, citizenship reform was being advanced by mainstream German political leaders as early as the 1970s.[37] As was true in Canada, changes in normative contexts profoundly shaped Germany's membership debates and policies. Unlike Canada, however, opponents of liberalization were able to exploit opportunities made available to them by virtue of Germany's institutional configuration when they concluded that it was in their interests to do so. As a result, policy making during much of the 1980s and 1990s was marked by highly symbolic, rhetorically charged debates that typically ended in non-decisions, policy drift, and awkward compromises that left all sides dissatisfied and were suboptimal from the standard of policy effectiveness.

Finally, it is important to note the importance of historical contingency in shaping the tenor of membership debates and policy making.[38] Canada's turn to a universalistic admissions regime occurred during a period of general economic prosperity, which coincided with efforts to distinguish Canada's national identity from that of Britain and the United States.[39] As Richard Alba persuasively argues, the extension of membership boundaries typically generates less opposition where prosperity limits the losses in social and economic standing of hitherto dominant groups (the theory of "non-zero sum mobility").[40] Conversely, Germany's transition occurred during a more fraught period, marked by the end of the postwar economic boom, the onset of unemployment, and the massive social-political disruption generated by the end of the Cold War and reunification.[41] Not surprisingly, under such conditions, calls for changes in membership boundaries *did* elicit concern among members of the broader public. Political entrepreneurs responded to and exacerbated this concern for self-interested political ends, transforming migration policy from an issue based on political consensus to one marked by divisiveness and often bitter acrimony.

Theorizing Normatively Driven Policy Change: Stretching, Unravelling, and Shifting

If, as I claim, broadly encompassing normative contexts influenced domestic politics and policy making, what were the conduits through which this normative context worked? Given the differences in the timing of change and the degree of contestation, were the dynamics of change similar or different in the two cases?

I identify three mechanisms through which the changing normative context influenced Canada's and Germany's immigration and citizenship policies: policy stretching, unravelling, and shifting. My use of the term "stretching" aims to capture the dynamic tension that arises when entrenched policy regimes that reflect taken-for-granted ideas, terminology, and practices carry over into new normative contexts. The result of such conjunctions is not abrupt and radical transformations in policy, as theories of punctuated equilibrium would suggest;[42] rather, change unfolds incrementally as policy makers seek to reconcile the unfamiliar demands of a newly emerging normative order with the deeply engrained, path-dependent logic of established policy frameworks.[43] As per evolutionary models of institutional change, extant policy regimes are adapted to meet these new demands through modest adjustments at their margins.[44]

Stretching is thus a variant of incrementalism,[45] albeit with an important twist: whereas standard incrementalist theories cast policy makers as modestly groping towards some new end in a cost-averse manner, in the sense understood here, their actions are directed towards preserving the overarching goals of the established policy regime. Stretching is not so much about "muddling through" policy challenges as it is about deflecting them in the name of staying true to established goals. It is a reactive strategy with a conservative purpose, similar to Peter Hall's conceptualization of "normal policymaking," wherein policy makers "adjust policy without challenging the overall terms of [established] policy paradigm[s]" through "first and second order change" – alterations to the settings of policy instruments and, on occasion, more substantive changes to the instruments themselves.[46]

With regard to the cases at hand, while the disjuncture between postwar norms and established immigration and citizenship policies was quickly registered by Canadian and German policy makers, they did not respond by searching for radically new solutions to the migration-membership dilemma. Rather, their initial response to the friction generated by this clash of discordant political logics was to stretch policies to address inconsistencies without abandoning the core premises and objectives of extant frameworks.[47] These initial changes were therefore instrumental and cosmetic, undertaken with the aim of diffusing criticism rather than altering prevailing policy objectives.

Contrary to policy makers' intentions and expectations, however, these modest responses propelled the unravelling of the policy frameworks they were meant to serve. Most important, attempts to answer critics with tactical concessions affirmed the normative validity of their claims. This had two important effects. First, it drew policy makers into discursive exchanges that privileged the language of their critics while further undermining the fundamental premises of established frameworks.[48] As per Thomas Risse's "spiral model" of norm diffusion,[49] a process of discursive "self-entrapment" drove the reform process forward, engendering what Seyla Benhabib usefully terms "democratic iterations[:] complex processes of public argument, deliberations, and exchanges through which universalist claims are contested and contextualized, invoked and revoked, posited and positioned."[50] Once they committed to speaking the language of rights, policy makers could not easily end their conversations or return to prewar tropes and standards in defending their positions.

Second, policy stretching enhanced domestic critics' standing and helped generate support for their projects. As demands for reform grew louder, more frequent, and increasingly sophisticated, policy makers were forced to make additional concessions that further undermined the coherence and administrative efficacy of existing policy paradigms. Over time, policy stretching reduced once-coherent frameworks to messy patchworks held together by contradictory principles working at cross-purposes.

The unravelling of established policy regimes created opportunities for the formulation of approaches to the migration-membership dilemma that were more consistent with the postwar normative context. The elaboration of alternative approaches to the migration-membership dilemma and their translation into public policy marked the transition from policy unravelling to policy shifting. The implementation of new approaches was subject to institutionally patterned political dynamics, which affected the timing of and degree to which new approaches to the migration-membership dilemma were entrenched in law, administrative practices, and governing mindsets.

In sum, changes in broadly encompassing normative contexts in the postwar period challenged Canada's and Germany's ability to shape their responses to the migration-membership dilemma as they had in the past. While both states were subject to comparable pressures and reacted in similar ways, their unique histories, conceptions of national identity, and political institutional configurations shaped the politics of membership in distinctive ways, leading to variation in the timing and nature of policy change. In important respects, however, change followed a similar pattern: policy makers in both countries responded to changing normative contexts by enacting small-scale, symbolic concessions in the name of mollifying critics and preserving extant regimes to the greatest extent possible. These small changes had powerful and unexpected consequences, opening the door to further challenges and, ultimately, the reorientation of membership policies in both countries.

Overview of the Book

Chapter 2 explores the origins of Canada's and Germany's initial solutions to the migration-membership dilemma, tracing their development from the turn of the twentieth century through the interwar period. I argue that forces unleashed by the second industrial revolution and improvements in transportation technologies increased the scale of international migration to new levels, forcing both countries to develop policies that regulated admissions, residency, and citizenship. By the end of the 1920s, Canada and Germany had developed distinctive policy frameworks entrenched in legislation, institutions, and practices. Exclusions based on prevailing notions of race and ethnicity were institutionalized to reinforce dominant conceptions of national homogeneity. Canada's and Germany's responses to the migration-membership dilemma during this period were in keeping with the prevailing normative context, reflecting the influence of scientific racism, integral nationalism, and contemporary understandings of state sovereignty. The chapter concludes by describing how the radicalization of *völkisch* nationalism under the Nazis and the racist exclusions dominating Canadian immigration policy intersected in the late 1930s, gravely influencing the fate of European Jews who were fleeing fascism.

Chapter 3 describes how normative contexts shifted as a result of the Second World War and its legacy. I discuss the impact of the Holocaust in this regard, linking the horror of Nazi barbarity to the emergence of the global human rights movement and the discrediting of scientific racism. The impact of decolonization on the international system is also explored. I then demonstrate how the normative context forged by these world-historical developments influenced Canada's and West Germany's approaches to the migration-membership dilemma in the early postwar period.

Policy makers in Canada and Germany reacted to changing norms by stretching familiar policy frameworks to co-opt real and anticipated criticism. This entailed dropping explicitly racist and otherwise morally dubious language and granting symbolic concessions to critics. In both cases, however, policy stretching generated unintended effects that drove policy unravelling. In Canada, the repeal of the Chinese Immigration Act and the enfranchisement of Asian Canadians granted this group political voice, which it used to lobby officials through the 1950s and 1960s. Concessions to other groups, including the establishment of an annual quota for immigration from India, Pakistan, and Ceylon, also signalled that the state recognized the dubious implications of continuing racial discrimination. In Germany, failure to implement effective mechanisms for ensuring the "rotation" of guest workers allowed millions of foreign workers to settle in the Federal Republic. Their presence prompted changes to policies concerning residency and family reunification, which, in time, challenged the ethnically exclusive nature of German citizenship law. In both Canada and Germany, then, incremental changes associated with policy stretching undermined the intellectual coherence and administrative efficacy of established policy frameworks, hastening their unravelling and opening space for the introduction of new ideas and initiatives.

The final part of the story documents the emergence and implementation of alternative solutions to the migration-membership dilemma. Chapter 4 analyzes the dismantling of racially discriminatory immigration policies in Canada from 1962 to 1967 and the institutionalization of a universal admissions policy in the Immigration Act, 1976. I argue that the rejection of discriminatory admissions criteria in 1962 was not driven by economic concerns, as is often claimed,[51] but by the need to respond convincingly to charges that Canadian immigration policy was racist. The introduction of civil rights legislation by federal and provincial governments and efforts to fashion a distinctive Canadian foreign policy based on principled opposition to colonialism and apartheid made it impossible to continue stretching the established immigration policy regime and necessitated a break with past practices. However, the changes introduced in 1962 failed to satisfy critics, who argued that the Canadian state's commitment to universal admissions criteria was a ploy meant to mask ongoing discrimination. I contend that the points system was developed as a response to critics' demands that Canada introduce a transparent set of criteria for judging immigrants' skills and education. It also addressed policy makers' concerns regarding the flow of sponsored immigrants from "non-traditional sources." Thus, the points system was not simply a tool to harness immigration for economic needs; it was also a unique innovation intimately linked to the liberalization of Canada's immigrant admissions regime.

Chapter 4 concludes with a discussion of the institutionalization of Canada's universalistic policy paradigm in the 1970s. I explain how political consensus in support of the new policy regime was maintained despite growing popular concern over the impact of "Third World" immigration on Canadian national identity. "New" immigrants' concentration in urban electoral ridings and demonstrated ability to mobilize in defence of their interests made them an important political constituency that no political party could afford to alienate – all the more so given the extremely competitive nature of the party system in the early-1970s and the disciplining function of Canada's single-member plurality ("first past the post") electoral system. Opponents of reform lacked an institutional venue for expressing their discontent and were therefore shut out of debates, which, in turn, limited their influence on policy making. The result was a process characterized by elite consensus and bereft of the partisan politics that was to be so decisive in Germany.

Chapter 5 examines policy shifting in Germany. Although the settlement of millions of guest workers in the Federal Republic led some officials to recognize the need for robust integration policies, their recommendations were largely ignored as the government of Helmut Schmidt opted for a policy of "temporary integration" based on the notion that Germany was "not an immigration country." The futility of this position was evident in the early 1980s as the number of foreigners in Germany increased and the need for their integration became undeniable. Yet, in marked contrast to the Canadian case, the shift from a failed policy of "temporary integration" to the recognition of Germany's de facto status as an immigration country stalled as "foreigners policy" (*Ausländerpolitik*) became politicized.

The period of Christian Democratic Union/Christian Social Union hegemony (1982-98) marked the breakdown of cross-party political consensus, with the Union parties initially opting to encourage the voluntary return of "foreigners," while their coalition partner, the Free Democratic Party, along with the Social Democratic Party, the Greens, and a determined coalition of civil society groups, demanded more liberal policies on residency, family reunification, and citizenship. Contrary to Rogers Brubaker's claim that the stasis of the 1980s and early-1990s reflected an elite consensus on the inviolability of ethnic German nationhood,[52] I demonstrate that change was effectively blocked by the standoff between conservatives and reformers – a confrontation exacerbated by changes in the German party system and federalism after unification.

Despite this, the period of the late-1980s and early-1990s witnessed the development of new solutions to the migration-membership dilemma. The election of the Social Democratic Party-Green coalition government in 1998 created an opportunity for the implementation of these ideas through the official recognition of Germany's status as an immigration country and the introduction of policies such as *jus soli*. Even here, however, political opposition to reform enabled by Germany's institutional configuration led to strained solutions that embodied conflicting principles. The most glaring of these compromises is the 1999 law's simultaneous embrace of *jus soli* and rejection of dual citizenship. As a result of this paradoxical combination, between the ages of eighteen and twenty-three, children born in Germany of foreign parents must choose between their German citizenship and that of their parents. I conclude with a brief synopsis of German citizenship policy making in the years since the 1999 reform, paying attention to the consequences of the compromises struck in the course of passing the 1999 reform.

In Chapter 6, in light of the insights generated by my case studies, I revisit the question of how broadly encompassing normative contexts shape politics and policy making. I argue that norms enable rights-based politics by changing the rules of the political game. While policy change is driven by domestic politics, we cannot make sense of similarities in broad outcomes without taking seriously the power of broader global norms and ideas. Hence, analyses of the role of norms should treat them as resources that influence politics rather than as definitive rules that dictate policy.

I conclude with a brief consideration of the ongoing politics of membership in Canada and Germany, paying particular attention to the re-emergence of religion in considerations of liberal-democratic nationhood. While both Canada and Germany have acknowledged the momentous social transformations wrought by postwar immigration, they are still searching for means of adapting national membership to the challenges of cultural plurality, particularly as it relates to religion. As such, the process of becoming multicultural – of adapting existing institutions, policies, and practices rooted in longheld assumptions to a new, more plural reality – constitutes an ongoing project whose importance is likely to increase in the years ahead.

2 Building Walls, Bounding Nations

Canada and Germany emerged as independent states in the latter part of the nineteenth century. Despite differences in geography, historical development, and regime type, similarities in the two states' approaches to the regulation of mass migration in this era of unprecedented globalization are striking.[1] Whereas migration was seized upon to meet the needs of rapidly expanding industrial and commercial agricultural sectors, restrictions aimed at guarding the nation against the "invasion" of "non-preferred" groups were also conceived, debated, and enacted. Globalization catalyzed a "double movement," facilitating the expansion of transnational migration on a hitherto unsurpassed scale, while also prompting a political response in the form of immigration controls designed to further national integration.[2] In Canada, efforts to keep out "unwanted races" culminated in a complex policy regime based on discriminatory admission and naturalization policies. In Germany, the threat of "Polonization" led to the development of a temporary labour recruitment model, while efforts to exclude Poles and East European Jews from national membership influenced the formulation of the highly restrictive *Reichs- und Staatsangehörigkeitsgesetz* (RuStAG [Citizenship Law]) of 1913. In both countries, solutions to the migration-membership dilemma were entrenched in durable institutions that shaped policy making in subsequent years. Exclusion based on race and ethnicity reinforced Canada's identity as a "white man's country" and Germany's ethno-cultural nationalism.

International Migration during the First Wave of Globalization

The years spanning the turn of the twentieth century were marked by a rapid surge in globalization. Vast networks of newly built transcontinental railways and transoceanic steamship lines enabled goods and people to move on an unprecedented scale with remarkable speed.[3] Improvements in technology, coupled with increased competition among providers, reduced the cost of travel significantly, enabling greater numbers of people to take advantage of these improvements.[4] The growth of the shipping industry helped to catalyze the expansion of emigration as "companies actively promoted their services and recruited passengers," much as they had in the past with regard to northwestern Europe, "but on a commensurately much larger scale."[5] The Hamburg-America line organized a network of agents in Russia and Eastern Europe from the 1870s onward; these agents played a key part in facilitating the movement of East European Jews to North America via the German port cities of Bremen and Hamburg.[6]

The emergence of a nascent worldwide communications network based on mass literacy and the proliferation of print media meant that information concerning hitherto far-off and unknown lands would be available to potential migrants.[7] States in search of "suitable" migrants, such as Canada and Australia, provided some of this information through extensive promotional campaigns that included printed literature, slide shows, and speaking tours.[8] Official and unofficial information, such as that provided by friends and relatives who had already emigrated, helped link sending and receiving regions in transnational networks; these, in turn, facilitated further movement.

The combination of steadily declining rates of mortality, improvements in the production and distribution of food, and the radical dislocation of traditional ways of life brought on by the second industrial revolution ensured that there was a large pool of dispossessed labourers who were willing to migrate in the hope of finding work:

> As land became more concentrated and production more specialized ... farmers found that the traditional system of service based on an annual contract providing housing as well as wages economically burdensome ... With the shift to short-term work, social ties and shared interests binding landlords to workers were severed, leaving large numbers without housing or sustenance ... As capital moved to urban sites and fled some regions altogether, the European countryside was deindustrialized; chances for finding village work disappeared and the pay rates for rural goods declined, reducing the ability of country workers to get by in the cottage economy.[9]

Through the course of the nineteenth century, the "great transformation" set in motion by industrialization contributed to the steady loosening of long-standing controls on internal movement.[10] As the real and perceived social repercussions of internal mobility were registered, more and more states followed Britain's lead and began to view emigration as a "safety valve" capable of offsetting the negative social impact of industrialization.[11] Thus, long-standing barriers to exit were loosened in countries throughout Europe, increasing the scope of transnational movement.[12]

These epochal changes had a direct impact on international migration. Turn-of-the-century globalization

> induced a vast expansion of international migrations to unprecedented and hitherto truly inconceivable levels. Most spectacularly visible, in the Atlantic region as a whole (including both within Europe and overseas) the combined international flows grew fourfold within a forty-year period, from 2.7 million for the 1871-1880 decade to over 11 million in 1901-1910. Overseas migration to the major receivers alone (Argentina, Brazil, Canada, and the United States) expanded in the same span by an even more dramatic fivefold factor, from 2.6 million to 12.9 million.[13]

Not only did the scale of immigration expand markedly but also the geographic range of sending countries. Industrial capitalism's penetration into Europe's southern and eastern hinterlands prompted a significant increase in migration from these areas.[14] Italy, the Austro-Hungarian Empire, Russia, and the newly independent Balkan states all experienced high rates of emigration during this time and quickly developed into important sending countries. Violence visited upon religious and national minorities, particularly East European Jews, also contributed to the great waves of emigration from these regions.[15]

The thrust of European imperialism into Asia prompted mass population movements from this part of the world as well – a process driven in large part by increasing demand for commodities such as natural rubber, palm oil, cotton, coffee, cocoa, tea, and sugar in Europe. These commodities were produced in plantations owned by white Europeans and worked, for the most part, by imported Asian indentured labourers – the preferred form of colonial labour in the era following the abolition of the slave trade.[16] "Coolie" labour was based on "short-term contracts bound by penal sanctions, linked to debts incurred in transit and invariably barbaric in its working conditions and levels of pay."[17] While indentured workers from India served as the key source of labour throughout the expanses of the British Empire, Chinese migration was also important, particularly in Southeast Asia and Australia, New Zealand, the United States, and Canada.[18]

In sum, turn-of-the-century globalization catalyzed and helped propel mass migration of hitherto unsurpassed scope and scale. More and more immigrants from increasingly variegated sources made their way to receiving states to work in factories and mines, build railways, plant and pick crops, and take up the other dirty, difficult, and poorly paid jobs offered to them, often raising the ire of the native workers they encountered.[19] Because rates of international migration accelerated so quickly, receiving states initially lacked the legal and administrative wherewithal to deal with this movement and therefore had to create mechanisms for managing flows and their social consequences.[20] Thus, this was also a period of extensive policy experimentation among receiving countries. While economic factors – principally employers' demands for cheap and abundant labour – weighed heavily on the minds of policy makers and helped sustain a period of relatively open borders, two other central preoccupations of the late nineteenth and early twentieth century – race and national identity – also played a key role in shaping incipient immigration and citizenship policies. The restrictions that were implemented were not simply barriers to movement; they were barriers to particular, racially defined peoples whose presence was deemed to be harmful to the development of the nation. Thus, a period of globalization and unsurpassed levels of international migration also witnessed the emergence of racially discriminatory immigration and citizenship policies.

Race and National Identity during the First Wave of Globalization

Among the most striking features of the late nineteenth and early twentieth centuries was the widespread appeal of racism, by which I do not mean simple racial discrimination – a pernicious and all too common feature of contemporary societies – but a pervasive, scientifically sanctioned belief in the superiority of the "white races" of northwestern Europe over other peoples within and beyond Europe.[21] Race thinking infused the programs of liberal and illiberal governments, informed discussion in polite and impolite company, and filled the pages of the popular press and learned scientific journals. Race and racially tinged integral nationalism were ubiquitous.

Ideas about race and the hierarchical relation of distinct human types qua races predate the first wave of globalization.[22] What was different about turn-of-the-century racism was its scientific moorings and the way it melded with concepts of nationhood.[23] Charles Darwin's *On the Origins of the Species* (1859) and *The Descent of Man* (1871) propelled the emergence of a widely accepted science of race that branched into specialized fields such as physical anthropology and eugenics.[24] The new, "scientific" racism

> assumed that the human family was not one but many ... [and] that those different families were marked out by their appearance, their abilities and, in some quasi-religious sense, by the purposes for which they had been created. And it supposed that those differences, since they were as we would say today, "genetically determined," could not be altered substantially by education, persuasion or example.[25]

Building on these core precepts, scholars devised intricate racial hierarchies that ranked groups according to their inherent traits and evolutionary development.[26] White Europeans of "Aryan," "Caucasian," "Anglo-Saxon," or "Teutonic" stock were deemed superior in all respects based on their genetic make-up.[27] Conversely, lower-level Europeans (e.g., "Mediterraneans") and non-Europeans (Asians, Africans, Jews, etc.) were considered inherently and irremediably inferior and threatening. Chief among the myriad concerns haunting race scientists was the spectre of dilution: "race mixing" would lead to the weakening of the superior white races and the emergence of impure, "mongrel breeds" lacking the biological capacity for advanced civilization.[28] Racial quarantine was advanced as a means of preserving the "stock" of superior races, upon which the future of civilization itself depended.[29]

Intellectual work along these lines mapped onto and reinforced other contemporaneous processes, including imperialism and nation building.[30] With regard to imperialism, scientific racism reinforced the notion that differences in human types sanctioned the subjugation of "inferior peoples" by white Europeans: "Subjects of Empire were seen as unworthy of self-rule, as backward, as culturally interior, and so forth."[31] This division of the world into civilized peoples subject to international law and custom, on the one hand, and uncivilized "savages," on the other, was reflected in imperial conduct: "Where no reciprocity of civilized behavior could be expected, European armies were taught they need not observe them – or indeed in some versions – any rules at all ... After all, savages were impressed only by force; fanaticism could be stopped only through an awesome demonstration of technological superiority."[32]

This outward orientation had an important domestic concomitant as assumptions along these lines "embedded themselves in immigration policies, in the treatment of indigenous peoples, in the teaching of history, and in the basic world views of all Western peoples, even those who possessed no formal colonies across the water."[33] Scientific racism helped to form a broadly encompassing global-level cultural code, "popularized through novels, plays, popular science literature, public lectures and museum displays,"[34] that embedded ideas of racial hierarchy into the "common sense" of the period. Categories used to define groups in national censuses helped reinforce the logic of racial difference by dividing populations into discrete groups whose identity was based on science and authorized by the authority of the state.[35]

The ubiquity of racial classifications and the linking of race with national identity help make sense of the striking similarity of immigration restrictions and controls across receiving states during the first phase of globalization. Ideas about racial suitability intersected with economic and national security concerns so that specific groups were deemed particularly dangerous. Policies were enacted to restrict the entry and incorporation of these groups, thus avoiding "contamination from ... those who would pass along their deficiencies."[36] Immigration policies thus complemented eugenics policies such as sterilization. Both sought to protect the nation from threatening (because inferior) groups: domestic in the case of eugenics, external/foreign in the case of immigration policy.[37]

Liberalism's comfortable co-existence with scientific racism and xenophobia during this period of policy innovation ensured that the equality it propounded was reserved for members of "civilized peoples." States enjoyed significant discretion in enacting highly illiberal laws barring the entry and incorporation of unwanted groups – whether or not they professed to uphold liberal-democratic principles. Hence, in terms of their efforts to use immigration to meet economic needs without disrupting the course of nation-building projects, Canada and Germany followed remarkably similar immigration and citizenship policy trajectories during this period. While the precise nature of their solutions to the migration-membership dilemma differed, they shared the goal of limiting the entry and incorporation of "inferior," and hence unwanted, groups.

Immigration Policy and the Construction of White Canada, 1869-1929

Colonization and Early Settlement
Immigration was limited during most of Canada's colonial history. France's efforts to settle colonists in the territory Jacques Cartier claimed for Francis I in 1534 were intermittent and unsuccessful. Only approximately ten

thousand colonists were settled in New France in the years preceding the British conquest in 1760.[38] Population growth, which had reached seventy thousand on the eve of the French defeat, was driven almost exclusively by natural increase. Britain's early hopes of quickly assimilating its new French Roman Catholic subjects also came to very little. In lieu of the hoped for influx of British subjects – and mindful of the security threat posed by revolutionary developments in its restive colonies to the south – Britain granted grudging recognition of the "French fact" in North America through the passage of the Quebec Act, 1774.[39]

The onset of the American War of Independence in 1775 gave rise to Canada's first wave of mass immigration. Approximately fifty thousand Loyalist refugees fled the incipient American republic and settled in British North America. Their arrival and demand for institutions befitting loyal subjects of the British Crown prompted another round of institutional change, leading to the creation of New Brunswick in 1784 and, significantly, the division of Quebec into Lower Canada (present-day Quebec) and Upper Canada (present-day Ontario) under the Constitution Act, 1791. The arrival of the Loyalists also helped to fix Canada's emerging political identity: although the Constitution Act recognized the position of the Roman Catholic Church and maintained established patterns of land holding in Quebec, both Upper Canada and Lower Canada were granted representative institutions along British lines.[40]

The years between 1830 and 1850 witnessed the second great wave of immigration to Canada as large numbers of British subjects displaced by new agricultural practices, technological change, and famine came to the New World. The population of British North America rose from approximately 250,000 in 1790 to 1.6 million in 1845. Close to half of the immigrants from Britain were Irish, many of them Catholic. They continued to arrive in large numbers up until the 1850s, driven by poverty and the devastating famine of 1847. Most of these immigrants were settled in Upper Canada and helped increase the population of the province from approximately ninety-five thousand in 1815 to 952,000 in 1851. Their presence helped spur the growth of agriculture, industrialization, and urbanization in Canada.[41] Deepening religious and class divides also helped drive an incipient democratic reform movement, which culminated in outright rebellion in 1837.[42]

Despite this influx, Canada's status as an immigration receiver was offset by its role as a major sending region. This was particularly true in the case of Lower Canada, where every year thousands of French Catholics departed for the mill towns of New England. Indeed, approximately 150,000 left for the United States in the 1850s alone. Mass emigration was also a factor in Upper Canada, with many Irish migrants remaining for only a short time before continuing their journeys southward, typically to New York or the American Midwest. Between 1860 and 1900 more people left Canada than entered it; for many, British North America served as a way station for a longer journey that would ultimately terminate in the United States.

During this period, Britain continued to struggle to find some means of dealing with the French Catholic challenge in Lower Canada. Renewed efforts at assimilation, spurred by Lord Durham's 1839 report, led to further institutional engineering. The merging of Upper Canada and Lower Canada into a single province was intended to take advantage of English Canada's growing population in order to "swamp" French Catholics. However, this effort, like others before it, failed, leading to further ruminations on the "question of Canada." The constitutional arrangement devised by the Fathers of Confederation in 1867 represented yet another attempt to deal with the consequences of Canada's dual colonial heritage. While it was designed to accommodate the presence of two "founding nations" – principally through the adoption of federalism – its admixture of monarchical principles, parliamentary institutions, and respect for English traditions gave it a distinctive identity. In the words of the new country's first prime minister, Sir John A. Macdonald, Canada was destined to be a "subordinate kingdom" in the Empire.[43]

From Laissez-Faire to Selectivity, 1869-1905

Even during the years of mass immigration between 1830 and 1860, Britain did not introduce measures that might be termed "immigration policies." What regulations were devised consisted of Passenger Laws, which were typically ignored by ships' captains, and measures to assist the movement of immigrants from their point of arrival to the interior of the country.[44]

Canada's first Immigration Act was passed in 1869, two years after Confederation. The act granted the federal government "authority to deny entry to paupers and the mentally ill or physically disabled." Subsequent amendments to the act passed in the 1870s broadened the government's ability to check the entry of the poor, sick, and disabled but did not touch on matters pertaining to national identity.[45] The absence of more robust controls in the 1869 act reflected Canada's continuing status as a country of emigration. Canada's most pressing problem vis-à-vis migration at this time was its inability to retain its own natural population increase. Each year tens of thousands of Canadians emigrated to New England, New York, or the US Midwest. Despite its best efforts, the Canadian government was unable to stem this out-migration from Britain and Europe. An estimated one-quarter of those who did cross the Atlantic to Canada subsequently moved on to the United States.[46]

Indeed, the US census of 1900 "counted 1.2 million Canadian-born in America, a number equal to a quarter of Canada's 1901 population."[47] The 1869 act was intended to check this trend and to assist in the settlement of Canada's vast western territories, thus complementing the Macdonald Conservatives' National Policy.[48] The hope was that greater governmental oversight would help encourage more immigrants to arrive and stay in Canada, thus assisting the building up of a domestic market and checking "American expansionist impulses."[49]

Although the Immigration Act, 1869, imposed a minimum of restrictions and complemented the prevailing laissez-faire philosophy of the time,[50] it established a number of important precedents that would define Canadian policy making in the years ahead. Most important, the act delegated extremely broad authority to the federal Cabinet. This permitted subsequent governments to change regulations governing admissions through orders-in-council, thereby avoiding the need to debate changes before Parliament.[51] While this institutional peculiarity of Canadian immigration policy making provided the executive with a great deal of flexibility in meeting challenges, it concentrated decision making in a relatively closed circle of policy makers, limiting democratic oversight and increasing the likelihood that decisions would be made to suit the whims of powerful political and private interests. Hence, while the executive was "strong," the autonomy of the state was compromised as powerful economic interests could exert significant influence on the shaping of immigration policy without having to work through the Legislature.

The shift to identity-based exclusions emerged with the expansion of migration at the close of the nineteenth century. As the numbers of immigrants entering Canada increased, so did their countries of origin. The building of the Canadian Pacific Railway (CPR) was accomplished in part by the labour of Chinese "navvies" who were recruited to perform the often dangerous tasks that the project required.[52] Southern and Eastern Europeans were also recruited to build the CPR, work in mines and forestry, and provide much needed labour for other economic sectors. The expansion of the railway and introduction of weather-resistant wheat facilitated the settlement of the west on a much greater scale, increasing rates of immigration.

With this success, however, came increased calls for the regulation of community and the guarding of the nation against the incursion of "inferior" foreigners. This was registered initially through the implementation of controls on Chinese immigration. British Columbia passed legislation prohibiting Asian immigration in 1884 and 1885 under the authority granted to it and other provinces through section 95 of the Constitution Act, 1867 (which deemed immigration and agriculture matters of concurrent federal-provincial jurisdiction).[53] Both statutes were annulled by the federal government through the power of "disallowance" granted it under section 90 of the Constitution Act, 1867. Ottawa's decision aimed to protect BC employers' rights to cheap labour. In Prime Minister John A. Macdonald's words: "It will be all very well to exclude Chinese labor, when we can replace it with white labor, but until that is done, it is better to have Chinese labor than no labor at all."[54]

While the prerogatives of employers and the national government blocked British Columbia's efforts to introduce laws that would exclude Asian immigrants outright, the federal government concluded that "British Columbia would have to be accorded some satisfaction if open violence in the province were to be avoided."[55] To this end, the Macdonald government introduced the Chinese Immigration Act, 1885. The act required all Chinese immigrants to pay a "head tax" of fifty dollars. Only diplomats, government representatives, tourists, merchants, scientists, and students were exempted. Ship captains were responsible for collecting the head tax and presenting a passenger list, along with the sum payable, to the port authorities before passengers were allowed to disembark.[56]

The continuing expansion of immigration in the late nineteenth century was also propelled by the reorganization of the immigration program by Prime Minister Wilfrid Laurier's minister of the interior, Clifford Sifton, after the Liberal Party's electoral victory in 1896. Under Sifton's leadership, Canada committed itself more firmly to the rapid settlement of the west through mass immigration of "agriculturalists." This entailed wooing would-be immigrants from Britain, the United States, Germany, and other northern European countries through promotional activities such as lectures, slide shows, and mobile exhibits. Printed materials in migrants' native languages, "finder's fees" for travel agents, and offers of free land were also used to attract potential settlers.[57] Because immigration from Britain, the United States, France, and Germany proved to be insufficient, the geographic range of preferred source countries was expanded to include Central and Eastern Europe.[58] Sifton famously declared that his idea of an ideal immigrant was a "stalwart peasant in a sheepskin coat born on the soil, whose forefathers have been farmers for generations, with a stout wife and a half-dozen children."[59] The Canadian government's overriding objective was to "promote the immigration of farmers and farm laborers."[60] As such, all Europeans (including white Americans) who fit the bill were welcome.

Sifton's preference for sturdy European "agriculturalists" necessitated the elaboration of an organizational structure capable of attracting the "good" immigrants while keeping out the "bad." This was accomplished through the reorganization of the Canadian immigration program and the formulation of policies aimed at regulating entry according to governmental preferences. Thus, policy moved from laissez faire to greater control. The Alien Labour Act, 1897, was enacted to limit Canadian employers' propensity to import contract labourers, particularly railway workers from the United States. A 1902 amendment to the Immigration Act was added to exclude "diseased persons." And in 1903 the head tax on Chinese immigrants was doubled, bringing it to $100; in 1903, the levy was raised still further to $500.[61]

Immigration, Citizenship, and Nation Building, 1905-14

The elaboration of identity-based exclusions was carried out under the tutelage of Sifton's successor, Frank Oliver. While Oliver shared Sifton's preference for farmers, he was less enamoured with the non-British migrants his predecessor had actively recruited. Speaking on behalf of his fellow western Canadians, Oliver noted:

> There is nothing we more earnestly resent than the idea of settling up the country with people who will be a drag on our civilization and progress. We did not go out to that country simply to produce wheat. We went to build up a nation, a civilization, a social system that we could enjoy, be proud of and transmit to our children; and we resent the idea of having the millstone of this Slav population hung around our necks in our efforts to build up, beautify and improve the country, and so improve the whole of Canada.[62]

As Oliver's comments make clear, Continental Europeans were regarded as impediments to nation building. At the same time, however, they met the needs of powerful economic actors. This generated a distinct political cleavage:

Those who tended to be concerned about issues of assimilability of immigrants and the preservation of Anglo-Canadian norms and values tended to support a selective and restrictive approach to immigration, as did those who wanted to limit labour supply in the interests of preserving wage rates and improving conditions at work. In contrast, those who benefited from inexpensive labour advocated an expansive, relatively unrestrained approach to immigrant admissions.[63]

Expansionists represented a small, if powerful, minority. Reflecting the prejudices of the time, churches, labour leaders, progressive intellectuals, physicians, academics, and members of the media agreed that Canada's moral fabric was threatened by the importation of "inferior races."[64] Anglo-Saxon angst was matched by French-Canadian nationalists' fear of being swamped by waves of non-French-speaking others. Henri Bourassa went so far as to argue that federal government funds would be better spent repatriating French-Canadian emigrants from New England than luring Eastern Europeans to western Canada.[65] French-Canadian nationalists also railed against the migration of European Jews, arguing that they hindered the economic and moral development of French-Catholic society.[66] Indeed, elements of the "new anti-Semitism" that was emerging in Europe during this period were increasingly common in Quebec and across Canada.[67] Like their European counterparts, Canadian anti-Semites such as Goldwin Smith and the founder of the Social Credit movement, Major Clifford Douglas, cast Jews as a wholly inassimilable "race" bent on exploiting host societies for selfish gain.[68]

Nativist reaction was not limited to hardcore racists. The continuing expansion of migration during the years before the First World War intersected with growing concerns among Canadian intellectuals regarding the challenge immigration posed to national integration. Among the most influential comments in this vein are found in J.S. Woodsworth's *Strangers within Our Gates*. Woodsworth's position is particularly important as it represents the mainstream of elite *progressive* opinion. As Kelley and Trebilcock note, "his writings and lectures reveal the degree of acceptability that notions of racial superiority held, even among those most sympathetic to the plight of the economically downtrodden and politically oppressed."[69] Woodsworth's analysis of Canada's immigration problem drew heavily from the dominant scientific discourse of the day, and he categorized immigrants' ability to assimilate into Canadian culture according to their ranking on what Richard Day calls the "Great Chain of Race": the prevailing racial hierarchy advanced by scientific race theories.[70]

Woodsworth's analysis of immigrant difference and its impact on Canadian identity led him to advance a two-pronged strategy for managing the migration-membership dilemma: On the one hand, Eastern and Southeastern Europeans should be subject to strenuous assimilation, the end of which was to transform them into acceptable, English-speaking citizens with manners and habits consistent with the dominant Anglo-Canadian national character. This would be accomplished through the work of local religious-based organizations and public educational systems. Conversely, those considered beyond the scope of assimilation – that is, non-Europeans – would be excluded outright via immigration restrictions. According to Woodsworth, inassimilable races were detrimental to Canada's national development and therefore "should be vigorously excluded."[71]

Woodsworth's proposed solutions to Canada's migration-membership dilemma were consistent with trends in broader elite opinion and, increasingly, governmental policy. The Immigration Act, 1906, set an important precedent by clarifying the criteria to be used to determine the suitability of would-be migrants.[72] Among the most important addition to the government's control apparatus was an expanded list of prohibited classes. The task of determining admissibility was left to "a board of inquiry comprising an immigration agent, medical officer, or any other officer or officers named by the minister [of the interior]."[73] The minister was also granted the power to hear and judge appeals to decisions reached by the boards of inquiry. Inadmissible immigrants and immigrants who became a public charge, committed a crime involving moral turpitude, or had become an inmate of a jail or hospital within two years of their landing were subject to removal from Canada. The act also included a more elastic provision granting the Cabinet the power to prohibit the landing of "any specified class of immigrants." The Cabinet was authorized to enact landing-money requirements, which could "vary according to the class and destination" of immigrants and "otherwise according to the circumstances."[74] In public pronouncements, Oliver made clear that the government was no longer interested in promoting the immigration of Continental Europeans.

The policy orientation of the Immigration Act, 1906, and subsequent regulations enacted in 1908,[75] were reinforced in a new immigration act introduced in 1910. A major innovation was the right of the Cabinet to enact regulations that excluded the entry of immigrants "belonging to any race deemed unsuitable to the climate and requirements of Canada or immigrants of any specified class, occupation, or character" and those immigrants who came to Canada other than by "continuous journey."[76] The state's deportation powers were also enhanced through the introduction of the concept of domicile, according to which Canadian domicile was obtained only after legal landing and three years of lawful residence in Canada. Immigrants lacking such a status would be subject to deportation if they became a member of an undesirable class, which included purveyors of moral turpitude (pimps, prostitutes, etc.), "convicted criminals, public charges, and inmates of jails, hospitals, and insane asylums."[77] Political radicalism was also deemed grounds for inclusion in the "undesirable" category and, consequently, deportation.[78]

Despite the thoroughness of the Immigration Act, 1910, its aim of restricting immigration to healthy, white, preferably British or American agriculturalists was limited by pressures brought to bear by employers keen on maintaining, if not expanding, supplies of cheap immigrant labour for decidedly non-agricultural enterprises such as mining, logging, railway construction, and saw mill operations.[79] The belated success of the National Policy in fostering Canadian-based industry came back to haunt immigration planners, whose long-term strategies were upset by employers' short-term economic interests.[80]

The solution, or solutions, to this dilemma included further elaborating formal immigration policy at the "front gate" and, significantly, allowing for continued access to officially non-preferred migrants through a widening "back door."[81] Back-door strategies included employers' active recruitment of foreign labourers with the tacit approval of the government. Recruitment was also carried out on behalf of employers by hundreds of private labour agencies that typically specialized in particular nationalities.[82] The end result during periods of economic expansion was a steady flow of precisely the type of migrants that Oliver, Canadian labour unions, and nativists sought to restrict: Continental Europeans – Italians, Poles, Ukrainians, Russians, and others – who were not "agriculturalists" but, rather, wage labourers.

Restrictions on the entry of "unsuitable races" were more comprehensive than were those directed at stemming the flow of Continental European labourers. This reflected the limits of employers' influence on governmental policy. Whereas non-preferred Europeans upset labour unions and provoked fears of swamping among Anglo- and French-Canadian nationalists, the potential entry of large numbers of non-white "races" generated acute discomfort at the highest levels of the state. The reasons for this discomfort were rooted in prevailing attitudes towards non-European peoples and the fear that anti-Asian nativism in British Columbia might threaten political stability in the province.

For a time, the federal government sought to manage Asian migration through a combination of restriction, as reflected in the Chinese Immigration Act, and limited back-door recruitment.[83] Thus, although both the federal government and the Privy Council accepted British Columbia's decision to prohibit the addition of Chinese persons on voting lists, thereby disenfranchising them both at the provincial and federal levels (as placement on provincial voting lists was a prerequisite for voting in federal elections), it consistently sided with the province's economic power brokers in striking down provincial legislation aimed at the total exclusion of Asians.[84] The Vancouver Riot of 1907 acted as a catalyst for the formulation of more definitive restrictions against "Asiatic" immigration.[85] The federal government responded to the riot by tightening restrictions against Asian migration, through the imposition of strict medical examinations, demands for a $200 "landing-money" payment to be paid upon arrival, and implementation of the "continuous journey" clause (an imaginative legal contrivance aimed especially at potential immigrants from British India). According to the clause, immigrants entering Canada had to arrive via continuous voyage from the country of their birth or citizenship with tickets bought in those same countries. Within days of enacting the provision, the Canadian government ordered the only shipping company operating direct service between India and Canada "to suspend its services, thereby obviating the possibility of making a continuous journey from India to Canada."[86] All of these innovations were passed as order-in-council in 1908 and were subsequently woven into the Immigration Act, 1910.[87] Furthermore, a "gentleman's agreement" was negotiated with the Japanese government to limit the number of visas granted for travel to Canada to four hundred per year.[88]

Although the Laurier government had also drafted an order-in-council to prohibit the landing in Canada of "any immigrant of the Negro race," it ultimately chose to restrict African-American immigration through more "informal" measures, including the strict interpretation of medical and character examinations.[89] The Department of Immigration made it clear that examinations made at the border would likely result in the rejection of most black immigrants: "So effective was the 'strict interpretation' policy that the number of black immigrants fell from 136 in 1907-1908 to seven in 1909-1910."[90] Other elements of Canada's "informal" policy to restrict

African-American immigration included convincing the CPR not to provide African Americans with services normally granted to prospective American immigrants.[91]

The regulatory apparatus constructed out of the 1908 orders-in-council and Immigration Act, 1910, was tested in May 1914 when the *Komagata Maru*, a ship carrying 376 passengers from the Punjab region of British India, set anchor in Vancouver harbour.[92] The owner of the vessel, Gurdit Singh, maintained that as British subjects all of the ship's passengers enjoyed an unimpeded right to enter any part of the British Empire, including Canada. This raised a fundamental challenge to Canada's authority to regulate membership via naturalization policy, at least as concerned British subjects. While the Immigration Act, 1910, "explicitly defined an 'alien' as a person who was not a British subject" and thus maintained the link between Canadian citizenship and British subjecthood, it also "carve[ed] out of British subject status a new legal subject, the Canadian citizen, which amounted to a container for British subjects with a physical connection by birth or domicile to Canadian territory."[93] Gurdit Singh's claim thus challenged Canadian legislators' authority to "produce an excludable other that would encompass British subjects."[94]

These constitutional niceties were not registered by the white citizens of British Columbia, who demanded that the would-be immigrants and fellow British subjects be prevented from landing and returned to India forthwith.[95] Canadian parliamentarians were also keen to concoct means of returning the ship and its crew to India as quickly as possible. The dilemma was ultimately settled by the courts, which ruled that the continuous journey clause, $200 landing fee requirement, and the parsing of British subject status and Canadian citizenship by the Immigration Act, 1910, were valid. In Audrey Macklin's words: "The court took a legally vacuous Canadian citizenship, reified and inflated it with febrile fantasy of white nationhood, and read it back as that which must be preserved through law."[96] Indeed, the Court's opinion demonstrated the degree to which legal principles had assimilated notions of racial difference and cultural incompatibility:

> In that our fellow British subjects of the Asiatic race are of different racial instincts to those of the European race – and consistent therewith, their family life, rules of society and laws are of a very different character – in their own interests, their proper place of residence is within the confines of their respective countries in the continent of Asia, not in Canada, where their customs are not in vogue and their adhesion to them here only gives

rise to disturbances destructive to the well-being of society and against the maintenance of peace, order and good government ... Better that peoples of non-assimilative – and by nature properly non-assimilative – race should not come to Canada, but rather that they should remain of residence in their country of origin and there do their share, as they have in the past, in the preservation and development of the Empire.[97]

The *Komagata Maru* was escorted out of Vancouver Harbour two months after it set anchor: "Its departure signaled the virtual cessation of Indian immigration to Canada ... Between 1914 and 1920, only one East Indian immigrant was admitted. Over the next twenty-five years, fewer than 650 settled in Canada."[98]

War, Recovery, and the Crystallization of White Canada, 1914-29

By 1914, the fundamental components of Canada's immigration policy regime were in place. In times of economic growth, a greater proportion of non-preferred groups would be allowed to enter Canada to assuage labour needs. During economic downturns, the main gate would be narrowed and the back door more thoroughly policed. Groups deemed unsuitable were subject to special restrictions and, increasingly after 1907, outright exclusion. Naturalization was used to police the boundaries of the nation internally, as was deportation, particularly during economic bad times. Conversely, the Canadian state also expended a great deal of effort in attracting preferred immigrants, particularly white agriculturalists from the British Isles, the United States, and northwestern Europe. Thus, the period during which Canada developed its immigration control apparatus also coincided with periods of massive immigration.[99] While not all of the newcomers met the standards set by the immigration bureaucracy, many did. Those who did not were subject to assimilative pressures, the ends of which were to transform second-rate foreigners into acceptable, English-speaking Canadians.[100]

The regime established during the early part of the twentieth century served as the basis for immigration policy making through the First World War, the interwar period, and beyond. The flexibility of the system and the extensive discretion granted to immigration officials allowed for rapid adjustments in policy in response to changing domestic and international conditions. Thus, during the early years of the First World War, "enemy aliens" crowding municipal welfare rolls were interned in camps and/or deported, through the combined exercise of immigration policy and the War Measures

Act.[101] When demands for war provisions, conscription, and entry of the United States into the war led to a shortage of labour for the war industries, policy was adjusted, the camps were emptied, and the "enemy aliens" were put to work.[102] Similarly, controls on non-preferred immigrants were tightened during the economic downturn that accompanied the initial postwar period and loosened once the economy improved. When supplies of preferred British and American immigrants did not keep up with employers' demands for labour, the government widened the gap for non-preferred Europeans through innovations such as the Railway Agreement.[103] At the same time, preferred migrants were recruited even more aggressively through the Empire Settlement Agreement and Farm Family Settlement Schemes, which provided transportation assistance and other incentives to British immigrants who were willing to become Canadian farmers.[104]

The interwar era also marked the definitive exclusion of "unsuitable races" as the need for unskilled labour in British Columbia diminished and racist xenophobia deepened throughout Canadian society. Innovations such as visa and passport requirements were introduced, and existing legislation and accompanying regulations were revised. An important amendment to Clause C of section 38 of the Immigration Act, 1910, was passed in 1919, allowing Canada to

> prohibit or limit in number for a stated period or permanently the landing in Canada or the landing at any specified port or ports of entry in Canada, of any immigrants belonging to any nationality or race or of immigrants of any specified class or occupation, by reason of any economic, industrial or other condition temporarily existing in Canada or because such immigrants are deemed unsuitable having regard to the climate, industrial, social, educational, labour, or other conditions or requirements of Canada or because such immigrants are deemed undesirable owing to the peculiar customs, habits, modes of life, and methods of holding property, and because of their probable inability to become readily assimilated or to assume the duties and responsibilities of Canadian citizenship within a reasonable time after their entry.[105]

Demands for the total exclusion of Chinese migrants voiced by a broad coalition, including the Trades and Labour Congress (TLC), the British Columbia Legislature, teachers' associations, war veterans' associations, the Retail Merchants Association of Canada, the Asiatic Exclusion League, and the Ku Klux Klan of Canada, among others, were answered by the Chinese Immigration Act, 1923.[106] In place of the head tax featured in its 1885 predecessor, the new act limited entry or landing of persons of Chinese origin (irrespective of their allegiance or citizenship) to: diplomatic and consular personnel; children born in Canada of Chinese race or descent who had left Canada for educational or other purposes; merchants (i.e., individuals who devoted their undivided attention to mercantile pursuits, had no less than $2,500 invested in an enterprise importing goods to Canada or exporting goods of Chinese or Canadian manufacture, and had conducted business for at least three years); and students coming to Canada to study at recognized Canadian educational institutions.[107] The act made no provision for the relatives of Canadians of Chinese descent or of persons of Chinese origin living in Canada. Several orders-in-council reinforced the aim of the 1919 amendment.

In sum, Canada succeeded in establishing a complex apparatus designed to ensure that immigration did not impinge on its status as a "white man's country." Limits on non-preferred Continental European migrants also reflected doubts as to the ability of the country to assimilate inferior whites without imperiling its racial composition and level of "civilization."[108] Growing anxiety over assimilative capacity and the dangers posed by the entry of even a small number of immigrants from unsuitable races reflected the influence of prevailing ideas pertaining to race and national identity held by intellectuals, civil servants, politicians, doctors, psychologists, social workers, progressive reformers, and members of the media.[109] By the late 1920s, there was virtual agreement as to the necessity of regulating immigration with an eye to maintaining the health and development of the nation. Thus, Canada's status as an immigration country was highly circumscribed by its equally important status as a nationalizing state.[110] Immigration was a necessary evil to be tolerated in order to satisfy labour market needs and to complete the process of westward expansion and consolidation.

Germans and Others: Migration and National Identity, 1871-1929

From Emigration to Immigration, 1871-90
In the years prior to and immediately after the founding of the second German Empire in 1871, the North German Confederacy and various political entities that came to form the *Kaiserreich* witnessed huge waves of emigration. German migrants' principle destination was the United States, though Argentina, Brazil, and Canada were also host to significant levels of

German immigration. Overseas emigration peaked between 1880 and 1893, when approximately 1.8 million persons left Germany.[111] Emigration helped to ease pressures produced by a steeply rising population and only trailed off after 1893 as a result of declining birth rates and increases in domestic employment opportunities generated by rapid industrialization.[112] Economic bad times in the United States also played a role in dissuading potential migrants from travelling overseas.

The expansion of the domestic labour market prompted increases in internal migration, from the agricultural regions of the Prussian northeast to the industrializing centres of western Prussia and the Ruhr region.[113] The shift from transatlantic to internal migration marked the acceleration of the second industrial revolution in Germany and the "transformation of millions of landless poor and smallholders into an industrial proletariat."[114] The reduction in transportation costs and the expansion of railways facilitated movement from farms to factories. Aggressive recruiting by western employers in the rural northeast also helped draw migrants from the countryside to Germany's urban-industrializing regions.

The period spanning 1871 and 1913 marked Germany's transformation from an agrarian state with powerful industry to a fully fledged industrial state with an agricultural base.[115] This profound shift in political economy had important implications for migration. The internal movement of Germans from east to west left landowners in Prussia's eastern provinces scrambling for workers. While competition with the United States and other agricultural producers on the international market necessitated cutting costs, the shift to higher-yield root crops required large numbers of workers who were willing to accept a demanding and entirely unpleasant form of labour.[116] The solution to this conundrum lay in the recruitment of foreign workers, principally from the nearest and most convenient sources at hand: the Austro-Hungarian Empire and the Russian Empire. As the elimination of feudal relations in both these empires had prompted a comparable displacement of the peasantry, there existed a large supply of potential workers who were willing to cross the border for relatively better wages in the German east. The fact that most of these workers were Poles, however, prompted a sharp reaction among those less enamoured with foreign labor. The settlement of Jewish traders, craftspeople, and shopkeepers who were expected to follow their traditional clientele to Germany also provoked consternation among German nationalists.[117]

The entry of large numbers of Polish foreign workers into Prussia raised fears that the newcomers would hinder the "Germanization" of the Prussian east (and its indigenous ethnic Polish minority) and lead instead to the "Polonization" of the region. As one editorialist put it:

> Polonization is taking place in certain regions that had previously been won over to Germanic customs, culture, and language. A wave of Polish immigration is inundating our eastern provinces. That wave grows ever larger, the greater the feeling of discontent among Poles in Russia. In this way, the Polish element is being continually augmented. And it is precisely those Poles emigrating from Russia who bring with them a high degree of dissatisfaction and longing for the liberation of Poland from Russian bondage. Here they fan flames that otherwise would probably be extinguished under the ashes. All this forces upon us the question as to whether it is not in fact necessary – to close the door tightly on any further expansion of Polish culture and their national-political conception.[118]

Thus, large-scale labour migration aimed at offsetting an economic crisis in agriculture ran headlong into a key source of German nationalist angst: the so-called "Polish Question."[119]

While the Prussian government recognized the need for labour among large landowners, the perceived negative impact of mass Polish migration outweighed it. In Bismarck's words:

> We could not concede that the need for manpower in the border regions was of greater importance than the political dangers and threat to the state posed by a Polonization of a large segment of the Prussian population. Though recognizing agriculture as the most important of all trades, we deem it as a lesser evil for the individual regions to suffer from a shortage of manpower than for the state ... to suffer any impairment.[120]

The threat of Polonization prompted swift and decisive action in the spring of 1885. In March, Bismarck ordered Prussia's provincial departments to deport some thirty thousand to forty thousand foreigners, principally Roman Catholic Poles but also a significant number of Jews. Prussian women married to foreign Poles were also expelled, along with their children.[121] Complementing the deportation policy was a strict prohibition on the recruitment of any Polish labourers from the Austrian and Russian empires as well as a policy of internal colonization that entailed the state's purchase of Polish-owned estates for resale to German settlers. Bismarck hoped that his deportation and colonization policies and continuation of the *Kulturkampf* in Polish Prussia would eventually neutralize Polish nationalism in the German east.[122]

Becoming a "Labour-Importing Country," 1890-1912

Although Bismarck's prohibition on foreign Polish labour generated criticism among agribusiness interests, their alignment with the "Iron Chancellor" endured, in part because the need for such labour had not yet reached crisis proportions. This would only come as the transformation of the countryside intensified in the years after the introduction of the anti-Polish decrees. The increasing popularity of sugar beet cultivation heightened demands for seasonal labour: whereas the ratio of required labour power in the heaviest working month to the lightest in grain farming was 1.6 to 1, for sugar beet production it stood at 4 to 1.[123] This need for seasonal agricultural workers further weakened the traditional rural economy and effectively transformed the remaining semi-independent farmers into rural wage labourers. Although labour shortages meant that these individuals could demand relatively high wages during the peak of the growing season, the instability of seasonal work and lack of social benefits prompted their flight from the countryside and a further narrowing of the labour market. By 1890, market pressures and increasing indebtedness prompted agribusiness interests to voice renewed demands for foreign labour. According to the district administrative head (*Regierungspräsident*) of Oppeln, there was no choice "but to reopen the closed frontiers and once more ... permit the entry of Russian-Polish and Galician laborers. By dint of their modest requirements and diligence [they would be capable of] providing agriculture with effective, longer-term relief."[124]

Demands from powerful economic interests for access to foreign labour compelled Bismarck's successor, Leo von Caprivi, to reconsider the ban on Polish labour migration – over the stern objections of the Prussian ministries of education, culture, and the interior. And yet the fear of Polonization that had prompted the initial policy response in 1885 had not abated. If anything, worries about the influence of foreign Poles on the Polish Question had intensified during the interim as national security concerns intersected with more general fears of swamping by "lower orders" from the east.[125] In order to satisfy demands for labour while simultaneously guarding against the perceived effects of migration on national integration, a system of tightly controlled temporary labour migration was conceived and enacted. The aim of the system was to ensure that Germany did not become a country of immigration but, rather, a "labour-importing country," in which migrant workers were utilized as a disposable labour force.[126]

The system established in 1890 allowed for the recruitment of foreign labour from Russia and Austrian Galicia for agricultural enterprises in Prussia's eastern provinces. Only unmarried labourers were permitted to enter, and permission to work was granted from April 1 to November 15 exclusively.[127] The introduction of mandatory rotation and a "closure period" (*Karenzzeit*) during which Polish workers were required to leave Prussia was meant to "impress upon both foreign workers and the local German population that such workers were merely aliens whose presence was tolerated and that their permanent settlement in Prussia was out of the question."[128] The decrees of 1890 therefore established a central pillar of Germany's migration policy: the rejection of immigration proper and pursuit of temporary labour recruitment in its stead.

The elaboration of migration control followed shortly thereafter as the large landowners who benefited most from the entry of foreign workers demanded that the Prussian state take measures to counter foreign workers' tendency to breach the terms of their contracts.[129] Demands for greater control also emerged among nationalist opponents of migration; in lieu of a total ban on Polish foreign workers, groups such as the Pan-German League (*Alldeutscher Verband*) urged greater surveillance and supervision of foreigners.[130] The Prussian ministries of culture and war also pushed for greater state oversight in the sphere of labour migration. State officials believed that leaving the recruitment of foreign workers solely to employers and their agents was not in the best interests of the state.[131]

The culmination of these pressures led the Ministry of Agriculture to establish the Prussian Farm Workers Agency (*Preußische Feldarbeiterzentrale*) in 1905, renamed the German Farm Workers Agency (*Deutsche Feldarbeiterzentrale*) in 1912. The agency was established as a private entity that functioned as a coordinating bureau for the Ministry of Agriculture.[132] It "was designed to bring under one roof all recruitment of foreign agricultural workers and ... totally eliminate any competition of commercial procurement agents and private middlemen." Moreover, the "concentration of employment activities in the hand of one agency would allow for the possibility ... to attract and hire elements less dangerous (from a national perspective) in place of the previously predominant Russian-Polish and Galician workers. In this way, the need in agriculture for foreign workers could be properly reconciled with the desire of the state, dictated by an interest in self-preservation, to protect itself ... against antinational immigration."[133]

The centralization of control under the Farm Workers Agency was assisted by the Prussian Ministry of the Interior's introduction of the "compulsory domestic permit" (*Inlandslegitimierungszwang*) in 1907. Initially meant only for Polish foreign labourers, by 1909 all foreign workers in Prussia were required to possess a permit card that noted their national origin and other personal data, along with the name of their employer. Inclusion of employers' names on the permit checked workers' exit option as those who engaged in "breach of contract" were subject to deportation if they ran afoul of the authorities. Change of employers could only be arranged with the authorized employer's blessing, and a second copy of the permit was kept on file to assist the police in tracking "illegal" migrants.[134] Despite the Labour Agency's monopoly on legitimization, the recruitment and distribution of foreign labourers was still largely left to private agencies. Control over the hiring of illegal foreign workers by western industrialists was also tempered by the recognition that industry could not function without foreign workers.[135] Thus, the centralization of control was supplemented by the continuation of intermittently policed back-door migration, which itself reflected differences among diverging interest groups (employers, nationalists, etc.) and the various Prussian ministries they sought to influence.[136]

The system of temporary labour migration enacted at the turn of the century facilitated massive transnational movements into Germany. On the eve of the First World War, Prussia alone accounted for nearly 1 million foreign migrant workers, in agriculture and industry.[137] Of these migrants, Poles from Austria-Hungary and Russia made up approximately 66 percent of all agricultural workers in Prussia in 1913 and 30 percent of the total labour force.[138] Whereas migrants from these countries occasionally took up longterm residence in Prussia and other German *Länder*, compulsory rotation helped maintain the seasonal character of Polish migration. For example, of the 270,496 Poles employed in Prussia in 1913, only 3,213 remained in the country at the end of the year.[139] While far from perfect, the regulatory mechanisms put in place to guard against the "Polonization of the East" helped to maintain a mass labour force that met the needs of East Elbian landowners and German industrialists while at the same time respecting Prussian state officials' interest in excluding "unwanted elements."

Despite the system's careful weighing of distinctly political concerns and advancement of an explicitly anti-Polish "defence policy" (*Abwehrpolitik*), nationalists remained apprehensive about the impact of eastern migration on German society. Sources of discontent ranged from the extreme right-wing Pan-German League and Society in Support of the Germans in the Eastern Marches (*Verein zur Förderung des Deutschtums in den Ostmarken*) to the National Liberals and leading academics, including Max Weber. Weber's position on the impact of foreign workers in the German east provides us with a revealing insight into the perceived threats posed by trans-national movement to Germany's national integration. It highlights the degree to which turn-of-the-century German liberals (albeit nationalist liberals) could assimilate what are by contemporary standards highly illiberal positions on nationality and immigration.[140]

According to Weber, the recruitment of foreign Poles and Slavs contributed to the "displacement" of native German peasants from the eastern lands. As the number of foreign workers increased, wage levels declined, thereby compelling those remaining German peasants whose superior cultural condition precluded them from stooping to the level of foreign workers to leave the land for the factories of Brandenburg and points further west.[141] Even more alarmingly, the "flooding" of Germany by "swarms of eastern nomads" threatened to derail the all-important project of raising the "domestic Polish proletariat to the German cultural level."[142] Given that many German-Poles were joining their German compatriots in migrating to the Ruhr region to work in its factories and mines, the mass migration of foreign Poles threatened not only the Polonization of the East but of the West as well. Weber's proposed solution to the threat of foreign labour was a reinstatement of the ban on Polish migration decreed by Bismarck: For the Kings of Prussia had not been called upon to "rule over a rural proletariat without a fatherland and over wandering Slavs alongside Polish peasants and depopulated latifunda ... but over German peasants alongside a class of large landowners whose workers know that they will be able to find their own future independence in their homeland."[143]

Weber's diagnosis and prescription was phrased much more radically by extreme right-wing elements. In the words of one editorialist:

> The inundation of our German lands with foreigners of an inferior character has led in those areas particularly affected to a level of general insecurity incompatible with the essence of an advanced cultural nation ... [T]he unbridled coarseness, ill-bred depravity, and licentious passion of these emissaries of foreign peoples will, wherever they come into contact with the morally dubious elements within our own peoples, corrupt the last vestige

of any positive qualities in those individuals and increase the danger of a general degeneration and decline into barbarism ... It is high time we started to search seriously for some remedy. We must endeavor to keep such persons at a far remove from the body of our nation.[144]

As Ulrich Herbert notes, "'patriotic' misgivings regarding the admission of foreign workers were widespread, extending all the way into the conservative wing of the Social Democrats."[145] Indeed, the challenge posed by the recruitment of foreign labourers vexed the German left throughout the years leading up to the First World War. Whereas the leadership of the *Sozialdemokratische Partei Deutschlands* (SPD), or Social Democratic Party, advocated international freedom of movement and solidarity with foreign workers, pressure from the rank and file prompted a strong current of protectionism as well. Part of the problem lay in the inability of the German trade unions to organize foreign workers.[146] So long as foreigners were regarded as unfair competitors and potential threats to the interests of "natives," internationalism was typically accompanied by calls for "prudent" restrictions on immigration.

Neither the nativist right nor organized labour succeeded in derailing the system of labour migration devised by Prussian administrators. Foreign labour was too important to both East Elbian landowners and industrialists throughout the Reich. As one speaker at the Sixth Congress of Labour Exchanges in Breslau put it, foreigners were needed to perform the "difficult, often dirty and disgusting jobs ... that a flabby or pampered working class ... prefers to avoid." Foreigners were not "genuine competition but rather ... a second-rate working-class, akin to Negroes in the eastern states of the US, the Chinese in California and Australia, coolies in the British West Indies, the Japanese in Hawaii."[147] Foreign labourers would serve as a cheap and expendable "reserve army," used to fuel economic expansion in good times and discarded with impunity during downturns.

"Unwanted Elements" and the Nationalization of Citizenship

Labour migration for agriculture and industry was not the only source of mass transnational movement into Germany at the turn of the twentieth century. This was also a period during which large numbers of East European Jews crossed into Germany either to continue their journey to North America or to settle in the Reich. Violence directed at Jews in the Russian Empire was a key factor behind this movement.[148] By the turn of the century, over 100,000 refugees emigrated from Russia each year and, by 1914, approximately 2.5 million had settled in the United States, England, France, Canada, and Argentina.[149] German shipping companies such as the Hamburg-America line sought to reap the economic benefits of this movement and went to great lengths to facilitate the flow of Jews through the port cities of Hamburg and Bremen.[150]

What was a boon for shipping companies triggered panic among anti-Semites and extreme nationalists. As was the case with Polish labour migrants, the movement of Jewish "transmigrants" through Germany prompted fear of imminent "floods" from the east and calls for greater control and exclusion.[151] Though demands for a complete ban on the entry of all East European Jews were voiced as early as 1895, the anti-Semitic right never succeeded in realizing this goal.[152] Trade treaties with the Austro-Hungarian and Russian empires placed a diplomatic barrier in front of such approaches, as did domestic political opposition to such explicit manifestations of anti-Semitism among members of the Catholic Centre Party and the SPD.[153] In place of more direct approaches for singling out Jews, German bureaucrats relied upon regulatory measures to effectively police national boundaries.

Efforts to minimize the impact of Jewish migration began at the state's outer borders. Control at the point of entry aimed to impede the settlement of Eastern Jews in Germany while permitting them to cross into the country to embark on ships destined for England or North America. Thus:

> German states bordering the Tsarist and Hapsburg empires organised an elaborate programme to concentrate Jewish travellers at frontier stations and expedite them out of the country. After undergoing health tests and delousing, transmigrants were herded into sealed trains and sent on to transit hostels located near major train terminals along the route to North Sea ports ... When the transmigrants reached Hamburg, they were detained in barracks ... until their ship departed. Government officials strove to isolate the transmigrants from the German populace and to ensure their quick evacuation from the *Reich*.[154]

Those Eastern Jews who managed to evade such controls had to secure a residency permit. Such permits were required of all transients and could only be obtained by registering with the local police. This allowed state officials to maintain a vigilant watch on all foreigners and limit the duration of their stays.[155] Expiration of a residency permit also opened the door to deportation – another key component of the regulatory framework. Eastern Jews were denied residency permits by authorities in Prussia's border areas "for fear of being 'flooded by foreign Jewish elements of the Slavic mother-tongue.'"[156] Other districts were also notorious for denying Eastern Jews permission to establish lawful residency, while still others admitted Jews only on a highly selective basis, often putting conditions on their stay that did not apply to members of other groups.[157]

The final line of defence against Eastern Jews and other "unwanted elements" lay in the manipulation of naturalization procedures.[158] In an effort to limit the discretion of local authorities in granting naturalization to East European Jews, the Prussian Ministry of the Interior assumed the power to vet all Jewish applications for citizenship. This limited the naturalization of first-generation Jewish migrants in Prussia.[159] Prussian officials also sought to offset more generous attitudes towards the naturalization of Jews and Poles in some of Germany's western *Länder*. This was to counter a tendency among some Jewish migrants to apply for naturalization in more liberal *Länder* and then return to Prussia in a much better legal position after their petitions had been accepted.[160]

Prussia's insistence on establishing greater uniformity in naturalization procedures was realized with the passage of the 1913 *Reichs- und Staatsangehörigkeitsgesetz* (RuStAG). The law marked an important turning point in the regulation of membership in Germany. Its reinforcement of the principle of descent (*jus sanguinis*) was intended to allow German emigrant men to maintain their German citizenship abroad (on the condition that they fulfilled their military service),[161] while at the same time limiting the ability of non-German foreigners to attain German citizenship in all but exceptional cases.[162] The latter dimension of the law served as a central means of ensuring that foreign migrants could continue to be used to satisfy economic needs without threatening the unity of the German nation.[163] The law also centralized naturalization policy by mandating that all applications for citizenship must gain the approval in principle of all the federal *Länder*. This granted Prussia, the state with the most restrictive policies at that time, the ability to block naturalizations in other, more liberal *Länder*.[164]

The shift to an increasingly exclusive citizenship regime based on the principle of descent did not simply mark the continuation of business as usual.[165] According to Dieter Gosewinkel, the 1913 law "codified a secular change in German citizenship policy during the 1800s, from territorially based to descent-based principles, and institutionalized this paradigm change for the twentieth century."[166] One of the catalysts for this break was the rise of nativist far-right nationalist groups.[167] These actors played an important role in placing immigration and citizenship policy in the context of both the Polish and Jewish "questions." Whereas outright bans on Jewish migration failed to yield necessary support among other parties and actors, a citizenship policy based on *jus sanguinis* that effectively sheltered the German *Volk* from infiltration by Poles and Jews *did* resonate across the political spectrum, granting what had been an extreme position greater acceptability. Indeed, during the parliamentary debates over the reform of the citizenship law in 1912-13, only left liberals, members representing the indigenous Danish and Polish minorities, and members of the SPD came out strongly in favour of a more open policy that included elements of *jus soli*. The SPD's Karl Liebknecht maintained that a foreign worker deemed worthy of being exploited ought also to be granted the opportunity to become a German citizen.[168] According to Liebknecht, only a "certain moral perversity" could lead one to deny the validity of this claim.[169] And yet it *was* strenuously denied, and not only by extreme nationalists. In responding to the SPD's proposals, Dr. Emil Belzer of the Catholic Centre Party stated that he did not care to endorse the "mass naturalization of Galician peddlers" or "thousands of poor agricultural workers"; rather, Belzer claimed that his party was "obligated to ensure that our municipalities are protected against the naturalization of morally or economically dubious elements."[170] Despite its veiled language, Belzer's statement illustrates that the 1913 law was in part a response to the challenge of mass migration of "unwanted elements" from Russia and Austria-Hungary. Negative reaction to Jews ("Galician peddlers") and Poles ("poor agricultural workers") helped to spur the nationalization of citizenship in Imperial Germany.

The Narrowing of Temporary Labour Migration and Citizenship, 1914-29

By the eve of the First World War, Germany had established the central pillars of its twentieth-century migration regime: temporary labour migration coupled with restrictive naturalization and citizenship policies. Not unlike what occurred in Canada, the war gave rise to circumstances that ratcheted up the degree of coercive power employed by the state against foreigners. The failure of the German army to secure a decisive victory early in the conflict produced heightened demands for labour in the German war economy.[171] Germany turned to several sources of labour to meet this demand, including captured prisoners of war (POWs) and civilian foreign workers, both from Russia (an enemy state) and Austria-Hungary (a key ally).[172] Coercion was used to extract labour from both POWs and civilian foreign labourers. Polish workers ordinarily required to return to their home states at the close of the rotation period were compelled to remain in Germany, against their will if necessary. Although the extraction of coerced labour from foreign civilian workers did not proceed without difficulties, it was an essential element of the German war economy. By the end of the war, approximately 2 million foreign workers, made up of both POWs and civilians, were serving the needs of the German war economy. As such, they were a "virtually indispensable" part of Germany's overall war effort.[173]

Following the end of the war, efforts were made to repatriate both POWs and civilian foreign workers to make room for returning German soldiers.[174] Germany's ravaged economy also required far fewer foreign workers. Indeed, the postwar era marked a spike in emigration, as German workers fled a tight job market, hyperinflation, and socio-political instability.[175] The decline of foreign labour in the interwar period was also due to the loss of agricultural lands in the east and the shift to corporatist economic relations under the Weimar Republic.

The shift to a more "organized" form of capitalism with origins in the war economy would have profound effects on German migration policy. Whereas controls on residency were directed almost exclusively against foreign Poles during the Imperial era, under the Weimar Republic they were expanded to encompass all foreign workers regardless of their nationality. The point was to enhance the standing of domestic workers vis-à-vis foreign competitors, thereby safeguarding the formers' interests.[176] This reflected the increased power of organized labour under the Weimar Constitution. Formal preference in hiring was granted to German workers, and foreign labour was reserved for only those cases in which domestic sources were unavailable. Furthermore, foreign workers were to be paid at the same rates as were German workers, thereby guarding against the use of foreign labour to undercut domestic wage rates. Finally, the admission of foreign workers was to be regulated by committees made up of representatives of both employers and organized labour.[177] The Labour Exchange Act (*Arbeitnachweisgesetz*) of 1922 formalized these new approaches to the regulation of foreign labour. Responsibility for recruitment and supervision of foreign labourers was centralized in the German Labour Agency and the Reich Employment Office (*Reichsamt für Arbeitsvermittlung*), respectively. The duration of work and residency permits was strictly limited to a maximum of twelve months for all foreign workers, except those who had established a long-term presence in Germany and therefore qualified for a "permanent visa" (*Befreiungsscheine*).[178] Taken together, these regulations allowed for the flexible use of foreign labour to meet particular economic needs.

The RuStAG of 1913 remained the law of the land concerning citizenship and, despite some shifting positions on naturalization practices across the *Länder*, naturalization remained difficult.[179] There were calls for the reorientation of naturalization by Prussian officials, which reflected the influence of Social Democrats in the state's postwar government. Demands included replacing the principle of descent with a principle of cultural affinity so that assimilated foreigners who considered themselves German, spoke German, and displayed German cultural habits might be considered for naturalization once residency requirements and other criteria (such as potential for military service) were satisfied. This assimilationist turn in interwar Prussia allowed for over 130,000 naturalizations between 1919 and 1931 (though the number of Jews granted citizenship remained relatively low).[180]

Prussia's approach to naturalization met with vociferous opposition, led in the main by Bavarian state representatives. For critics of the Prussian reform line, culture was simply too imprecise a category; conservatives claimed that ambitious foreigners were adept at mimicking German cultural habits in their efforts to further their selfish commercial and economic interests.[181] Cultural affinity, as measured through language use or particular habits, simply could not take the place of descent in terms of defining German nationality. In the words of the Bavarian foreign minister: "It cannot be concluded that the Eastern Jew somehow bears an affinity to German nationality on the basis of their use of the German language."[182]

For the Bavarian foreign minister, the simple fact that one was an Eastern Jew severely limited any possibility of "true" acculturation and hence successful incorporation into the German *Volk*. This way of thinking about identity and difference reflected the growing influence of the "new anti-Semitism" in Weimar-era Germany, especially among conservatives. The melding of scientific racism and traditional anti-Semitism that had begun at the turn of the century was taken several steps further during the interwar years, resulting in a scientifically sanctioned view of the nation as constituting a biologized entity threatened by "contamination" from "culturally distant foreigners." Under such a worldview, the "assimilability" of Jews and other suspect groups was rendered inconsequential; by the late-1920s, more and more German officials came to accept the view that no amount of assimilation could alter this essential fact.[183]

Thus, the boundary distinguishing Germans from non-Germans during the Weimar period took on a more radical character. The economic crash of 1929, the growing importance of "racial health" among public authorities, and the rejection of liberal-democratic principles by adherents of organic nationalism thwarted attempts to shift this line outward and increased the likelihood that the *völkisch* conception of German nationality, embraced by many in the last days of the Weimar Republic, would be radicalized under the Nazis.

Conclusion

Canada and Germany responded to the challenge of mass migration at the turn of the century in comparable ways, despite important differences in geographic location, regime type, national traditions, and immigration experiences. Both states constructed systems that aimed to exploit migration for economic and other requirements while blocking the entry and incorporation of groups deemed "unsuitable" with regard to the project of national integration. In Canada, this entailed the outright exclusion of "Asiatics," Africans, and, by the end of the 1920s, most Continental Europeans, particularly Jews. Thus a period of mass immigration prompted by the National Policy was limited to groups deemed assimilable: immigration flows were shaped to meet nation-building imperatives. In Germany, an elaborate array of migration controls, residency requirements, and naturalization procedures allowed for the harnessing of international migration for economic purposes while simultaneously limiting migrants' access to social incorporation and national membership. In Zolberg's pithy but accurate epigram, foreign workers were "wanted but not welcome."[184] In both states, economic, political, and ideological factors, including ideas concerning the suitability of particular "races," came together to influence responses to the migration-membership dilemma. By the interwar period, each country's respective policy regime had been elaborated and was set firmly in place.

The economic crash of 1929 would effectively halt migration to both Canada and Germany. Canada ceased to be an "immigration country," and economically burdensome and potentially threatening foreigners were deported en masse.[185] In Germany, the Depression boosted the fortunes of Hitler's National Socialist Workers Party; the Nazis successfully exploited the economic catastrophe to seize power and end the Weimar Republic's democratic experiment in 1933. Whereas Jews had faced harsh discrimination in migration and naturalization policies during both the Imperial and Weimar eras, they were now subject to a fundamentally different kind of prejudice whereby even those who already enjoyed the relative security of

German citizenship were threatened. The undermining of the legal pos-
ition of German Jews, which culminated in the passage of the Nuremberg
Laws in July 1935, codified what had been state-sponsored illegality and
oppression in a new, racist legal order.[186] The terror visited upon Germany's
Jews on the evening of November 9, 1938 – the "night of broken glass"
(*Kristallnacht*) – spelled out the Nazis' intentions: to drive out German
Jews by whatever means necessary. As Göring noted in the wake of the
event, *Kristallnacht* made it clear to the world that "the Jew cannot live in
Germany."[187]

If the Nazis' persecution and expulsion of Jews marked a pathological
turn in German anti-Semitism, Canada's response to the refugees' plight
illustrated the degree to which restrictive immigration controls oriented
state policies. In the words of Irving Abella and Harold Troper, "the single-
mindedness with which the Nazis murdered the vast majority of European
Jews was seemingly matched by the determination of Canada to keep out
these same people."[188] Abella and Troper's detailed account of Canada's conduct in the face of the mass flight of European Jews makes clear that the
Depression afforded Canadian government officials "a dramatic opportunity to complete [the] process of restriction begun in the boom years of the
1920s."[189] European Jews had long been considered "incorrigibly urban" by
immigration officials and were therefore deemed unsuitable for work on
farms, the only occupation open to would-be migrants during the Depression
era. Given that Order-in-Council PC 659 (1930) effectively banned all non-
agricultural workers who were of non-American or non-British stock,
Canada effectively shut itself off from the rest of the world: "For the remainder of the decade – and indeed beyond – a determined Canadian government fought every attempt by the wretched European refugees to breach
this protective wall of orders-in-council."[190]

The legacy of Germany's persecution of European Jews, and Canada and
other states' gross indifference to their plight, would have a tremendous impact on normative standards in the post-Second World War era. The terrible excesses prompted by racist thinking and its related policies would
help alter prevailing normative standards among states claiming the status
of liberal democracies. Even so, both Canada and (West) Germany revisited
their earlier responses to the migration-membership dilemma when faced
with the renewal of mass migration in the postwar period. And while the
rise of human rights and consequent transformation of liberalism would
come to discredit the discursive grammar of race and extreme nationalism

and create new space for differing immigration and citizenship polices in the postwar period, the unravelling of prewar regimes would prove to be a difficult, time-consuming process. Thus, the importance of both countries' initial attempts to regulate community would have important long-term consequences that extended far beyond their period of enactment.

3

Between Two Worlds

The Second World War marked a crucial watershed in attitudes towards race, ethnicity, state sovereignty, and human rights.[1] The Nazis' exclusion of whole groups of people from the national community because of their "racial" characteristics revealed the frightening excesses of race thinking and the fragility of rights in the face of unconstrained state sovereignty.[2] The calculated mass murder of 6 million Jews, half a million Roma, and thousands of Communists, Social Democrats, homosexuals, church activists, and "ordinary decent people who refused complicity in the new politics ... of barbarism"[3] posed a daunting moral, political, and legal challenge to the architects of the postwar order.[4]

The Allies' initial response to this challenge was the prosecution of perpetrators of "crimes against humanity" through the Nuremberg War Crimes Trials (1945-46).[5] A broader array of state delegates, international jurists, and activists forming an incipient "international community" also hammered out the outlines of the postwar doctrine of human rights, as enshrined in the Preamble of the Charter of the United Nations (UN) and the Universal Declaration of Human Rights (UDHR).[6] In stark contrast to the normative context of the late nineteenth and early twentieth centuries, the emerging postwar order featured a discursive grammar grounded in the principles of equality, dignity, and self-determination.[7] Article 2 of the UDHR holds that these principles are universal, applying to all peoples "without distinction of any kind, such as race, colour, sex, language, religion, political or other opinion, national or social origin, property, birth or other status" or "the jurisdictional or international status of the country or territory to which a person belongs, whether it be independent, trust, non-self-governing or under any other limitation of sovereignty."[8] The prewar distinction between civilized, racially superior peoples subject to the rule of law and uncivilized, inferior subjects governed by a combination of paternalism and force was formally rejected in favour of an ethic of equality premised on individuals' membership in a shared human community.[9] Actions contrary to this ethic could now be held up against emerging human rights standards and criticized accordingly.

The scar of Nazism also quickened the discrediting of scientific racist discourse in the postwar period. While scholarly challenges to biological racism had been mounted in the 1920s and 1930s, "opposition to Nazism shaped in dramatic fashion the refutation of racism as a legitimate intellectual stance ... [T]he uniqueness of Nazism underscored the immanent wickedness of racism ... Once racism was rejected, the edifice was shaken."[10] Race went from being a scientifically sanctioned "biological phenomenon" to a "social myth," responsible for "an enormous amount of damage, taking a heavy toll in human lives [and] causing intolerable suffering."[11] The United Nations Scientific and Cultural Organization's 1950 declaration that there was no scientific justification for race discrimination provided postwar reformers with a powerful means of challenging discriminatory public policies that had relied on racist theories for justification.[12] Without the authority of science to support them, racist policies were reduced to mean-spirited barriers to progress and an affront to supporters of equality.[13]

The unravelling of colonialism in the wake of the Second World War reflected and reinforced the ascendant ideas of equality and self-determination. This too marked a decisive break with the past:

> Before the war prevailing public opinion within Western states – including democratic states – did not condemn racial discrimination in domestic social and political life. Nor did it question the ideas and institutions of colonialism. In the minds of most Europeans, equality and democracy could not yet be extended successfully to non-Europeans. In other words, these ideas were not yet considered to be universal human rights divorced from any particular civilization or culture. Indeed, for a century or more race had been widely employed as a concept to explain the scientific and technological achievements of Europeans as compared to non-Europeans and to justify not only racial discrimination within Western states but also Western

domination of non-western peoples. Racial distinctions thus served as a brake on the extension of democratic rights to people of non-European descent within Western countries as well as in Western colonies.[14]

The war removed this "brake" by discrediting the doctrine of racial superiority and advancing the principles of racial equality and self-government.[15] The Second World War thus granted decisive leverage to long-simmering anti-colonial campaigns and helped quicken the collapse of the colonial system, hastening the emergence of a strikingly different international order.[16] This marked a profound shift in human history: "Never before ... had so revolutionary a reversal occurred with such rapidity. The change in the position of the peoples of Asia and Africa and in their relations to Europe was the surest sign of the advent of a new era."[17]

Decolonization helped to entrench the principles of equality and self-determination in world politics. The demise of empire "transformed the image and reality of the international system" as diverse ways of life once managed by empire were "accommodated in an international system of several hundred states."[18] Each of these states was granted a voice in international affairs, which could be exercised through membership in international organizations such as the UN and during the course of bilateral negotiations with fellow states: "The Asian, African, and Arab states that coalesced into the self-conscious 'Third World' ... shifted debates that determined the universality of rights ... [T]heir very presence was an essential prerequisite to any genuine claim of legislating on behalf of all nations."[19]

The emerging Cold War rivalry augmented postcolonial states' role in international relations. The Superpowers' struggle to secure competing "spheres of influence" in the "Third World" generated a process of progressive one-upmanship aimed at currying favour among newly independent countries:[20] "As the Soviet Union started to play to the gallery of the General Assembly, and the British and Americans plotted their turn to 'dish the Russians,' the 'small nations' ... were able to advance their own concerns, now often linked to the human rights agenda, in surprising ways."[21] Postcolonial states used their new-found authority to extend the principle of racial equality through the General Assembly's 1960 Declaration on the Granting of Independence by Colonial Countries and Peoples, and the 1963 Declaration on the Elimination of All Forms of Racial Discrimination.[22] The latter was elevated into a legally binding treaty in 1965, when the Convention on the Elimination of All Forms of Racial Discrimination was passed by a unanimous vote.[23] Postcolonial states also pressed their interests in other venues, notably the Commonwealth, where issues of racial equality often dominated discussions.[24]

At the domestic level, the revolution in postwar norms transformed the nature of minority-majority relations.[25] This was most obvious in the American Civil Rights Movement but was also true with regard to relations between indigenous peoples and whites in settler countries such as the United States, Australia, and Canada.[26] As was the case in the international sphere, paternalism and hierarchy were confronted by the newly ascendant principles of equality, dignity, and self-determination, which together formed a powerful discourse on behalf of groups hitherto subject to discrimination.[27] Domestic liberalism, which had readily adapted itself to race thinking and integral nationalism in the past,[28] was thus challenged by the human rights universalism of the postwar period. At the same time, struggles for equality in particular national contexts fed back into the international human rights movement through the globalization of discourses and techniques and the proliferation of rights claims. The "thickening" of the postwar normative context was driven by the dynamic interplay of domestic and global levels, mediated in important ways by non-governmental associations and an expanding array of transnational activists.[29]

The establishment of the Council of Europe in 1949 and the passage of the European Convention on Human Rights (ECHR) in 1950 aligned Western Europe's postwar development with the emerging global human rights movement.[30] The ECHR would serve as a "source of legitimacy and politico-moral commitment," anchoring the project of European integration in a distinctive normative basis.[31] The steady development of transnational ties via economic and political integration, under the terms of the 1950 "Schuman Plan" and the founding of the European Coal and Steel Community in 1951, also served to pool sovereignty and to align European states' interests in such a way that the nationalist rivalries that had sparked destructive conflicts in the past might be avoided.[32] The establishment of the European Economic Community (EEC) through the 1957 Treaty of Rome marked another important step in this project by committing its members (Belgium, Luxembourg, France, Italy, the Netherlands, and West Germany) to pursuing the harmonization of their economic policies and working to further liberalize the movement of goods, currencies, and labour.[33] As the EEC expanded to include more members, commitments to human rights and pooled sovereignty served as markers of a new European identity, which states with very different histories and cultures could claim in common. Although the "European project" has fallen far short of its more star-struck advocates' predictions and aspirations, it nevertheless "stands out as one of the [world's] most far-reaching and successful attempts at [building] an international human rights protection regime."[34]

In sum, the post-Second World War period marked a decisive shift in normative contexts, from one in which race, hierarchy, and discrimination were credible and widely acknowledged to one in which their legitimacy was increasingly rejected. The emerging normative context was given systematic form through human rights instruments, the doctrines of equality and self-determination, and anti-racist discourse. Norms helped propel the refashioning of the international system and contributed to important changes in the domestic politics and policies of liberal-democratic states. The postwar period thus constituted a "critical juncture" of the highest order in the history of membership politics in liberal-democratic states.

Yet immigration and citizenship politics and policy making in Canada and Germany followed a distinctive path. In both cases, the influence of the postwar normative context was mediated by the continuing sway of policy regimes developed in the prewar era. Rather than addressing the discrepancies generated by the clash of old and new orders head on, policy makers in Canada and Germany adapted more familiar policy regimes to new demands through what at the time were considered relatively modest concessions. As I demonstrate below, these efforts to "stretch" extant regimes to meet the requirements of a new normative order ultimately failed. Once the normative validity of their critics' positions was acknowledged, officials could not end the conversation or turn back the clock. Small-scale, incremental changes aimed at meeting the demands of a new normative order while staying true to the fundamental aims of established policy regimes led to their eventual unravelling, creating a need for more substantive changes in the future.

Opening the Gates Selectively: Canadian Immigration Policy, 1945-60

Economic Growth, European Refugees, and Renewed Immigration: 1945-47

Immigration to Canada all but ceased during the Great Depression and the Second World War, bottoming out at 7,445 in 1943.[35] Under the terms of Privy Council Order P.C. 1931-695, admissible classes were limited to healthy British subjects or US citizens not likely to become public charges; their wives or fiancées and unmarried children under eighteen; and "agriculturalists" having sufficient means to establish independent farms.[36]

While restrictions enacted during the Great Depression and war aimed at limiting entry generally, the exclusion of non-preferred groups was total.[37] During the war, German, Italian, and Japanese minorities were classified as "enemy aliens" and subjected to harsh treatment. Japanese Canadians had their fishing boats seized by order of the Royal Canadian Navy, saw their property confiscated and sold, and were forced to relocate away from the British Columbia coast into the Canadian interior in a massive violation of civil rights.[38] Many were also served deportation orders at the end of the war, and, despite court rulings invalidating the government's demands, several hundred left.[39]

The decision to resume immigration after the war came as a result of unexpected economic growth and concomitant labour shortages, on the one hand, and pressure to help alleviate the plight of refugees in postwar Europe, on the other.[40] With regard to economic expansion, the state's active role during the war catalyzed the rapid expansion of Canadian industry.[41] Pent-up consumer demand and improved access to plentiful natural resources such as petroleum, natural gas, and uranium helped maintain expansion in the postwar years, as did rapid population growth and readily available sources of foreign capital investment, principally from the United States.[42] In what proved to be a period of unprecedented economic expansion and prosperity, Canada's GNP jumped from $5.7 billion in 1939 to $36 billion in 1962. Unemployment remained low throughout this period and real incomes nearly doubled as Canada emerged as the world's fourth most prosperous industrial state.[43]

The combination of rapid economic expansion and historically low birth rates during the Depression and war led to labour shortages.[44] These domestic "pull" factors were joined by "push" factors, most notably the plight of thousands of refugees and "Displaced Persons" (DPs) in Europe. Canada was among the few countries in the world capable of accepting these refugees and was under international pressure to ease their plight and guard against political instability in Europe. Despite this merging of internal and external factors, the Canadian government approached immigration warily. Outright anti-Semitism expressed in postwar public opinion polls made the refugee issue politically sensitive, and fear of a postwar economic slump led the King government to initially resist calls for renewed immigration.[45]

Persistent lobbying on the part of employers, churches, and ethnic organizations, as well as the federal government's own interest in responding to its allies' demands and maintaining a population large enough to ensure Canada's sovereignty over its vast territory, came together to clinch the

decision to reintroduce immigration. The first statement of the government's postwar position on immigration was presented in a speech before
Parliament given by Prime Minister William Lyon Mackenzie King on May
1, 1947. Given its influence on immigration policy making in the immediate
postwar period, it is worth citing at length:

> The policy of the government is to foster the growth of the population of
> Canada by the encouragement of immigration. The government will seek
> by legislation, regulation and vigorous administration, to ensure the careful
> selection and permanent settlement of such numbers of immigrants as can
> advantageously be absorbed in our national economy ... With regard to the
> selection of immigrants, much has been said about discrimination. I wish
> to make quite clear that Canada is perfectly within her rights in selecting
> the persons whom we regard as desirable future citizens. It is not a "funda-
> mental human right" of any alien to enter Canada. It is a privilege. It is a
> matter of domestic policy ... There will, I am sure, be general agreement
> with the view that the people of Canada do not wish, as a result of mass im-
> migration, to make a fundamental alteration in the character of our popula-
> tion. Large-scale immigration from the Orient would change the
> fundamental composition of the Canadian population. Any considerable
> Oriental immigration would, moreover, be certain to give rise to social and
> economic problems of a character that might lead to serious difficulties in
> the field of international relations.[46]

King's statement captured the Janus-faced quality of early postwar thinking
on immigration, race, and nationality in Canada. On the one hand, it recognized that certain kinds of discrimination based on notions of racial hierarchy were no longer acceptable; on the other hand, it harkened back to
prewar concepts and language through its juxtaposition of European and
"Oriental" "stocks" and tacit acceptance of the idea that race and national
character were connected.[47] As Alan Green notes, "these biases, if not enshrined in the 1910 Immigration Act and its 1919 Amendment, had evolved
in various Orders-in-Council over the ensuing decades."[48] Canada's postwar
response to the migration-membership dilemma thus remained remarkably
static. This was true of the government's take on the "human rights" of immigrants as well. In line with previous practice, the Cabinet maintained
total discretion over the selection and treatment of migrants. Immigration
remained a "privilege" granted to immigrants at the pleasure of the state.

Even at this early stage, however, the government was forced to make concessions to critics who complained that the use of racial discrimination in Canadian immigration and citizenship policy clashed with Canada's commitments to postwar liberal principles. In a meeting of the federal Cabinet during which the Chinese Immigration Act, 1923, was discussed, the minister of external affairs, Louis St. Laurent, conceded: "Under the United Nations Charter, Canada has undertaken to avoid discrimination based on religion, color or sex, and to respect fundamental human rights ... [T]he present policy of exclusion ... could not be successfully defended in United Nations discussions."[49] Determined lobbying on the part of the Committee for the Repeal of the Chinese Immigration Act and diplomatic pressure from the Chinese government moved the government to strike the act in 1947 in order to stem criticism and to avoid possible embarrassment at the UN.[50]

Measures aimed at doing away with discriminatory naturalization regulations soon followed, lifting bars to citizenship for Chinese and other groups that had long faced discrimination in this area.[51] British Columbia removed barriers to the enfranchisement of Chinese and South Asians in 1947, giving members of both groups the right to vote in federal elections and to enter professions such as "accountancy, law, and pharmacy whose members had to be on the voters list."[52] The federal government lifted restrictions to the enfranchisement of Japanese Canadians in federal election in 1948; British Columbia followed suit in 1949.[53] As Carol Lee notes, the widening of the franchise was driven in the main by the Co-operative Commonwealth Federation (CCF), a left-of-centre party whose leaders took up the charge of anti-racism after the war, and a "coalition of concerned citizens, led by the liberal press, religious leaders, and community organizations," including groups representing Chinese, Japanese, and South Asian Canadians.[54]

Moves to enfranchise previously excluded groups were in accord with a more general reorientation of Canadian citizenship policy after the Second World War. The Citizenship Act, 1946, established a distinctive Canadian citizenship anchored in statute and reflective of Canada's growing independence from Britain: up until this time Canadian citizenship had been a corollary of British subjecthood.[55] The act would also set the ground rules for naturalization,[56] and it would serve as an instrument for drawing Canadians of different European ethnic origins together in a common Canadian national identity.[57] Hence "during the first inaugural [citizenship] ceremony organized in January 1947, the first certificate of Canadian citizenship was given to the prime minister, but the second went to 'Wasyl Elnyiak, one of the first Ukrainians to farm in western Canada.'"[58]

Despite these changes in citizenship policy, the goal of restricting the entry and incorporation of non-white immigrants remained a principal aim of state policy. Chinese immigration fell under the terms of P.C. 1930-2115, which limited the range of admissible "Asiatics" to the wives and children (under eighteen years of age) of Canadian citizens; other immigrant groups could apply to bring their family members to Canada after they secured legal residency. Given that "Asia" was defined in a "geographical" sense to include virtually every country in the Eastern Hemisphere outside of Europe, boundaries against all non-whites remained high.[59] Repeal of the Chinese Immigration Act and reforms to naturalization procedures therefore stood as symbolic gestures meant to appease critics while staying true to the aims of the established policy regime. Changes to citizenship law could be pursued at a relatively low cost, given that access to citizenship for previously excluded groups would continue to be checked by discriminatory admissions policies.

Back to the Future? Towards a New Immigration Act, 1947-52

Initial efforts to increase the immigration of preferred stocks included expanding the range of relatives who could be sponsored by foreign-born Canadian citizens through orders-in-council and broadening the list of admissible classes to include agricultural workers, miners, and lumber workers with guaranteed employment in Canada. Order-in-Council P.C. 2856 (June 9, 1950) enlarged the range of admissible European immigrants to include all those who satisfied the minister of citizenship and immigration that they were suitable with regard to "the climatic, social, educational, industrial, labour, or other conditions or requirements of Canada." Applicants also had to prove that they were not undesirable owing to their "probable inability to become readily adapted and integrated into the life of the Canadian community and to assume the duties of Canadian citizenship within a reasonable time after [their] entry."[60] Recruiting efforts in Great Britain and Western Europe were also stepped-up to increase the number of preferred immigrants coming to Canada.

In 1950, Germans were taken off the "enemy aliens" list and allowed to apply for entry under the conditions set for Europeans. Prohibitions against contract labour were also scrapped, and the pool of European DPs was "skimmed" to ensure that Canada's decision to assist in what was framed as a humanitarian endeavour would benefit Canadian employers and facilitate the entry of much needed labour.[61] Even here, however, ethnic preferences were in play, and certain refugee groups, such as Estonians and other "Balts," were much sought after, while others, especially Jews, were less appealing to Canadian field officers charged with making selections.[62] Guidelines regulating the sponsorship of refugees by family in Canada were also interpreted strictly to ensure that those admitted were of "preferable stock."

Pressure for a further widening of the gates continued to be exerted by employers, churches, and ethnic associations. In an unprecedented move, organized labour indicated that it would not oppose increased immigration outright, so long as it had a say in the program's development and was able to ensure that the interests of its members were taken into account.[63] In practical terms, this meant a more rigorous policing of the "back door" and the establishment of quasi-corporatist structures to grant labour a greater voice in setting immigration policy.

Perhaps the most important such consultative body established during this period was the Standing Committee of the Senate on Immigration and Labour. The committee was active from 1946 through to 1953 and published reports in 1946, 1947, and 1948.[64] It canvassed the opinion of business associations, transport companies, organized labour, community organizations, civil servants, ethnic lobby groups, and humanitarian organizations, including churches. A surprising degree of consensus regarding the need for a renewed immigration was expressed both in written submissions to the committee and in its own reports. The latter noted that Canada needed mass migration for population growth, economic development, and to ensure that it shouldered its share of the postwar humanitarian relief burden. The committee also noted that Canada required a "well-considered and sustained policy of immigration" and therefore recommended that the Immigration Act be revised. While the committee was generally bullish on immigration, it also warned that entries should not exceed Canada's "absorptive capacity" – that is, that immigration ought not to contribute to unemployment, reduce the standard of living, or otherwise endanger the Canadian economy.[65] This point reflected a key concern among representatives of organized labour, who tempered their support for renewed immigration with arguments against employers' use of foreign labour to drive down their members' standards of living.

With regard to the selection criteria, the Canadian Congress of Labour (CCL) stood against racial discrimination.[66] In its submission to the Standing Committee of the Senate on Immigration and Labour, the CCL argued:

Racial discrimination should have no place in our immigration policy. People from some countries may, because of their background, education, or customs fit into Canadian life more easily than people from some other countries, and such factors may properly be taken into account. But "race" (however defined) or nationality ought not to be considered at all.[67]

Although the committee also opposed discrimination based on race and religion, it did so only in so far these related to "Canada's traditional pattern of immigration and her strong European orientation."[68] Thus, while the committee held that "any suggestions of discrimination based upon either race or religion should be scrupulously avoided both in the Act and in its administration," limitations on "Asiatic" immigration should stand, as they were based on presumably legitimate "problems of absorption."

The Standing Committee's demand that all Europeans, irrespective of nationality and religion, be treated equally marked an important change rooted in Canada's wartime experience. The Canadian state went to great lengths during the war to ensure the loyalty of its immigrant population;[69] while coercion was used to police "enemy aliens," under the auspices of the Nationalities Branch of the Department of National War Services, a new emphasis on "integration" was developed for traditionally non-preferred European groups. This entailed greater respect for immigrants' cultures and a turn away from assimilation. It also called for a more positive depiction of Continental Europeans in order to gain Anglo-Canadians' sympathy and to bolster Canadian unity. Hierarchies among European races were therefore rejected and emphasis was placed on publicizing the essential contributions of all European immigrant groups. Moreover, the notion that Canada was the product of a "mixture" of white European nationalities was propounded. Distinctions among French, Anglo-Saxon, German, and Italian "races" were renounced in favour of a view that all Europeans – and therefore all white Canadians – were a product of mixture. As the pamphlet *Canadians All* put it, "none of our national groups from Europe is really alien to the rest of us."[70]

Thus, Italians, Slavs, Jews, and Greeks, among others, came to be regarded as legitimate Canadians who were officially on a par with their Anglo- and French-Canadian counterparts. However, racialized differences between whites and non-whites proved far more durable. No similar efforts were made to propagate the equality of Chinese or African Canadians. Indeed, even the CCL qualified its anti-racism by noting that the changes it demanded did not entail throwing open the gates for Chinese immigration and thus transforming Canada's identity.[71] Canada's other key union, the

Trade and Labour Congress (TLC), did not even share the CCL's tempered anti-racism. Speaking on behalf of the TLC, Percy Bengough noted that the union recognized "the need for selection and the exclusion of all races that [could not] properly be assimilated into the national life of Canada."[72]

The government responded positively to several of the Standing Committee's recommendations. Among the most important steps taken was the establishment of the Department of Citizenship and Immigration in 1950, which replaced the Immigration Branch of the Department of Mines and Resources.[73] Among the new department's most pressing challenges was to come up with an acceptable policy for regulating non-white immigration. A candid working paper bluntly laid out the dilemma confronting Canadian policy makers, echoing the concerns raised by Louis St. Laurent four years earlier: "The problem of Asiatic immigration into Canada is twofold: an international problem of avoiding the charge of racial discrimination and a domestic sociological and political problem of assimilation." Canada's membership in the UN carried with it an "unqualified obligation to eliminate racial discrimination in its legislation." This effectively meant supporting the UN's goal of "promoting and encouraging human rights and ... fundamental freedoms for all without distinction as to race, sex, language or religion." Further, Canada's statements in the General Assembly regarding the competency of the UN to intervene in domestic affairs of member states indicated that Canada favoured a "wide interpretation" of the provisions of the Charter. Claims to sovereign jurisdiction in domestic matters would therefore be open to challenge. As such, Canada was vulnerable to charges of hypocrisy:

> Because of these provisions of the Charter against racial discrimination and the unequivocal position taken by the Canadian delegation at the ... General Assembly, the Canadian delegation at any future session would be placed in an extremely embarrassing position if a delegation from some Asiatic country were to raise the question of the existence of racial discrimination in Canadian legislation, among other matters, in respect to immigration.[74]

Given the obvious risks to Canadian international prestige, the brief recommended that steps be taken to avoid or at least minimize the likelihood of such an outcome. Here, however, "sociological and political factors" – specifically, the perceived difficulty in assimilating "Asiatics" – intervened to foreclose certain options, such as the equal treatment of Asians in immigration regulations. Thus, the problem could only be resolved by "revising

[Canadian] immigration legislation so as to avoid the charge of racial discrimination and yet so effectively limiting Asiatic immigration as to prevent aggravation of the Asiatic minority problem and at the same time initiating measures to encourage the assimilation of the existing Asiatic minority groups in Canada." Based on the available options, the report concluded that a quota system might provide a suitable means of addressing Canada's postwar immigration dilemma.[75]

Although some officials eagerly embraced the quota option, others felt that the cost of adopting such an approach would exceed its benefits. Opponents of quota schemes drew on the experience of the United States to argue that they set rigid limits on the recruitment of preferred immigrants while still leaving governments vulnerable to accusations of discrimination. Failure to reach consensus on the desirability of quotas for non-white immigrants led to a compromise: the quota solution would only apply to immigration from Canada's South Asian Commonwealth partners, India, Pakistan, and Ceylon.[76] Other non-white migration would continue to be managed through administrative regulations and orders-in-council. Thus, the government concluded agreements with India, Pakistan, and Ceylon (present-day Sri Lanka) that established yearly immigration quotas for each of these Commonwealth partners. According to the terms of the quotas, 150 Indians, 100 Pakistanis, and 50 Ceylonese were to be granted access to Canada on a yearly basis. In addition, Canadian citizens could sponsor their wives, husbands, unmarried children under 21, fathers over 65, and mothers over 60. It was hoped that the move might limit the damage that Canada's discriminatory polices were causing in the Commonwealth.[77]

The regulation of "Asiatic" migration from other sources (e.g., Hong Kong) and that of other restricted classes would be dealt with under the terms of Orders-in-Council P.C. 2115 and 2856[78] and the new Immigration Act, which was passed in 1952 and came into effect on June 1, 1953. Rather than coming up with new measures to deal with the changed normative context described in the report cited above, Canada's circa-1952 response to the migration-membership dilemma bore a striking resemblance to those of the past. The near-total discretion granted to the minister of citizenship and immigration and his officers was maintained along with a long list of prohibited classes. According to the act, the Governor-in-Council was empowered to prohibit or limit the admission of persons because of their:

1 Nationality, citizenship, ethnic group, occupation, class, or geographical area of origin

2 Peculiar customs, habits, modes of life, or methods of holding property
3 Unsuitability vis-à-vis climatic, social, industrial, educational, labour, health, or other conditions or requirements existing temporarily or otherwise, in Canada or in the area or country from or through which such persons came to Canada
4 Probable inability to become readily assimilated or to assume the duties and responsibilities of Canadian citizenship, within a reasonable time after admission.[79]

Despite shifts in language, such as the replacement of "race" with the term "ethnic group," the intent of the list was very much in line with past practice. As per King's 1947 statement, immigration was to be closely regulated to ensure to the greatest extent possible that Canada's "national character" remained essentially white European. While appeals to the judgments of immigration officers could be made, the final arbiter of such disputes was the minister of citizenship and immigration since the act explicitly forbade the interference of courts. This was true for deportation decisions as well. While the act's elucidation of the terms constituting legal "domicile" in Canada provided some clarification, it also placed migrants who lacked this status in an extremely precarious position by maintaining the state's total discretion in deciding deportation cases.[80] This extraordinary discretionary power facilitated the state's policing of boundaries both with regard to non-preferred ethnic groups and to individuals deemed to be threatening as a consequence of their perceived ideological orientations.[81]

Continuity and Criticism, 1952-60

Policy making up to and including the Immigration Act, 1952, consisted of efforts to stretch Canada's established immigration and citizenship policy regime to meet the demands of a more liberal global normative context. However, policy stretching failed to satisfy external and internal critics of Canadian immigration policy. Their efforts would maintain pressure on the government, leading to further concessions and, over time, the steady unravelling of the established policy regime.

With respect to foreign affairs, Canada's championing of progressive positions in the United Nations and British Commonwealth made maintenance of discriminatory migration policies increasingly difficult. Canada's Caribbean partners in the British Commonwealth – Jamaica, Barbados, Trinidad, and the other island states making-up the "British West Indies" – were among the most vocal critics of Canadian immigration policy. A report prepared for the new minister of citizenship and immigration in 1957 noted:

> Most of the island governments have a positive almost aggressive approach to the question of migration privileges for their people. Public statements by responsible officials indicate the belief that a federated British West Indies within the Commonwealth will be able by consistent pressure to persuade Canada to ease its Immigration Regulations. The goal is complete equality for British West Indies' residents with other British subjects under the Immigration Act and Regulations.[82]

Such pressure was channelled through Canadian diplomatic representatives in the Caribbean who forwarded complaints to their superiors at the Department of External Affairs in Ottawa. In turn, external affairs regularly queried the Department of Citizenship and Immigration as to what might be done to counter complaints of discrimination and increase the scope of immigration from the West Indies. Caribbean governments also made their position clear to British officials who were asked to convey their message to the government of Canada.[83] British officials readily complied: concern regarding rates of immigration from the West Indies was generating tensions in some British towns and cities, and British officials hoped that Canada might open its gates to a greater number of immigrants from the Caribbean to "share the burden."

Officials in the Department of Citizenship and Immigration responded to these demands by insisting that Canada had limited room for manoeuvre:

> Our immigration policy is based on the principle that Canada desires to foster the growth of the population by the encouragement of immigration through legislation and vigorous administration to ensure the careful selection and permanent settlement of such number of immigrants as can be advantageously absorbed into the national economy ... [I]mmigration must not have the effect of altering the fundamental character of the population and Canada is perfectly within her rights in selecting persons whom we regard as desirable future citizens.[84]

Invocations of "official policy" and reference to fundamental principles became increasingly problematic in light of developments in Canadian foreign policy. Changes in international politics were pushing Canada to take increasingly liberal positions in the UN and the British Commonwealth.

Decolonization in Africa and Asia transformed power relations in both organizations and placed racial discrimination at the top of their agendas. By 1961, African, Asian, and Latin American members constituted two-thirds of the UN General Assembly, and anti-racist resolutions were becoming sharper and more frequent.[85] As Canada's ability to play an independent role in world affairs depended on the preservation and functioning of both organizations,[86] it could not afford to sit back when crises arose over the international community's handling of matters pertaining to racial justice.

Among the most important challenges confronting the Commonwealth during this period was the debate over South Africa's membership. Non-white member states argued that there was no place in the organization for racist regimes and demanded that their partners come out strongly against apartheid. The massacre of sixty-nine peaceful protestors in Sharpeville only two months before the Commonwealth's 1960 conference raised the stakes of the debate and increased tensions. During the 1960 conference, non-white members made it clear that the future of the organization would depend on how the apartheid issue was resolved. In an effort to avoid a split that could imperil the Commonwealth's future, Canada's Prime Minister, John Diefenbaker, came out strongly against the principle of racial discrimination during the Commonwealth's 1961 conference in London.[87] In a statement to the Canadian Broadcast Corporation (CBC), Diefenbaker declared: "in a Commonwealth composed of many races and colours, and with an overwhelming majority of colour other than white ... the principles of equality, without regard to race or any other consideration, must be generally acceptable to all member nations."[88]

Diefenbaker's crusading anti-racism was a source of concern among diplomatic personnel charged with administering Canadian immigration policy. Canadian consular officials understood that their country's public stand against race discrimination could easily be turned against it if and when immigration matters were raised. In their view, Canada was courting trouble by believing that it could take a leading role against racism internationally while maintaining discriminatory controls against non-whites in its immigration policies.[89] Their opinion was born out as critics of Canadian immigration policy never tired of pointing out Canada's reluctance to implement the principles it espoused abroad in its own legislation. These charges dogged Canadian leaders and complicated relations with partners in the Commonwealth and UN.

Domestic critics, such as the Canadian Council of Churches, the Canadian Jewish Congress, the Negro Citizenship Association, and the

Canadian Congress of Labour, also drew attention to Canada's continuing use of racial categories.[90] Advocacy groups challenged the government's oft-stated commitment to anti-discrimination, civil rights, and liberal democratic principles by exposing its maintenance of discriminatory immigration policies and administrative practices.[91]

The language employed by advocacy groups took full advantage of the discursive resources made available by the discrediting of racist science and the linking of racial discrimination to Nazism. In an angry public letter written in response to the minister of citizenship and immigration's denial of a request for family unification – on the grounds that the applicant would be unable to adapt to life in Canada because of her socialization in a tropical climate – a representative of the Brotherhood of Sleeping Car Porters argued that the minister's argument stood as "a masterpiece of ... Fascistic racialism." The letter went on to note:

> Evidently the good Minister ... has been drinking from the fountain of racism, whose intellectual source is such chauvinist propagandists as Huston Chamberlin of Germany, Arthur de Gobineau of France, if not Thomas Dixon of notorious Ku Klux Klansman fame. The anthropological offerings of whom have long since been completely discredited and exploded as mere myths and fantasies and are only worthly [sic] of being consigned to the ash can of oblivion from which they ought never to emerge ... In fact the old notion that Negroes could not endure the cold weather like white men and hence would die out if they attempted to live in the northern part of the United States is on a par with the psychological and sociological anachronism of a Negro being without a soul and wholly incapable of comprehending the so-called white man's civilization.[92]

Domestic critics also reminded officials of their commitments to international human rights and the elimination of discrimination based on race, colour, or creed. In its 1960 brief to the minister of citizenship and immigration, the Joint Committee of Oriental Associations of Calgary joined these two themes, noting:

> The world is embarking on a new era of international negotiations aimed at understanding, and co-existence of opposing cultures, as a solution to the grievances that have in the past led to wars. We cannot speak as a nation with sincerity and force in such matters if we continue certain absolute discriminatory bars to people of particular races and colour ... The present

government has gained wide support ... as a government which respects fundamental human freedoms as evidenced by the advocation [sic] of the Bill of Rights. It is respectfully submitted that we, as Canadians, should restrict those discriminatory aspects of our immigration policy as much as possible.[93]

The Canadian government's reaction to charges of discrimination was to continually adjust regulations to pre-empt or at least blunt the force of criticisms, while endeavouring to meet the objectives set out in King's 1947 statement. Officials introduced a number of changes in an effort to respond to critics and make good on promises to apply immigration regulations in a fairer and more sensitive manner. These included doubling India's annual quota from 150 to 300 persons, expanding the annual quota of female domestic workers from the British West Indies (established in 1955) from 230 to 280, and reconsidering previously rejected applications for sponsorship to increase the number of entries from China and other non-preferred countries.[94] Officials also made a point of informing critics of these moves in order to demonstrate their sensitivity to their concerns. Thus, in a letter to a member of the Christian Citizenship Society, Minister of Citizenship and Immigration Ellen Fairclough noted that special provision was being made "for the admission from Asian countries of wives and minor children and in some instances fiancées as well as aged parents of persons residing in Canada." The minister noted that nearly twenty-two thousand immigrants from Asia had been granted admission to Canada between 1955 and 1959, 55 percent of whom were Chinese.[95]

Critics of Canadian immigration policy were not impressed by the department's efforts. Far from providing solutions to the government's problems, the stretching of the system to accommodate internal and external critics' demands was compounding problems. For example, the government's effort to assuage Canada's East Indian community by doubling India's annual immigration quota prompted Pakistan to demand that its quota also be doubled.[96] While Canadian officials were well aware that acceding to Pakistan's demand would run the risk of encouraging similar requests from other Commonwealth countries, they had little choice but to comply, given that rejecting Pakistan's demand would likely lead to further accusations of discrimination and perhaps even a public airing of Canadian policies in the Commonwealth. Similarly, while efforts aimed at increasing the number of Chinese immigrants through ministerial discretion and orders-in-council failed to satisfy domestic advocacy groups, potential alternatives that remained wedded to traditional principles – such as quotas – were also open to charges of discrimination and were, therefore, of little practical use.[97]

There is evidence that Minister of Citizenship and Immigration Fairclough intended to respond to these pressures by pursuing a more comprehensive strategy. Indeed, she proposed that the Cabinet consider appointing a royal commission on immigration to allow the public to express its opinion on immigration matters, particularly regarding the classes of persons that Canada should seek as immigrants.[98] The proposal stalled, and discussions of reform were largely limited to the confines of the civil service. The Cabinet did authorize the Department of Citizenship and Immigration's intention to begin work on non-discriminatory immigration regulations in April 1960,[99] and Fairclough announced the government's interest in devising standards to be "applied consistently to all who seek admission to [Canada]" in a speech to the House of Commons on June 9 of the same year.[100] The culmination of these efforts would be the 1962 Immigration Regulations, discussed in Chapter 4.

In short, Canadian officials found that cosmetic solutions aimed at mollifying international and domestic opinion while preserving the essential features of the prevailing system were inadequate. Policy stretching could not disguise the fact that discriminatory immigration policies did not fit with either the emerging postwar normative context or Canada's carefully crafted image as a progressive "middle power"; rather, continuing pressure from domestic advocacy groups, external actors, and others led to further concessions. As stretching gave rise to unravelling, the coherence and utility of the established framework diminished, making Canada's immigration policies inconsistent and increasingly difficult to administer. This, in turn, created opportunities for the introduction of new solutions to the migration-membership dilemma in accord with prevailing norms.

The Return and Demise of Temporary Labour Recruitment: Germany, 1945-73

Postwar Rebuilding and Refugee Incorporation, 1945-55

In contrast to Canada, Germany emerged from the war a defeated and divided country under foreign military occupation. The shifting of Germany's eastern borders and compulsory transfer of ethnic German minorities from Poland, Czechoslovakia, and other East European countries under section 13 of the Potsdam Protocol created a refugee crisis of epic proportions, with upwards of 9 million persons entering the Western zones of occupation alone.[101] The refugees joined millions of internally displaced Germans, civilian foreign workers, prisoners of war, and returning German servicemen – along with approximately 200,000 concentration camp prisoners – contributing to a highly mobile and chaotic situation, marked by shortages of housing and food and high unemployment. The strain on resources prompted by the refugee influx gave rise to growing disaffection among the local population and friction between newcomers and natives.[102]

West Germany's rapid economic revival helped to diffuse what many feared was a potentially dangerous refugee problem.[103] Several factors contributed to this outcome. Perhaps most important, Germany's industrial capacity remained relatively intact after the war, despite the Allies' extensive aerial bombing campaign.[104] Remarkably, "the German armaments industry reached its production peak in the summer of 1944, and even in the first quarter of 1945 ... was at a level almost double that of 1941."[105] The Nazis' use of forced foreign labour on a mass scale also allowed Germany's war economy to continue functioning at a high level throughout the period leading up to the German surrender in 1945. By the end of the war, the German economy was dependent on the forced labour of approximately 8 million foreign workers (*Fremdarbeiter*).[106]

The combination of relatively robust industrial capacity and significant foreign assistance, as exemplified by the Marshall Plan, accelerated the expellees' integration into West Germany's postwar labour market. Industrial production in West Germany tripled between 1949 and 1959 and unemployment fell from 9 to 1 percent – despite an increase in the active labour force from 13.6 to 19.6 million. Expellees and refugees from East Germany served as a useful replacement for the millions of recently departed forced labourers, contributing to the expansion of the economy.

Towards Mass Labour Recruitment, 1955-59

Improvements in West Germany's economic fortunes in the 1950s led to a tightening of the labour market.[107] Although unemployment remained a key political issue, especially with regard to expellees, there was concern that insufficient labour power would dampen growth in geographical regions and economic sectors experiencing expansion. Agitation from employers and concern among some in the federal government with maintaining growth prompted renewed interest in the recruitment of foreign labour. In 1955, the president of the Confederation of German Employers (*Bundesvereinigung der deutschen Arbeitgeberverbände* – BDA), Hans Paulssen, cautiously noted that the recruitment of foreign workers could allow for a necessary expansion of the workforce.[108] Employers emphasized that many European countries were eager to shed their own unemployed citizens and urged West German policy makers to do more to facilitate such movements.

The Italian government also raised the issue of coordinated labour migration during Economics Minister Ludwig Erhard's visit to Rome in 1954. Italian leaders were keen to reduce levels of domestic unemployment and benefit from remittances earned by workers abroad. Although German negotiators did not express the same level of enthusiasm as did their Italian interlocutors, talks continued through 1954 and 1955.

Erhard's discussions with the Italians over foreign workers generated media attention, provoking a sharp reaction in Germany, where the ministers of Labour, Agriculture, and Expellees expressed their disagreement with the economics minister's plans. Erhard responded to these concerns by noting that several factors, including anticipated improvements in the defence industries, expansion of the federal armed forces, and an expected decline in West Germany's birth rate, necessitated the taking of "prophylactic measures."[109] Foreign workers could take up the relatively unskilled positions in agriculture and industry made available by German workers who were being trained for skilled occupations in an increasingly advanced industrial economy.[110] Foreign workers' mobility, flexibility, and lower levels of consumption would allow them to be deployed as a low-skilled industrial reserve and economic buffer, facilitating German workers' upward climb into more technologically sophisticated occupations.[111] The government's and employers' pledge to honour the trade unions' demand that foreign workers be treated as equals in terms of pay rates and benefits also eased fears of wage competition.[112] Thus, Erhard and West German employers sold foreign labour recruitment as a benefit for business and labour alike. The government's insistence that recruitment would serve as a temporary measure to deal with short-term problems in the labour market for which there was no other alternative limited criticism of the proposed policy.[113]

The German-Italian Agreement on Worker Recruitment was signed in Rome on December 20, 1955.[114] According to the agreement, Italian workers would be selected by a recruitment commission organized under the auspices of the Federal Institute of Labour, with the assistance of the Italian Labour Administration. Employers would forward requests for foreign workers to local employment offices and pay a recruitment fee for each worker. Announcements of job openings were sent to the Federal Employment

Administration in Munich and then forwarded to the Employment Administration office in Milan, which distributed notices to the Italian Labour Administration officials.[115] Successful job candidates were directed to the German Employment Administration office in Milan, where they were given documents confirming their identity, lack of criminal record, and marital and family status. After a thorough medical examination, German doctors and officials would decide on a prospective recruit's suitability for work in Germany. In the case of a positive decision, contracts in both Italian and German were signed and the worker was issued a renewable twelve-month *Legitimationskarte* that served as a work permit. Upon arrival in West Germany, foreign workers registered with the local employment office and then the police, who issued a temporary residence permit (*Aufenthalts-erlaubnis*). Accommodations were to be provided by the employer, as per guidelines formulated by the Federal Ministry of Labour and Social Affairs.[116] Upon expiry of their contracts, foreign workers were to return home and be replaced by fresh recruits.

The regulation of foreign workers' rights and status in West Germany fell under the terms of the circa 1938 *Ausländerpolizeiverordnung* (APVO – Police Decree on Foreigners), which was re-implemented without parliamentary debate in 1951 in response to concerns raised by interior ministers at both the federal and state levels regarding the need for some instrument for regulating the presence of foreigners in the country.[117] The regulation's major objective was to increase state power over aliens. Given that APVO was a Nazi revision of a Weimar-era statute, the lines of descent tracking the legal dimension of foreigners policy in postwar Germany were clear.[118] The decision to opt for temporary recruitment based on twelve-month work permits, protection of domestic labour through the re-imposition of the Weimar-era *Inländerprimat* (priority of nationals), and discursive framing of foreign workers as a reserve army of labour and economic buffer all reflected a return to familiar ways of envisioning and managing the migration-membership dilemma.[119]

The return to established practices was also evident in the area of citizenship policy. While the Nazis' explicitly racist citizenship and naturalization laws were annulled, the division of Germany granted new life to the principle of descent (*jus sanguinis*) and the 1913 *Reichs- und Staatsangehörigkeitsgesetz:*[120] "Retaining the principle of descent [allowed] the Federal Republic to maintain the idea of a single German nation despite the division of Germany and the foreign administration of the eastern territories."[121] This

was clearly expressed in Article 116 of the Basic Law (*Grundgesetz*), according to which "everyone is a German who holds German citizenship or who,
as a refugee or expellee of German *Volkszugehörigkeit*, or as a spouse or
descendant of such a person, has been admitted to the territory of the
German Empire as it existed on December 31, 1937."[122]

The revival of *jus sanguinis* reflected the Federal Republic's interest in
casting itself as the legitimate heir of the German Reich and sole representative of "all Germans."[123] Descent-based citizenship helped maintain the notion of a unified nation that persisted in spite of the country's partition into
separate, ideologically antagonistic states. Thus, refugees of "German stock"
(*Volkszugehörigkeit*) fleeing East Germany, the Soviet Union, and other Eastern and Central European states could claim equal footing as Germans once
they entered the Federal Republic.[124] This appeal to the bonds of descent was
further strengthened with the passage of the Federal Expellee Law of 1953
(*Bundesvertriebenen- und Flüchtlingsgesetz* – BVFG), the sixth paragraph of
which states: "Members of the German *Volk*, within the meaning of this law,
are those who in their homeland have maintained and acknowledged
German identity and can confirm it through such evidence as descent, language, upbringing, or culture."[125]

While the Basic Law's sanctioning of a descent-based citizenship regime
was rooted in the realities of postwar European geopolitics, its wholeheart-
ed embrace of universal human rights reflected the framers' resolve to set
postwar Germany on a path towards democratic governance and the rule of
law. As the German Constitutional Court put it: "underlying the Basic Law
are principles for the structuring of the state that may be understood only
in the light of historical experience and the spiritual-moral confrontation
with the previous system of National Socialism."[126] Hence, Article 1 of the
Basic Law holds that "human dignity is inviolable. To respect and protect it
shall be the duty of all state authority." A further range of universal fundamental rights (*Jedermann Grundrechte*), including "the right to equality before the law without disadvantage or favour stemming from sex, parentage,
race, language, homeland and origin, faith, or religious or political opinions," are granted to all persons in Germany, regardless of their citizenship
status.[127] Thus, while the Basic Law reserves certain rights for German citizens,[128] its protection of fundamental human rights has created a "constitutional ambivalence" towards the rights of foreigners, granting them standing
based on their personhood. As noted in Chapter 5, this constitutional ambivalence would come to play an important role in determining the rights
and status of foreigners in the Federal Republic in later years.

Expansion and Entrenchment, 1959-66

Foreign worker recruitment was limited in size and scope during the 1950s, with approximately 167,000 workers entering West Germany between 1955 and 1959. Recruitment picked up after 1959 as a result of continuing economic growth and the building of the Berlin Wall, which stopped the flow of East German refugees into the Federal Republic and deprived employers of a hitherto important source of labour. Other factors, including a shrinking working-age population, the introduction of mandatory military service, a shorter workweek, low rates of female participation in the labour market, and longer stints of postsecondary education for West German students, led to heightened demands for foreign labour.[129] Potential "sending" countries were also eager to secure recruitment agreements to help shed excess labour and to improve trade balances through the receipt of remittances. Consequently, recruitment contracts along the lines of the Italian model were signed with Greece (1960), Spain (1960), Turkey (1961), Portugal (1964), and Yugoslavia (1968). Hence, a framework meant to administer relatively modest numbers of mostly seasonal labourers was adapted to mass recruitment.[130] Whereas 85,000 foreign workers entered the Federal Republic in 1959, 259,000 arrived in 1961, with the total number of foreigner workers surging to 549,000 in 1961 and topping 1 million in 1964.[131] The expansion of the metalwork and engineering industries also meant that seasonal agricultural workers were no longer the primary target group for employers; rather, "employers' organizations and the Federal Ministry for the Economy demanded that as many foreign workers as possible should be recruited and that conditions should be shaped as to encourage foreigners to come for long-term employment."[132] The Federal Office for Labour Placement and Unemployment Insurance (*Bundesanstalt für Arbeitsvermittlung und Arbeitslosenversicherung*) urged support for the state's foreign labour recruitment project, noting that, "given current economic developments, the German population [would] have to come to terms with the idea of living together with greater numbers of foreign workers."[133]

Agreement on the need to foster economic growth encouraged consensus and limited public debate on the issue. The notion that foreign workers could be sent "back home" when the economic situation worsened and German jobs were put at risk was also widely held. Foreign workers were seen as something of a bargain, consuming far less in social services than they contributed by way of taxes. Moreover, as Rita Chin notes, "the heavy burden of guilt inherited by the Federal Republic for the genocide of the Holocaust, committed in the name of a pure German *Volk*, made West

German leaders anxious to demonstrate a new sense of openness to non-Germans."[134] Labour Minister Theodor Blank maintained that the guest worker program allowed for the "merging together of Europe and the rapprochement between persons of highly diverse backgrounds and cultures in the spirit of friendship a reality."[135] Guest worker recruitment was thus a highly advantageous means of advancing the Federal Republic's foreign policy interests and pursuing "normalcy."[136]

That being said, the rising number of "guest workers"[137] in West Germany did prompt some observers to question whether viewing foreign labour recruitment as a provisional, short-term process still made any sense, given the sharp rise in numbers and the propensity of increasing numbers of workers to settle in the Federal Republic. By the mid-1960s, the notion of a "foreigner problem" was being voiced, as were questions as to the "economic, political, and ethnological" limits of labour recruitment. In the words of one observer: "We will have to get used to the idea that everything that is connected with foreign labour – accommodations, family apartments, schools, cultural institutions, and so forth – will remain continuously on the agenda."[138] Similarly, another editorialist urged Germans to summon the "courage to no longer speak of guest workers but rather of immigrants" as doing so would allow for a more serious consideration of the consequences of settlement, particularly as regarded housing policy and family reunification.[139] And, in a statement prefiguring Yasemin Soysal's argument for postnational citizenship by almost thirty years, Eberhard de Haan observed that the "foreign worker of today" was "the European citizen of tomorrow," given that European citizenship was largely predicated on mobility rights granted to European *workers.* "Based on this reasoning," de Haan continued, "the term 'guest worker' must be struck from Germany's national vocabulary if Germany is to move beyond self-serving nationalist illusions."[140]

German officials were aware of the rapid increase in the number of foreigners in the country. They were also conscious of the fact that guest workers were being joined by family members in Germany. The first serious effort to counter these trends came with the 1961 recruitment agreement with Turkey.[141] The original agreement included a strict two-year maximum stay clause, requested by the Federal Ministry of the Interior to make the temporary nature of labour agreement explicit. However, before anyone was actually forced to return to Turkey under the terms of the clause, the BDA, supported by the Federal Ministry of Economics, demanded a revision of the agreement. Employers were impressed by how well Turkish workers performed on the job and felt that it would cost too much to train new workers every two years.[142] Not surprisingly, they lobbied vigorously for the removal of the maximum-stay clause. Federal Ministry of the Interior officials attempted to strike a compromise by acceding to employers' requests while checking immigration through a proposed amendment to the recruitment agreement that set strict limits on Turkish workers' family reunification rights. In essence, the proposed amendment denied Turkish workers the right to sponsor spouses and minor children. Turkish officials balked at this proposal, arguing that it would subject its workers to unfair discrimination. Several federal ministries also questioned the political merits of such a move, noting that the discriminatory bent of the proposal would raise unwanted criticism and damage Germany's efforts to enhance its image abroad. Once again, the Federal Ministry of the Interior relented. The revised recruitment agreement with Turkey implemented in 1964 lacked both a maximum-stay clause and special restrictions on family reunification.

In the meantime, migration continued to expand, and more and more guest workers opted to stay in Germany for longer periods, often being joined by spouses and children. This prompted further concern among politicians and policy makers. On the one hand, a new "Foreigners Law" was passed in 1965, replacing the 1938 *Ausländerpolizeiverordnung*. Concern that APVO's unsavoury history might lead to an embarrassing situation for Germany led to calls for a new more "liberal and open-minded" law, which would "demonstrate to the whole civilized world that the Federal Republic of Germany [was] striving to overcome the ill-fated past through positive regulations."[143] In truth, the new law did very little to improve the rights of foreign workers in West Germany. Article 2 instructed officials only to grant or extend residence where the foreigner's presence did "not injure the interests of the Federal Republic of Germany."[144] "Liberalization" was approached from a cosmetic point of view rather than from a principled one: "Under the guise of eradicating one more vestige of the Nazi past, the Bundestag created a legal instrument that gave the state more control and discretionary power over foreign workers and their efforts to settle in West Germany."[145]

Indeed, at the same time, federal and state interior ministers were working behind the scenes to craft guidelines to guide administrative decisions "on the ground." Their "Fundamental Principles of Foreigners Policy" (*Grundsätze der Ausländerpolitik*) represented a renewed attempt to formalize the rotation principle and hinder family reunification in order to discourage permanent settlement.[146] There were four elements in the interior ministers' demands: First, the range of migration-sending countries would be narrowed to exclude non-Europeans – with the exception of citizens of the

United States, Canada, Australia, New Zealand, and Israel; second, control over entry would be strengthened, especially with regard to migrants who entered the Federal Republic with tourist visas; third, efforts would be made to halt settlement and encourage rotation (this would be accomplished through the implementation of a three-year limit to residency); and fourth, family reunification would only be granted to migrants who had been in the country for three or more years and could demonstrate the provision of "adequate living space." The intent of the interior ministers' guidelines was punctuated by the first recorded instantiation of what would become a familiar refrain: "The Federal Republic of Germany is not an immigration country."

Once again, reaction to the interior ministers' efforts was sharply critical. Both the economics and foreign ministries complained that the guidelines were far too restrictive and cast Germany in a negative light.[147] Thus, the three-year residency limit was rejected. A series of exceptional regulations were also formulated to deal with various objection to, and problems with, the interior ministers' guidelines. For example, the interior ministers had "simply ignored" guarantees of freedom of movement granted to citizens of EEC member states under Article 48 of the 1957 Rome Treaty.[148] Germany's strong endorsement of the project of European unification and economic liberalization made shirking this condition extremely difficult as doing so would both call into question its efforts to cast itself as a rehabilitated, progressive European state and anger Italy, an important ally, stalwart proponent of freedom of movement, and major source of guest workers. As Karen Schönwälder notes, by the 1960s it was clear that the signing of the Rome Treaty in 1957 constituted "a political step ... that entailed a loss of control over migration processes and the settlement of foreigners."[149] Foreign policy considerations also arose from the fact that several of the recruitment agreements provided for family reunification after only one year. Again, the federal government would be placed in an awkward position if it allowed bilateral treaties to be circumvented by administrative regulations formulated in the bureaucratic shadows and not formally endorsed by the federal government.

In light of reactions to its proposals, the Federal Ministry of the Interior was forced to back down and be satisfied with the maintenance of its demand that family reunification only be allowed where foreigners demonstrated proof of adequate housing. The no-non-Europeans provision was also left intact and provided helpful cover for a widely held antipathy towards migration from Africa and Asia.[150] Despite these "victories," advocates of control were deprived of the means needed to aggressively block the settlement of guest workers in the Federal Republic. In the absence of a mechanism for compelling rotation, de facto immigration would continue.

The sharp rise in unemployment that accompanied the recession of 1966-67 eased officials' worries as recruitment was scaled back and foreign workers' applications for extensions of their residency permits were denied, prompting the return of some 245,000 foreign workers between September 1966 and February 1967. By the end of June 1967, there were approximately 300,000 fewer foreign workers in the Federal Republic than there had been the year before.[151] For many, the guest workers' apparent willingness to return home provided proof of the model's successful functioning.[152] The debate over foreign workers lost momentum as the Federal Republic struggled to regain its economic footing, and other issues, including the incipient student movement and war in Vietnam, captured the West German public's attention.

Towards the "Recruitment Stop," 1967-73

The resumption of recruitment after the end of the recession in 1967 led to a sharp increase in the number of migrants in the Federal Republic. By 1969, the number of foreign workers exceeded 1 million, and in the autumn of 1970 almost 2 million foreign migrants worked in West Germany.[153] By 1973, West Germany was host to approximately 2.6 million foreign workers, constituting approximately 11.9 percent of the total labour force. Initial reaction to the resumption of mass recruitment was reminiscent of the early 1960s, with government officials emphasizing the positive and relatively inexpensive contribution of guest workers to West Germany's economic development.[154] Given that robust economic growth was crucial to the successful pursuit of the Brandt government's reform agenda, there was general consensus that foreign workers would be needed to make good on promises for a more equitable and socially just West Germany.[155]

Questions arose as to the government's ability to manage the mass recruitment of foreign workers as it became increasingly clear that labour migration would indeed entail significant costs. A study undertaken by the Federal Institute of Labour found that, as of 1968, over 50 percent of male foreign workers had been in the Federal Republic for four or more years. Furthermore, 41 percent were living with their spouses in Germany.[156] Though many migrant families were engaged in the labour market, by 1967 upwards of 815,000 foreign citizens in the Federal Republic were unemployed. By 1973, this figure had risen to 1.37 million.[157] The reality of what in

truth amounted to a process of permanent immigration was once again setting in and, with it, the growing awareness that social costs related to school-
ing, housing, health, and a myriad of other areas would inevitably follow.[158]
Articles in newspapers and magazines also debated the merits of improving
foreign workers' access to German citizenship.[159] To many contemporary
observers, Germany was on the cusp of a significant transformation: would
decision makers seek to limit or even reverse the changes wrought by migration or embrace Germany's emerging status as an "immigration country"
and advance the "integration" of foreign workers?[160]

Responses to this weighty question were mixed. Conservative governments in Bavaria, Schleswig-Holstein, and other *Länder* pushed for a tougher line and were in favour of independently assuming greater control in
limiting foreign workers' residency rights. On Bavaria's initiative, the *Länder*
introduced a series of "Principles for the Granting of Residency Rights"
(*Grundsätze für die Erteilung der Aufenthaltsberechtigung*), calling for a
five-year maximum stay for all foreigners.[161] This time, representatives of the
BDA stood in favour of compulsory rotation, arguing that it represented a
practical means of maintaining foreign worker recruitment while minimiz-
ing its social costs.[162]

Attempts to implement the principles generated a storm of protest
against "forced rotation" (*Zwangsrotation*).[163] Trade unions and other civil
society actors argued that the federal government should eschew such
brutal measures and instead do more to secure and improve the status and
rights of foreign workers in the Federal Republic. Protest actions along these
lines included the drafting of an alternative to the 1965 Foreigners Law that
tapped into the language of human rights.[164] A petition in favour of the alternative proposal drew the signatures of 150 prominent West Germans and
won the support of both the Roman Catholic and Protestant churches and
the *Deutscher Gewerkschaftsbund* (DGB), or German Trade Union Federation, in 1971.[165] In early 1973, the DGB put forward its own "Demands for
the Reform of the Aliens Law," according to which foreign workers' security
should be increased by both limiting officials' discretion in granting residency permits and making deportation decisions subject to review by a special committee.[166]

The Brandt government's response to these developments was ambiguous. On the one hand, after giving the matter serious consideration, Brandt's
Cabinet rejected compulsory rotation and agreed with reformers that
more must be done to integrate foreign workers into West German society.
The 1971 Ordinance on Work Permits (*Arbeitserlaubnisverordnung*) was

introduced to allow foreign workers employed for more than five years to obtain a special five-year work permit that was not dependent on changes in the economy and labour market.[167] In January 1972, the federal government made clear its rejection of forced rotation by pledging that no legal instruments would be used to enforce limits on foreigners' stay in West Germany.[168] Furthermore, steps were taken to amend regulations to the citizenship law that discriminated against the foreign husbands of German women, particularly those from "developing countries." In response to criticism from the *Interessengemeinschaft der mit Ausländern verheirateten Frauen* and the left wing of the SPD's parliamentary group (*Fraktion*), the government amended the law, making it easier for foreign husbands to apply for citizenship.[169] In 1974, the Bundestag (spurred in part by court decisions that rejected the constitutionality of the rule holding that children could only inherit German citizenship from their German father) passed legislation allowing for the passing of nationality through German mothers, thus ensuring that children from all mixed marriages would acquire German citizenship at birth.[170] Residency rights for foreign spouses were also improved in 1972 through an amendment to the regulations for administering the Foreigners Law.[171]

Brandt also underscored his government's principled opposition to rotation on a number of occasions. In a speech given at the Opel auto plant in Rüsselsheim on June 26, 1973, he declared:

> We should never leave the impression that the Federal Republic of Germany is exploiting foreign workers as some kind of reserve army of labour that one can haul into the country and then ship out. That would be socially irresponsible, inhumane and entirely uneconomical. Whether German or foreign, people for us are not "material," with which we feed a gigantic economic machine as we desire. The economy is there to serve people – and above all those people whose efforts make its successes possible ... The spirit of social responsibility therefore compels us to reject forced rotation ... The state and administration alone cannot solve the foreign worker question. Solidarity is required both in the workplace and, where possible, during off-hours. It is precisely in this way that a people proves that it is a good neighbour.[172]

Despite such lofty declarations of principle, Brandt was unable to make a consequent move towards accepting the reality of mass immigration and enacting suitable policies. Like most German political elites at that time,

Brandt clung to the hope that a significant number of guest workers would return to their home countries voluntarily. This is not to say that more far-ranging approaches were not discussed. In the weeks leading up to the 1972 federal election, the federal interior minister, Hans Dietrich Genscher, attracted significant press coverage by proposing a two-pronged response to Germany's migration-membership dilemma. On the one hand, Genscher argued that Germany had reached the "limits of receptiveness" and should therefore scale down its foreign recruitment policies; on the other hand, he wondered whether it would not make sense to formulate a "real immigration policy" that offered migrants who had effectively cut off ties to their former countries a "real chance at integration in our country."[173] Genscher was not alone in this regard. In June 1971, the deputy leader of the SPD's parliamentary *Fraktion*, Hans Apel, asked whether it was not time to liberalize access to citizenship for long settled foreign workers and their families. Similarly, the SPD's Hermann Buschfort called for the easing of naturalization provisions for foreign workers, arguing: "current practices [are] no longer sustainable if the goal of our political efforts is a united Europe."[174]

While doubtlessly important, the more radical alternatives advanced by Genscher, Apel, Buschfort, and others were not embraced by their colleagues; rather, the SPD-FDP coalition's "Action Program," introduced in June 1973, consisted of six points:

1   Housing provided by employers would have to conform to new Employment Administration guidelines

2   Entry and settlement would be dependent on the absorptive capacity of receiving areas as set down by federally established criteria

3   The recruitment tax on employers would be raised to help pay for language and job training and housing construction as well as administrative costs

4   Further taxes on employers would be considered if the desired consolidation did not occur

5   Illegal entry would be fought more effectively

6   Rotation would be rejected.[175]

Despite its nod to solidarity, the Action Program passed over questions regarding how settled migrants ought to be dealt with in the longer term. This revealed the extent to which the logic of temporary recruitment continued to guide official thinking on these issues. The SPD-FDP government's inability to break with this logic was symbolized by Brandt's characterization of settled foreign workers as "co-citizens with their own particular status."[176]

Although the government was also keen to wind down its recruitment policy at this time, it was wary of provoking negative reactions among employers and sending countries. In late 1973, the oil crisis provided an opportunity to act: using the looming energy crisis as a pretext, Labour Minister Arendt announced that Cabinet had directed the Employment Administration to temporarily halt recruitment on November 23, 1973. Arendt noted that the step was a "precautionary measure to stem the employment of foreigners." Those who remained employed in Germany had no cause for concern, though the outcome of the energy crisis might require further action.[177] The government immediately deferred sixty thousand pending recruitment requests and notified foreign governments that their workers would no longer be needed. Labour Minister Arendt defended the decision by noting that, although foreign workers could not be treated as slaves and simply abandoned once the economy ran into trouble, German workers' interests took precedence during periods of retrenchment. Thus, the Federal Republic's use of foreign labour was once again reduced to an economic exercise. As Arendt made clear in December 1973:

> The Federal Republic of Germany does not consider itself to be an immigration country in the classical sense. Our principal position is that people who come to our country to work should voluntarily return to their home countries after a time, and contribute to the further development of their country.[178]

To the dismay of German officials, the recruitment stop reinforced immigration trends as millions of foreign workers opted to stay in Germany for fear that they would be shut out of the Federal Republic if they returned to their home countries. Having decided to remain, many arranged for their spouses and minor children to join them. Thus, while the proportion of working males declined, that of dependent women and children increased.[179] The recruitment stop also gave rise to shifts in the national composition of the foreign population, with migrants from Italy, Spain, and Greece opting to return to their home countries in greater numbers than did foreign workers from Turkey. This reflected improving economic and political conditions in the former countries. Italy's, and later Spain's, Greece's, and Portugal's membership in the European Community (EC, the successor to the EEC) also granted migrants from these countries rights of movement that Turkish nationals lacked. Consequently, the Turkish population in the Federal Republic grew from 469,000 in 1970 to approximately 1.5 million in 1984, representing the largest single national group in the country.[180]

Family reunification migration quickened the growth of migrant communities in West German cities, so that by the mid-1970s one could speak of genuine "ethnic" neighbourhoods in urban centres, "with their own shops, bars, churches, mosques and clubs."[181] In 1973, 26.5 percent of the employed labour force in Stuttgart was foreign; in Frankfurt the figure stood at 22.1 percent.[182] Wittingly or not, Germany had developed into a diverse immigration country. Yet, aside from a few notable exceptions, thinking on integration remained mired in the logic of the prevailing "guest worker" system. This glaring anomaly would drive the unravelling of established policies in the years ahead.

Conclusion

The resumption of mass migration in Canada and West Germany after the Second World War was marked by the intersection of changed normative contexts and prewar policy frameworks. In both countries, policy makers reached back to familiar solutions to the migration-membership dilemma, while at the same time carefully excising elements of older policies that could no longer be sustained in light of changing norms. Thus, Canada attempted to administer an immigration system that did not discriminate on the grounds of race but *did* aim to exclude non-white Europeans to the greatest extent possible. West Germany implemented a temporary labour recruitment program that eschewed compulsory rotation and hence allowed for the long-term settlement of foreign workers in the Federal Republic, albeit in the absence of policies designed to facilitate their integration.

In both cases, older policies fitted uncomfortably with changed social and political conditions. Domestic and international critics drew attention to this lack of fit and pressed for reforms. Canadian and German policy makers responded to these criticisms by tinkering at the margins of their respective systems, trying to accommodate critics while maintaining the essentials of their migration policy regimes. However, such tinkering could only suffice for a time; in both cases, the growing anomalies generated by changed contexts would lead to more profound transformations in the future. Ultimately, policy stretching and unravelling would lead to shifting.

In Canada, policy unravelling led to the collapse of the country's established membership regime in the 1960s. By 1967, the essential features of a new system were in place. They were entrenched in the Immigration Act,

1976. In Germany, the halting of labour recruitment in 1973 was advanced as a means of reasserting state authority in a field many feared was spiralling out of control. Yet millions of "provisional co-citizens" (*Mitbürger auf Zeit*) remained in the Federal Republic, crystallizing what had long been a de facto immigration process and intensifying questions about their residency rights and access to German citizenship. Worsening economic conditions, fraying political consensus, and the re-emergence of populist xenophobia influenced the ways in which German policy makers addressed these questions, such that fundamental changes to the Federal Republic's membership regime were only enacted some twenty years after the "temporary" halt to foreign labour recruitment announced in November 1973. While changes in a common normative context drove Canada and Germany to reconsider their responses to the migration-membership dilemma in the postwar period, distinctive political dynamics would result in significant differences in the nature of their responses.

4

Dismantling White Canada

By the end of the 1950s, it was becoming clear that the strategy of stretching immigration policies to meet the expectations of the postwar normative context had failed. Domestic and international critics were not satisfied with the incremental changes introduced by Canadian governments in the preceding years and continued to demand that Canada live up to its commitments to anti-discrimination and human rights by fundamentally reforming its immigration policies. Within Canada, demands for change were being voiced by an expanding range of actors, with academics and influential members of the print and broadcast media complementing the long-standing work of ethnic associations, liberal religious organizations, trade unions, and civil liberties groups. Internationally, Canada's partners in the Commonwealth and the United Nations continued to press Ottawa to honour its oft-stated commitments to racial equality.

Domestic and international critics' arguments were strengthened by developments in and outside of Canada. The American Civil Rights Movement's rise to prominence increased popular support for non-discrimination, as did the ongoing process of decolonization in Africa and Asia – a development that enjoyed Canada's strong backing in the Commonwealth and UN. Furthermore, the passage of anti-discrimination legislation in Canada, at both the provincial and federal levels,[1] contrasted with the maintenance of a discriminatory immigration policy – a point not lost on either elites or the general public. A growing number of politicians, particularly members of Parliament (MPs) representing constituencies with high concentrations of immigrants, also pressed for more substantive changes to Canada's immigration policy regime. For their part, immigration officials were frustrated by a badly frayed system whose blurred mandate made it increasingly difficult to administer and defend.

These factors came together to prompt a search for new solutions to the migration-membership dilemma that would offer critics proof that Canada's positions on anti-discrimination and civil rights were not empty gestures, while also injecting a measure of coherence into a policy regime stretched to the point of collapse. The years spanning the 1960s and early 1970s thus marked a period of transition, from the policy stretching and unravelling of the early postwar years to policy shifting.

Policy shifting was facilitated by fortuitous timing and the effects of Canada's political institutional configuration. The move to a truly universal admissions regime through the introduction of the "points system" in 1967 occurred during a period of general optimism fuelled by postwar economic prosperity. The successful entrenchment of the 1967 Immigration Regulations in the Immigration Act, 1976, despite a negative turn in economic conditions and growing antipathy towards immigration in the mid-1970s, was facilitated by the dynamics of Canada's political institutions. Immigrants who had benefited from the liberalization of policy in previous years were concentrated in competitive urban ridings key to both the federal Liberal and Conservative parties' electoral fortunes. Canada's single member plurality (SMP) electoral system encouraged the building of winning electoral coalitions that included immigrant voters – a trend that had roots in the 1950s. As such, it made very little sense for politicians to take an anti-immigration position or otherwise to challenge the cross-party political consensus that had emerged around immigration policy in the preceding years.

In marked contrast to developments in Germany, the shift to a new immigration policy regime in line with the prevailing normative context was achieved relatively quickly and smoothly in Canada. The perceived political benefits of maintaining support for a liberal admissions regime outweighed those of responding to significant but diffuse anti-immigration public opinion. This, in turn, solidified cross-party consensus, leaving opponents of reform without a politically efficacious means of challenging liberalization.

Towards the Points System

The 1962 Immigration Regulations

While the token reforms of the late 1950s did little to assuage critics of Canadian immigration policy, they did accelerate the unravelling of the regime, making it increasingly difficult to administer and defend. In light of this, immigration officials set about reorienting Canada's admissions regime away from race and more firmly towards work-related skills. Their efforts informed the Immigration Regulations of 1962. Scholars have assumed that the turn to a non-discriminatory, "skills-based" immigrant admissions system at this time was driven by changes in Canada's economic needs and reductions in the number of potential migrants in Europe. Alan Green nicely captures this view, noting that "the major changes in immigration control ... were economic in nature ... [C]hanges in the state of the economy were decisive, while political influences were marginal."[2] This position needs to be reconsidered. While there certainly was growing consensus within the Department of Citizenship and Immigration on the need to revamp the immigration program and focus recruitment on skilled workers, professionals, and entrepreneurs,[3] there is little evidence to suggest that officials believed that this would necessarily entail active recruitment from "non-traditional" sources.[4] Rather, the two issues developed along parallel but quite distinct lines. The subsequent linking of the two objectives in 1961-62 was driven by *political* rather than by economic reasons. That is to say, the shift to universal skills-based selection criteria in 1962 was primarily aimed at mollifying domestic and international critics of racial discrimination rather than at opening up new sources of skilled migrants. While the goal of attracting skilled immigrants to Canada reflected a contemporaneous view emerging from within the bureaucracy,[5] it did not drive the decision – changes in normative contexts and related political developments did.

This becomes clear when one considers how officials characterized the 1962 reforms. According to Director of Immigration W.R. Baskerville, the purpose of the change was to "abolish racial discrimination from [Canada's] policy," while making it clear that Canada would "still give preference in [its] selection of immigrants to those countries which have traditionally supplied [its] immigrants."[6] Similarly, in a memorandum to Cabinet outlining the department's proposed measures, Minister of Citizenship and Immigration Ellen Fairclough noted that the "principal criticisms of Canada's ... immigration legislation" was that "it [was] based on racial or colour discrimination."

As such, the foremost objective of the revised regulations was "the elimination of any valid grounds for arguing that they contain any restrictions or
controls based on racial, ethnic or colour discrimination."[7] This would be
accomplished through the amendment of Regulation 20, which, according
to Fairclough, constituted "the heart of Canada's immigration policy" and
main target of criticism.[8]

The proposed changes to Regulation 20 were unique in that they elimin-
ated "all reference to questions of nationality, geography or regions of the
world."[9] In place of such criteria:

> The new Regulation 20 (a) lays primary stress on selectivity based skills
> and qualifications as the main conditions for admissibility, without regard
> for any other factor. If an applicant can qualify on these grounds and has
> sufficient means to establish himself in Canada until he finds employ-
> ment, or alternatively has a firm employment opportunity or plan for self-
> establishment in Canada, he comes within the admissible classes.[10]

The chief effect of the new regulations would be the elimination of "all
grounds for charges of discrimination" and placement of "emphasis hence-
forth on the skills, ability and training of the prospective immigrant himself,
and on his ability to establish himself successfully in Canada."[11]

The amended Immigration Regulations were tabled in the House of
Commons on January 19, 1962. In her address to the House, Fairclough
noted that the new regulations would

> improve the position of nationals of all countries without weakening the
> position of any. The chief beneficiaries will be the Asians, Africans and na-
> tionals of Middle Eastern countries ... for the first time unsponsored appli-
> cants from these parts of the world with the necessary qualifications will be
> admissible to Canada ... Next to Asians, Africans and nationals of Middle
> Eastern countries, persons from the Central and Latin American countries,
> including the West Indies, stand to benefit. Nationals of these countries will
> for the first time come within the admissible classes on the basis of their
> education, training and skills.[12]

Fairclough's statement makes clear that the intended beneficiaries of the reforms were the previously inadmissible classes and their advocates, both in
Canada and abroad. Far from being the product of economic forces, the new

Immigration Regulations would serve a distinctly political end by granting the government a more effective means of countering accusations of racism and discrimination.[13]

Related policies also speak to the political nature of the 1962 reforms. The government decided to limit sponsorship rights of non-Europeans and maintained an official but unpublicized policy of maintaining a preference for immigrants from Canada's traditional sources – that is, the United States and Europe. Whereas Canadian citizens hailing from European and Western Hemisphere countries were able to sponsor a full range of family members and relatives, including children over the age of twenty-one, married children, siblings and their corresponding families, and unmarried orphaned nieces and nephews under the age of twenty-one, citizens from non-European and non-Western Hemisphere countries were limited to sponsoring members of their immediate family and a narrower range of relatives. The decision to restrict the sponsorship rights of citizens from Asia, Africa, and most of the Middle East (with the exception of Egypt, Israel, and Lebanon) was meant to limit the impact of the policy changes on immigration flows. Officials feared that the granting of full sponsorship rights to migrants from Africa and especially Asia would prompt a flood of non-white minorities whose presence could catalyze a negative backlash among white Canadians.[14] The "security threat" posed by potential Communist infiltrators also led officials to opt for maintaining limits on Chinese sponsorship rights.[15]

Similar anxieties stood behind the decision to interpret the 1962 reforms passively, allowing unsolicited applications from non-traditional sources but only actively recruiting immigrants from the United States, Western Europe, and the British Isles. While acknowledging that they were "bound by the provisions of the new Immigration Regulations to *service* applications anywhere in the world," Canadian officials insisted that there was nothing preventing them from concentrating their promotional efforts on encouraging immigration from traditional sources.[16] The Canadian government's decision to forego the establishment of immigration offices in the Caribbean and to maintain limited administrative capacity in Asia and other parts of the "Third World" was derivative of such thinking.[17]

Whether the "political" approach that characterized the 1962 regulations would satisfy domestic and international critics of Canadian immigration policy remained to be seen. In a memorandum written before the tabling of the revised Immigration Regulations, the director of immigration correctly noted that, while the changes succeeded in establishing a broad legal standard, they did not "define the means by which it [was] going to be interpreted in administrative practice."[18] In essence, the government had reformed the immigration policy "superstructure" while leaving its administrative "base" in place, thereby exposing it to scrutiny:

> As long as the critics could see a concrete geographical basis for our selective policy, they never suspected that our major tool of control was the number and size of immigration offices in various parts of the world. This was so little apparent that it escaped, not only outside observers, but a good many departmental officials, even Ministers. Now, with the "blind" gone, it would be reasonable to expect that more searching questions will be asked, as soon as the Department starts reporting on its achievements under the new deal. Will the new policy result in changes in the composition of the flow? Whether it does or not, critics, on both sides, are going to ask for explanations.[19]

Continuing Discrimination?

The 1962 reforms generated a generally positive, if guarded, response. On the one hand, the media, advocacy groups, and foreign governments welcomed the government's decision to formally repeal racial and ethnic criteria in its admissions policies; on the other hand, the overall impact of the changes was subject to speculation. The headline on the front page of the Toronto *Globe and Mail* the day after the regulations were tabled nicely captured this ambiguous response: "Canada Unlocks Its Doors to All Who Possess Skills: Bias Ends – On Paper at Least." In an accompanying report, the newspaper noted that distinctions based on national origin were maintained in sponsorship rules and that the minister had herself stated that she "did not expect any major change in Canada's pattern of immigration" as a result of the new regulations.[20] An editorial in the *Globe and Mail* two days later noted that, while the changes would help "clear Canada of the reproach of practicing racial discrimination in its immigration policy," whether the new rules would actually work in practice would "depend on how they are enforced." The editorial went on to note:

> The great danger of the situation is in the fact that enforcement will be in the hands of immigration Department officials whose whole training and tradition has emphasized the necessity of excluding persons from "undesirable"

parts of the world. There is a real risk that these men will interpret the rules regarding education and skills so rigidly and pedantically that no more immigrants will be in fact admitted than before.[21]

An accompanying story on Chinese-Canadian reactions to the announcement of the new regulations underscored doubts regarding the efficacy of the new rules among members of the community.[22]

The Department of Citizenship and Immigration's own review of mainstream and "ethnic" press responses to the announcement of the new regulations revealed that a good deal of the coverage was marked by similar scepticism:

> Columnists pointed out that acceptable skills were still comparatively rare among colored people. Since many such applicants came from countries where the opportunities for education and training were limited, they would continue to have difficulty in meeting Canada's standards. It was also noted that the new immigration regulations gave immigration officials greater responsibility and more individual discretion than ever before and concern was expressed over the way it might be used. One columnist asked pointedly why the Minister had not abolished discrimination in relation to sponsored relatives ... Chinese-Canadian reaction was mixed. While a number seemed happy, some expressed "bitter disappointment" over the lingering limitation of the sponsorship of relatives. Others saw "a sign of limited friendship" in the new regulations but felt there were "hidden restrictions" in the "invisible background." Too much power, the majority felt, was left in the hands of immigration officials. Applicants, they averred, could always be rejected on the ground that they lacked sufficient skills, education, etc.[23]

Doubts as to the effectiveness of the new regulations were warranted. As noted, the 1962 regulations were a political gesture meant to appease domestic and international critics without changing the composition of immigration flows. The maintenance of preferred sources persisted and efforts were redoubled to improve recruitment efforts in those parts of the world.[24] Beyond the fact that immigration from non-traditional sources would not be encouraged and administrative capacity stood far below that needed to carry out a truly global immigration program,[25] critics were correct to note that the vagueness of the new regulations and the discretion left to immigration officers would be used to restrict the flow of non-white immigrants.

Immigration officials' reticence was based in part on doubts as to whether even well-qualified non-white immigrants could successfully adapt to life in Canada and be accepted by Canadians. These concerns were used to justify a double standard in

the *administrative* application of the Regulations ... [We] recognize, for example, the greater difficulties that are faced by a West Indian who tries to find employment in Canada, as compared to a Western European. This may justify and even require a somewhat more exacting interpretation of adequacy in terms of skills and settlement arrangements in the case of the West Indian, since we know for a fact that the cards will be stacked against him to some extent in Canada, and that therefore he needs more skills or more resources if he is to have an even chance with the others. This kind of discrimination, in my opinion, can be justified and defended.[26] (Emphasis in original.)

Another memorandum on the subject states:

Although we are trying to remove racial and national distinctions from our selection it is a fact that because our examination facilities are concentrated in Europe non-Europeans at present have a harder time to get into Canada. Applications which are "paper screened" are approved only if the applicant is obviously well qualified while our visa officers in Europe in direct contact with applicants often approve the admission of someone who is not particularly well qualified but is very suitable personally. I think we must also admit that someone from a society totally unlike ours is going to have trouble establishing himself in Canada unless he is very well qualified. Therefore there may be a *natural* tendency in immigrant selection to demand better qualifications of some immigrants than others, for example, East Indian compared to Irish or Germans. This distinction is not a deliberate thing and our instructions to staff emphasize that all applicants should receive equal treatment but I believe it is a *natural* consequence of our officers' efforts to assess the applicant's ability to settle successfully in Canada.[27] (Emphasis added.)

Hypothetical concerns about the entry of qualified immigrants from societies "unlike" Canada's took on practical effect in the field. In a letter to the acting chief of operations (Administrative Services) in the Department of

Citizenship and Immigration, Canada's immigration attaché in New Delhi noted:

> I have found on several occasions that well-educated and otherwise well-qualified persons are simply unacceptable as immigrants due to the [sic] rigidly inflexible social attitudes, or obvious lack of suitability to a Canadian environment, stemming mainly from religious, racial, or class prejudices.

The official went on to note that "Anglo-Indians ... because of their mixed blood, Christian faith, and Westernized outlook" would fare better and thus recommended "taking in a carefully selected number of those well-qualified people whose potentialities [were] being suppressed [in India]." Yet settling on such prospects would be difficult; while there were "substantial" numbers of Indians who believed that their "prospects would be better in a country like Canada," most would prove ineligible:

> Herein lies perhaps the most important, and yet most tedious, burden at this post – sifting through the enormous quantity of chaff in order to garner the relatively few grains of fertile wheat.[28]

Canadian officials' reaction to events in Great Britain, where rioting in opposition to immigration from the West Indies and other New Commonwealth countries was fuelling demands for immigration restriction, also tempered their support of non-discrimination in Canada's immigration policy.[29] Notwithstanding the non-discriminatory bent of the 1962 Immigration Regulations, immigration officials maintained that Canada's interest in preserving social peace and maintaining an active immigration program justified its reserving "the right ... to decide its own social and racial composition" by refusing "to accept immigrants whose presence would cause severe disruptions or drastic change."[30]

The 1962 regulations were thus Janus-faced. Viewed from one side, they dramatically broke with past practice by formally rejecting the principled use of race, nationality, and culture in determining the suitability of immigrants. As political scientist David Corbett put it at the time: "The important thing is that the Immigration Regulations are now framed to emphasize skills, occupation and family sponsorship, and to subordinate preferential treatment of applicants from selected parts of the globe."[31] At the same time, it is important to stress that the reform was meant to appease domestic and international critics of racial discrimination while not altering the composition of immigration flows – and hence Canadian society – to any appreciable degree. From this angle, the 1962 regulations might reasonably be deemed an instance of, albeit dramatic and consequential, policy stretching. While the hard tone of Mackenzie King's 1947 statement was replaced with a more cosmopolitan cadence, the aim of immigration policy as it related to nation building remained strikingly similar.

These built-in limits to Canada's 1962 reforms did not go unchallenged. Governments in the West Indies questioned whether the rules were being applied fairly regardless of applicants' skin colour,[32] and the under-secretary of state for external affairs noted that the response to the new regulations among countries in South American, Central America, Africa, and noncommunist China was "disappointingly low."[33] Canadian immigration officials in the field were also keenly aware that the 1962 amendments had not solved their problems and duly registered their concerns. Canadian diplomatic personnel in the West Indies and Pakistan complained of not having enough resources to process long overdue applications or to answer requests for information from local residents.[34] Contrary to expectations, the issue of race refused to recede; rather, it continued to occupy a prominent place in discussions of Canadian immigration policy making.

Resolving the two outstanding issues pertaining to racial equality – sponsorship rights and global administrative capacity – would prove to be difficult. With regard to sponsorship, Canada's liberal position on family reunification, as set out in the Immigration Act, 1952, was now seen as a serious problem. In the immediate postwar period, employers' demands for low-skilled workers justified a liberal approach to sponsorship, which facilitated large flows from Southern Europe. By the late-1950s, changing labour market needs and concern regarding the social consequences of large-scale sponsorship prompted a reconsideration of this approach. Policy makers were particularly alarmed by the phenomenon of "chain migration," whereby primary migrants (selected under prevailing admission schemes) sponsored their more distant relatives, who, in turn, sponsored even more distant relatives, effectively bypassing any system of immigration selection. Officials believed that chain migration was leading to a surfeit of undereducated and unskilled immigrants, particularly from Italy, Greece, and Portugal, who were ill-suited to the needs of Canada's changing economy.[35] Moreover, uncontrolled sponsored immigration was seen as having "contributed powerfully to the growth of large and, to a considerable extent, self-contained ethnic communities in Montreal and Toronto and, to a more limited degree, in certain other cities."[36]

The Diefenbaker government's preferred solution to the quandary of chain migration lay in narrowing the range of family members eligible for sponsorship to spouses and minor-age children. This qualified right to sponsorship would hold for all Canadian citizens and landed immigrants. The Conservatives tried to implement this approach in March 1959, through the passage of Order-in Council P.C. 1959-310. The move evoked protest, however, especially among Italian Canadians, who believed the measure unfairly targeted them.[37] Their intensely negative reaction convinced the Conservatives to rescind their decision in order to avoid further alienating an increasingly important segment of urban voters.[38] The episode demonstrated that sponsorship was a politically loaded issue to be handled with care.

The problem of global administrative capacity involved questions of resource allocation: so long as non-whites were perceived as threats to social and political stability, the shifting of resources to pay for expansion would be resisted and the preference for opaque decision-making procedures that allowed for the maintenance of double standards would endure. What was needed was both a politically acceptable non-discriminatory solution to the sponsorship dilemma and the determination to reform the administrative component of Canadian immigration policy. Despite Diefenbaker's genuine embrace of equality and human rights, his government was unable to resolve these challenges, allowing the issue of racial discrimination in Canadian immigration policy to linger.

The 1966 White Paper on Immigration Policy

The federal election of June 18, 1962, saw the Conservative Party's majority in the House of Commons contract to ninety-two seats, leaving Diefenbaker to preside over a weakened minority government. Diefenbaker was forced to resign a few months later, in the wake of a Cabinet revolt and two lost confidence votes on February 5, 1963. Despite campaigning effectively in the weeks leading up to the election of April 18, 1963, "Dief the Chief" was relegated to leader of the Official Opposition as the Liberal Party under the leadership of Lester B. Pearson secured enough seats in the House of Commons to form a minority government.[39]

Pearson thus inherited the problems associated with the 1962 reforms and, like his predecessor, was forced to defend Canada against continuing charges of racism. In November 1963, the *Globe and Mail* noted the lack of any substantive change in the number of non-whites who were being admitted into Canada and asked whether the 1962 Immigration Regulations were "being applied equally to coloured and white immigrants." The editorial went on to demand that the newly appointed Liberal minister of citizenship and immigration, Guy Favreau, "take action to correct abuses where they may be found."[40] Domestic advocacy groups whose constituents were subject to sponsorship limits criticized the perpetuation of double standards and demanded that equality be granted to all groups.[41] Foreign governments also made a point of reminding Canadian officials that a lack of administrative capacity outside of Canada's traditional sources of immigration suggested that the much heralded move to a universal immigration policy was, at best, as yet incomplete. Japan's ambassador to Canada, Hisanaga Shimadzu, stated that he "would [have] like[d] to [have] see[n] some positive action by the Canadian Government" with respect to immigration from Japan. His colleague, Kazuo Wachi, suggested that delays in setting up a Canadian immigration office in Tokyo were based on "an unwritten bar on Japanese immigrants." Wachi urged that Canada's "door ... be thrown wide open."[42]

Given the Liberal Party's promises to liberalize immigration policy prior to and during the 1963 election campaign,[43] and Pearson's lofty ambitions for Canada in the area of foreign policy, accusations of racism became increasingly difficult to ignore.[44] Presidents Kennedy's and Johnson's much publicized efforts to reform the United States' immigration policies also put pressure on Pearson to follow suit.[45] During a press conference in Jamaica on November 30, 1965, Pearson formally acknowledged the reality of a double standard in admissions procedures and sponsorship rights and pledged to make good on Canada's promise to remove racial discrimination "in fact as well as in theory."[46] He intimated that his government was considering new means of regulating admissions and would reveal the details of its consideration shortly. In a sop to his partners in the Commonwealth, Pearson also agreed to a long-standing request that Canada introduce a temporary farm labourer program to employ workers from Jamaica and other Caribbean countries.[47]

The decision to eliminate the lingering vestiges of racial discrimination in Canada's immigration policy aggravated a perennially thorny issue: despite the Pearson government's official positions on issues of race and discrimination, officials in the Department of Citizenship and Immigration continued to be troubled by the prospect of greater levels of sponsored migration from "non-traditional sources."[48] Pearson's pledge to repeal the discriminatory provisions of the 1962 Immigration Regulations meant that some other means had to be found to maintain control over sponsored flows, lest

Canada face the prospect of admitting "massive waves of newcomers unprepared for Canadian life."[49] While the admission of "unskilled" and "poorly educated" Greeks, Italians, and Portuguese was troubling enough to immigration officials,[50] they believed that similar flows of sponsored immigrants from the West Indies, Asia, and other "non-traditional sources" would create a "double disability" as a result of the immigrants' "racial variance from the Canadian majority and lack of occupational qualification."[51] Immigration officials were convinced that the sponsorship "time bomb" had to be confronted lest matters spin out of control.[52]

Stepped-up efforts to meet these challenges coincided with the reorganization of Canada's immigration policy apparatus. In December 1965, Pearson called for the Department of Immigration and Citizenship and the Department of Labour to be merged into the new Department of Manpower and Immigration, which was to be led by the recently appointed minister of citizenship and immigration, Jean Marchand.[53] The move signalled that immigration would be dealt with in a more technocratic manner, such that immigrant admissions better complemented the government's labour market policies. Marchand's reputation as a progressive also suggested that concerns regarding race discrimination in Canadian immigration policy would be dealt with seriously.[54]

The White Paper on Immigration Policy,[55] tabled in the House of Commons on October 14, 1966, tackled the issues of race and sponsorship head on. It made clear that there could no longer be any room for discrimination on the grounds of race, ethnicity, or religion and committed Canada to establishing a universal immigration policy. Foreign policy considerations were key in this regard: "Any discrimination, in the selection of immigrants, creates strong resentments in international relations."[56] The White Paper also emphasized the benefits of a consistent immigration program targeting skilled immigrants capable of adjusting to Canada's "highly complex industrialized and urbanized society." At the same time, however, it warned of the economic and social consequences of uncontrolled sponsored immigration. Unskilled and poorly educated immigrants, it maintained, were at risk of becoming burdens: finding themselves unable to keep up with innovations linked to technological change, they would slip into the ranks of the unemployed, compounding labour market deficiencies and adding to the costs of Canada's social welfare system. Moreover, the tendency of immigrants to concentrate in large cities – principally Montreal and Toronto – threatened the emergence of "ghetto-like slums" that would offset the advantages of increased cosmopolitanism.[57] For the authors of the White Paper, sponsored migration was not simply an economic problem: it was also a looming threat to social cohesion.

The White Paper's policy recommendations followed from its analysis. First, Canada would accentuate its effort to recruit well-educated and highly skilled immigrants capable of quickly settling in the country and contributing to its economic development. Second, Canada would move away from a "tap-on, tap-off" approach to a more consistent immigration program capable of attracting well-educated, skilled, and flexible workers from other industrialized countries. Policy makers believed that the difficulty in convincing such immigrants to come to Canada instead of staying in their home countries or opting to immigrate to the United States or Australia was exacerbated by Canada's failure to communicate its intentions consistently through the operation of an aggressive immigration program. This would require both a commitment to raising immigration's stature on the public policy agenda and investing the financial resources needed to maintain an activist program. Third, remaining discrimination in the realm of sponsorship rights would be ended. Finally, the White Paper announced the government's intention to reform the immigration appeals process by granting the Immigration Appeals Board the power to deal conclusively with appeals to deportation orders. Expansion of the Assisted Passenger Loans scheme to countries outside of Canada's traditional immigration sources was also recommended, thus ending a long-standing discriminatory practice.

The White Paper's solution to the perceived dangers of uncontrolled sponsored migration came in two parts. First, the sponsored stream would be split into immediate dependents (spouses and minor-age children), to be admitted as a matter of course, and a second category of more distant relatives whose admissibility was subject to qualifications – namely, the possession of primary education and some work-related skill that was in demand in Canada.[58] Second, while all landed immigrants would enjoy the right to sponsor the same array of dependents and "eligible relatives," after a six-year adjustment period only Canadian citizens would be able to sponsor the full range of relatives stipulated under the proposed system. Policy makers believed that tying sponsorship rights to the acquisition of citizenship would introduce a "delaying effect" as naturalization required five years residence. This, in turn, would dampen the sponsored movement's "potential for explosive growth."[59] Although they did not say so publicly, officials also believed that the requirement that more distant relatives possess "minimal education requirements" would limit sponsored flows from Asia and Africa.[60]

The authors of the White Paper were confident that they had settled on a means of effectively limiting uncontrolled sponsored immigration that did not risk provoking the ire of "ethnic groups" wary of the government's efforts to curtail – or perhaps even eliminate – the sponsorship program.[61] Such optimism proved to be badly misplaced. Opinions expressed by ethnic groups, churches, labour unions, and others to the Special Joint Committee of the Senate and House of Commons on Immigration – appointed by the government to examine and report on the White Paper – were often stinging.[62] Senior civil servants charged with defending the White Paper were subjected to particularly fierce questioning by witnesses and committee members who correctly judged the White Paper's citizenship requirement to be a mechanism for slowing the flow of sponsored immigrants.[63] Advocacy groups' challenges to the architects of the White Paper served as a stark warning of the political costs to be borne by any government that was willing to tamper too aggressively with the existing rules on sponsorship. MPs representing constituencies with high proportions of immigrant and ethnic voters took the hint, joining "the chorus of those protesting against the implementation of the White Paper's recommendations to limit sponsorship."[64]

The fierce rebuke of the government's proposal for restraining sponsored immigration was accompanied by probing questions concerning precisely how immigration officials intended to replace racial and cultural criteria with those relating to education and skills with regard to independently selected immigrants. While the vast majority of the witnesses appearing before the Special Joint Committee endorsed the elimination of discrimination in Canada's admissions system, many questioned how criteria relating to education and skills would be applied in the absence of clearly defined standards. Without transparency, pronouncements regarding the government's intention to seek out the best and brightest immigrants, regardless of their race, ethnicity, and religion, continued to ring hollow.[65]

While the White Paper did not fulfill its role as an "exercise in persuasion for a particular policy,"[66] responses to it did clarify the remaining challenges to reform, prompting further reflection on the part of senior civil servants. Policy makers remained convinced that much of the analysis and recommendations that formed the White Paper were basically sound, but they also understood that more would be needed to gain the support of the Special Joint Committee, the media, and interest groups. As such, the Special Joint Committee's "intelligent criticism" gave senior officials in the Department of Manpower a "mandate" for fundamental change.[67]

The Points System

To this end, Minister of Citizenship and Immigration Marchand appointed an internal taskforce to devise admissions rules that (1) divided the sponsored stream into dependent and non-dependent relatives as per the White Paper; (2) employed a standard set of selection criteria; and (3) were based on the principle of universality.[68] The group was led by Deputy Minister Tom Kent, a highly regarded civil servant and friend and confidante of Prime Minister Pearson, who replaced the principal architect of the White Paper, C.M. Isbister, just before its release. While Kent shared Isbister's belief that sponsored flows needed to be brought under control,[69] he felt that criticisms of the White Paper – of which he was a principal recipient during the hearings of the Special Joint Committee – were deserved: the document was vague and lacked a clear statement of principles.[70] What was needed, in his view, was some means of identifying, defining, and attaching relative weight to "the various factors affecting a person's ability to settle successfully in Canada."[71] This would grant immigration officers a consistent means of assessing the potential of immigrants and remove any lingering suspicions concerning the criteria used to judge a person's suitability for admission into Canada. Both Kent and Marchand insisted that whatever solution was arrived at, it had to be universal in terms of its application and completely free of racial bias.

After spending several months on the project, the taskforce produced a proposal that satisfied these core requirements. According to the scheme, prospective immigrants would be assigned a score of one to ten "assessment points" in nine categories. The first five categories – age, education, training, occupational skill in demand, and personal qualities – related to "the immigrant's prospects of successful establishment in Canada." The other four categories – knowledge of English or French, presence of relatives in Canada, arranged employment, and employment opportunities in area of destination – were intended to determine "the speed and ease with which [the immigrant] is likely to get settled initially."[72] Primary applicants scoring fifty assessment points or higher would be admitted as "independent immigrants" and would enjoy the right to sponsor dependents as well as more distant "nominated relatives." Nominated relatives were also subject to the proposed assessment system but would be evaluated on a narrower set of criteria. The fact that a relative was sponsoring them was deemed an automatic advantage that would facilitate their settlement in Canada. Sponsored dependents did not have to qualify under the assessment scheme. However, they were subject to security screening and could be prevented from entering

Canada as a result of a criminal conviction or holding executive office in a "Communist, Neo-Nazi, or Neo-Fascist or other subversive or revolutionary organization."

Simulated tests of the new system were "highly encouraging."[73] Although the broadening of sponsorship rights would lead to increases in sponsored flows, officials believed the points system could be used to control this movement by regulating the number of nominated relatives granted entry according to labour market conditions.[74] While this was not a perfect solution, it did offer some means of controlling sponsored flows in a transparent, non-discriminatory, and politically acceptable fashion.[75] More generally, officials believed that they had crafted a system that satisfied both political and policy requirements. In the words of the minister of manpower and immigration: "Both the efficiency and the humanity of the selection process will be increased and be seen to be increased."[76]

Officials in the Department of Manpower and Immigration devised a promotional strategy "to gain the understanding and earn the support of the interested publics."[77] The "interested publics" to be reached included both "ethnic groups and ethnic media, news media and Members of Parliament" at "home" and "foreign governments (through diplomatic representatives in Canada), immigration personnel and travel agencies ... abroad." The principal "theme" to be stressed in the department's outreach efforts was that the new regulations would "serve the manpower needs of the growing Canadian economy" while also ensuring that Canada's Immigration Regulations were administered in a universally applicable, non-discriminatory manner that recognized the importance of family relationships and that combined efficiency and compassion.

In contrast to reaction to the White Paper, reaction to the "points system" was positive. The Special Joint Committee approved of the new Immigration Regulations in April 1967; the Cabinet followed suit shortly thereafter, and they were quickly implemented and came into effect in October 1967. The press and public were also receptive. The *Globe and Mail* noted that the new policy removed "discrimination against would-be immigrants from many countries in Asia and [was] aimed at making procedures more flexible."[78] The *Toronto Star* reported that Minister of Manpower and Immigration Jean Marchand had come close to the elusive goal of eliminating "outright racial discrimination" and opening Canada to increased levels of immigration.[79] Although the points system maintained a "good deal of subjective assessment" on the part of immigration officers, the new system was "a good deal better than the hit-and-miss system that [had] applied before."[80] The points system also offered Canadian politicians a way of demonstrating the purity of Canada's intentions to the rest of the world. Immigration had been placed on a progressive footing, in line with the image Canadian officials wished to project both domestically and internationally.[81] Kent believed that he and his team had succeeded in both rationalizing and civilizing the process of immigrant selection.[82]

Marchand, Kent, and their colleagues succeeded in crafting a relatively transparent, non-discriminatory immigration policy that opened Canada up to large-scale immigration from Asia, Africa, the Middle East, and other "non-traditional" sources for the first time in the country's history. Other reforms implemented during this time, including the expansion of the Assisted Passenger Loans Scheme, the opening of immigration processing facilities outside of Europe, and the establishment of the Immigration Appeals Board, secured the institutional prerequisites for an immigration regime open to qualified applicants regardless of their "race," ethnicity, religion, and culture. Moreover, the government repealed a circa 1957 regulation and once again allowed non-resident foreigners in Canada to apply for landed immigrant status from within the country. The results of these changes in policy and administrative structure were registered immediately as immigrants from Asia, the West Indies, and other formerly proscribed areas entered Canada in much larger numbers than ever before.

The more liberal tenor of the times was also evident in the area of refugee policy. Canada accepted some twelve thousand refugees from Czechoslovakia in the wake of the Soviet Union's violent termination of the Prague Spring in 1968,[83] and it signed the 1951 UN Convention Relating to the Status of Refugees in 1969, making it an official party to a formal international agreement regulating states' reception of refugees and asylum seekers. In 1972, Canada responded to a request by the British government to assist in relocating some fifty thousand Asian Ugandans expelled by Uganda's military dictator, Idi Amin. Canadian officials seized "the opportunity to confirm Canada's rejection of racial discrimination" by providing a haven for 7,069 non-European refugees.[84] The decision was noteworthy in that "the issue of race played almost no part in the government's decision."[85] Canada's response to the plight of Chilean refugees who were seeking sanctuary in the wake of General Augusto Pinochet's violent overthrow of Salvador Allende's socialist government in 1973 was rather less hospitable. Foreign policy considerations, economic interests, and an enduring ideological aversion to left-wing academics, activists, and intellectuals among its immigration and security personnel slowed Canada's response, despite intense lobbying on the part of the United Nations high commissioner for refugees, the Canadian Council of Churches, and other advocacy groups: "Nevertheless, Canada ultimately admitted 6,990 Chileans."[86]

The fact that changes to Canada's Immigration Regulations in 1967 provoked virtually no organized political opposition speaks to the uniformity of elite opinion at this time.[87] Several factors help explain this consensus. First, the buoyancy of the Canadian economy engendered a generally optimistic attitude towards immigration that encouraged agreement among business, labour, the state, and civil society organizations. Second, opposition to the reforms would have been interpreted as support for the old system, which had been successfully framed as racist. Whereas Minister of Citizenship and Immigration Jack Pickersgill could defend Canada's "discriminatory immigration policy" to members of the press in 1954,[88] shifts in the political meaning of words such as "discrimination" in the intervening years meant that any politician obtuse enough to utter a similar statement in 1967 would have opened him- or herself up to intense criticism.

Efforts to cast Canada as a tolerant oasis in a turbulent continent also helped shape the tone of elite political discourse. The "Other" against which official Canadian identity was constituted at this time was an amalgam of intolerance, assimilation, and national chauvinism projected onto select entities, including opponents of the Civil Rights Movement in the United States and Quebec nationalists.[89] The most striking manifestation of this re-engineering of Canadian identity was Prime Minister Pierre Trudeau's introduction of an official policy of multiculturalism in 1971. The moment ostensibly marked the Liberal government's implementation of recommendations advanced by the Commission on Bilingualism and Biculturalism, a body appointed by Lester Pearson in 1963 to

> inquire into and report upon the existing state of bilingualism and biculturalism in Canada and to recommend what steps should be taken to develop the Canadian Confederation on the basis of an equal partnership between the two founding races, taking into account the contribution made by the other ethnic groups to the cultural enrichment of Canada and the measures that should be taken to safeguard that contribution.[90]

Pearson and the commission's co-chairs, André Laurendeau and Davidson Dunton, were keen to "work out a practical response to the growing threat of separatist nationalism in Quebec" that reaffirmed Canada's identity as a partnership between "two founding races."[91] Canadians who did not trace their origins to one of Canada's two "charter groups" balked at what they saw as the privileging of French and English Canadians and lobbied intensely for greater recognition. They succeeded to a degree in that the fourth and final volume of the commission's recommendations, published in 1968, focused on "The Cultural Contribution of Other Ethnic Groups."

In his statement to the House of Commons on October 8, 1971, Trudeau rejected his predecessor's support of the "two founding races" doctrine, maintaining: "Although there are two official languages [in Canada], there is no official culture, nor does any ethnic group take precedence over any other. No citizen or group of citizens is other than Canadian, and all should be treated fairly."[92] While the aim of ensuring fair treatment provided support for policies geared towards cultural retention, Trudeau also emphasized the importance of individual freedom, which would be "hampered" if immigrants were "locked for life within a particular cultural compartment by the accident of birth or language." It was therefore "vital ... that every Canadian, whatever his ethnic origin, be given a chance to learn at least one of the two languages in which this country conducts its official business and politics."

Trudeau believed that a "policy of multiculturalism within a bilingual framework" would support the "cultural freedom of Canadians" while helping to "break down discriminatory attitudes and cultural jealousies." Cultural recognition was thus qualified by a robust integrationist position based on shared citizenship. Extending this liberal conceptualization of Canadian identity further, Trudeau argued that if national unity were to mean anything in a "deeply personal sense," it must be "founded on confidence in one's own individual identity; out of this can grow respect for that of others and willingness to share ideas, attitudes and assumptions." A "vigorous policy of multiculturalism" would "help create this initial confidence" and thus assist in forming "the base of a society ... based on fair play for all."

Like the liberalization of Canada's Immigration Regulations in 1967, the announcement of the federal government's official multiculturalism policy enjoyed broad cross-party political support, drawing little in the way of criticism outside of Quebec, where some saw it as a slight to their province's special status in the Canadian federation.[93] In English Canada, immigration reform and multiculturalism were very much in keeping with Canadians' view of themselves as a progressive, modern, and forward-looking people, no longer tethered to Britain and eager to craft a distinctive civic identity.[94] As we see below, optimism about Canada's ability to carry out this project would be tested in the years ahead as worsening economic conditions and changes in Canadian society provoked renewed considerations of the migration-membership dilemma.

Impact and Entrenchment: The Immigration Act, 1976

Changing Immigration Patterns

The 1967 Immigration Regulations prompted a significant increase in the volume of annual immigration flows, with totals reaching 122,006 in 1972, 184,200, in 1973 and 218,465 in 1974.[95] While policy makers had anticipated some increase in overall levels of immigration as a consequence of the new regulations, they were caught unprepared by the rapid growth and size of these movements. This was due to the unforeseen convergence of two components of the new rules. While section 34 of the Immigration Regulations allowed tourists to apply for landed immigrant status from within Canada, the Immigration Appeal Board Act "gave anyone who had been ordered deported the right to appeal [their deportation decision] to the Board, no matter what his or her status under the Immigration Act."[96] Consequently, large numbers of visitors began to arrive in Canada with the intention of staying, applying for landed immigrant status and, if refused, submitting an appeal to the Immigration Appeal Board, which had the power to permit them to stay in Canada on compassionate or humanitarian grounds. Presumably, the longer they stayed and the more successfully they settled in, the more compelling those grounds would be.[97]

Immigration officials feared that the growing number of in-land applications and the related malfunctioning of the appeals process were allowing immigrants who would otherwise not be granted immigrant status to remain in the country indefinitely, challenging the very premises of the skills-oriented system established in 1967.[98]

Officials reacted to these developments by revoking the right to submit in-land applications through the passage of P.C. 1972-2502 in November 1972, days after the governing Liberals failed to secure a majority in the October 30 federal election.[99] Further efforts aimed at assuring Canadians that the government had not "lost control" of its immigration policy followed. In January 1973, the new minister of manpower and immigration, Robert Andras, introduced regulations requiring all visitors staying in Canada for more than three months to register with the department upon entry. Rules tightening non-residents' access to the labour market were also implemented.[100]

While these changes checked the flow of visitors entering Canada to apply for immigrant visas, they did not address concerns raised by the large number of overstayers already in the country or the backlog of outstanding cases confronting the Immigration Appeals Board. These points were addressed in August 1973 through the introduction of a temporary amnesty program aimed at encouraging overstayers to apply for landed immigrant status. The government also tightened appeals procedures and expanded the size of the Immigration Appeals Board.[101]

Officials in the Department of Manpower and Immigration believed the changes introduced in 1972 and 1973 only addressed the symptoms of more fundamental problems in Canada's immigration policy regime and requested authorization for a general policy review to culminate in the passage of a new immigration act. Andras supported their position and urged his Cabinet colleagues to give him the opportunity to develop legislation to replace the outdated Immigration Act, 1952. The decision to review Canada's immigration policy was announced in the House of Commons on September 17, 1973. Andras called for the formation of a special task force, the Canada Immigration and Population Study Group, to prepare a green paper on immigration and population to be published in six months. In the meantime, deteriorating economic conditions prompted growing concern. In February 1974, the Immigration Regulations were amended "so that all independent immigrants (including nominated relatives) intending to enter the labour force had to have a firm job offer in order to be admitted."[102]

In August of 1974, Andras presented a memorandum to his Cabinet colleagues drawing on research undertaken by the special task force.[103] His report noted that the points system was "open-ended" in that it determined "the composition, but not the size or source of the immigrant movement to Canada." While Canadian officials had anticipated increases in annual flows, "worsening economic conditions in various parts of the world added to the stimulus to immigrate." Moreover, the global economic downturn had caused other immigrant-receiving countries, such as Australia and New Zealand, to limit their admissions, deflecting more demand to Canada. Based on these trends and in the absence of changes to the selection system, Canada could expect "landings of 251,000 in 1975, 295,000 in 1976, and 350,000 in 1977."

The proportion of nominated relatives making up annual flows, already significant at 23 percent, was destined to grow to 27 percent by 1977. Given that Canada's admissions rules tilted "selection in favour of source countries where families are large and family ties are strong – a characteristic of underdeveloped and developing countries," a growing proportion of future flows would be made up of sponsored immigrants from "underdeveloped and developing countries" in general and from Asia in particular. Unless the government acted quickly to address these trends, the 350,000 immigrants expected to arrive in 1977 would "represent a much larger immigrant movement than Canadians ha[d] been accustomed to ... significantly different than those of the past." Based on past trends, these immigrants would "concentrate in Toronto, Montreal and Vancouver, where urban friction already exist[ed]." At that point, the usefulness of past trends for predicting future outcomes diminished: "No one can say how rapid can be a change in the social character of a community before ethnic and racial tensions get out of hand. Many signs suggest that we are reaching that point in a number of Canadian centres today."

Andras thus recommended that "steps be taken to stabilize the [immigration] movement" in a manner that did not "prejudge the immigration policy review and the legislation resulting from it" or create "bottlenecks" in the labour supply. Specifically, he recommended that independent applicants and nominated relatives receive credit for a job offer in Canada only if the Department of Manpower and Immigration certified that suitable qualified Canadian citizens or permanent residents were not available to take the job. This would "eliminate the 'creation' of jobs solely to gain the admittance of friends and relatives." Andras also recommended using "a number of regular administrative steps" within the normal range of his responsibilities to maintain the "annual immigration movement within some 10% of 200,000 persons for 1975, 1976, and 1977." Dealing with the "changing composition of the movement" would require a third step aimed at checking the "growth of the nominated movement." Here, Andras recommended that "10 of the 15 to 30 bonus points ... awarded for kinship [under the points system] be awarded only if the applicant has a definite prearranged job or is destined to a designated vacancy." This third proposal was expected to "reduce the nominated movement by 40% overall ... and reduce the shift from the developed to the developing countries."

Andras' memorandum hit a nerve: the Cabinet agreed with all three of his recommendations, adding that "public announcements on this subject ... be worded to stress that compassionate and humanitarian grounds could be used in place of the newly restricted nominated class where circumstances warrant."[104] Andras was also instructed to "report back to Cabinet after Caucus consultation," presumably to discuss his colleagues' reactions to the proposed changes. His follow-up memorandum to the Cabinet, dated September 25, 1974, noted that his proposals were "criticized as being (a) too complicated and (b) directed too conclusively at the nominated category."[105] In response, Andras proposed a "simpler" approach whereby "after totalling all the points to which an applicant is entitled, the visa officer will deduct 10 points unless the applicant has satisfactory evidence of bona fide arranged employment or is coming to a 'designated vacancy' [i.e., an occupation designated by the Department of Manpower and Immigration as experiencing labour shortages]." Arranged employment would be defined as "employment for which no qualified Canadian citizen or landed immigrant is available." Tying policy squarely to labour market concerns, while not distinguishing between independent and sponsored immigrants, was considered the best means of avoiding charges of racism. Despite continuing misgivings among members of the Liberal Party caucus and Cabinet, Andras' revised proposal was deemed an acceptable compromise; the minister announced the implementation of the new regulation on October 22, 1974.[106]

The *New York Times* covered Andras' announcement on its front page, reporting that "the principal impact" of the new regulation would be to stem "the flow of nonwhite immigrants."[107] Citing "official figures," the article noted: "The number of immigrants from the Caribbean has nearly tripled, from 4,000 in the first half of 1972 to 11,000 in the first six months of [1974]. The flow from Africa is increasing at a rate of 230 per cent, and from South Asia by 177 per cent." The *New York Times* story included quotations from Canadian broadcast journalists. The publicly funded Canadian Broadcast Corporation's Brian Stewart opined: "Canada is becoming a multiracial country at a staggering rate, and there's just no simple guarantee that we'll be able to handle the phenomenon better than others." While the privately owned Canadian Television Network's Bruce Phillips warned: " [A] large proportion of the nonwhites now coming to Canada have few skills and little education. They have been consigned to the lowest rung of the economic ladder. Most of them are congregating in major cities and we are putting in place all the elements of ghetto situations and all that portends for the future."

The 1974 Green Paper

The Canada Immigration and Population Study Group submitted the long overdue Green Paper to Cabinet in October 1974. Both the Liberal Party caucus and opposition MPs rejected the government's suggestion that public consultation be pursued through a national conference on immigration

policy, demanding instead that Parliament play a leading role in the formulation of a new immigration act. With Minister of Manpower and
Immigration Andras' support, they succeeded in persuading Prime Minister
Trudeau to appoint a Special Joint Committee of the Senate and House of
Commons on Immigration Policy. The committee was instructed to review
the Green Paper, organize public hearings, and receive briefs from interested individuals and groups.[108] On February 3, 1975, the government announced the formation of the Special Joint Committee (SJC) and tabled the
Green Paper in the House of Commons.[109]

In keeping with precedent, the Green Paper was to present policy options without necessarily advocating a particular position. Yet, despite its
intended neutrality, the Green Paper's tone and language reflected the Department of Manpower and Immigration's apprehension about the course
of immigration in the years following the shift to a universal admissions
system. Worries about the size and "quality" of the sponsored movement
were joined by what the *Globe and Mail* characterized as a delicate dance
around the subject of race.[110] The *New York Times* noted that Canadians
were embarking on a "comprehensive national debate on Canada's immigration policy" in general and on the future of non-European immigration in
particular. The *Times* reported that some believed that "the government
ha[d] already decided on a no-blacks policy, and [was] just trying to figure
how to implement it."[111]

It was not difficult to see why critics were doubtful of the sincerity of the
public consultation process. The Green Paper made much of the fact that,
until 1967, Europeans accounted for approximately 80 percent of total immigration. By 1974, this figure had fallen to under 40 percent. Conversely,
non-European immigration increased significantly. Whereas total flows
from India stood at 2,233 persons in 1966, by 1974 this figure had climbed
to 12,868. Similar increases were registered for immigration from the
Caribbean, Asia, and other previously restricted source regions. By 1974,
Hong Kong, Jamaica, India, the Philippines, and Trinidad stood among
Canada's top ten immigration source countries.[112] Moreover, while initial
rounds of applications from non-European source countries tended to include a disproportionate percentage of independent immigrants selected
under the provisions of the points system, subsequent movements featured
a growing proportion of sponsored relatives.[113] While nominated relatives
had to meet some requirements under the points system, doubts were expressed about their employability in a period of tightening labour markets.

The Green Paper went on to note that Canadians were "concerned about the consequences for national identity that might follow any significant change in the composition of the population," and it referred to other unspecified cases where the introduction of "new racial groups into the population outstripped the ability of societies to adapt to ... changes harmoniously." The implication was that Canada might be headed for similar problems:

> Intensifying demands for housing, transit facilities, community services and just plain space mean that the calls the migrant makes on the receiving community's hospitality become more onerous, and are seen to be so. There is no getting away from a fairly high degree of social tension, if not outright friction, in modern urban living. Newcomers may easily become the focus of frustrations and antagonisms that are no less socially disruptive for being quite out of proportion with the actual size of the immigrant group involved.[114]

What was truly surprising was that matters had not already spun out of control:

> The rapid increase during the past few years in the number of sources of significant immigrant movements to this country – with those from certain Asian and Caribbean nations now larger than some traditional European flows – has coincided with the latest and most dynamic phase of post-war urban expansion in Canada. It would be astonishing if there was no concern about the capacity of our society to adjust to a pace of population change that entails novel and distinctive features. What is more surprising is the resilience Canadian society has demonstrated in accommodating so many foreign migrants with so little stress.[115]

The Green Paper suggested that this "astonishing" resilience on the part of Canadians should not be overtaxed. While not calling for a more restrictive solution, the document went out of its way to point out the dangers of maintaining present policies. Some means of reasserting control over immigration flows had to be developed lest Canadians lose their patience and "racial incidents" multiply. Interestingly, the Green Paper made no mention of the federal government's official multiculturalism policy but did recommend that immigration be regulated to ensure that Canada's status as a bilingual country was not jeopardized.[116]

Four potential policy options for meeting the immigration challenge were presented. The first entailed retaining the present "responsive" system of immigration management and not setting a ceiling on total yearly admissions. A second option would link immigration more closely to economic objectives: the "nominated relatives" category would be dropped and all immigrants save dependents and refugees would have to satisfy strict admissions criteria geared towards ensuring their employability. Option three was the most contentious as it entertained the possibility of setting "explicit targets for the number of visas to be issued annually on a global, regional and possibly post-by-post [i.e., country-by-country] basis." Such a policy could "enable the immigration program to be deliberately related to national demographic/population growth policies as these are developed." The fourth option called for the establishment of a global ceiling for the total immigration movement, "specifying the priorities to be observed in the issuance of visas to different categories of immigrants within that ceiling." A regular process of consultation with the provinces and other stakeholders would help determine both the number of immigrants to be accepted and the order in which different classes of applications would be processed: "With the over-all ceiling and priorities established, a forecast would then be made of the number of applicants in each priority group from each source country and area of the world." Such an approach would "avoid some of the dilemmas inherent in establishing, in advance, visa quotas on a regional or country-by-country basis, as would be the case under option three."[117]

Reaction and Consultation: The Special Joint Committee

The Green Paper generated sharp reactions even before it was released. Of particular concern was the government's position on immigration from the "Third World." Leaked reports of the Green Paper's contents prompted many to wonder whether Canada was contemplating "curbs on immigration from non-traditional areas."[118] The leader of the federal Conservative Party, Robert Stanfield, confronted Prime Minister Trudeau with these concerns during a debate in the House of Commons on October 16, 1974, compelling Trudeau to pledge that Canada would not depart from a "policy which is universal and non-discriminatory in its selection criteria."[119] Many remained wary of the government's plans despite Trudeau's reassurances.

Reaction to the Green Paper widened after the document was tabled. Opinions were expressed in the press and channelled through the SJC, which held fifty days of public hearings in twenty-one cities across Canada.[120] The committee received 1,873 statements from individuals and organizations in the form of letters of opinion, formal briefs, and oral testimony. Representations to the SJC revealed an important split in public opinion. Eighty-three percent of briefs received from individuals were highly critical of Canadian immigration policy and demanded tighter controls on immigration from the "Third World."[121] A Toronto-based writer expressed the commonly held view that immigration was leading to urban decay, bemoaning immigrants' habit of "spitting on the street" and allowing their children to "[relieve] themselves in public." Others argued that immigration from Africa, Asia, and the West Indies was upsetting "Canada's racial composition," thus threatening the maintenance of Canada's "distinct national identity." An Edmonton-based writer declared that immigration should be limited "to Anglo-Saxon-Celts and Nordic-Germanic peoples," while a fellow resident of Edmonton maintained that officials should "exclude all non-whites [and] institute a program of deportation of non-whites in the Dominion." Another Toronto-based writer demanded that officials "look into the cultural shock the native born Canadian [was] sustaining." Many of the letters received by the SJC also expressed fears of increasing racial tensions in cities and the threat of racial violence along the lines of that being experienced in the United States and Great Britain.

Conversely, virtually every organized delegation testifying before the SJC disapproved of the Green Paper's pessimistic tone and criticized its preoccupation with immigration from "non-traditional sources."[122] In this vein, the Immigration Policy Action Community of the Vancouver Chinese Community noted that the Green Paper insidiously raised the issue of the rapid increase of immigrants from Asian and Caribbean nations, implicitly contravening the principle of universality and supplying "ammunition to the arsenal of racists and bigots in Canada."[123] Similarly, a spokesperson for the Armenian Congress noted that even the suggestion of restrictions based on geography were insulting to "the thousands of people from Asia and Africa who have taken up Canadian citizenship and are working towards a better Canada."[124] Twenty-nine East Indian associations appeared before the SJC, calling for the maintenance of a non-discriminatory immigration policy and the broadening of sponsorship rights and categories. Representatives of European immigrant associations also argued against restrictions on sponsorship rights and voiced their support for an expansive immigration policy. Other groups, including churches and labour unions, criticized the Green

Paper's fixation on putative problems related to the immigration of non-whites and underscored the claim that Canada was a "multicultural society," in which no national group was dominant. The Green Paper's failure to address humanitarian concerns regarding refugees was also criticized.

The SJC opted for a compromise opinion, granting tacit endorsement for the tightening of immigration policy but rejecting any move to limit flows according to geographical origin. In its final report, tabled in the House of Commons on November 6, 1975, the SJC recommended that the immigration program be scaled back to approximately 100,000 immigrants per year. Within this overall figure, a target number of independent immigrants would be determined after the total number of sponsored applicants had been calculated. The committee also proposed changes to the points system, including the outright elimination of the nominated class and the awarding of more points to independent applicants with a relative already in Canada. The SJC recommended that less credit be given for educational attainment and more emphasis be placed on work-related experience. Sponsorship provisions should be expanded to allow Canadian citizens over twenty-one to sponsor parents under sixty years of age. Other recommendations included the establishment of a separate program for refugees and the removal of the 1952 act's ban on homosexuals. At the same time, the SJC recommended that immigration policy "continue to be fair and non-discriminatory on the basis of race, creed, nationality, ethnic origin and sex, and that this principle be formally set out in the new Act." The SJC also suggested that discrimination be countered through educational and community programs that encouraged inter-group understanding. Better enforcement of human rights legislation would "protect Canadians and immigrants alike from racial and ethnic discrimination."[125]

The SJC's position was endorsed by employers and the Progressive Conservative opposition. Echoing analyses presented in the Green Paper, the Conservative's immigration critic Jake Epp stated that the nominated class drove down the overall quality of Canada's immigration flow. Conversely, "MPs representing constituencies with high immigrant concentrations opposed the abolition of the nominated class, on the grounds that family reunification should not be limited to the nuclear family."[126] Civil society groups in general and associations representing ethnic groups in particular also stood against the dismantling of the nominated class, arguing that humanitarian considerations should outweigh narrow economic interests. Defenders of the nominated class emphasized that understandings of "family" differed across cultures and that imposing one view over another was unfair.[127]

The government ultimately sided with the defenders of the nominated class. Although an initial bill prepared under Andras' watch followed the lead of the SJC by eliminating the nominated class and expanding the range of relatives falling under the sponsored dependent class, Andras' successor as minister of manpower and immigration, Bud Cullen, abruptly reversed the government's position by preserving the nominated class in a revised bill. Cullen also opted to maintain the earlier bill's expansion of the sponsored dependent class – effectively expanding the new immigration law's provisions on family reunification. Jake Epp criticized Cullen's decision, arguing that it was based on "purely political" reasoning that ignored evidence produced by his department. Cullen defended the bill before the Commons Standing Committee on Labour, Manpower and Immigration by "alternatively appearing as the champion of family reunification and downplaying the family element in the nominated class."[128] His predecessor's misgiving regarding the nominated class's deficiencies had clearly given way to a more expansive position on family reunification within the Cabinet. While Epp was clearly not convinced by Cullen's reasoning, neither he nor his party opted to politicize the issue further.

The Immigration Act, 1976

The Immigration Act, 1976, was passed with near unanimous support, gaining Royal Assent in August 1977 and taking effect on April 10, 1978. The act implemented sixty of the SJC's sixty-five recommendations and, for the first time, clearly enunciated the fundamental objectives of Canadian immigration policy. These included:

1 Promotion of economic, social, demographic, and cultural goals
2 Endorsement of family reunification
3 Fulfillment of Canada's international obligations under the United Nations Convention and 1967 Protocol relating to refugees
4 Nondiscrimination in immigration policy.[129]

The act established four categories of immigrants: "family class" dependents, assisted relatives, independent immigrants, and refugees. Aside from changes in wording and the entrenchment of Canada's obligations under the UN Convention Relating to the Status of Refugees in statute, the typology differed little from that established under the reforms of 1967. Under the act, independent and assisted relatives would be subject to differing versions of the points system, while family class dependents would gain entry so long as they met basic health and security requirements.[130] Conversely, the act broke new ground by including a provision for federal-provincial consultations in immigration planning and setting an annual quota for admissions. Furthermore, the 1952 act's litany of "prohibited classes" was replaced by broader categories that denied entry to individuals likely to imperil public health or security or place an undue burden on health or social services. The prohibition against the admission of homosexuals was also struck down.

Given the gloomy circumstances that so influenced the work of the Immigration and Population Study and the dismal tone of the Green Paper, the relatively liberal tenor of the Immigration Act, 1976, and strong political consensus that accompanied its passage through Parliament are puzzling. At the very least, one would have expected a more restrictive law that limited flows of sponsored immigrants, and more frequent and aggressive attempts on the part of politicians to exploit the anti-immigrant sentiment that was very much in evidence in the early 1970s. Yet what emerged from the policy-making process was a compromise that retained a modified version of the sponsorship provisions of the 1967 Immigration Regulations and enjoyed strong cross-party support. Moreover, the Trudeau government passed a significantly liberalized Citizenship Act in 1977, which reduced the residency requirement from five to three years and provided for a "wholly permissive stance on the issue of multiple nationality," with very little in the way of parliamentary debate.[131]

In his attempt to make sense of these counter-intuitive outcomes, John Wood points out that there were very good *political* reasons behind the maintenance of a relatively expansive policy backed by cross-party consensus. Wood notes that the influence of the SJC went beyond providing the government with useful recommendations. It also sent an important political signal: MPs serving on the SJC "were impressed by the publicity-catching and vote-mobilizing ability of minority ethnic organizations," which "represented the largest proportion ... of all organizations that appeared before the SJC."[132] These ethnic organizations' political leverage was increased as a consequence of the Liberal government's unpopularity in 1976-77 and the uncomfortably close margin of victory it had enjoyed in a large number of ridings in the 1972 federal election.[133] These very competitive ridings tended to be in metropolitan areas and therefore contained a high proportion of "ethnic" voters whose support was essential for victory – doubly so given Canada's SMP electoral system, which offers no rewards for second place.

Wood also notes that, during the course of drafting the 1976 act, at least four cabinet ministers and several other members of the Liberal caucus warned that a policy of tighter controls "could do damage to a party that was already in difficulty."[134] The ministers whom Wood interviewed acknowledged that their electoral success "depended on minority ethnic support."[135] Given that ethnic groups came out strongly against proposed restrictions to sponsored immigration, it is not surprising that Cullen's view won out over Andras' in the formulation of the penultimate version of the Immigration Act. According to Wood, both the Immigration Act, 1976, and the Citizenship Act, 1977, were part of a more general strategy on the part of the Liberal Party to harness the support of new ethnic voters. The reduction of the residency requirement in the new Citizenship Act would allow immigrants who arrived in the early 1970s "to become citizens – and grateful voters – in time for the coming general election."[136]

Like their Liberal counterparts, Conservative Party MPs in competitive urban constituencies had good reason to reject policies that might alienate a significant proportion of their electorate. They continued to compete with the Liberals for the votes of "new urban-ethnic Canadians" and were keen to improve their standing among other voters who might be won over from the Liberals and the New Democratic Party (NDP): women, workers, and the young.[137] Stirring up a populist reaction under such circumstances did not make good political sense and would do little to enhance their new leader Joe Clark's appeal among "swing" voters. While parliamentary convention made some opposition to the Liberals' immigration bill inevitable, political considerations militated against expanding the scope of the debate by whipping up and drawing on popular opposition to sponsored immigration.

Conclusion

The maintenance of cross-party political consensus during a period of economic difficulty and growing concern regarding the consequences of changing immigration patterns allowed for the passage of a relatively liberal immigration act and the entrenchment of a new approach to the migration-membership dilemma. Rather than turning back or standing still, Canada pressed ahead in redefining its identity in a manner that accorded to postwar human rights norms. Political considerations – principally parties' interests in competing for the votes of new Canadians – helped steer Canadian politicians away from divisive anti-immigrant positions. Anti-immigration sentiment thus constituted an untapped resource, lying fallow for want of a political catalyst.[138]

Cross-party political consensus facilitated the further liberalization of Canadian membership policies through the 1980s. The entrenchment of multiculturalism in section 27 of the 1982 Charter of Rights and Freedoms, according to which the "Charter shall be interpreted in a manner consistent with the preservation and enhancement of the multicultural heritage of Canadians," was overseen by Liberal prime minister Pierre Trudeau.[139] Not to be outdone, Brian Mulroney's Progressive Conservative government entrenched Canada's official multiculturalism policy in statute through the passage of the Multiculturalism Act, 1988.[140] A year later the Conservatives severed the long-standing link between annual immigration flows and prevailing economic conditions by committing Canada to maintaining an expansive immigration policy regardless of fluctuations in the unemployment rate. While the decision was defended in terms of meeting Canada's changing labour market needs, the potential "electoral benefits [that] might accrue from an expansive immigration policy" likely played a role as well.[141]

The Reform Party briefly challenged the political consensus on immigration policy in the late 1980s and early 1990s.[142] Reform emerged as a populist alternative to the Progressive Conservative and Liberal parties, in part by rejecting what it deemed were politically correct positions on immigration and multiculturalism. This strategy helped the party achieve a breakthrough in the 1993 election, when a faltering economy and rising unemployment fuelled a backlash against immigration.[143] While Reform's success in 1993 doubtlessly influenced the Liberal government of Jean Chretien to make adjustments to Canada's immigration policy,[144] it soon became apparent that populist opposition to immigration and multiculturalism came at a cost. Having established a solid base of support in western Canada, Reform needed to make inroads into seat-rich Ontario if it was to compete against the Liberals for national office (the Progressive Conservatives were decimated in the 1993 election, dropping from 151 seats to two). Yet, just as its opposition to Quebec's demands for recognition as a "distinct society" made it a non-entity in that province, Reform's anti-immigration and anti-multiculturalism positions severely limited its standing among immigrant voters in Ontario.[145] The Liberal Party did its part by reminding immigrant voters of the party's past positions, effectively framing it as a dangerous threat with a "hidden" anti-Canadian agenda.

In time, Reform and its successor, the Canadian Alliance, put aside the immigration card, coming full circle, as it were, after merging with the Progressive Conservative Party in December 2003. The "new" Conservative Party has embraced an expansive immigration policy, defended official multiculturalism, and, after winning a minority government in 2006, offered a series of apologies to groups victimized by Canada's racist immigration policies in the late nineteenth and early twentieth centuries.[146] During the campaign leading up to the federal election of May 2, 2011, the Conservative Party's leader, Prime Minister Stephen Harper, campaigned aggressively for the votes of new Canadians, attending religious ceremonies, donning "ethnic" attire in numerous meet-and-greet sessions, granting interviews to the "ethnic press," and promising to maintain an expansive immigration policy. Strikingly, the former Reform Party activist offered a robust defence of Canada's multiculturalism policy during the televised English-language leaders' debate, arguing:

> What Canadians need to understand about multiculturalism is that people who make the hard decision to ... come here, they first and foremost want to belong to this country ... They also at the same time will change our country. And we show through multiculturalism our willingness to accommodate their differences, so they are more comfortable. That's why we're so successful integrating people as a country. I think we're probably the most successful country in the world in that regard.[147]

The election saw the Conservatives secure a majority government in part through their success in Ontario, where they won 73 of the province's 106 federal seats, including 32 of 47 seats in the Greater Toronto Area, where immigrants make up 50 percent of the total population.[148] Whether the Conservatives' victory can be attributed to increased support among immigrant voters is open to question. What is clear is that they tailored their campaign to compete for immigrant voters and, in so doing, reinforced the durable cross-party political consensus that facilitated policy shifting in the 1970s and that continues to shape membership politics in Canada in distinctive ways.

5

Guest Workers into Germans

The decision to forgo the implementation of compulsory rotation during the recruitment era allowed "guest workers" to extend their stays and settle in West Germany. This de facto mass immigration challenged German officials' claims that the Federal Republic was "not an immigration country" and raised questions regarding foreign workers' membership status. The social integration of the so-called "second generation" was of particular concern.[1] The number of migrant children under sixteen had risen from 364,000 in 1969 to 768,000 in 1974; by 1982 it had climbed to 1,183,203.[2] Many of these children had been born in West Germany and all were entitled to attend public schools. Unfortunately, the German school system proved to be woefully unprepared to cope with the situation. A 1975 report on the social situation of second-generation migrants by the Catholic welfare organization Caritas warned of the emergence of a "generation without prospects."[3]

The challenges raised by the emerging second generation made it clear that the 1973 recruitment stop had addressed only one dimension of the migration-membership dilemma – that concerning the admission of foreign workers. It did not address the membership status and prospects of settled migrants and their children. The settlement of millions of migrants and the emergence of a large second-generation cohort socialized in Germany but categorized as "foreigners" raised vexing problems that cut to the heart of the temporary labour migration model, challenging Germany's identity as a democratic *Rechtsstaat* and hampering its leadership role in the project of

European integration. Yet, notwithstanding a few notable exceptions, initial responses by German officials remained mired in the logic of the guest worker model and fell far short of what was needed.

When the limits of the established regime and consequent need for change were acknowledged, policy shifting was hampered by the collapse of cross-party political consensus and the politicization of "foreigners policy" (*Ausländerpolitik*). In contrast to Canada, in Germany a combination of institutional factors and timing ensured that the expansion of membership boundaries to include migrants and their families would be a slow and fractious affair.[4] Policy shifting occurred, capped by the 1999 citizenship reform, but it was marked by compromises that weakened the new regime's effectiveness as a motor of integration. The long, rancorous battle that transformed what was to be a relatively welcoming immigration law into the rather restrictive Act on the Residence, Economic Activity and Integration of Foreigners in the Federal Territory (Residence Act), 2004, demonstrated the degree to which migration remained a highly contested subject in German politics, despite the significant liberalization of membership policies that marked the period under consideration.

Integration and Return, 1973-82

Policy making during the period following the announcement of the recruitment stop was oriented towards integrating settled migrants temporarily while also encouraging their return to their home countries. Efforts to encourage return were often heavy-handed. On November 13, 1974, the Federal Ministry of Labour passed an administrative decree denying work permits for non-EC sponsored children and spouses entering Germany after the "key date" of December 1, 1974. In 1975, the federal government chose to deny non-EC foreign residents full child benefits for children living outside of Germany. Freedom of movement within Germany was also curtailed in 1975 through a decree barring migrants from moving into "overburdened" urban districts with foreign populations of 12 percent or more.[5]

Invariably, these policies either failed or backfired. The deadline for work eligibility prompted a rush of family reunification migration and created a cohort of immigrants barred from the labour market and thus dependent on social assistance. The "key date" was therefore changed to January 1, 1977; regulations were revised again in 1980 and 1981, and waiting periods were introduced to govern the entry of dependents into the labour market.[6] The result was a confusing profusion of regulations that satisfied no one. The denial of full child benefits for children outside of Germany compelled many migrants to have their children join them in the Federal Republic. Finally, employers complained that the "anti-ghettos" scheme added further strictures to an already inflexible labour market. Beyond this, the policy proved difficult to enforce and was rescinded in 1977.[7]

Efforts to "assist" migrants' return to their home countries through administrative deportations were checked by West Germany's courts. In its landmark "Indian" decision of 1978, the Federal Constitutional Court greatly enhanced settled migrants' residency rights.[8] The case involved a construction worker from India who had first entered Germany in 1961 for occupational training. His residency permit had been extended annually between 1967 and 1972 and he applied for naturalization in 1972 but was turned down. In 1973, his application for a renewal of his residency permit was denied by local officials, who argued that his intention to settle permanently in Germany – as evidenced by his application for naturalization – contravened state interests because the Federal Republic was "not a country of immigration." The state administrative court upheld the local officials' decision and went a step further in justifying the verdict by citing a 1966 regulation that recommended the restriction of non-European nationals who were seeking entry and work in the Federal Republic – the so-called "no non-Europeans" policy discussed in Chapter 3.

The Federal Constitutional Court reversed the decision, holding that the prior routine renewals of the applicant's residency permit had created a constitutionally protected "reliance interest" in continued residence based on the constitutional principle of *Vertrauensschutz* (protection of legitimate expectations), derived from Article 19 of the Basic Law (the *Rechtsstaatsprinzip*). The Court argued that, although officials were entitled to exercise discretion in their implementation of regulations, both their decisions and the regulations themselves had to accord with more general principles inherent in the rule of law. The repeated extension of the complainant's residency permit had fostered his integration into German society, while simultaneously deepening his alienation from India. The decision to deny his residency request and order his deportation failed to take this into account and therefore contravened his constitutionally protected interests. The Court maintained that a reversal in immigration policy could not "justify [the] expulsion of foreign workers after the government had induced their de facto settlement, despite their legal status as temporary residents and an official policy of discouraging 'immigration.'"[9]

The Court's decision in the "Indian case" was in line with its 1973 ruling overturning the deportation orders of two Palestinian students. The students' expulsion was part of the anti-terrorism campaign that emerged after the terrorist attack on Israeli athletes at the 1972 Munich Olympics. The students' ties to Palestinian political organizations were deemed grounds for their classification as security risks and this, in turn, was used to justify their deportation. The Court ruled that this inference was illegal, arguing that the "public interest [had to be] balanced against the private interests of the respective foreigner, that is, the impact of the deportation on his economic, professional, and private life ... as well as on his other social ties." Taken together, the Court's rulings in the "Arab" and "Indian" cases struck a blow to the discretionary powers accorded to the state through the 1965 Foreigners Law and related regulations. The cases solidified migrants' status as bearers of human rights guaranteed under the Basic Law and placed further limits on the state's ability to reverse immigration processes through deportation and the termination of residency rights.[10]

The intervention of the Federal Constitutional Court forced the government to devise a more comprehensive strategy. An initial step in this direction came with the appointment of a joint *Bund-Länder* commission on the future of *Ausländerpolitik* in August 1976. The commission was instructed to develop policies that dealt with the post-recruitment reality while keeping sight of the fact that West Germany was not a "country of immigration." Its report, tabled on August 4, 1977, reflected the ambivalence of its mandate. The commission recommended that: (1) the recruitment stop be maintained to restrict further labour migration from non-EC countries; (2) foreigners be encouraged to return to their countries of origin; and (3) the legal status of families remaining in the Federal Republic be enhanced and their integration into West German society promoted.[11]

While the commission's finding concerning integration represented a slight unravelling of the temporary labour framework, its recommendations pertaining to migration and return reinforced its basic premises.[12] A similar outcome marked the review of naturalization regulations (*Einbürgerungs-richtlinien*) in 1977.[13] The ruling SPD-FDP coalition and predominantly CDU-led *Länder* governments succeeded in fleshing out the rather thin regulations that had been in place until then and establishing a comprehensive set of criteria for judging naturalization applications. However, the conditions remained highly restrictive. They included a ten-year residency requirement, proficiency in spoken and written German, renunciation of former nationality, and evidence of a "voluntary and lasting orientation towards Germany" based on the "applicant's entire attitude towards German culture." The requisite "commitment to Germany" meant that applicants had to abstain from any connection with "émigré organizations." Further-more, naturalization could only be considered if it was in the "public inter-est"; the "personal and economic interests of the applicant" could not serve as "decisive factors." The regulations specified that the "public interest" be based on the principle that the Federal Republic of Germany was not a country of immigration and did not seek to increase the number of its cit-izens through naturalizations. An exorbitant fee of three months' salary served as an exclamation point to the regulations' unreceptive message to prospective applicants.

Both the recommendations of the *Bund-Länder* Commission and the 1977 naturalization regulations reflected the degree to which entrenched principles continued to shape policy makers' approaches to the migration-membership dilemma during this period. The nod to integration in point three of the commission's recommendations and the slight opening granted to non-ethnic Germans in the naturalization regulations indicated that there was agreement that some elements of the regime required modifica-tion. Yet the scope of change was limited. The mantra-like repetition of the "principle" that West Germany was "not an immigration country" demon-strated an unwillingness to acknowledge the reality that confronted the Federal Republic in the aftermath of mass labour recruitment.

An important exception to this line of thinking was the 1979 report of the Federal Republic's first commissioner for the integration of foreign workers and their families, Heinz Kühn.[14] Kühn, the former minister-president of North Rhine-Westphalia and a prominent member of the SPD, explicitly rejected past policies and called for the recognition of West Germany's status as an immigration country.[15] His recommendations included granting local voting rights to settled migrants, improving access to all levels of edu-cation for immigrant children, and simplifying naturalization rules for second-generation migrant youth.[16]

Taken together, Kühn's recommendations formed a coherent, long-term vision for improving foreign residents' legal status and encouraging their integration into West German society.[17] Unfortunately, they were largely ig-nored. The CDU/CSU was generally hostile to Kühn's suggestions and made a point of declaring its opposition publicly.[18] The reaction of Kühn's com-rades in the SPD was only slightly warmer.[19] Wary of being cast as "soft" on the foreigners issue during the upcoming 1980 federal election, Chancellor Helmut Schmidt claimed that Kühn's proposals went "against the core in-stincts" of the party's supporters.[20] Not surprisingly, a government state-ment issued in March 1980 reiterated that permanent settlement must be treated as an exception. At the same time, however, the SPD-FDP coalition recognized the need to expedite integration in order to avoid social problems. While Kühn's recommendation that migrant youth be granted naturalization as a right was rejected, the easing of naturalization requirements for the second generation was deemed a politically acceptable alternative.[21] A bill along these lines was drafted and prepared for submission to the Bundestag and Bundesrat. New programs to assist integration were also proposed and spending for programs already in place was increased.[22]

The Crumbling Consensus, 1980-82

The politicization of *Ausländerpolitik* cast even these modest reforms into doubt. Cross-party consensus began to break down in the late 1970s and early 1980s. Several factors lay behind this, including high rates of unemployment and rising public anxiety regarding immigration, which was heightened as a result of an increase in asylum applications in 1979-80.[23] The growing presence of immigrant families in large German cities and the real and perceived strain on infrastructure this caused also played a role in increasing public awareness. While these factors certainly provided grounds for public discontent, they did not prompt the breakdown of cross-party consensus in and of themselves. As pointed out in Chapter 4, comparable conditions in Canada during the mid-1970s also led to a sharply negative shift in public opinion and threatened the politicization of immigration policy making. Yet, the potential for such politics was never actualized and consensus was maintained. In Germany, a durable cross-party consensus stretching back to the beginning of the recruitment phase in the mid-1950s collapsed. Why?

Shifts in the strategy of the CDU/CSU were crucial. Members of the Union parties, at both the federal and state levels, began to take a much harder line on *Ausländerpolitik* after their defeat in the 1980 federal election.[24] The reasons for this shift included principled opposition to Germany's becoming an "immigration country" and an interest in mobilizing public discontent for electoral advantage. The high levels of public concern regarding migration promised some gain if properly exploited; conversely, the still marginal influence of pro-immigrant actors and near total disenfranchisement of migrants limited the costs of such a strategy. The vote-wielding and advantageously positioned "urban ethnics" that raised the costs of anti-immigrant politics in Canada were absent in West Germany.

Furthermore, the shadows of the Nazi past that had so thoroughly discredited right-wing nationalist sentiment and set strict limits to acceptable public discourse in the late 1960s and 1970s had begun to recede by the early 1980s.[25] There were calls among many in the CDU/CSU leadership to rehabilitate the German nation – to bury guilt over crimes long past and allow Germany to enjoy its well-earned status as a "normal" country. In Franz-Josef Strauß's estimation, West Germans had earned the right "not to be constantly reminded of Auschwitz."[26] Similarly, the CDU's Alfred Dregger called "upon all Germans to step out of Hitler's shadow," adding that "we must become normal."[27] A CDU resolution in the Bundestag in November 1981 declared unabashedly that the German Federal Republic was a "national unitary state," which as a constituent part of a "divided nation" did not permit "the commencement of an irreversible development to a multi-ethnic state."[28]

Karen Schönwälder notes that the early 1980s witnessed the "racialization" of migration politics in Germany, through the media and conservative politicians' designation of certain groups – especially Turks but also non-European refugees and asylum seekers – as "culturally inassimilable."[29] Christine Morgenstern similarly points out that such cultural arguments allowed critics of migration to engage in "racism without races."[30] This marked a break with the more restrained language of the 1960s and early 1970s.[31] Incendiary concepts such as *Überfremdung* (foreignization) were granted a renewed legitimacy by mainstream conservatives and used to mobilize public political support for tougher policies on asylum and family reunification.[32] Repeated references to "floods" of asylum seekers and threats to "German ways of life" in the print and broadcast media reinforced negative views of foreigners, transforming migration from a rather minor political issue in partisan terms to a matter of utmost importance.[33] Although references to "race" were carefully avoided, "culture" was used as a proxy to distinguish Germans from non-Germans and to justify exclusionary policies.[34] Turks, in particular, were considered to be inassimilable on the basis of their culture; for conservatives such as Dregger, the notion that Turks would be willing to become German was altogether absurd. As such, discussions of naturalization were entirely beside the point. The only real solution to Germany's migration problem lay in the return of Turks to their "natural and historical home."[35]

The Schmidt government struggled to maintain consensus by emphasizing its commitment to implementing tighter controls on migration and insisting that the need to integrate foreigners in no way constituted a retreat from the principle that Germany was not an immigration country.[36] In December 1981, the Cabinet approved guidelines formulated by the Federal

Ministry of the Interior that set stricter limits on family reunification. Among other measures, the maximum age of child dependents was lowered from eighteen to sixteen. At the same time, the Social-Liberal coalition sought to answer calls for the modernization of Germany's migration policies by developing policies aimed at facilitating the integration and naturalization of second-generation migrant youth.[37]

These efforts to preserve cross-party consensus failed. The Union parties claimed that the government was still unprepared to act decisively and continued to campaign for tougher policies at the *Land* level.[38] The opposition also struck a blow to the federal government's integration measures in 1982 by blocking a bill on simplified naturalization in the Bundesrat.[39] During the debate on the naturalization bill, the CDU/CSU argued that the government's intention to naturalize migrant youth who satisfied an eight-year residency requirement would transform a "foreigner problem" into a "German social problem," generating increased political tension and instability. The CDU/CSU insisted that naturalization could only be bestowed in order to acknowledge an individual's successful integration; its use as a means of facilitating integration was flatly rejected.

Concerns raised by members of the SPD and FDP regarding the CDU/CSU's politicization of *Ausländerpolitik* were beaten back by conservatives who argued that "polite" language was no longer appropriate. In Helmut Kohl's words:

We are all concerned about and wish to warn against the emergence of xenophobia in our country. However, the situation threatening to develop here, notwithstanding the theses of some aspiring right-wing extremists ... has absolutely nothing to do with nationalism or chauvinism ... So long as we fail to come up with effective measures to deal with the concrete problems that exist in our schools, in the emergence of ghettos in certain parts of our cities and, above all, in regard to limiting further immigration, tensions will continue to rise. Those who go on about tolerance and integration in these circumstances, without doing anything to ameliorate the situation, have no idea as to how feeble such concepts seem in the tension-filled reality of cities such as Frankfurt, Berlin, and my own Ludwigshafen.[40]

The breakdown of the social-liberal coalition in 1982 and the establishment of a CDU/CSU-FDP government under Kohl's leadership put an end to efforts to salvage cross-party consensus and gave the CDU/CSU an opportunity to pursue a harder line. Kohl included *Ausländerpolitik* among West

Germany's top policy challenges in his announcement of the new coalition's agenda (*Regierungserklärung*) on October 13, 1982. Policy making would be driven by three fundamental principles: (1) the integration of foreigners who continued to "live among us," (2) maintenance of the recruitment stop and limits on family reunification, and (3) encouragement of return through policies that facilitated repatriation. Although integration remained an aim of governmental policy, the onus was shifted to reducing migration and expediting return.[41]

The "Lost Decade," 1982-90

Whither Integration?

In October 1982, Kohl appointed a *Bund-Länder* commission to confer with representatives of the federal ministries, state and local governments, and social groups on the topics of migration and integration policy. The commission was instructed to present its recommendations to the government before the general election slated for March 1983 and dutifully submitted its report on February 24, 1983. Its recommendations were unremarkable; for the most part, they echoed those offered by its 1976 predecessor, though the accent was placed on the principles enunciated by Kohl in his *Regierungserklärung*. Thus, settled foreigners should be integrated, immigration sharply controlled, and return encouraged.[42] More specific recommendations included setting concrete standards for the granting of unlimited residency status; regulating family reunification by law rather than by the administrative guidelines set in 1981; devising a new category of residency for students and short-term residents; demarcating specific reasons for denial of residency permits in law; and simplifying naturalization for second-generation foreigners.[43]

The ambivalence of the report's recommendations reflected the divisions that marked the commission's work. Whereas the federal ministries of interior and finance, along with the state representatives of Baden-Württemberg, West Berlin, and Bavaria, pushed for a harder line on family reunification and rules governing residency – including dropping the maximum age for *Kindernachzug* (child migration) from sixteen to six and setting stringent rules for residency and deportation – the Foreign Office, the federal commissioner for foreigners affairs, and state representatives of Hessen and Bremen demanded maintenance of the status quo or, in some cases, the introduction of more liberal policies. Advocacy groups, including the Protestant and Roman Catholic churches and their respective social welfare organizations (Diakonisches Werk and Caritas), supported their positions.[44] The German Trade Unions Federation (DGB) accepted the principles set out in Kohl's *Regierungserklärung* and the notion that Germany was not an immigration country, but it rejected the hard-line policies on family migration, residency, and deportation pushed by Interior Minister Friedrich Zimmermann (CSU) and the CDU/CSU-governed *Länder*.[45]

The work of the commission also exposed a rift within the federal government. The FDP's interior affairs spokesperson, Burkhard Hirsch, had criticized Interior Minister Zimmermann's position on *Kindernachzug* before the release of the commission's report, noting that the protections granted to the sanctity of the family under the Basic Law were "human rights" that applied to Germans and non-German residents alike. Zimmermann's "radical and unprecedented moves" would not only breach constitutional principles but also damage the standing of the Federal Republic internationally as no other liberal democratic country prohibited the migration of minors in such a draconian fashion. Hirsch argued that the Federal Republic had to place greater emphasis on recognizing migrants' human dignity and do more to ensure the integration of migrant youth through investments in education and training.[46] Following the publication of the commission's report, Hirsch maintained that his party's parliamentary group would continue to honour humanitarian principles in its migration policies and reject any efforts to bring Germany's position on family reunification rights for dependent children below the standards of other "Western democracies."[47] Similarly, the federal commissioner for foreigners affairs, the FDP's Liselotte Funcke, rejected Interior Minister Zimmermann's efforts to restrict family reunification, arguing that such a move would be both "anti-family" and "unconstitutional."[48]

Unease over the interior minister's repeated public statements on child migration also emerged from within the CDU, with the party's social-Catholic wing distancing itself from Zimmermann and aligning itself with the more liberal position of the FDP. A working group of CDU jurists in Rheinland-Pfalz maintained that the Federal Ministry of the Interior's proposal would contravene Article 6 of the Basic Law, which guaranteed the sanctity of the family and marriage to citizen and non-citizen families alike.[49] In light of such serious internal disagreement, the federal Cabinet elected to end discussions of child migration. Nevertheless, the debate intensified, as Federal Ministry of the Interior officials continued to press for restrictions to family reunification. The Foreign Office responded by highlighting the potential political repercussions of restricting migration flows from Turkey, a key NATO ally. Foreign Minister Hans-Dietrich Genscher reminded his Cabinet colleagues that Germany had long-standing agreements with Turkey regarding family reunification that it could not easily dismiss. In an emergency meeting called to deal with what was fast becoming a full-blown Cabinet crisis, Genscher warned that he would resign his post if these commitments were not honoured.[50] This "weapon of last resort" was effective in so far as Zimmermann dropped his insistence on lowering the age for *Kindernachzug* to six.

Following the CDU/CSU's landslide victory in the federal election of March 1983,[51] the CDU/CSU-FDP coalition government acted on its commitment to "encourage return" by passing a new law – the aptly titled Law for Encouraging the Willingness of Foreigners to Return (*Gesetz zur Förderung der Rückkehrbereitschaft von Ausländern*). The legislation offered unemployed foreigners a refund of their pension contributions and a DM10,500 grant for deciding to return to their home countries. An additional DM1,500 was be added for spouses and children.[52] The "return premium" (*Rückkehrprämie*) came into effect on December 1, 1983, and was to remain in force until December 31, 1984. While the program contributed to a slight drop in the total number of foreigners in Germany, the number of repatriations in 1983-84 did not vary significantly from past years. New family migration and high birth rates among migrants ensured that the government would be unable to honour its earlier pledge to decrease the total number of foreigners in the Federal Republic by 1 million. By 1988, the total number of foreigners had nearly returned to its 1983 level. In 1989, it surpassed it and stood at 4.85 million individuals, or 7.7 percent of the total population.[53]

The government's "buy-out" policy prompted indignation and criticism among advocacy groups.[54] Churches, unions, welfare organizations, and a small but growing number of immigrant associations all argued that the Kohl administration was sending the wrong message to migrants, hindering their integration. Successful integration, they argued, required a greater sense of security. As of 1983, only 95,000 foreign workers from non-EC countries, or roughly 5 percent of those eligible, possessed a long-term residency permit.[55] The other 95 percent had to apply for yearly renewals and were subjected to the whims of officials who still enjoyed great discretion under the terms of the 1965 Foreigners Law. Advocacy groups also supported the maintenance of the sixteen-year maximum age for dependent children; many demanded that the age of eligibility be raised to eighteen or even twenty-one. The birth of foreign children in Germany and their socialization in German society highlighted the need for citizenship policy reforms for the second generation. Proposals advanced by the SPD and the FDP focused on simplifying naturalization procedures and making naturalization a right for all migrant youth who satisfied basic residency requirements.[56] Advocates of reform also noted that the effective disenfranchisement of first-generation adult migrants challenged the Federal Republic's status as a democratic *Rechtsstaat*. Demands for local voting rights were aimed at addressing this glaring democratic deficit.[57]

The "Zimmermann Draft Law"

Prior to its collapse, the Schmidt government had pledged to replace the 1965 *Ausländergesetz,* and the SPD continued to press this demand while in opposition.[58] Criticism of the existing law had been building since the late 1960s. Opponents questioned the discretion granted to officials and decried the lack of residency and other basic rights the law provided to migrants.[59] The CDU/CSU-led government maintained its predecessor's interest in crafting a new law but for quite different reasons: conservatives wished to introduce more restrictive guidelines to check the tendency of some SPD-governed *Länder* (such as Bremen) to interpret regulations pertaining to family reunification in what they deemed was too liberal a fashion. The Federal Ministry of the Interior had made a first attempt to introduce principles for a new law in 1983-84 but was stymied by opposition from the FDP and segments of the CDU. Work on a new law only resumed following the CDU/CSU-FDP's victory in the 1987 general election. Interior Minister Zimmermann made it known that he planned to enact a new law promptly and a first draft was completed in January 1988.[60] It was leaked to the press and excerpted in the weekly news magazine *Der Spiegel*.[61] The draft consisted of two laws: the first addressing the integration of foreign workers who had come to Germany as a result of the Federal Republic's recruitment policy and the second designed to restrict immigration and decrease the number of foreigners in Germany.

The "Foreigners Integration Law" (*Ausländerintegrationsgesetz*) made no reference to naturalization and maintained officials' discretion in granting unlimited residency permits. It expressed the Federal Ministry of the Interior's grudging acceptance of settled migrants' distinctive legal standing, as expressed in the Federal Constitutional Court's decisions in the "Arab" and "Indian" cases. Conversely, the "Foreigners Entry Law" (*Ausländeraufnahmegesetz*) featured draconian measures aimed at preventing further immigration.[62] Chief among these was the stipulation that residency permits only be granted if the applicant's stay was consistent with the interests of the

Federal Republic. Permits would be extended for a maximum of eight years, at which point a decision would be made either to award an unlimited residency permit or to terminate the foreigner's stay in Germany. Under the terms of the draft law, unlimited residency was an exceptional status, granted only in individually justifiable cases. Renewal of yearly permits would depend on the foreigner's intention to return to his or her country of origin. Thus, in a cruel legal pirouette, foreigners who had consistently maintained their intention to leave in order to secure extensions of their one-year permits would then be compelled to request an unlimited residency permit, signalling their intention to remain in the Federal Republic.

The draft Foreigners Entry Law also revived hard-line positions on family reunification. *Kindernachzug* would be limited to children up to the age of six, except in what officials' deemed "extraordinary circumstances." Administrative regulations designed to limit the migration of spouses would also be inscribed into law. Fees for residency permits would be raised and grounds for expulsion expanded to include disparagement of the Federal Republic and its institutions and a host of other offences.[63]

The draft legislation's central aim, as set out in its accompanying commentary, was to "safeguard [Germany's] national characteristics" by limiting further migration to the greatest extent possible. Failure to do so entailed the "abandonment of societal homogeneity," which was "primarily determined by membership in the German nation." Left uncontrolled, migration would wreak havoc on Germany's national identity:

> Germany's common history, heritage, language, and culture would lose their unifying and defining nature. The Federal Republic would develop little by little into a multicultural society, which would inevitably be burdened with minority problems.[64]

The text sent "shock waves" through advocacy groups, opposition parties, the FDP, and segments of the CDU.[65] Diakonisches Werk strongly criticized the draft's tone and content, noting that its elevation of the state's interest in reducing migration to paramount status made the granting of residency rights an "act of mercy" beyond the scope of the rule of law.[66] The DGB described the "Zimmermann Plan" as "backwards-looking, inhumane, and mired in the nationalist thinking of the past century."[67] The Greens, who had scored a major breakthrough in the 1987 federal election and enjoyed an enhanced profile during this period, argued that the new law would make the flawed 1965 act appear "downright liberal" in comparison. The Greens'

Erika Trenz went on to note that such a law would set itself against "basic constitutional principles, such as human dignity and the rule of law." While the "Federal Republic could not be compared to the Germany of the National Socialists or Apartheid South Africa," the draft law and the spirit that informed it were "nevertheless racist."[68] Members of the SPD drew similar parallels in their comments on the draft law. The mayor of Bremen, Klaus Wedmeier (SPD), argued that the draft's "conceptual coupling of 'national identity' and 'societal homogeneity' must be firmly rejected":

> In a period of European integration, with the increasing mutual entwinement of states and peoples, and in view of the experiences which have linked Germans with nationalist arrogance and racist delusions of superiority, it would be fatal to make [such] antiquated conceptions the basis of our policy on foreigners.[69]

More troubling from the point of view of the government were the reactions of members of the CDU and FDP. The Christian Democratic Workers Association (*Christlich-Demokratische Arbeitnehmerschaft* [CDA]) argued that structural factors, such as the ageing of the working population and the imminent collapse of the social security system, would soon make it necessary to *renew* migration to meet labour market needs. The CDA also noted that the need for fundamental change was driven by changes in political and normative contexts:

> Given that human rights have come to play such a decisive role in our foreign policy, the generous administration of family reunification and asylum rights is no longer only mandated by our constitution, but rather *is essential to the credibility and long-term success of our foreign policy.*[70] (Emphasis added.)

The CDU's Committee on Social Affairs (*Sozialausschüsse*) criticized Zimmermann for "provoking panic" among the German public and unwittingly "playing into the hands" of right-wing extremists.[71]

The FDP's senior interior affairs spokesperson, Burkhard Hirsch, came out strongly against the federal interior minister, arguing that the plan to drop the age for child migration to six was "inhumane" and "extraordinarily narrow minded."[72] The federal commissioner for foreigners affairs and FDP party member Liselotte Funcke was similarly dismayed as her office had produced a brief in December 1987 to help steer policy making in a more

liberal direction. Funcke had recommended a number of fundamental liberalizing reforms, including the granting of unlimited residency permits
after eight years; improved residency rights for spouses; independent
residency rights for children born or raised in Germany; child migration
up to eighteen years of age; the right of children born or raised in Germany
to return to the Federal Republic after returning to their parents' home
countries (*Wiederkehroption*); simplified naturalization for first-generation
migrants after eight years of legal residency; and as-of-right naturalization
for migrant children.[73]

The episode was a disaster for the government, the Federal Ministry of
the Interior, and Zimmermann personally. The minister attempted to play
down the draft's significance by referring to it as an intradepartmental "ex-
pert opinion" not endorsed by the ministry's political leadership.[74] But his
qualifications came too late; the affair had unleashed a politically damaging
debate that embarrassed the Kohl government. Critics of the Zimmermann
draft succeeded in casting it as outdated and outside the range of prevailing
European and liberal-democratic norms. Zimmermann was demoted to
transport minister as part of a Cabinet shuffle in April 1989. The CDU's
Wolfgang Schäuble succeeded him as interior minister.

The "New" Foreigners Law of 1990

The debate over the reform of the 1965 Foreigners Law continued through
1989. Opposition to the Zimmermann plan mobilized a broad coalition in
favour of liberal reforms. Civil society actors were joined by the opposition
SPD and Greens as well as by the governing FDP. For its part, the CDU/CSU
was determined to pass a new law while it maintained control of both the
Bundestag and the Bundesrat, thereby avoiding a legislative defeat or the
prospects of bargaining with the opposition. The Union parties were also
concerned that their majority in the Bundesrat might be lost as a result of
the state election in Lower Saxony scheduled for May 13, 1990.[75] Furthermore,
there were fears that the debate unleashed by the Zimmermann draft might
benefit the far right-wing *Republikaner* party in the Bavarian state election
in September 1990.[76] The success of the far right in the 1989 Berlin *Senat*
race suggested that politicization was beginning to work *against* the Union
parties at the state and local levels.[77] Hence, Schäuble was under considerable pressure to bring recalcitrant members of his own party and the FDP
on board to form a "minimum winning coalition" as quickly as possible.

Schäuble accepted a new draft composed by a working group headed by
representatives from the CDU, the CSU, the FDP, and senior civil servants

from the interior and justice ministries after taking up his post in April 1989.[78] The draft was designed to secure inter- and intra-party consensus and thus drew from policy proposals advanced by the CDU's Committee on Social Affairs and the FDP.[79] The most objectionable features of the Zimmermann plan were discarded, while more liberal measures, including clearer rules for granting unlimited residency as a right, were incorporated.[80] The law also introduced simplified naturalization for migrant youth aged sixteen to twenty-one who had lived in the Federal Republic for at least eight years. The fee for naturalization was dropped from the punitive three months salary to a more reasonable DM100, and the principle of encouraging return was scrapped. Beyond these changes, the draft added little that was new and instead consolidated many of the administrative and regulatory changes that had arisen in the years since the passage of the 1965 Foreigners Law.[81] Rules governing child migration and the sponsorship of spouses reverted to those implemented by the SPD-FDP coalition in 1981.

The Schäuble draft steered a middle course, avoiding the harshness and rhetorical excesses of the Zimmermann plan while preserving the overall aims of the prevailing policy framework. As such, it represented a further example of policy stretching. Politically, the strategy was successful. Schäuble succeeded in gaining the support of the FDP leadership and most recalcitrant CDU members. Although the CSU's Edmund Stoiber complained that the new draft was far too liberal,[82] neither he nor the CSU stood in the way of the federal interior minister's efforts to push the bill through Parliament before the state election in Lower Saxony. Thus, intra-coalition consensus was secured.[83]

Criticism of the law and the government's tactics continued during the course of the debates that accompanied the legislation's passage. Censure came from the opposition SPD and the Greens as well as from advocacy groups, including the DGB, the Protestant and Roman Catholic churches, welfare organizations, and immigrant associations. Critics demanded clearer and less complicated conditions for the conferral of unlimited residency permits, more expansive sponsorship rights, simplified naturalization procedures, dual citizenship, and explicit recognition of the Federal Republic's de facto status as an "immigration country."[84] In Berlin, migrants fashioned placards with the motto *Wir sind auch das Volk* (We are also the people), evoking and effectively extending the motto used by protesters in East Germany in the months leading up to the fall of the Berlin Wall in November 1989.[85] Members of the SPD complained that, despite its more moderate tone, the Schäuble draft law remained mired in the logic of an "antiquated nationalism." The Greens and some church activists went further, demanding that the entire edifice of foreigners policy be replaced with laws based on "multicultural principles."[86] The vision of a "multicultural society" advanced in their proposals entailed respect for migrants' cultural identities and a "dialogue" among groups in the Federal Republic.[87] Support for multiculturalism was shared by segments of the SPD and even some members of the CDU.[88] The Greens also sought to change the language of migration politics and were the first German political party to consistently refer to former guest workers as "immigrants." This marked an important shift in discourse that was taken up by advocacy groups.[89]

This spirited opposition to Schäuble's bill was largely symbolic and did not lead to any further amendments. The government used its majority to push its legislation through the Bundestag in April 1990; the law was approved by the Bundesrat on May 11, 1990, two days before the crucial election in Lower Saxony, in which the SPD's candidate for minister president, Gerhard Schröder, beat the CDU incumbent and, in so doing, broke the Union parties' dominance of the German upper house, setting the stage for a period of divided government.

Tragedy, Reflection, Stasis, 1990-98

From Euphoria to Barbarism

The debates leading up to the passage of the 1990 Foreigners Law demonstrated both the resilience of established policy orientations and their limits. The Federal Ministry of the Interior's efforts to introduce hard-line measures were checked by opposition forces who pointedly demonstrated the lack of fit between Interior Minister Zimmermann's position and the prevailing normative context through their evocations of the unassailable right to human dignity guaranteed by the Basic Law (and upheld by prevailing European standards) and pointed reminders that Germany's foreign policy interests would suffer if policies towards migrants were interpreted as illiberal backsliding by the international community. Critics' efforts delayed the legislative process and ultimately led to the passage of a law that further stretched the established framework through its more expansive provisions on residency and naturalization.

Critics were clearly not satisfied with the 1990 law and continued to press for more robust integration measures. The emergence of second- and third-generation "foreigners" and extremely low rates of naturalization among long-settled migrants led many to reject the 1913 citizenship law and demand the introduction of *jus soli*, less stringent naturalization criteria, and dual citizenship. By 1990, the Green Party, the SPD, the FDP, and even leading members of the CDU came to endorse these positions, often pointing out that Germany lagged behind its European partners in this regard.[90] Academics, journalists, and others joined them. German reunification removed a key justification for the maintenance of the 1913 RuStAG and convinced a growing number of actors that the time had come to modernize Germany's antiquated nationality law, bringing the newly united Federal Republic and its membership policies into the European mainstream.[91]

Yet, significant changes to German citizenship policy would not be implemented until nearly ten years after reunification. The lack of major reforms was not due to the overwhelming force of a widely shared national tradition but, rather, was a consequence of political factors that deepened the ideological-political splits that had begun to emerge in the early 1980s. Among the most important issues blocking agreement was the bitter debate over asylum that dominated German politics in the early 1990s.[92] Asylum was not a new issue:[93] the number of asylum seekers entering Germany increased steadily during the late 1980s as a result of political changes in Eastern Europe and deteriorating political, social, and economic conditions in the Middle East, Africa, and Asia. However, the end of the Cold War compounded matters by dissolving restrictions on exit in the countries of the former Eastern Bloc and catalyzing refugee-generating violence in southeastern Europe.[94] As a result, the number of asylum seekers entering Germany spiked in 1991, 1992, and 1993, and the issue became more salient within German society and politics.

The Union parties raised the stakes of the debate by demanding the repeal of Article 16(2) of the Basic Law: "Persons persecuted on political grounds shall have the right of asylum." The CDU/CSU argued that Article 16(2) hindered the normal exercise of state sovereignty, leaving Germany vulnerable to "overwhelming floods" of asylum seekers.[95] However, Article 16(2) was one of the framers' clearest acknowledgments of Nazi crimes,[96] and its repeal represented much more than a shift in asylum policy: for many it marked the desecration of symbolic memory and a dangerous affirmation of a resurgent German nationalism.[97] The Union parties' welcoming attitude towards co-ethnic resettlers (*Aussiedler*) who were also entering Germany in huge numbers in the late 1980s and early 1990s deepened these suspicions, particularly among those on the left of the political spectrum.

Undaunted by such criticism, the CDU/CSU embarked on a nationwide campaign to generate popular support for the repeal of Article 16(2). As per the instructions of the CDU's general secretary, Volker Rühe, Union politicians across Germany told their constituents that every new asylum seeker entering the Federal Republic was an "SPD asylum seeker."[98] Verbal and written attacks on the SPD escalated in the summer of 1990 in anticipation of the first post-unification federal election that December. More disturbingly, the government failed to speak out against attacks on asylum seekers and migrants, which were occurring with ever greater frequency. Rather than condemning the attacks, some politicians in the Union parties argued that the SPD's failure to back the abolition of Article 16(2) was forcing the German people to take matters into their own hands. Indeed, the Bavarian interior minister, Edmund Stoiber, claimed that "necessary" changes to the Basic Law would only come about as a result of the people themselves "lighting a fire under the ass" of the "old guard" in Bonn.[99]

Following its success in the December 1990 federal election, during which it continued to politicize the asylum issue, the CDU/CSU stepped up its campaign to amend the Basic Law. Union politicians made a point of linking foreigners with issues such as welfare abuse and criminality, while also stressing that the German people could no longer cope with overwhelming "floods" of outsiders stretching the reasonable limits of their endurance.[100] The popular press echoed these claims in exaggerated and sensational reports.[101] The result of this agitation was a steep increase in public concern over asylum and migration policy, as reflected in public opinion polls in 1991 and 1992.[102]

The government's indifference to irresponsible speech among leading politicians and incidents of racist violence was such that Commissioner for Foreigners Affairs Funcke resigned in protest.[103] Her resignation letter noted that rising levels of xenophobia in the five new *Länder* was an "alarm signal" that must be heeded lest the situation spin out of control. Chancellor Kohl accepted her resignation, ignored her warning, and delayed the appointment of a new commissioner for several months, displaying what in hindsight can only be judged an appalling indifference to growing problems.[104]

The violence feared by Funcke and others exploded in September 1991 in a week-long anti-foreigner riot in the eastern city of Hoyerswerda. The event was marked by gangs of youths shouting "Foreigners out" and setting fire to apartment units used to house asylum seekers. Police guarding the buildings were attacked with stones and firebombs and eventually quit the scene, leaving the victims at the mercy of the mob. The response of the crowd that gathered to take in the spectacle made the event all the more disturbing: many expressed sympathy for the attackers, while others applauded and shouted their approval.[105] Similar events occurred throughout Germany in the weeks and months that followed, culminating in a four-day pogrom in Rostock-Lichtenhagen in August 1992, in which over one thousand assailants stormed a residence for asylum seekers and Vietnamese foreign labourers, setting fire to the building, breaking windows, and terrorizing those inside. The official tally of racially motivated attacks jumped from a dismal 2,426 in 1991 to an astonishing 6,336 in 1992.[106] These events were greeted with alarm both in Germany and abroad. Yet, Union politicians remained largely indifferent. Indeed, the CDU's Dieter Heckelmann maintained that the events in Rostock were not an expression of racism but, "rather[,] of a fully justified discontent over the mass abuse of the right to asylum."[107]

Pressure from local party leaders led the SPD leadership to signal its interest in ending the asylum debate through a compromise, according to which support for the amendment of Article 16(2) would be exchanged for a pledge by the government to introduce a new immigration law that regulated refugee flows, co-ethnic migration, and labour migration through quotas.[108] The idea was flatly rejected by the CDU/CSU. Chancellor Kohl increased pressure on the Social Democrats by warning that failure to repeal the right to asylum would lead to the deepening of the crisis and a potential "state of emergency."[109] A little more than two weeks after Kohl made his statement, right-wing extremists in Mölln set fire to the home of a Turkish family, killing a ten-year-old girl, her grandmother, and the grandmother's fourteen-year-old niece. Nine other people were also injured in the attack.[110] Yeliz Arslan, the youngest victim, burned to death in her bed. In a chilling scene broadcast on that evening's television news broadcasts, her grieving mother exclaimed that her daughter was neither an "asylum seeker" nor a "Kurd," but a "real Turk," born and raised in Germany.[111]

From Tragedy to Mobilization

The tragedy in Mölln provoked shock and an outpouring of sympathy for the victims and their families. On the evening of the attack, six thousand residents of the town took part in a spontaneous demonstration against xenophobia. In the days and weeks that followed, hundreds of thousands took to the streets throughout Germany in demonstrations, protest marches, and candlelight vigils.[112] For many, Mölln exposed the perverse workings of a system that made foreigners out of millions of long-settled migrants and their German-born children, while conferring instant citizenship to "ethnic Germans" whose only connection to the Federal Republic lay in their claim to German descent. The tragedy thus served as a turning point in policy terms: grief and indignation were channelled into demands for change, with the abolition of the 1913 RuStAG – now widely seen as isolating Germany in the international community and shackling it to its disastrous ethnonational past – emerging as a unifying theme.

Reform advocates highlighted the incompatibility of a citizenship law based on descent with a Western European liberal-democratic society transformed by immigration. The DGB and Protestant Church Council of Germany demanded that *jus soli* be introduced to facilitate the incorporation of long-settled foreign workers and their families.[113] Leading academics also voiced their dissatisfaction with established citizenship and immigration policies and called for drastic changes that recognized Germany's de facto status as an immigration country, as did the new federal commissioner for foreigners affairs, Cornelia Schmalz-Jacobsen, and a growing number of politicians.[114] The president of the Federal Republic, Richard von Weizsäcker (CDU), made an impassioned plea on behalf of citizenship reform, arguing that, despite their official categorization as foreigners, the victims in Mölln were "our people."[115] In von Weizsäcker's view, the established law's failure to recognize this fact pointed to its incompatibility with Germany's liberal values and long-term interests.[116] Similarly, the chief justice of the Federal Constitutional Court, Roman Herzog, argued that individuals born and raised in Germany were already "German" in so far as they spoke German and were integrated into German society. They should therefore be offered easier means of acquiring German citizenship, even if this meant greater tolerance of dual citizenship.[117] A number of prominent German intellectuals and authors joined forces with the Green Party to mobilize grassroots support for nationality reform through a signature campaign in support of dual citizenship.[118] The campaign eventually included the SPD, the FDP, trade unions, churches, immigrant associations, and a multitude of concerned individuals and groups, such as members of the German national soccer team and even some CDU politicians.[119] It received significant press coverage and succeeded in provoking sustained discussion on citizenship reform. The goal of collecting 1 million signatures was reached within eight months, an unrivalled achievement in the history of the Federal Republic.[120]

Domestic pressure was joined by international condemnation. The peculiarity of Germany's "blood-based" citizenship regime and the phenomenon of second- and third-generation "domestic foreigners" drew the attention of the international press, as did the Kohl administration's dubious handling of the "asylum problem." The British *Independent on Sunday* reported that crimes such as the murder of Yeliz Arslan were the "result of a systematic campaign of the government to depict foreigners as a problem."[121] A 1992 report by the human rights organization Helsinki Watch concluded that the German government had failed to give "clear and unwavering support for the protection of foreigners."[122] The American news magazine *Newsweek* pointed out the inherent injustice of Germany's "atavistic law of *jus sanguinis*," which enabled "[a] farmer in Kazakhstan whose ancestors left the Rhine Valley 250 years ago" to be granted German citizenship, while excluding "a second generation Berliner whose grandparents came from Ankara."[123] The *Times* of London noted that Germany's "anachronistic [citizenship] law" was "a real obstacle in creating a sensible multicultural society in Germany" in that it did "little to discourage the xenophobia of the fringe nationalists." The *Times* maintained that "the main source of paralysis for Bonn [was] the fear that citizenship [would] become an issue in [the] next year's general campaign." Chancellor Kohl was encouraged to "shrug off these party political considerations and take the lead on citizenship."[124] Similar opinions were expressed in publications throughout Europe and North America.

German diplomats warned that news of the murders in Mölln was damaging Germany's image abroad, with possible long-term implications for the Federal Republic's foreign policy interests. Foreign Minister Klaus Kinkel intimated that "he had not attended a meeting in Brussels, Luxemburg or anywhere else in the world where the topic [of right-wing extremism] had not been raised."[125] Germany's ambassador to the United States, Immo Stabreit, reported that Germans who were planning to visit the United States in the spring should expect "to encounter a changed atmosphere."[126] He went on to note that, during the course of presenting his credentials to outgoing president George H.W. Bush, Bush surprised him by asking: "What is going on in Germany?" – clarifying in the same breath that he was not seeking to engage in diplomatic small talk but rather requesting information on the recent attacks on migrants. Stabreit's report added: "unless we succeed in getting matters under control, those of our friends, who have helped us thus far, will grow quiet and gradually hold themselves back." Jürgen Sudhoff, a German diplomat based in Paris, reported that Stabreit's report of reactions in the United States "mirrored" those he was experiencing in France. While his French colleagues were still couching their concerns in a friendly manner, Sudhoff predicted that this would quickly change for the worse if Germany did not successfully confront and eliminate the violent excesses of the previous months: "This will have consequences for everyone ... each German exporter who wants to sell, each tourist who wants to vacation on a sunny shore."

Starbreit's and Sudhoff's gloomy forecasts were prescient: The US State Department issued warnings to Americans travelling to Germany, prompting a wave of concern among German business leaders regarding how outsiders' views of the Federal Republic might harm their bottom line.[127] Seeking to counteract such feelings, major German firms, such as Lufthansa, BMW, and Siemens, published full-page advertisements in major German dailies denouncing extremist violence and pledging solidarity with migrants.[128]

Domestic and international reactions to Mölln renewed efforts to broker a deal on asylum policy. On December 6, 1992, the CDU/CSU-FDP coalition and the SPD's parliamentary group entered into the so-called "asylum compromise."[129] Under the terms of the accord, the government agreed to extend the naturalization provisions of the 1990 Foreigners Law by making the granting of citizenship a right for all applicants who satisfied residency and other conditions. The SPD also extracted a pledge from the government to limit the entry of co-ethnic resettlers through yearly quotas and other measures.[130] A separate status for refugees who were fleeing civil wars was also established to allow for the acceptance of de facto refugees who were escaping crisis zones in the Balkans. In return, the SPD agreed to modify Article 16(2). Specifically, a new paragraph was inserted holding that the right to asylum granted under what became paragraph one of the new Article 16a ("Persons persecuted on political grounds shall have the right of asylum"):

> may not be invoked by a person who enters the federal territory from a member state of the European Community or from another third country in which the standards of the Convention Relating to the Status of Refugees and of the Convention for the Protection of Human Rights and Fundamental Freedoms are assured. Countries outside the European Community, to which the criteria of the first sentence of this paragraph apply, shall be determined by statute subject to the consent of the *Bundesrat*. In the cases specified in the first sentence of this paragraph, measures to terminate an applicant's stay may be pursued without regard to any legal challenge that may have been raised against said measures.[131]

In essence, the amended article entailed withholding the right to asylum for asylum seekers entering Germany from "safe third countries." As all the states sharing borders with Germany were deemed "safe," the right of asylum was effectively suspended for asylum seekers entering by land.[132] An accompanying change to section 18a of the Asylum Law (*Asylverfahrensgesetz*) plugged the remaining gap left to asylum seekers who arrived by airplane: Frankfurt International Airport was deemed an "extraterritorial" space. This being the case, constitutional provisions would not apply; instead, asylum seekers' applications would be considered under a new "fast-track" basis. Rejected applicants would have recourse to a limited appeals process and would be sent back to their home countries once the process was completed – a task made easier as a result of changes to deportation procedures.[133] The amended Article 16a was voted into law on May 26, 1993, and came into effect on July 1, 1993.

The qualification of Germany's constitutionally enshrined right to asylum was justified as necessary in order to both control large-scale asylum flows and to render German law consistent with efforts to harmonize the emerging European Union's immigration and asylum policy. While the Treaty of European Union, agreed upon in December 1991 and set to take effect November 1, 1993, formalized and extended long-standing rights to freedom of movement for citizens of EU member states, the Schengen Agreement of June 1985 (an intergovernmental accord concluded by Belgium, the Netherlands, France, and West Germany and set to take effect on January 1, 1990) envisioned the removal of internal border controls and the establishment of common external borders and visa policies regulating the admission of third-country nationals. Freedom of movement would thus be liberalized for EU citizens and others (e.g., tourists) inside the evolving European space but sharply regulated for those outside.[134] German conservatives welcomed these changes as they allowed for the Europeanization of migration control – "shifting" a sensitive issue "up and out" of the Federal Republic's highly charged domestic political arena.[135] Whereas European standards had long been used by progressive actors to criticize hard-liners' attempts at limiting migration (recall the reactions to the Zimmermann draft law discussed above), they could now be used to defend calls for tougher controls.

In a deadly coda to the brutality of the preceding months, five members of the Genç family, three young girls and two women, were burned to death by extremists who set fire to their home in Solingen on May 29, 1993. Seven others, including an infant, were badly injured in the attack.[136] Violence continued to intensify across Germany, with 3,365 attacks recorded in the first six months of 1993 alone. Migrants of Turkish descent took to the streets in spontaneous, angry, and sometimes violent demonstrations to express their bitter disappointment with the government's failure to rein in extremists.[137] The Turkish government added its voice to the protests: Turkey's ambassador in Bonn, Onur Öymen, warned his compatriots to brace for more attacks and urged them to purchase fire extinguishers and secure their doors,[138] while Turkey's president, Suleyman Demirel, called on German lawmakers to do more to protect foreigners.[139] Demirel's demand was repeated by a group of lawmakers in the Israeli Knesset, who signed an appeal urging their counterparts in Bonn to stand up against "such dangerous developments,"[140] and in over 1 million postcards to Kohl bearing the message "I am angry" (*Ik ben woedend*), sent by individuals in the Netherlands mobilized by a radio campaign.[141] Commenting on the international reaction to the events in Mölln and Solingen, Foreign Minister Kinkel despaired that Germany's allies were "beginning to have doubts about the Germans."[142]

The international press's condemnation of the German government's handling of immigration and citizenship policy intensified following the Solingen attack. Once again, Germany's "blood-based" citizenship law was cast as a particularly egregious affront to liberal-democratic principles and human rights.[143] The *Times* of London complained that, despite the promises made in the wake of the Mölln attacks, not enough had been done either to protect or to integrate the "millions of former guest workers who have been living in legal limbo."[144] While the public demonstrations and declarations of the past months suggested that the overwhelming majority of Germans rejected racism, the country had nevertheless "fallen prey to a criminal rabble of alienated youths."

> What is needed is vision and leadership at the very top. Helmut Kohl has again refused with threadbare excuses to make the gestures of atonement the tragedy demands. The fact remains that the laws on citizenship in Germany, *of all countries*, are based on blood. Until this is changed, the ghosts of Germany's past will not be exorcised, nor its current crisis properly addressed. (Emphasis added.)

Syndicated columnist Gwynne Dyer likened Germany's ethnic nationhood to that of the Bosnian Serbs, arguing that the maintenance of a blood-based law was scandalous for a country "like Germany, with its special historical burden."[145] Even more provocatively, the *New York Times*' William Safire argued that the 1913 RuStAG was "allied to Hitler's 'master race' fulminations and his search for polluting 'Jewish blood.'"[146]

Safire's column elicited a letter from the German embassy's press and information counsellor in Washington, DC, Gottfried Haas. Haas rejected any connection between Germany's nationality law and the "Nazi era ideology of blood and soil," insisting:

> The principle of nationality by descent is the traditional European way of determining citizenship, with roots in the French Revolution of 1789. It was then seen as a progressive principle for ending an aspect of absolutism that subjected men to the will of the state in which they were born.[147]

While Haas was correct to note that *jus sanguinis* was considered a "progressive" means of granting citizenship in the late eighteenth century,[148] the intensity of reactions to the events in Mölln and Solingen, as expressed by Safire and other key players in an increasingly connected global public sphere, suggested that the standards for judging the normative validity of liberal-democratic states' citizenship policies – and Germany's in particular – had since changed in quite fundamental ways.

Still reeling from domestic and foreign criticism of its conduct after the Mölln murders, the Kohl administration quickly responded to the Solingen attacks. In a move with clear political motivations, Kohl stated that he would consider the introduction of "temporary" dual citizenship to encourage Turkish migrants to naturalize. The federal Justice Minister, Sabine Leutheusser-Schnarrenberger (FDP), signalled that the government would shortly introduce a bill along these lines.[149] The Cabinet also took steps to toughen laws against right-wing extremists, and the chancellor pledged to engage in discussions with civil society groups over what ought to be done to improve the conditions of foreigners in Germany.[150] In a moving address given during a memorial for the Genç family in Cologne's Main Mosque on June 3, 1993, President von Weizsäcker highlighted the importance of acknowledging and responding positively to migrants' profound sense of fear and frustration. While admitting that improving migrants' citizenship rights would likely not deter violent extremists, von Weizsäcker argued that it would enhance their "self-esteem and whole attitude to life" and allow them to "finally rid themselves of the stigma of being second-class co-citizens." Von Weizsäcker pressed his colleagues in the CDU/CSU to recognize that accepting dual citizenship might assist in this regard: "We do not wish to stamp as foreigners those men and women who have for years, indeed decades, proven that Germany is also home to them as citizens. For that they need not deny their bonds of ancestry."[151]

By July 1993, there was general agreement between the government and opposition regarding the need for a sustained campaign against the extreme right and substantive changes to Germany's citizenship law. This suggested that reforms would soon follow – an expectation Kohl encouraged in a special address to the Bundestag on June 16, 1993.[152] However, there was still no consensus as to precisely what form changes should take. Whereas the SPD, Greens, FDP, and a minority in the CDU supported the introduction of dual citizenship and *jus soli*, and the establishment of a "modern" nationality premised on "republican" principles, the CSU and conservatives in the CDU rejected these options, arguing instead for limited changes that upheld the principles of the established regime. Changes to the naturalization provisions of the 1990 Foreigners Law, agreed to in the asylum compromise and implemented in July 1993, were in line with this more conservative approach.[153] In April 1994, the government voted against an initiative for dual citizenship advanced by the SPD. However, at the urging of the FDP and liberal elements in the CDU, Kohl pledged that reform of the 1913 RuStAG would be a key government objective after the 1994 election.[154]

Stasis

Following its narrow victory in the 1994 federal election, the CDU/CSU-FDP coalition government moved to honour its pledge to reform Germany's citizenship law. However, the key element in the government's reform plan – the so-called "child citizenship law" (*Kinderstaatszugehörigkeitsgesetz*) – was an unwieldy and unpopular contrivance. According to the scheme, foreign children born in Germany could, upon application before the age of twelve, obtain a legal status on a par with German children, providing one parent was born in Germany and both parents could prove at least ten years residence. If his or her application was accepted, the child would be granted a temporary status equal to, but distinct from, German citizenship; the child citizenship status could be converted to full nationality only if the child succeeded in obtaining release from his or her previous citizenship within one year of reaching the age of majority.[155] Failure to apply for full citizenship would lead to the automatic termination of the status once the child turned nineteen. The status was not recognized by international law and did not exclude children from the terms of the Foreigners Law, leaving them vulnerable to deportation.[156]

The child citizenship proposal did little to improve the legal standing of migrants and thus fell far short of what opposition parties and civil society groups demanded.[157] The Berlin-based Federation of Turkish Immigrants called the proposal a "laughable compromise" aimed at fooling the public into believing that the government was intent on improving the lot of migrants.[158] Berlin's commissioner for foreigners affairs, Barbara John (CDU), criticized the government for trying to pass a reform that only granted a "little bit of equality."[159] Taking a harder tone, Sabine Kriechhammer-Yagmur of the German Association for Bi-National Families noted that the proposal was "absolutely idiotic" and marked "a step backward."[160]

Differences of opinion over citizenship policy within the coalition help explain why the proposal was so convoluted. Conservatives in the CSU were unwilling to accept dual citizenship and *jus soli* in any form: the child citizenship proposal represented their maximal concession. The FDP's poor result in the 1994 election limited its influence within the government and put it at a disadvantage in negotiations over the agreement. The CDU was also split, with reformers and conservatives disagreeing over the extent of reforms. The child citizenship law offered Kohl a means of formally honouring his promise to liberalize Germany's citizenship policy without antagonizing conservatives in the CDU/CSU. The result was an exercise in policy stretching par excellence.

Efforts to move the debate forward continued through the mid-1990s. Citizenship reform was advocated by an impressive range of academics, intellectuals, journalists, and opinion leaders and, as the success of the signature drive demonstrated, enjoyed a good measure of public support.[161] The opposition parties also continued to press for reforms. In 1995, the SPD called for *jus soli* for third-generation foreigners, discretionary naturalization after five years, and acceptance of dual nationality.[162] Legislation introduced by the Green Party was even more far-reaching and included a legal right to citizenship after eight years, *jus soli* for the second generation, and acceptance of dual nationality.[163] The Greens also settled a long-running internal party battle and came out in favour of an immigration law that regulated flows through annual quotas. This marked an important turn in the party's approach to immigration policy and brought an end to earlier calls for "open borders."[164]

In an unexpected move, a group of junior CDU parliamentarians dubbed the *Junge Wilde* broke with their party's leadership and offered an alternative to the child citizenship proposal that included provisions for full *jus soli* and a compromise position on dual citizenship, whereby children would maintain their parents' nationality along with their German nationality until they reached the age of majority, at which time they would have to choose one or the other. Peter Altmaier, one of the group's members, noted that, given the circumstances, the proposal was a reasonable and appropriate compromise that "remained well behind the regulations of other western states."[165] The *Junge Wilde* proposal gained the support of 150 prominent CDU members, including thirty-one members of the CDU's Bundestag caucus.[166] It was also welcomed by the FDP leadership as a way out of its commitment to the child citizenship proposal. Thus, by 1996, there existed a numerical majority within the Bundestag in favour of fundamental changes to German nationality law. The potential for a broadly acceptable cross-party consensus was tantalizingly real.

Hardliners led by the CSU's Edmund Stoiber moved to quash this development by rejecting the *Junge Wilde* proposal and pressuring the CDU leadership to veto the plan. Kohl did so at the CDU's party conference in October 1996.[167] This effectively ended whatever possibility may have existed for working out a compromise with the opposition parties, making it clear that Union hardliners would prefer a non-decision on citizenship to a law that included *jus soli*.[168]

Thus, the impetus for reform reverted to the opposition parties and the FDP. A bill calling for dual citizenship for children born in Germany was introduced into the Bundesrat by the SPD-Green controlled governments of Hessen, Hamburg, and Lower Saxony in 1997. The SPD and Greens enjoyed a majority in the upper house and pressed for a vote on the bill in the Bundestag, forcing members of the FDP to choose between their principled support for reform and their interest in preserving a coalition with the Union parties. Given the government's thin majority in the Bundestag, a legislative defeat was possible. In an effort to avoid a potentially disastrous outcome, the Union parties warned the FDP that failure to vote against the opposition bill would lead to the dissolution of the government. Thus, the FDP leadership opted to enforce party discipline, with several of its members, including Cornelia Schmalz-Jacobsen and Burkhard Hirsch, abstaining from the vote.[169] The institutional logic of coalition government effectively blocked the will of a cross-party majority, granting the 1913 RuStAG a further lease on life.

The Contentious Politics of Reform, 1998-2000

The Red-Green Coalition's Citizenship Reform
The SPD's victory in the 1998 federal election and its selection of the Alliance 90/Greens as its coalition partner created a unique opportunity to fundamentally reform Germany's membership regime. Both parties had

long advocated the introduction of dual citizenship, *jus soli*, and (somewhat less enthusiastically in the case of the SPD) an immigration law. It soon became clear that the new government would focus its energies on citizenship reform. A statement in its coalition agreement affirmed that Germany had experienced an "irreversible process of immigration." Given this fact, the government pledged to assist in the "integration of those immigrants who live [in Germany] on a permanent basis and ... [who] accept [Germany's] constitutional values."[170] Towards this end, the Red-Green coalition pledged to introduce a new citizenship law that included a reduction of the residency requirement for naturalization from fifteen to eight years for foreign-born applicants and from eight to five years for individuals born or raised in Germany.[171] Furthermore, dual citizenship would be tolerated to facilitate the naturalization of long-settled foreign residents. The most significant reform addressed the attribution of citizenship for children born of foreign residents. According to the new government's plan, citizenship would be granted through the principle of *jus soli*. Moreover, the children could maintain their parents' nationality, thereby becoming dual citizens.

The proposed citizenship reform promised to fundamentally transform the institutional grounding of German nationhood. Children of qualified immigrant parents born in Germany would no longer be "foreigners" but, rather, German citizens with equal rights and responsibilities. The easing of barriers to dual citizenship would also make it easier for the millions of immigrants who satisfied the new law's residency requirements to naturalize. This would help resolve Germany's glaring democratic deficit and change the face of German politics by granting a hitherto weak segment of the population increased political voice and power. Government officials went to great lengths to laud the revolutionary character of the reform. According to Chancellor Gerhard Schröder, the reform of the citizenship law would bring German policy into line with its EU partners and demonstrate that "our national consciousness depends not on some 'law of descent' of Wilhelmine tradition but on the self-assured democracy we now have."[172]

The "Signature Campaign" and 1999 Hessen State Election
The government was confident that the citizenship reform would be passed into law quickly and did not expect the proposal to generate significant opposition.[173] There was even hope that the move could advance the SPD's political interests by granting citizenship to millions of immigrant voters who might express their gratitude by renewing the party's mandate in upcoming elections. These expectations were misplaced. The arch-conservative

minister president of Bavaria, Edmund Stoiber, greeted the citizenship proposal with alarm, arguing hyperbolically that it presented a greater threat to Germany than the terrorism of the Red Army Faction.[174] His CSU colleague, Wolfgang Zeitlmann, warned that the reforms would imperil German identity, lead to Islamic parties in the Bundestag, and provoke uncontrolled waves of immigration, undermining the integration of migrants already in Germany.[175]

Opponents of the proposed citizenship reform sought to get around the government's majorites in the Bundestag and Bundesrat through a signature drive modelled, ironically, after the Green Party's 1992-93 campaign for dual citizenship.[176] Reluctantly, the CDU's leader, Wolfgang Schäuble, accepted the idea. He and other party brass believed that something dramatic had to be done to raise the party's fortunes in the wake of its drubbing in the 1998 election. A populist campaign might motivate the party's core and ready it for the upcoming *Länder* elections in Hessen and Baden-Württemberg. The Union parties were also keen to "avoid ceding the issue of citizenship reform to the extreme right" and therefore moved to outflank the *Republikaner* and German People's Union (*Deutsche Volksunion* [DVU]).[177]

To mollify the CDU moderates, the campaign against the "double passport" included a call for integration that proposed increased funding for German language courses and the further liberalization of naturalization policy. These gestures were enough to convince moderates to accept Schäuble's choice of strategy at a party conference in January 1999, though many did so grudgingly.[178] The emphasis on integration also granted CDU/CSU politicians a means of deflecting accusations that they were again stoking anti-immigrant passions and undermining the safety of foreigners in the Federal Republic. Some Union politicians even argued that their position would *benefit* foreigners by improving their prospects of integration.

The signature-drive commenced in January 1999, several weeks before the government had even introduced a bill, accumulating over 3.5 million signatures in six weeks. It combined an assortment of messages, including claims that the government's citizenship plan would unfairly privilege foreigners, threaten social peace by enabling migrants with ulterior motives (e.g., Islamists) to claim the advantages of citizenship, turn Germany into a "multicultural playground," and throw the gates open to waves of new immigration.[179] The argument regarding "fairness" proved to be particularly potent, tapping into Germans' *Neid-Gefühle* (feelings of envy).[180]

The government was caught off-guard by the signature campaign and failed to mount an effective defence of its policies.[181] Although important civil society actors, including the Roman Catholic and Protestant churches, unions, the liberal media, and even several members of the CDU came out strongly against the signature drive,[182] the popular opposition to dual citizenship generated by the campaign succeeded in raising the Union parties' visibility and increasing media coverage of the CDU's electoral campaign in Hessen. To the delight of Roland Koch, the CDU's candidate for minister president in Hessen, the signature drive succeeded in mobilizing CDU voters and improved turnout on election day.[183] In the end, the SPD finished on a par with its results in 1995, but the Greens slipped, suffering a 4 percent loss. Koch and the CDU carried the day and now were in a position to block the government's reform in the Bundesrat.[184]

The Optionsmodell

Without its majority in the upper house, the government was forced to enter into negotiations with the FDP to gain the necessary votes to pass the law in the *Bundesrat*. Although the Greens argued that the coalition should fight to maintain the proposal in its original form, both Chancellor Schröder and the SPD'S party leader, Oscar Lafontaine, preferred to settle matters quickly. Ultimately, the SPD adapted elements of an FDP proposal (ironically modelled after the *Optionsmodell* of the *Junge Wilde*) that limited the scope of dual citizenship.[185] According to the revised law, which was passed by the Bundestag on May 7, 1999, and cleared the Bundesrat on May 21, 1999, children granted German citizenship under the principle of *jus soli* would maintain their parents' nationality until they reached the age of majority (eighteen), at which time they would have until their twenty-third birthday to choose between the two. Dual nationality would be officially discouraged in the conferring of citizenship via naturalization, and criteria pertaining to language competence and loyalty to the constitution would be required of applicants. Furthermore, the fee for naturalization was raised to a flat rate of DM500. Thus, although the new law's adoption of *jus soli* in the attribution of nationality represented a major innovation, the CDU/CSU succeeded in eliminating, or at least weakening, the acceptance of dual citizenship, dealing the government and reform advocates a heavy blow.[186]

The CDU/CSU's politicization of the citizenship reform proposal reflected hardliners' principled objections to the introduction of *jus soli* and dual citizenship into German nationality law. This was clear in the statements of Stoiber, Zeitlmann, and others in the CSU and, to a lesser extent, the CDU. However, the decision to politicize the issue and risk what could have developed into a potentially dangerous populist reaction was also driven by political reasoning. The CDU/CSU was aware that the absence of dual citizenship in Germany's nationality law had dissuaded hundreds of thousands of immigrants from naturalizing and thus becoming German voters. Given that research consistently revealed that current and potential immigrant voters overwhelmingly supported the SPD and Greens, there were very real political costs in enfranchising a large number of immigrants in a relatively short period of time.[187] Other political factors, including leadership issues, fears of being upstaged by the extreme right, and the desire among many in the CDU to do something to take the media attention off their 1998 election failure and multiple scandals, made a populist move on the scale of the signature campaign more acceptable than it might otherwise have been. Finally, the prospect of using the citizenship issue to unseat the SPD-Green coalition in Hessen, and thus upset the federal government's majority in the Bundesrat, offered further incentives to reject compromise and opt instead for an aggressive populist strategy.

In the final analysis, a combination of principled opposition to changes in German nationality law and institutionally shaped political machinations came together to block consensus. The result was a reform that fell short of what the SPD-Green government had planned and many reform advocates had long hoped for. Nevertheless, hardliners in the Union parties did not regard this as a victory and fought a hard, though ultimately futile, final battle to block the implementation of the *Optionsmodell*.[188] Their continuing opposition to the new law and bitter disappointment with its passage illustrates that, for all its limitations, the citizenship reform of 1999 marked a crucial shift in Germany's membership policies.[189]

Coda: The Battle over Immigration Policy

The Red-Green government's decision to introduce an immigration law came as a surprise to many. The SPD had rebuffed the Greens' request for a law during negotiations over their coalition agreement in 1998, arguing that Germany had already exceeded its tolerance for immigration.[190] The SPD felt the German public was not ready to accept an immigration law and therefore preferred to deal only with citizenship reform during the government's first term.[191] This greatly disappointed the Greens and cast a pall over the negotiations.[192]

The impetus for a change in policy was driven by business. German employers argued that they were ill-prepared to meet the challenges generated by the revolution in information and communication technologies, and petitioned the government to facilitate the recruitment of foreign-born "computer experts" to satisfy demands for trained personnel.[193] Acting independently of his Cabinet colleagues and eager to establish his credentials as a business-friendly "innovation chancellor," Gerhard Schröder responded to these demands by introducing a so-called "Green Card" visa initiative that envisioned the recruitment of up to twenty thousand qualified applicants from East European and non-European countries such as India.[194] This time, attempts by the CDU to politicize the issue failed and the initiative went forward.[195] In the meantime, concerns about Germany's shrinking population increased in the wake of a highly publicized report of the UN's Population Division, which argued that the country's social security system and social market economy were threatened by demographic decline. Although immigration was not offered as a cure-all, the report made clear that, without it, Germany's situation, like those of other advanced industrial countries, would worsen.[196]

The success of the Green Card initiative, the emergence of the demographic question, and pressure from employers, the FDP, the Greens, and other advocacy groups persuaded the SPD to move forward with a new immigration law. In July 2000, Interior Minister Otto Schily announced the formation of an independent commission on immigration and asylum policy to be chaired by former Bundestag president and senior CDU member Rita Süssmuth. The twenty-one-member commission, which included representatives from churches, unions, industry, local government, the Office of the United Nations High Commissioner for Refugees, and academia, was instructed to come up with concrete proposals for the reform of all facets of Germany's immigration policies.[197] The government also intended to use the commission to build on public interest sparked by the Green Card announcement and to create popular support for its proposed immigration law. A parallel commission chaired by Saarland's minister president Peter Müller was appointed by the CDU. Müller made it clear that he was in favour of an immigration law, stating that it was illusory to believe that "one could maintain a wall around national labor markets alone in a world marked by flows of goods, capital, and services."[198] The leader of the CDU's parliamentary group, Friedrich Merz, also signalled that his party was prepared to bargain, as did Bavaria's interior minister Günther Beckstein

(CSU).[199] Both the German and foreign press devoted extensive coverage to these developments, increasing expectations that a consensus position on immigration policy would soon be reached.

The CSU's position toughened in November 2000 as its leader Edmund Stoiber made his party's support for an immigration law dependent on the government's satisfaction of several demands, including the replacement of the amended constitutional right to asylum with an "institutional guarantee."[200] The Union parties' insistence that integration be founded on immigrants' respect for Germany's "leading culture" (*Leitkultur*), based on Christianity, Judaism, classical philosophy, humanism, Roman law, and the Enlightenment, also raised the hackles of the SPD and Greens and increased doubts as to the CDU/CSU's willingness to compromise.[201] Still, there was strong support for an immigration law among the FDP, employers, and the Protestant and Roman Catholic churches – actors that the CDU/CSU could not easily ignore. Furthermore, the media had come out in favour of the immigration law and elite opinion was generally positive. Thus, rather than rejecting the government's immigration proposal outright, the Union parties left open the possibility that a compromise solution might be crafted.

After nine months of extensive hearings, the Süssmuth Commission tabled its report. In dramatic fashion, its opening statement noted:

> Germany needs immigrants. An overall plan defining clear goals is needed to structure immigration to Germany as well as integration: in order to meet its humanitarian responsibilities, to contribute to the safeguarding of economic prosperity, to improve the co-existence of Germans and immigrants to Germany as well as to foster integration.[202]

In a marked departure from past practices, the report also recommended a yearly immigration quota to help address both labour market needs and Germany's acute demographic decline. A portion of the yearly intake would be selected according to a "points system" that ranked applicants according to their education, skills, knowledge of the German language, and other criteria. Recommendations were also made for managing family reunification, asylum, and integration.[203] In sum, the commission's report offered a detailed set of recommendations that pointed towards the development of a migration regime not unlike those of the classic settler countries. The *Washington Post* reported that: "the new proposals, combined with changes last year in citizenship law, could put immigrants in Germany on largely the same legal ground as those in the United States, Canada, or Britain – a wide-reaching change for a country that has long defined itself racially and has formally eschewed immigration for almost 100 years."[204]

Shortly after the Süssmuth Commission tabled its report, the government produced a draft law composed by the Federal Ministry of the Interior.[205] The draft was less ambitious than one might have expected given the Süssmuth Commission's recommendations and offered clear evidence that the SPD was willing to take relatively tough positions in areas such as family reunification and asylum in order to reach a consensus position with the Union parties – even if this meant upsetting its coalition partner, the Greens. However, the Union parties were unimpressed by Interior Minister Schily's efforts and made it clear that their support for regulated labour migration would depend on significant restrictions to both asylum flows and family reunification. This would entail, among other things, the replacement of the constitutional right to asylum with an "institutional guarantee" and the lowering of the maximum age for *Kindernachzug* to six.

The Union parties' emphasis on using any new law to strictly *limit* migration intensified after the terrorist attacks in New York and Washington on September 11, 2001. Repeated efforts by the SPD-Green coalition to broker a cross-party compromise with the CDU/CSU were denied,[206] and the Union parties' candidate for chancellor for the September 2002 election, Edmund Stoiber, took to sharply criticizing the law, noting that Germany's high unemployment made any talk of new immigration ridiculous.[207] After further attempts at mollifying the CDU were rejected, the government abandoned its efforts to broker consensus, settled its own differences, and sent a revised bill forward. The Bundestag passed the law on March 1, 2002.[208] In a historic vote preceded by intense politicking, the law cleared the Bundesrat by the narrowest of margins.[209] Citing irregularities in the vote, the Union parties claimed that the Bundesrat sanction was unconstitutional and brought the case before the Federal Constitutional Court.[210]

After studiously avoiding the issue to soften his image among moderate "swing" voters, chancellor candidate Stoiber invoked the threat of mass migration during the end-run of the September 2002 election campaign – precisely one day after the Union parties fell behind the SPD in opinion polling for the first time in the race. In hindsight, it is clear that Stoiber had kept the immigration issue in reserve in case he needed to rally support. However, the tactic failed to mobilize the sort of reaction generated by the 1999 signature drive in Hessen. Given the SPD's slight margin of victory in the election, it is possible that the Union's decision to play the immigration card so late in the game may have cost it the campaign by alienating swing voters and mobilizing enfranchised immigrants to come out strongly in favour of the Greens and the SPD on the day of the election. Some embittered CDU politicians were convinced that the "foreigner vote" cost the party the contest.

The Union parties did however enjoy something of a victory in December 2002, when the Federal Constitutional Court ruled that the Bundesrat vote contravened constitutional guidelines and suspended application of the law. Thus, what was to be a major turning point in Germany's immigration policy was postponed until the passage of a significantly altered law in July 2004. The period preceding the passage of the law was marked by strained efforts to carve out a compromise that captured parts of each side's positions.[211] This clumsy balancing act helps explain the restrictiveness of what was to be a policy instrument for facilitating immigration.[212] Although the Act on the Residence, Economic Activity and Integration of Foreigners in the Federal Territory (Residence Act), 2004, did little to open Germany to immigration, it did simplify residency policies while also advancing a more coherent approach to integration.[213] Under Section 43 of the act, the federal government pledged to support the integration of legally resident foreigners through the introduction of integration courses established to impart "adequate knowledge of the [German] language" and information regarding Germany's "legal system, culture and history." Section 45 of the Residence Act called for the federal government to develop additional integration measures organized by the federal and state governments. The haphazard approach to settlement and integration that emerged out of the guest worker period was to be carefully evaluated and reformed, with an eye to better coordinating the work of the federal, state and municipal governments and civil society organizations.

Conclusion

The expansion of membership boundaries to include guest workers and their children proved to be a long and drawn-out affair, marked by disagreement and acrimony. In contrast to the Canadian case, the breakdown of cross-party political consensus led to a prolonged period of stasis that allowed older boundaries to persist despite their lack of fit with prevailing international norms and domestic political principles. While traditions of nationhood influenced the politics of immigration and citizenship in

Germany, there was little in the way of consensus on what German nationhood ought to entail; rather, membership politics was driven by competing positions on precisely this point. The logic of coalition government, electoral competition, and federalism shaped competing actors' political strategies, making it difficult to generate agreement on what was needed to address the consequences of mass labour recruitment. Relatively poor economic conditions and high unemployment further hindered policy innovation, as did the challenges that emerged in the wake of German unification. By the mid-1990s, the terrible costs of maintaining Germany's established citizenship policies had become clear, and consensus on the need for reforms such as the introduction of *jus soli* had emerged. The fact that the fundamental features of the 1999 citizenship reform were already proposed by CDU politicians in 1996 underscores both the degree of consensus at this time and the important ways in which Germany's political institutions allowed a relatively small but powerful group of reform opponents to block progress. Simply put, highly charged partisan politics extended the period of policy stretching and unravelling, delaying the introduction of measures needed to integrate Germany's "domestic foreigners."

The ultimate results of policy shifting also bore the imprint of politicization. The *Optionsmodell's* awkward melding of *jus soli* and opposition to dual citizenship promises to create an administrative and political quagmire, as, in the years to come, hundred of thousands of young men and women born and raised as German citizens are forced to decide between their German nationality and that of their parents.[214] Similarly, opposition to dual citizenship has played a role in dampening the integrative function of the 1999 reform as regards naturalization. While the number of naturalizations per annum peaked at an all-time high of 186,688 in 2000, it has since fallen, reaching a post-reform low of 94,470 in 2008 – out of a foreign population of 6.73 million, of whom some 4 million are estimated to fulfill the residence requirement for naturalization.[215] In the field of immigration policy, a law initially aimed at opening the Federal Republic up to the world's "best and brightest" was, through the alchemy of legislative bargaining, transformed into a tool for strictly limiting admissions. While the Residence Act's accent on integration marks a long overdue acceptance of Germany's status as an immigration country, German political elites' embrace of this new identity remains halting.[216] In the final analysis, policy shifting in Germany must be characterized as a qualified revolution: doubtlessly crucial but undeniably limited.

6 Conclusion

This book explores Canada's and Germany's responses to the migration-membership dilemma in the twentieth century. I explain why two countries so determined to limit cultural diversity through the application of restrictive immigration and citizenship policies during the first half of the twentieth century found themselves transformed into highly diverse, multicultural societies by its end. I argue that Canada and Germany's identities as liberal-democratic countries, and their interest in developing progressive identities in pursuit of their foreign policy and domestic political interests, made it extremely difficult for them to maintain, in the post-Second World War period, the restrictive policies they had developed in the late nineteenth and early twentieth centuries. The postwar period was marked by the emergence and entrenchment of a global human rights culture, driven by reactions to the Holocaust and the discrediting of scientific racism, unfettered state sovereignty, and colonialism. Older principles that had given support and sustenance to discriminatory membership policies were rejected, leaving Canada and Germany vulnerable to charges of hypocrisy when they sought to reapply these policies after 1945.

This lack of fit between postwar norms and identities, on the one hand, and prewar solutions to the migration-membership dilemma, on the other, was highlighted by domestic and international critics of racial and ethnonational discrimination, catalyzing a long-term process of policy change. As my case studies demonstrate, this process entailed a distinctive brand of incrementalism, whereby, in the hope that symbolic concessions would satisfy and hence silence them, Canada and Germany did as little as possible in responding to critics' rights claims. This strategy failed. Once emboldened, critics did not relent; rather, the politics of norm contestation was iterative: concessions were met by further and more consequential demands so that, in time, policy stretching became counterproductive and self-defeating. The unravelling of established policy regimes created opportunities for the introduction of more substantive reforms to membership policies, in line with prevailing normative standards.

My emphasis on the role of critics is meant to underscore that norms are not self-actualizing constraints on state behaviour, in the manner suggested by the Stanford School sociologists and their postnationalist acolytes. Normative standards were not announced from on high and absorbed by pliant domestic actors; nor did they compel domestic political actors to behave in norm-governed ways through some invisible, talismanic force. Rather, broader normative *contexts* influenced membership policy making in Canada and Germany by reconfiguring the terrain of postwar politics – recasting liberal-democratic states' interests and providing critics of discriminatory immigration and citizenship policies a powerful discursive resource with which to challenge defenders of the old order. Claims to just treatment on the part of excluded individuals and groups succeeded most impressively where they intersected with states' pursuit of their interests, as was the case both in Canada's efforts to preserve the Commonwealth in the late-1950s and early-1960s and the Brandt government's interest in casting itself as a distinctively progressive political force in German politics during the late 1960s and early 1970s. More generally, political claims drawing on postwar norms put the onus on leaders to justify their decisions in a manner that was consistent with prevailing global standards. When they failed to do so, critics could rightly claim that they had failed to live up to their self-declared principles and identities.

While all this points to a common pattern of political contestation and change, my case studies also reveal important variations in political processes in Canada and Germany – variations that influenced the timing and nature of their respective outcomes. These variations, in turn, were based on differences in the two countries' traditions of nationhood and political institutions. Canada's history and identity as an immigration country was consequential in so far as immigrants enjoyed a relatively clear path to citizenship once they were admitted. Hence, despite their largely symbolic character, the lifting of racially discriminatory naturalization rules in the late 1940s and the slight loosening of admissions criteria in the 1950s and early 1960s created a cohort of active ethnic minority citizens who could mobilize in response to threats to restrict immigration in the mid-1970s. Canada's political institutions amplified new Canadians' political strength, thereby necessitating that their interests be acknowledged and upheld. Hence the reforms of the late 1960s were successfully entrenched in the Immigration Act, 1976, despite a downturn in the economy and a backlash against non-white immigration in the mid-1970s.

The situation in Germany was very different. Although policy stretching, evidenced in the rejection of compulsory rotation in the 1960s and early 1970s, allowed for the settlement of temporary foreign workers and their families, citizenship remained an elusive goal. This was not due to a consensus among Germany's political elite regarding the inviolability of an ethno-national conception of German nationhood. As I indicate in chapters 3 and 5, a good number of German political elites believed that citizenship policy had to be reconfigured to better integrate former guest workers and their children if the Federal Republic was to live up to its status as a *Rechtsstaat*. By the mid-1990s, this view was shared by a majority of Germany's political parties. Yet, Germany's political institutions allowed a small but powerful minority of reform opponents to block the liberalization of Germany's citizenship law during the Kohl administration's final term in office. Even when the left-of-centre SPD-Green coalition did move to introduce fundamental reforms, conservatives in the Union parties were able to exploit veto points in Germany's political system to dilute the integrative power of the new law by qualifying its *jus soli* provision and rejecting its tolerance of dual citizenship.

In both Canada and Germany, then, politics played a key role in steering the course of norm-driven change. While both countries found themselves transformed into diverse multicultural societies by the end of the twentieth century, their respective routes differed in important ways, with respect to both the timing of change and the precise nature of their responses to the migration-membership dilemma.

Looking beyond the story told in the preceding chapters, we might ask whether the force of the postwar normative context that so influenced the course of politics and policy making in Canada and Germany from the end of the Second World War through to the turn of the most recent century will continue to shape liberal-democratic states' responses to the migration-membership dilemma. Are liberal-democratic states' membership regimes still expanding in an inclusionary direction? Or are we witnessing the exhaustion of the post-Second World War moment and the dawning of a new, more sinister era in the politics of membership?

There is certainly evidence in support of the pessimistic view. The 1990s and early 2000s were marked by the emergence of extreme right-wing parties across Europe, often riding a wave of anti-immigrant sentiment.[1] Even in countries like Canada and Germany, where the far-right parties are marginal at best, policies regarding asylum seekers have been toughened in an effort to respond to a restive public's anger at "queue jumpers" and to satisfy security interests.[2] In the sphere of citizenship policy, we have seen an interesting convergence among liberal-democratic states, whereby liberalization driven by the adoption of *jus soli* and the tolerance of dual citizenship has been balanced by moves to revalue nationality, by making the conferral of citizenship via naturalization conditional upon immigrants' passing of exams, swearing of oaths, and, in Britain, satisfactory conduct during a period of "probation," during which nationality may be withdrawn in cases of anti-social behaviour.[3]

And, in a book with "multiculturalism" in its title, I would be remiss for overlooking the abuse that this term has taken of late, blamed as it is for stifling debate through the imposition of political correctness; encouraging ethnic separatism and the establishment of "parallel societies"; counselling the rejection of common national identities; implicitly endorsing reprehensible practices rooted in patriarchy (such as forced marriage, female genital mutilation, honour-related violence, etc.); and providing cover for religious fundamentalists bent on exploiting multicultural tolerance to further their destructive projects. Critics contend that multiculturalism manages to do all this simultaneously, aided by well-meaning liberals who see only the good of diversity while wilfully rejecting its challenges and the "hard work" of building a socially cohesive society.[4]

These trends have been interpreted as portents of an aggressive civic integrationism, through which liberal-democratic states employ illiberal means to discipline newcomers into becoming safe and productive liberal subjects.[5] Like nationalists, the advocates of "identity liberalism" seek to exclude outsiders in the name of social homogeneity, with the caveat being that homogeneity is understood in terms of members' acceptance of and loyalty to liberal principles, such as gender equality, respect for same-sex relationships, and unfettered freedom of speech.[6] The "Other" that identity liberals seek to exclude is the deeply conservative, tradition-bound adherent of illiberal traditions and worldviews. In what amounts to a recasting of liberalism along lines that would have been familiar to Carl Schmitt, self-described liberals have argued in favour of carefully distinguishing liberalism's friends from its enemies through the application of "tough" immigration, citizenship, and integration laws and policies.[7]

Even this rather gloomy reading of contemporary liberal states' responses to the migration-membership dilemma is rejected by scholars and activists who herald an even more dangerous state of affairs, wherein Islamophobia and blatant racism have joined forces to reconfigure membership policies in a manner not unlike those of the dark days of the 1920s. While the biological racism of the late nineteenth and early twentieth centuries may indeed have been relegated to the ash heap of history, a more recent but similarly insidious "cultural" racism, which openly embraces claims to the superiority of the "West," has taken its place, shaping discussions of immigration, integration, and citizenship policy in ways that have led to the tightening of membership boundaries through the imposition of discriminatory policies and practices.[8]

I cannot offer a well developed response to this debate here, but I would like to draw on recent trends in the politics of membership in Canada and Germany to sketch a (cautiously) more optimistic position pertaining to where liberal-democratic states presently stand and are likely to go with regard to the politics of membership.

In contrast to the more pessimistic views noted above, I believe the reverberations created by the world-changing events of the mid-twentieth century, and the collapse of prewar membership regimes that they instigated, continue to shape membership politics in Canada, Germany, and other liberal-democratic countries. This is particularly true with respect to the accommodation of new religious minorities. The boundaries of secular societies in Europe and North America, which have all been founded on the bedrock of Christianity, are shifting as claims to equal treatment by and on behalf of religious minorities are being voiced with increasing frequency. In this sense, the process of "becoming multicultural" is ongoing.

One of the most striking examples of this trend is Germany's ongoing efforts to "integrate" Islam into its elaborate system of church-state institutions. Beginning in 2006, the Federal Ministry of the Interior has hosted a recurring "Islam Conference," drawing together federal, state, and municipal officials and representatives of Germany's Muslim faith communities. Conference participants have focused on resolving a number of practical challenges, including how to fund and administer Muslim religious instruction in Germany's public schools, train imams in Germany, and steer German Islam in a direction compatible with Germany's secular political institutions. Also, through the gathering and dissemination of research and the encouragement of greater responsibility on the part of the German media, the Islam Conference has aimed at assuaging the hysteria around Islam. The process has not simply recognized Muslim groups; it has also spurred the creation of the Coordinating Council for Muslims, a peak association representing Muslims' interests in Germany.[9]

The Islam Conference's results to date have been mixed.[10] The large umbrella organizations that make up the Coordinating Council disagree on a range of issues, making the formulation of common positions difficult. The extent to which these organizations can claim to represent Muslims in Germany is highly contested. Meetings have been marked by boycotts and progress has been slow. Nevertheless, there are signs of movement ahead. For example, a framework for incorporating Islamic religious instruction into Germany's public schools has emerged and is on the cusp of being implemented in Hamburg and other federal states. There are similar efforts afoot to devise standards for the training of imams in German universities. Guidelines aimed at improving the media's coverage of Islam have also been developed, through close interactions among faith groups, government officials, journalists, editors, and media representatives. Gender-related issues, including matters pertaining to discrimination in the labour market and issues of patriarchy and violence in the private sphere, have also been aired. More important, the German Islam Conference has provided a mechanism for working through these and other challenges inherent in religiously diverse societies.

The courts in Canada and Germany have also played an important role in facilitating the incorporation of religious minorities.[11] The Supreme Court of Canada has developed and employed the doctrine of "reasonable accommodation" to assist in balancing the right to freedom of religious expression under the Charter of Rights and Freedoms with other important rights and social expectations, such as freedom of speech and safety.[12] The Supreme Court's 2006 decision in *Multani v. Commission scolaire Marguerite–Bourgeoys* provides a vivid illustration of this point.[13] In its decision, the Court upheld the right of Sikh student Gurbaj Singh Multani to wear his ceremonial dagger, or kirpan, to school. The case was prompted by a Montreal school board's attempt to prohibit the wearing of kirpans on school property through a "zero tolerance" policy on dangerous objects. School board officials argued that kirpans should be completely banned from schools in order to ensure students' safety, pursuant to its code of conduct. Multani and his supporters countered by arguing that such a ban would infringe upon his constitutional right to religious freedom under section 2(a) of the Canadian Charter of Rights and Freedoms. They also noted that other provinces, including Ontario and British Columbia, allowed students to wear kirpans in school, so long as they were sheathed, blunt, and worn under clothing. The fact that kirpans had never been used to threaten students' safety in Ontario and British Columbia – and Quebec, for that matter – was also noted, as was Multani's willingness to abide by a compromise solution reached initially by school officials and later upheld by the Quebec Superior Court, whereby he could wear his kirpan to school so long as it was sealed inside his clothing.

The Supreme Court of Canada agreed, arguing that the potential threat to student safety posed by Multani's wearing of his kirpan in school was minimal and in no way sufficient to authorize the school board's infringement of his right to freedom of religion. The interpretation of the board's "zero-tolerance" ban on all weapons in schools as applied to the kirpan was deemed an unreasonable infringement on religious freedom and, as such, was overturned in a unanimous 8-0 decision. Hypothetical threats to student safety could not serve as grounds for restricting the exercise of religious freedom because allowing them to do so would have undermined the value of the kirpan as a religious symbol and sent the message "that some religious practices do not merit the same protection as others."

I do not want to suggest that the process of accommodating demands for inclusion among religious minorities in Canada and Germany has always been smooth, as in many instances it has been anything but. Debates over so-called "Sharia law" tribunals in Ontario, the niqab in Quebec, and the construction of mosques in Cologne and other German cities have been marked by populist hyperbole and expressions of "identity liberalism," "civic integrationism," and, at times, garden variety racism.[14] But this should not surprise us: membership politics is distinctively patterned by the logics of political institutions. Highly structured forums such as courts and the German Islam Conference engender distinctive political logics, problem solving in the case of the latter and legalistic in the case of the former. Partisan political arenas, such as legislatures, the opinion pages of newspapers, and talk radio shows generate a rather different logic, which, too often, encourages a politics of fear and intimidation. Here too, however, we must be conscious of differences in political contexts: even the most self-interested of politicians will be wary of offending religious minorities where their votes are prized; this calculation, in turn, will be mediated by the rate at which immigrants naturalize, their concentrations in politically salient areas, and their overall "weight" in political terms. Once again, politics will play a role in mediating claims to religious equality underwritten by global norms and domestic liberal principles.

Here we may note that the expansion of membership boundaries in Canada and Germany during the periods analyzed in this book provides added support for my cautiously optimistic forecast. As immigrants and ethnic minorities in Canada and Germany assume greater political voice and power by taking up and practising formal citizenship, their claims should take on added force. As noted above, claims to just treatment are more likely to succeed where powerful actors judge it in their interests to consider them carefully. In liberal-democratic states there are few interests more important to their holders than the desire of politicians to be elected. This being the case, we may indeed see in the longer term a further expansion of membership boundaries in liberal-democratic states, as members of once marginalized groups take on the rights of citizenship and become active players in the politics of membership. What is beyond doubt is that the migration-membership dilemma will continue to shape the development of liberal-democratic states far into the future.

Notes

CHAPTER 1: INTRODUCTION

1 Aristide Zolberg, "Contemporary Transnational Migrations in Historical Perspective: Patterns and Dilemmas," in *US Immigration and Refugee Policy: Domestic and Global Issues*, ed. Mary M. Kritz (Lexington: Lexington Books, 1983), 16.

2 Zolberg, "Contemporary Transnational Migrations," 16.

3 See Aristide R. Zolberg, "International Migrations in Political Perspective," in *Global Trends in Migration: Theory and Research on International Population Movements*, ed. Mary M. Kritz, Charles B. Keely, and Silvano M. Tomasi (New York: Center for Migration Studies, 1981), 5-8; "Wanted but Not Welcome: Alien Labor in Western Development," in *Population in an Interacting World*, ed. William Alonso, 37-73 (Cambridge: Harvard University Press, 1987); Rainer Bauböck, "Integration in a Pluralistic Society: Strategies for the Future" (Working Paper, Institute for Advanced Studies, Vienna, May 1993), 2-4; Elizabeth Petras, "The Role of National Boundaries in a Cross-National Labour Market," *International Journal of Urban and Regional Research* 4, 2 (1980): 157-94; Michael Walzer, "The Distribution of Membership," in *Boundaries: National Autonomy and Its Limits*, ed. Peter G. Brown and Henry Shue (Totowa, NJ: Rowman and Littlefield, 1981), 2.

4 Peter Schuck, "Immigration Law and the Problem of Community," in *Clamor at the Gates: The New American Immigration*, ed. Nathan Glazer (San Francisco: ICS Press, 1985), 285-86.

5 See, for example, Rainer Geißler, "Multikulturalismus in Kanada – Modell für Deutschland?" *Aus Politik und Zeitgeschichte* B 26, June 23, 2003, 19-25. More generally, see Eytan Meyers, "Theories of International Immigration Policy – A Comparative Analysis," *International Migration Review* 34, 4 (2000): 1254.

6 Theda Skocpol a   Margaret Somers, "The Uses of Comparative History in
   Macrosocial Inqui   *Comparative Studies in Society and History* 22, 2 (1980): 183;
   Adam Przeworski,   thods of Cross-National Research, 1970-1983: An Overview,"
   in *Comparative Po   Research: Learning from Experience*, ed. Meinolf Dierkes,
   Hans N. Weiler, and   'ane Berthoin Antal (Brookfield, VT: Gower, 1987), 38-41.
   For a more skeptical   on the method of most different cases see John Gerring,
   "Case Selection Tech   's for Case-Study Analysis: Qualitative and Quantitative
   Techniques," in *The O.   *Handbook of Political Methodology*, ed. Janet M. Box-
   Steffenmeier, Henry E.   , and David Collier (Oxford: Oxford University Press,
   2008), 671-75.
7 Warren E. Kalbach, "Grov   d Distribution of Canada's Ethnic Populations, 1871-
   1981," in *Ethnic Canada: 'ties and Inequalities*, ed. Leo Driedger, 82-110
   (Toronto: Copp Clark Pitma,   1.
8 Alain Bélanger and Éric Car   enfant, "Ethnocultural Diversity in Canada:
   Prospects for 2017," *Canadian   '*ends* (Winter 2005), Statistics Canada –
   Catalogue 11-008.
9 Peter Katzenstein, *Policy and Politics i.*   *The Growth of a Semisovereign
   State* (Philadelphia: Temple University Pr
10 Jürgen Gerdes, Thomas Faist, and Beate Rieple,   ivow . me
   Politics of Dual Citizenship in Germany," in *Dual Citizenship in Europe: From
   Nationhood to Social Integration*, ed. Thomas Faist, 45-76 (Aldershot: Ashgate,
   2007); Simon Green, "Between Ideology and Pragmatism: The Politics of Dual
   Nationality in Germany," *International Migration Review* 39, 4 (2005): 921-52;
   Christian Joppke, "Mobilization of Culture and the Reform of Citizenship Law:
   Germany and the United States," in *Challenging Immigration and Ethnic Relation
   Politics: Comparative European Perspectives*, ed. Ruud Koopmans and Paul Statham,
   145-61 (New York: Oxford University Press, 2000); Andreas Klärner, *Aufstand der
   Ressentiments: Einwanderungsdiskurs, völkischer Nationalismus und die Kampagne
   der CDU/CSU gegen die doppelte Staatsbürgerschaft* (Cologne: PapyRossa, 2000).
11 Martin Dolezal, Marc Helbling, and Swen Hutter, "Debating Islam in Austria, Germany and Switzerland: Ethnic Citizenship, Church-State Relations and Right-Wing
   Populism," *West European Politics* 33, 2 (2010): 171-90; Joel Fetzer and J. Christopher
   Soper, *Muslims and the State in Britain, France, and Germany* (Cambridge: Cambridge University Press, 2005); Andreas Golberg, "Islam in Germany," in *Islam:
   Europe's Second Religion*, ed. Shireen T. Hunter, 29-50 (Westport, CT: Praeger,
   2002); Matthias Koenig, "Incorporating Muslim Migrants in Western Nation-States:
   A Comparison of the United Kingdom, France, and Germany," *Journal of Inter-
   national Migration and Integration* 6, 2 (2005): 219-34; Bundesamt für Migration
   und Flüchtlinge, *Muslimisches Leben in Deutschland*. Im Auftrag der Deutschen
   Islam Konferenz (Nürnberg: Bundesamt für Migration und Flüchtlinge, 2009).
12 Rogers Brubaker, *Citizenship and Nationhood in France and Germany* (Cambridge,
   MA: Harvard University Press, 1992); Christian Joppke, "The Legal-Domestic
   Sources of Immigrant Rights: The United States, Germany, and the European Union,"
   Comparative Political Studies 34, 4 (2001): 339-36; Virginie Giraudon, "Citizenship

Rights for Non-Citizens: France, Germany, and the Netherlands," in *Challenge to the Nation-State: Immigration in Western Europe and the United States*, ed. Christian Joppke, 272-319 (New York: Oxford University Press, 1998); Adrian Favell, *Philosophies of Integration: Immigration and the Idea of Citizenship in France and Britain* (London: Macmillan, 1997); Stephen Castles, "How Nation-States Respond to Immigration and Ethnic Diversity," *New Community* 21, 3 (1995): 293-308; Anthony M. Messina, *The Logic and Politics of Post-WWII Migration to Western Europe* (Cambridge: Cambridge University Press, 2007); Herman Kurthen, "Germany at the Crossroads: National Identity and the Challenges of Immigration," *International Migration Review* 29, 4 (1995): 914-38.

13 For a similar argument emphasizing the interplay of domestic cultural traditions and political institutions, see James F. Hollifield, *Immigrants, Markets, and States: The Political Economy of Postwar Europe* (Cambridge: Harvard University Press, 1992).

14 Variations of this strategy are employed in Sven Steinmo, *Taxation and Democracy* (New Haven: Yale University Press, 1993); and Ellen Immergut, *Health Politics: Interests and Institutions in Western Europe* (New York: Cambridge University Press, 1992).

15 Ira Katznelson, "Structure and Configuration in Comparative Politics," in *Comparative Politics: Rationality, Culture, and Structure*, ed. Mark Irving Lichbach and Alan S. Zuckerman (Cambridge: Cambridge University Press, 1997), 107. I have also drawn inspiration from Charles Tilly, *Big Structures, Large Processes, Huge Comparisons* (New York: Russell Sage Foundation, 1984); Jeffrey Haydu, "Making Use of the Past: Time Periods as Cases to Compare and as Sequences of Problem Solving," *American Journal of Sociology* 104, 2 (1998): 339-71; Philip McMichael, "Incorporating Comparison within a World-Historical Perspective: An Alternative Comparative Method," *American Sociological Review* 55 (1990): 385-97; Richard Simeon, "Studying Public Policy," *Canadian Journal of Political Science* 9, 4 (1976): 548-80; Reinhard Bendix, "Concepts and Generalizations in Comparative Sociological Studies," *American Sociological Review* 28, 4 (1963): 532-39; Aristide R. Zolberg, "Beyond the Nation-State: Comparative Politics in a Global Perspective," in *Beyond Progress and Development*, ed. J. Berting and W. Blockmans, 42-69 (Aldershot: Gower Publishing, 1987).

16 Aristide R. Zolberg, "A Nation by Design: Immigration Policy in the Fashioning of America," paper presented at the 2002 meeting of the American Political Science Association, Boston, August 28, 4-5. Also see Aristide R. Zolberg, *A Nation by Design: Immigration Policy in the Fashioning of America* (New York/Cambridge, MA: Russell Sage Foundation/Harvard University Press, 2006), 11-15.

17 Aristide R. Zolberg, "International Migration Policies in a Changing World System," in *Human Migration: Patterns and Policies*, ed. William H. McNeill and Ruth S. Adams, 244-51 (Bloomington: Indiana University Press, 1978); "Bounded States in a Global Market: The Uses of International Labor Migrations," in *Social Theory for a Changing Society*, ed. Pierre Bourdieu and James S. Coleman (New York/Boulder: Russell Sage Foundations/Westview Press, 1991), 311-12.

18 John W. Meyer, John Boli, George M. Thomas, and Francisco O. Ramirez, "World Society and the Nation-State," *American Journal of Sociology* 103, 1 (1997): 153. See

also John Boli and George M. Thomas, "World Culture in the World Polity: A Century of International Non-Governmental Organization," *American Sociological Review* 62, 2 (1997): 171-90; Martha Finnemore, "Norms, Culture, and World Politics: Insights from Sociology's Institutionalism," *International Organization* 50, 2 (1996): 325-47; Michael A. Elliot, "Human Rights and the Triumph of the Individual in World Culture," *Cultural Sociology* 1, 3 (2007): 343-63; Matthias Koenig, "Institutional Change in the World Polity: International Human Rights and the Construction of Collective Identities," *International Sociology* 23, 1 (2008): 95-114.

19 Meyer et al., "World Society and the Nation-State," 153.

20 Alan C. Cairns, *Citizens Plus: Aboriginal Peoples and the Canadian State* (Vancouver: UBC Press, 2000), 41. John Skrentny takes a similar route in explaining the United States' "minority rights revolution." See his *The Minority Rights Revolution* (Cambridge, MA: Harvard University Press, 2002). The role of global forces in shaping the American Civil Rights Movement is explored by Thomas Borstelmann, *The Cold War and the Color Line: American Race Relations in the Global Arena* (Cambridge, MA: Harvard University Press, 2001); Mary L. Dudziak, *Cold War Civil Rights: Race and the Image of American Democracy* (Princeton, NJ: Princeton University Press, 2002); Philip A. Klinkner and Rogers M. Smith, *The Unsteady March: The Rise and Decline of Racial Equality in America* (Chicago: Chicago University Press, 1999).

21 Yasemin Nuhoğlu Soysal, "Changing Citizenship in Europe: Remarks on Postnational Membership and the National State," in *Citizenship, Nationality and Migration in Europe*, ed. David Ceasarini and Mary Fulbrook (London and New York: Routledge, 1996), 21.

22 Saskia Sassen, "The *de facto* Transnationalizing of Immigration Policy," in *Challenge to the Nation-State: Immigration in Western Europe and the United States*, ed. Christian Joppke (New York: Oxford University Press, 1998), 72. See also David Jacobson, "New Border Customs: Migration and the Changing Role of the State," *UCLA Journal of International Law and Foreign Affairs* 443 (1998-99): 450-51; David Jacobson, "State and Society in a World Unbound," in *Public Rights and Public Rules: Constituting Citizens in the World Polity and National Policy*, ed. Connie L. McNeely (New York: Garland Publishing, 1998), 53; David Jacobson and Galya Benraieh Ruffer, "Social Relations on a Global Scale: The Implications for Human Rights for Democracy," in *Dialogues on Migration Policy*, ed. Marco Giugni and Florence Passy, 25-44 (Lanham: Lexington Books, 2006); and Linda Bosniak, *The Citizen and the Alien: Dilemmas of Contemporary Membership* (Princeton, NJ: Princeton University Press, 2006).

23 Jeffrey Checkel, "Norms, Institutions, and National Identity in Contemporary Europe," *International Studies Quarterly* 43 (1999): 85.

24 Checkel, "Norms," 91.

25 Amy Gurowitz, "Mobilizing International Norms: Domestic Actors, Immigrants, and the Japanese State," *World Politics* 51 (1999): 417.

26 In his previous work, Christian Joppke maintained that "all Western constitutions ... contain a catalogue of elementary human rights, independent of citizenship, which are to be protected by the state and thus limit its discretionary power. Universal human rights are not the invention of the United Nations in 1945, but of liberal

nation-states in the late eighteenth century." See his "Immigration Challenges the Nation-State," in *Challenge to the Nation-State: Immigration in Western Europe and the United States*, ed. Christian Joppke (New York: Oxford University Press, 1998), 18. The domestic sources of "rights-based liberalism" are also emphasized in James F. Hollifield, "The Politics of International Migration: How Can We 'Bring the State Back In?'" in *Migration Theory: Talking across Disciplines*, ed. Caroline Brettell and James F. Hollifield (New York and London: Routledge, 2000), 149.

27 Christian Joppke, *Selecting by Origin: Ethnic Migration in the Liberal State* (Cambridge, MA: Harvard University Press, 2005), 49.

28 Audie Klotz, "Norms Reconstituting Interests: Global Racial Equality and US Sanctions against South Africa," *International Organization* 49, 3 (1995): 460-62; Stefano Guzzini, "A Reconstruction of Constructivism in International Relations," *European Journal of International Relations* 6, 2 (2000): 149; Antje Wiener, "Contested Compliance: Interventions on the Normative Structure of World Politics," *European Journal of International Relations* 10, 2 (2004): 200; Peter J. Katzenstein, "Introduction: Alternative Perspectives on National Security," in *Cultural Norms and National Security*, ed. Peter J. Katzenstein, 11-25 (Ithaca: Cornell University Press, 1996); Emanuel Adler, "Seizing the Middle Ground: Constructivism in World Politics," *European Journal of International Relations* 3, 3 (1997): 322.

29 Martha Finnemore and Kathryn Sikkink also highlight the importance of "world time." See "International Norm Dynamics and Political Change," *International Organization* 52, 4 (1998): 909.

30 Robert Huttenback, *Racism and Empire: White Settlers and Colored Immigrants in the British Self-Governing Colonies, 1830-1910* (Ithaca: Cornell University Press, 1976); Marilyn Lake and Henry Reynolds, *Drawing the Global Colour Line: White Men's Countries and the International Challenge of Racial Equality* (Cambridge: Cambridge University Press, 2008); Paul Gordon Lauren, *Power and Prejudice: The Politics and Diplomacy of Racial Discrimination* (Boulder, CO: Westview Press, 1996); Mark Mazower, "Paved Intentions: Civilization and Imperialism," *World Affairs* 171, 2 (2008): 72-85.

31 Jana Grekul, Harvey Krahn, and Dave Odynak, "Sterilizing the 'Feeble-Minded': Eugenics in Alberta, Canada, 1929-1972," *Journal of Historical Sociology* 17, 4 (2004): 358-84; Randall Hansen and Desmond King, "Eugenic Ideas, Political Interests, and Policy Variance: Immigration and Sterilization Policy in Britain and the US," *World Politics* 53 (2001): 237-63.

32 Hugh Heclo, *Modern Social Politics in Britain and Sweden* (New Haven, CT: Yale University Press, 1974).

33 Ann Swidler, "Culture in Action," *American Sociological Review* 51, 2 (1986): 273-86.

34 Ellen M. Immergut, "The Rules of the Game: The Logic of Health Policy-Making in France, Switzerland, and Sweden," in *Structuring Politics: Historical Institutionalism in Comparative Analysis*, ed. Sven Steinmo, Kathleen Thelen, and Frank Longstreth (Cambridge: Cambridge University Press, 1992), 58; George Tsebelis, "Decision Making in Political Systems: Veto Players in Presidentialism, Parliamentarism, Multicameralism, and Multipartyism," *British Journal of Political Science*, 25 (1995):

289-325; Peter Gourevitch, "The Second Image Reversed: The International Sources of Domestic Politics," *International Organization* 32, 4 (1978): 905.

35 Ninette Kelley and Michael Trebilcock, *The Making of the Mosaic: A History of Canadian Immigration Policy* (Toronto: University of Toronto Press, 1998), 449.

36 For an excellent discussion of the role of institutions in structuring membership politics and policy making in Germany see Simon Green, *The Politics of Exclusion: Institutions and Immigration Policy in Contemporary Germany* (Manchester: Manchester University Press, 2004).

37 I discuss early calls for the reform of Germany's citizenship policy in Chapter 5. See also Rita Chin, *The Guest Worker Question in Postwar Germany* (Cambridge: Cambridge University Press, 2007), 104-5.

38 Paul Pierson, "Not Just What, But *When*: Timing and Sequence in Political Processes," *Studies in American Political Development* 14 (2000): 72-92; Tulia G. Falleti and Julia F. Lynch, "Context and Causal Mechanisms in Political Analysis," *Comparative Political Studies* 42, 9 (2009): 1153-54; Hansen and King, "Eugenic Ideas," 239, 260-62; Charles Tilly, "Why and How History Matters," in *The Oxford Handbook of Contextual Political Analysis*, ed. Robert Goodin and Charles Tilly, 417-37 (Oxford: Oxford University Press, 2006).

39 Robert Bothwell, Ian Drummond, and John English, *Canada since 1945*, rev. ed. (Toronto: University of Toronto Press, 1989), 287-314; José E. Igartua, *The Other Quiet Revolution: National Identities in English Canada, 1945-1971* (Vancouver: UBC Press, 2006).

40 Richard Alba, "Connecting the Dots between Boundary Change and Large-Scale Assimilation with Zolbergian Clues," *Social Research* 77, 1 (2010): 173.

41 Ulrich Herbert, *Geschichte der Ausländerpolitik in Deutschland: Saisonarbeiter, Zwangsarbeiter, Flüchtlinge* (Munich: C.H. Beck, 2001), 231-334; Douglas B. Klusmeyer and Demetrios G. Papademetriou, *Immigration Policy in the Federal Republic of Germany: Negotiating Membership and Remaking the Nation* (New York: Berghahn Books, 2009), 144-58; Konrad H. Jarausch, *After Hitler: Recivilizing Germans, 1945-1995* (Oxford: Oxford University Press, 2006), 229-38.

42 Stephen Krasner, "Sovereignty: An Institutional Perspective," *Comparative Political Studies* 21, 1 (1988): 66-94.

43 Arthur Stinchcombe, *Constructing Social Theories* (New York: Harcourt, Brace and World, 1968), 101-28; Paul Pierson, "Public Policies as Institutions," in *Rethinking Political Institutions: The Art of the State*, ed. Ian Shapiro, Stephen Skowronek, and Daniel Galvin, 114-34 (New York: New York University Press, 2006); Paul Pierson, "Increasing Returns, Path Dependence, and the Study of Politics," *American Political Science Review* 94, 2 (2000): 251-67; Paul Pierson, "When Effect Becomes Cause: Policy Feedback and Political Change," World Politics 45, 4 (1993): 595-628; James Mahoney, "Path Dependence in Historical Sociology," *Theory and Society* 28, 4 (2000): 507-48; James Mahoney, "Analyzing Path Dependence: Lessons from the Social Sciences," in *Understanding Change: Models, Methodologies, and Metaphors*, ed. Andreas Wimmer and Reinhart Kössler, 129-39 (New York: Palgrave Macmillan, 2006); Kathleen Thelen, "Historical Institutionalism in Comparative Politics," *Annual Review of Political Science* 2 (1999): 369-404.

44 Kathleen Thelen, "How Institutions Evolve," in *Comparative Historical Analysis in the Social Sciences*, ed. James Mahoney and Dietrich Rueschemeyer, 208-40 (Cambridge: Cambridge University Press, 2003); Ito Peng and Joseph Wong, "Institutions and Institutional Purpose: Continuity and Change in East Asian Social Policy," *Politics and Society* 36, 1 (2008): 64-65. The evolutionary approach to change advanced by Thelen and others should not lead us to neglect the importance of "critical junctures" in instigating modest adaptations. See Giovanni Capoccia and Daniel Kelemen, "The Study of Critical Junctures: Theory, Narrative, and Counter-factuals in Historical Institutionalism," *World Politics* 59 (2007): 341-69. As my conceptualization of normative contexts suggests, I regard the postwar period as a critical juncture in the history of liberal-democratic states' management of the migration-membership dilemma. Colin Hay's notion of "punctuated evolution" offers one way of squaring these differing accounts of institutional change. See Colin Hay, *Political Analysis: A Critical Introduction* (New York: Palgrave, 2002), 162-63.

45 Charles Lindblom, "The Science of Muddling Through," *Public Administration Review* 19, 2 (1959): 79-88; Charles Lindblom, "Still Muddling, Not Yet Through," *Public Administration Review* 39, 6 (1979): 517-26; John Forester, "Bounded Rationality and the Politics of Muddling Through," *Public Administration Review* 44, 1 (1984): 23-31.

46 Peter Hall, "Policy Paradigms, Social Learning and the State: The Case of Economic Policymaking in Britain," *Comparative Politics* 25, 3 (1993): 279, 281-83. See also Peter Hall, "Policy Paradigms, Experts, and the State: The Case of Macroeconomic Policy-Making in Britain," in *Social Scientists, Policy, and the State*, ed. Stephen Brooks and Alain-G. Gagnon, 53-78 (Westport, CT: Praeger, 1990).

47 Karen Orren and Stephen Skowronek, "Beyond the Iconography of Order: Notes for a New Institutionalism," in *The Dynamics of American Politics: Approaches and Interpretations*, ed. L. Dodd and C. Jillson (Boulder, CO: Westview Press, 1994), 321; Robert C. Lieberman, "Ideas, Institutions, and Political Order: Explaining Political Change," *American Political Science Review* 96, 4 (2002): 704.

48 Vivian Schmidt, "Discursive Institutionalism: The Explanatory Power of Ideas and Discourse," *Annual Review of Politics* 11 (2008): 315.

49 Thomas Risse, "International Norms and Domestic Change: Arguing and Communicative Behavior in the Human Rights Arena," *Politics and Society* 27, 4 (1999): 526-56; "'Let's Argue!': Communicative Action in World Politics," *International Organization* 54, 1 (2000): 1-39; Thomas Risse and Kathryn Sikkink, "The Socialization of International Human Rights Norms into Domestic Practices: Introduction," in *The Power of Human Rights: International Norms and Domestic Change*, ed. Thomas Risse, Stephen C. Ropp, and Kathryn Sikkink, 1-38 (Cambridge: Cambridge University Press, 1999).

50 Seyla Benhabib, "Claiming Rights across Borders: International Human Rights and Democratic Sovereignty," *American Political Science Review* 103, 4 (2009): 698-99.

51 Alan G. Green, *Immigration and the Postwar Canadian Economy* (Toronto: Macmillan-Hunter Press, 1976), 34-35; Peter Li, *Destination Canada: Immigration Debates and Issues* (Toronto: Oxford University Press, 2003), 23.

52 Brubaker, *Citizenship and Nationhood*, 174.

CHAPTER 2: BUILDING WALLS, BOUNDING NATIONS

1　On the turn of the twentieth century as a period of globalization, see David Held, Anthony McGrew, David Goldblatt, and Jonathan Perraton, *Global Transformations: Politics, Economics and Culture* (Stanford: Stanford University Press, 1999); Jeffrey G. Williamson, *Globalization and the Poor Periphery before 1950* (Cambridge: MIT Press, 2006); Kevin H. O'Rourke and Jeffrey G. Williamson, *Globalization and History: The Evolution of the Nineteenth-Century Atlantic Economy* (Cambridge: MIT Press, 2001).

2　The notion of a "double movement" is drawn from Karl Polanyi's *The Great Transformation: The Political and Economic Origins of Our Time* (Boston: Beacon Press, 1957).

3　Geoffrey Barraclough, *An Introduction to Contemporary History* (New York: Basic Books, 1964), 42-43; Aristide R. Zolberg, "Global Movements, Global Walls: Responses to Migration, 1885-1925," in *Global History and Migrations*, ed. Wang Gungwu (Boulder, CO: Westview Press, 1997), 282-83; Aristide R. Zolberg, "Contemporary Transnational Migrations in Historical Perspective: Patterns and Dilemmas," in *US Immigration and Refugee Policy: Global and Domestic Issues*, ed. Mary M. Kritz (Lexington, MA: Lexington Books, 1983), 25; Eric Hobsbawm, *The Age of Empire, 1875-1914* (New York: Vintage Books, 1989). On the expansion of railroad lines, see Peter J. Hugill, *World Trade since 1431: Geography, Technology, and Capitalism* (Baltimore: Johns Hopkins University Press, 1993), 174.

4　Walter Nugent, *Crossings: The Great Transatlantic Migrations, 1870-1914* (Bloomington: Indiana University Press, 1992), 31-33; Zolberg, "Global Movements," 283.

5　Zolberg, "Global Movements," 283.

6　Jack Wertheimer, *Unwelcome Strangers: East European Jews in Imperial Germany* (New York: Oxford University Press, 1987), 13-14.

7　Hobsbawm, *Age of Empire*, 29-30.

8　Ninette Kelley and Michael Trebilcock, *The Making of the Mosaic: A History of Canadian Immigration Policy* (Toronto: University of Toronto Press, 1998), 118-19.

9　Zolberg, "Global Movements," 284.

10　John Torpey, *The Invention of the Passport* (New York: Cambridge University Press, 2000), 57-92.

11　Hugh J. M. Johnston, *British Emigration Policy, 1815-1830: "Shovelling Out Paupers"* (Oxford: Clarendon Press, 1972); Held et al., *Global Transformations*, 292; Zolberg, "Global Movements," 285.

12　Aristide R. Zolberg, "The Exit Revolution," in *Citizenship and Those Who Leave: The Politics of Emigration and Expatriation*, ed. Nancy L. Green and François Weil, 33-62 (Urbana and Chicago: Illinois University Press, 2007).

13　Zolberg, "Global Movements," 285. See also Dudley Baines, "European Labor Markets, Emigration and Internal Migration, 1850-1913," in *Migration and the International Labor Market, 1850-1939*, ed. Timothy J. Hatton and Jeffrey G. Williamson (New York: Routledge, 1994), 44-45.

14　Nugent, *Crossings*, 43.

15　Michael Marrus, *The Unwanted: European Refugees in the Twentieth Century* (New York: Oxford University Press, 1985); Norman Naimark, *Fires of Hatred: Ethnic*

Cleansing in Twentieth-Century Europe (Cambridge, MA: Harvard University Press, 2001), 57-84. For a more skeptical take on the so-called "persecution thesis of Jewish emigration," see Leah Platt Boustan, "Were Jews Political Refugees or Economic Migrants? Assessing the Persecution Theory of Jewish Emigration, 1881-1914," in *The New Economic History: Essays in Honor of Jeffrey G. Williamson*, ed. Timothy J. Hatton, Kevin H. O'Rourke, and Alan M. Taylor, 267-89 (Cambridge: MIT Press, 2007).

16 Aristide R. Zolberg, "Wanted but Not Welcome: Alien Labor in Western Development," in *Population in an Interacting World*, ed. William Alonso, 44-54 (Cambridge, MA: Harvard University Press, 1987); Dirk Hoerder, *Cultures in Contact: World Migrations in the Second Millennium* (Durham, NC: Duke University Press, 2002), 366-498; Robin Cohen, "East-West and European Migration in a Global Context," *New Community* 18, 1 (1991): 10; Michael Geyer and Charles Bright, "World History in a Global Age," *American Historical Review* 100 (1995): 1034-60.

17 Held et al., *Global Transformations*, 294; P.C. Campbell, *Chinese Coolie Emigration* (London: King and Son, 1923).

18 For background, see Tin-Yuke Char, "Legal Restrictions on Chinese in English-Speaking Countries in the Pacific," *Chinese Social and Political Science Review* 16, 3 (1932): 474-86.

19 Leslie Page Moch, "The European Perspective: Changing Conditions and Multiple Migrations, 1750-1914," in *European Migrations: Global and Local Perspectives*, ed. Dirk Hoerder and Leslie Page Moch (Boston: Northwestern University Press, 1996), 126.

20 John Torpey, "States and the Regulation of Migration in the Twentieth-Century North Atlantic World," in *The Wall around the West: State Borders and Immigration Controls in North America and Europe*, ed. Peter Andreas and Timothy Snyder, 31-54 (Lanham: Rowman and Littlefield, 2000).

21 Elazar Barkan, *The Retreat of Scientific Racism: Changing Concepts of Race in Britain and the United States between the World Wars* (Cambridge: Cambridge University Press, 1992), 2; Paul Gordon Lauren, *Power and Prejudice: The Politics and Diplomacy of Racial Discrimination*, 2nd ed. (Boulder, CO: Westview Press, 1996), 36-40.

22 For background and discussion, see J.W. Burrow, *The Crisis of Reason: European Thought, 1848-1914* (New Haven, CT: Yale University Press, 2000), 68-108; Neil MacMaster, *Racism in Europe, 1870-2000* (Houndmills: Palgrave, 2001), 31-57; Audrey Smedley, *Race in North America: Origin and Evolution of a Worldview* (Boulder, CO: Westview Press, 1993); Nancy Stepan, *The Idea of Race in Science* (Hamden, CT: Archon Books, 1982).

23 E.J. Hobsbawm, *Nations and Nationalism since 1870: Programme, Myth, Reality*, 2nd. ed. (Cambridge: Cambridge University Press, 1993), 107. Michael Mann notes: "Increasing social density, state infrastructures, and linguistic and sometimes also religious community gave racism a national definition ... Ideologists for the Anglo-Saxon, the Frank, the Teuton, the Slav 'race' developed a mythological history of common descent. In the 1900s, British politicians and popular writers used the word 'race' in a perfectly routine way to refer to the British people, in discussing the

problems of the Empire, and in regard to economic rivalry with Germany – even with the United States. Thus racism was not unitary but split, as Europe had always been split, between the transnational and the national." See Michael Mann, *The Sources of Social Power*, vol. 2: *The Rise of Classes and Nation-States, 1760-1914* (Cambridge: Cambridge University Press, 1993), 581-82. See also Bruce Baum, *The Rise and Fall of the Caucasian Race: A Political History of Racial Identity* (New York: NYU Press, 2006), 132-52.

24 John Solomos and Les Black, *Racism and Society* (Houndmills: Macmillan Press, 1996), 45; Baum, *Rise and Fall*, 129-30. On the emergence of the eugenics movement in Germany, see Paul Weindling, *Health, Race and German Politics between National Unification and Nazism, 1870-1945* (Cambridge: Cambridge University Press, 1989).

25 Anthony Padgen, *Peoples and Empires: Europeans and the Rest of the World, from Antiquity to the Present* (London: Weidenfeld and Nicholson, 2001), 146.

26 Michael Banton and Jonathan Harwood, *The Race Concept* (London: 1975); George L. Mosse, *Toward the Final Solution: A History of European Racism* (New York: H. Fertig, 1978).

27 For a summary of debates among race scientists on how "superior" white races ought to be categorized, see Baum, *Rise and Fall*, 132-52.

28 Padgen, *Peoples and Empires*, 151.

29 James A. Tyner, "The Geopolitics of Eugenics and the Exclusion of Phillipine Immigrants from the United States," *Geographical Review* 89, 1 (1999): 56-57.

30 MacMaster, *Racism in Europe*, 40-41.

31 Alan Cairns, "Empire, Globalization, and the Fall and Rise of Diversity," in *Citizenship, Diversity and Pluralism*, ed. Alan Cairns, John C. Courtney, Peter MacKinnon, Hans J. Michelmann, and David E. Smith (Montreal and Kingston: McGill-Queen's University Press, 1999), 38.

32 Mark Mazower, "An International Civilization? Empire, Internationalism and the Crisis of the Mid-Twentieth Century," *International Affairs* 82, 3 (2006): 557. See also Marilyn Lake and Henry Reynolds, *Drawing the Global Colour Line: White Men's Countries and the International Challenge of Racial Equality* (Cambridge: Cambridge University Press, 2008), 336; Lauren, *Power and Prejudice*, 47-48.

33 Cairns, "Empire," 38. This point is also at the centre of Hannah Arendt's discussion of imperialism in *The Origins of Totalitarianism*, 3rd ed., rev. (New York: Harcourt, Brace, Jovanovich, 1973).

34 Andreas Fahrmeir, *Citizenship: The Rise and Fall of a Modern Concept* (New Haven, CT: Yale University Press, 2007), 113. See also John Willinsky, *Learning to Divide the World: Education at Empire's End* (Minneapolis: University of Minnesota Press, 1998).

35 David I. Kertzer and Dominique Arel, "Censuses, Identity Formation, and the Struggle for Political Power," in *Census and Identity: The Politics of Race, Ethnicity, and Language in National Censuses*, ed. David I. Kertzer and Dominique Arel, 1-42 (Cambridge: Cambridge University Press, 2002); Debra Thompson, "Seeing Like a Racial State: The Census and the Politics of Race in the United States, Great Britain and Canada" (PhD diss., University of Toronto, 2010).

36 Kay J. Anderson, "The Idea of Chinatown: The Power of Place and Institutional Practice in the Making of a Racial Category," in *Immigration in Canada: Historical Perspectives*, ed. Gerald Tulchinsky (Toronto: Copp Clark Longman, 1994), 230.

37 Randall Hansen and Desmond King, "Eugenic Ideas, Political Interests, and Policy Variance: Immigration and Sterilization Policy in Britain and the US," *World Politics* 53, 2 (2001): 237-63; Frank Dikötter, "Race and Culture: Recent Perspectives on the History of Eugenics," *American Historical Review* 103, 2 (1998): 467-78.

38 Kelley and Trebilcock, *Making of the Mosaic*, 28.

39 J.M.S. Careless, *Canada: A Story of Challenge* (New York: St. Martin's Press, 1965), 103.

40 W.L. Morton, *The Canadian Identity* (Toronto: University of Toronto Press, 1965), 25.

41 Kelley and Trebilcock, *Making of the Mosaic*, 44.

42 Donald Creighton, *Dominion of the North: A History of Canada*, rev. ed. (Toronto: Macmillan, 1957), 204-62.

43 Cited in Morton, *Canadian Identity*, 44.

44 Kelley and Trebilcock, *Making of the Mosaic*, 45-47.

45 See Canada, Manpower and Immigration, *The Immigration Program* (Ottawa: Information Canada, 1974), 5.

46 John Herd Thompson and Morton Weinfeld, "Entry and Exit: Canadian Immigration Policy in Context," *Annals of the American Academy of Political and Social Science* 538 (1995): 186.

47 Ibid. See also Leon E. Truesdell, *The Canadian-Born in the United States, 1865-1930* (New Haven, CT: Yale University Press, 1943), 9-37.

48 Reg Whitaker, *Canadian Immigration Policy since Confederation* (Ottawa: Canadian Historical Association, 1991), 4. The National Policy consisted of a "comprehensive system of tariffs designed to promote Canadian manufacturing in steel, textiles, coal, and petroleum products, and via a Canadian Pacific Railway, to facilitate the internal exchange of agricultural and industrial products between western and eastern Canada." See John Herd Thompson and Stephen J. Randall, *Canada and the United States: Ambivalent Allies* (Athens, GA: The University of Georgia Press, 1994), 56. See also Donald V. Smiley, "Canada and the Quest for a National Policy," *Canadian Journal of Political Science* 3, 1 (1975): 40-62.

49 Kelley and Trebilcock, *Making of the Mosaic*, 62.

50 Alan G. Green, "A Comparison of Canadian and US Immigration Policy in the Twentieth Century," in *Diminishing Returns: The Economics of Canada's Recent Immigration Policy*, ed. Don J. DeVoretz (Ottawa: The C.D. Howe Institute, 1995), 37.

51 Green, "Comparison," 38.

52 Vic Satzewich, "Racisms: The Reactions to Chinese Migrants in Canada at the Turn of the Century," *International Sociology* 4, 3 (1989): 313-14; Patricia E. Roy, *A White Man's Province: British Columbia Politicians and Chinese and Japanese Immigrants, 1858-1914* (Vancouver: UBC Press, 1989), 39; Bruce Ryder, "Racism and the Constitution: The Constitutional Fate of British Columbia Anti-Asian Immigration Legislation, 1884-1909," *Osgoode Hall Law Journal* 29 (1991): 646; David Goutor, *Guarding the Gates: The Canadian Labour Movement and Immigration, 1872-1934* (Vancouver: UBC Press, 2007), 27.

53 Ryder, "Racism and the Constitution," 641.

54 Statement in House of Commons in 1883. Cited in Ryder, "Racism and the Constitution," 647. See also Goutor, *Guarding the Gates*, 27; and Peter Ward, *White Canada Forever: Popular Attitudes and Public Policy toward Orientals in British Columbia* (Montreal and Kingston: McGill-Queen's University Press, 1978), 55.

55 R.A. Huttenback, "The British Empire as a 'White Man's Country': Racial Attitudes and Immigration Legislation in the Colonies of White Settlement," *Journal of British Studies* 13, 1 (1973): 131.

56 Fiona Tinwei Lam, "The Pursuit of Cultural Homogeneity and Social Cohesion in Immigration and Naturalization Policy: The Example of the Chinese in Canada," (LLM thesis, University of Toronto, 1994), 12. See also Charles A. Price, *The Great White Walls Are Built: Restrictive Immigration to North America and Australia* (Canberra: Australian National University Press, 1972); and Ward, *White Canada Forever*.

57 Canada, *Immigration Program*, 6. See also Harold Martin Troper, *Only Farmers Need Apply: Official Canadian Government Encouragement of Immigration from the United States, 1896-1911* (Toronto: Griffin House, 1972); and Paul W. Gates, "Official Encouragement to Immigration by the Province of Canada," *Canadian Historical Review* 15, 1 (1934): 24-38.

58 The decision to allow "block settlements" made Canada an attractive destination for German and Russian Mennonites and Russian Doukhabors.

59 Cited in Freda Hawkins, *Critical Years in Immigration: Canada and Australia Compared* (Kingston and Montreal: McGill-Queen's University Press, 1989), 6.

60 Sifton to Laurier, 1901, cited in Valerie Knowles, *Strangers at Our Gates: Canadian Immigration and Immigration Policy, 1540-1990* (Toronto: Dundurn, 1992), 62.

61 Huttenback, "British Empire," 133.

62 Cited in Hawkins, *Critical Years*, 8.

63 Kelley and Trebilcock, *Making of the Mosaic*, 132-33.

64 Ibid. See also Howard Palmer, *Patterns of Prejudice: A History of Nativism in Alberta* (Toronto: McClelland and Stewart, 1982), 17-61.

65 Whitaker, *Canadian Immigration Policy*, 8-9; Howard Palmer, "Ethnicity and Politics in Canada: 1867-Present," in *From "Melting Pot" to Multiculturalism: The Evolution of Ethnic Relations in the United States and Canada*, ed. Valeria Gennaro Lerda (Rome: Bulzoni Editore, 1990), 172.

66 See Michael Brown, "From Stereotype to Scapegoat: Anti-Jewish Sentiment in French Canada from Confederation to World War I," in *Antisemitism in Canada: History and Interpretation*, ed. Alan Davies (Waterloo, ON: Wilfrid Laurier University Press, 1992), 46.

67 Lauren, *Power and Prejudice*, 37.

68 John Boyko, *Last Steps to Freedom: The Evolution of Canadian Racism* (Winnipeg: Witton and Dwyer, 1995), 88-89.

69 Kelley and Trebilcock, *Making of the Mosaic*, 134-35.

70 Richard J.F. Day, *Multiculturalism and the History of Canadian Diversity* (Toronto: University of Toronto Press, 2000), 127. The following section draws from Day's excellent analysis of *Strangers within Our Gates*.

71 J.S. Woodsworth, *Stangers within Our Gates: Or, Coming Canadians* (Toronto: University of Toronto Press, 1972), 202.

72 Green, "A Comparison of Canadian and US Immigration Policy," 38.

73 Kelley and Trebilcock, *Making of the Mosaic*, 136.

74 Green, "A Comparison of Canadian and US Immigration Policy," 38.

75 These included a 1908 order-in-council barring immigrants whose passage was financed by a charitable society in their home country (unless the charity was approved and recognized by the Canadian government) and another requiring that immigrants entering Canada arrive via continuous voyage from the country of their birth or citizenship with tickets bought in those same countries. The first regulation aimed at checking the flow of British "paupers" whose passage to Canada was assisted by British municipalities eager to "off-load" their poor. The second was aimed at barring the entry of Japanese and East Asian immigrants and arose in response to growing anti-Asian sentiment in British Columbia, which exploded in the 1907 Vancouver Riot. See Mabel Timlin, "Canada's Immigration Policy, 1896-1910," *Canadian Journal of Economics and Political Science* 26, 4 (1960): 523-28.

76 Kelley and Trebilcock, *Making of the Mosaic*, 136.

77 Ibid., 137.

78 Ibid.

79 Ibid., 139.

80 Whitaker, *Canadian Immigration Policy*, 9.

81 Aristide R. Zolberg, "The Main Gate and the Back Door: The Politics of American Immigration Policy, 1950-1976" (unpublished manuscript, Council on Foreign Relations, 1978).

82 Kelley and Trebilcock, *Making of the Mosaic*, 139. See also Robert F. Harney, "The Padrone System and the Sojourner in the Canadian North, 1885-1920," in *Immigration in Canada: Historical Perspectives*, ed. Gerald Tulchinsky, 249-64 (Toronto: Copp Longman, 1994).

83 Ryder, "Racism and the Constitution," 668.

84 Ryder, "Racism and the Constitution"; Ward, *White Canada Forever*, 55.

85 For details concerning the riot, see Ward, *White Canada Forever*, 53-78; Roy, *White Man's Province*, 185-228.

86 Audrey Macklin, "Historicizing Narratives of Arrival: The Other Indian Other," in *Storied Communities: Narratives of Contact and Arrival in Constituting Political Community*, ed. Hester Lessard, Rebecca Johnson, and Jeremy Webber (Vancouver: UBC Press, 2010), 49.

87 See Frank Oliver's summary of his government's positions on the issue of "Asiatic Immigration" in Canada, House of Commons, *Debates*, March 2, 1914, 1220-22.

88 Huttenback, "British Empire," 134; Roy, *White Man's Province*, 209-13.

89 The order-in-council was drafted in response to a slight increase in the number of black American settlers in the Prairie provinces. According to Harold Troper, the order-in-council was probably vetoed by Prime Minister Laurier as it would "likely [have] raise[d] undesired diplomatic problems with the United States." See Harold Martin Troper, "The Creek-Negroes of Oklahoma and Canadian Immigration,

1909-1911," *Canadian Historical Review* 53, 3 (1972): 272-88; Troper, *Only Farmers Need Apply*, 140. See also Palmer, *Patterns of Prejudice*, 35-37.

90 Kelley and Trebilcock, *Making of the Mosaic*, 156.

91 Troper, *Only Farmers Need Apply*, 144.

92 For background, see Kelley and Trebilcock, *Making of the Mosaic*, 150-52.

93 Macklin, "Historicizing Narratives," 58.

94 Ibid.

95 Kelley and Trebilcock, *Making of the Mosaic*, 150.

96 Macklin, "Historicizing Narratives," 59. The harmonization of naturalization across the British dominions, which culminated in the New Naturalization Act, 1914, tightened naturalization requirements and granted the secretary of state absolute discretion in the granting of citizenship along with the power to revoke the citizenship of naturalized immigrants. See H.F. Angus, "The Legal Status in British Columbia of Residents of Oriental Race and Their Descendants," *Canadian Bar Review* 9, 1 (1931): 10. Requirements for naturalization included: five years residence or five years service to the Crown; an intention to continue to reside in Canada or serve the Crown; good character; and a knowledge of English or French. The grant of citizenship lay within the absolute discretion of the secretary of state. Reasons for rejection were not required and appeal was impossible.

97 Cited in Macklin, "Historicizing Narratives," 59.

98 Kelley and Trebilcock, *Making of the Mosaic*, 152.

99 Nearly 3 million immigrants arrived in Canada between 1896 and 1913. Nearly half of this total entered the country from 1910 to 1913. See Canada, *Immigration Program*, 10.

100 Raymond Breton, "From Ethnic to Civic Nationalism: English Canada and Quebec," *Ethnic and Racial Studies* 11, 1 (1988): 88-89; Joseph Levitt, "Race and Nation in Canadian Anglophone Historiography," *Canadian Review of Studies on Nationalism* 8 (1981): 1-16; David Nock, "Patriotism and Patriarchs: Anglican Archbishops and Canadianization," *Canadian Ethnic Studies* 14 (1982): 85-100.

101 For details see Kelley and Trebilcock, *Making of the Mosaic*, 170-71; David J. Carter, *Behind Canadian Barbed Wire: Alien, Refugee and Prisoner of War Camps in Canada, 1914-1916* (Calgary: Tumbleweed, 1980).

102 Donald Avery, *Reluctant Host: Canada's Response to Immigrant Workers, 1896-1994* (Toronto: McClelland and Stewart, 1995), 74-75.

103 On the Railway Agreement see Palmer, *Patterns of Prejudice*, 91-122.

104 Kelley and Trebilcock, *Making of the Mosaic*, 189-94.

105 Cited in Hawkins, *Critical Years*, 17.

106 Patricia E. Roy, *The Oriental Question: Consolidating a White Man's Province, 1914-1941* (Vancouver: UBC Press, 2003), 73-74.

107 Ibid., 73-74; Hawkins, *Critical Years*, 19-20; Kelley and Trebilcock, *Making of the Mosaic*, 203.

108 W. Burton Hurd, "The Case for a Quota," *Queen's Quarterly* 36 (1929): 145-59.

109 Kelley and Trebilcock, *Making of the Mosaic*, 209-15; W.A. Carrothers, "The Immigration Problem in Canada," *Queen's Quarterly* 36 (1929): 516-31.

110 Reflecting on the impact of policy on Canada's development, a Canadian immigration official noted that the maintenance of an overwhelmingly white society was due "in no small measure to the immigration policy that ha[d] been pursued for years. The immigration regulations reflect[ed] the immigration policy and while there [was] not what one would call a colour line, there [was] something that [came] very close to a race line." See Letter from Birks, Ottawa, April 8, 1942, Library and Archives Canada, RG 76, vol. 338, file 553-36-644, pts. 1-8, "Admission of Coloured Domestics from BWI: Policy and Instructions."

111 Klaus J. Bade, *Vom Auswanderungsland zum Einwanderungsland? Deutschland 1880-1980* (Berlin: Colloquium Verlag, 1983), 18.

112 Klaus J. Bade, "German Emigration to the United States and Continental Immigration to Germany in the Late Nineteenth and Early Twentieth Centuries," *Central European History* 13 (1980): 348-77.

113 Saskia Sassen, *Guests and Aliens* (New York: The New Press, 1999), 53.

114 Klaus J. Bade, "Labour, Migration, and the State: Germany from the Late 19th Century to the Onset of the Great Depression," in *Population, Labour and Migration in 19th- and 20th-Century Germany*, ed. Klaus J. Bade (New York: St. Martin's Press, 1987), 62.

115 Bade, "Labour," 62. See also J.A. Perkins, "The Agricultural Revolution in Germany, 1850-1914," *Journal of European Economic History* 10 (1981): 71-118.

116 Ulrich Herbert, *A History of Foreign Labor in Germany, 1880-1980: Seasonal Workers, Forced Laborers, Guest Workers*, trans. William Templer (Ann Arbor: University of Michigan Press, 1990), 9.

117 Zolberg, "Wanted but Not Welcome," 65.

118 *Die Post*, March 11, 1885, cited in Herbert, *History of Foreign Labor*, 11.

119 See William H. Hagen, *Germans, Poles, and Jews: The Nationality Conflict in the Prussian East, 1772-1914* (Chicago: University of Chicago Press, 1980); Hans-Ulrich Wehler, "Polenpolitik im deutschen Kaiserreich," in *Krisenherde des Kaiserreichs 1871-1918* (Göttingen: Vandenhoeck und Ruprecht, 1979), 129-200; Klaus J. Bade, "Kulturkampf auf dem Arbeitsmarkt: Bismarcks Polenpolitik 1885-1890," in *Innenpolitische Probleme des Bismarck-Reiches*, ed. Otto Pflanze, 121-42 (Munich: R. Oldenbourg, 1983); Witold Molik, "Die preußische Polenpolitik im 19. und zu Beginn des 20. Jahrhunderts: Überlegungen zu Forschungsstand und – Perspektiven," in *Nationale Minderheiten und staatliche Minderheitenpolitik in Deutschland im 19. Jahrhundert*, ed. Hans Hennig Hahn and Peter Kunze, 29-40 (Berlin: Akademie Verlag, 1999); and Wertheimer, *Unwelcome Strangers*, 19.

120 Cited in Herbert, *History of Foreign Labor*, 12. See also Bade, "Labour," 66-67; and Karen Schönwälder, "Invited but Unwanted? Migrants from the East in Germany, 1890-1990," in *The German Lands and Eastern Europe: Essays on the History of Their Social, Cultural and Political Relations*, ed. Roger Bartlett and Karen Schönwälder (Houndmills: Macmillan, 1999), 200.

121 Herbert, *History of Foreign Labor*, 13. See also Helmut Neubach, *Die Ausweisungen von Polen und Juden aus Preußen 1885/86* (Wiesbaden: Harrassowitz, 1967); Eli Nathans, *The Politics of Citizenship in Germany: Ethnicity, Utility and Nationalism* (Oxford: Berg, 2004), 121-23.

122 Robert Lewis Koehl, "Colonialism inside Germany: 1886-1918," *Journal of Modern History* 25, 3 (1953): 261. Andreas Fahrmeir notes: "The measure was part of Bismarck's more general plan to create a German Empire in which German was the sole language, and Protestantism the main religion, at a time when migration and demographics were making the Chancellor's native Prussia increasingly Polish and Catholic." See Andreas Fahrmeir, *Citizenship: The Rise and Fall of a Modern Concept* (New Haven, CT: Yale University Press, 2007), 89.

123 Herbert, *History of Foreign Labor*, 14.

124 Ibid., 17.

125 Schönwälder, "Invited but Unwanted," 206-07; Geoff Eley, "German Politics and Polish Nationality: The Dialectic of Nation Forming in the East of Prussia," in *From Unification to Nazism: Reinterpreting the German Past*, ed. Geoff Eley, 200-28 (London: Allen & Unwin, 1986).

126 Martin Forsberg, "Foreign Labour, the State and Trade Unions in Imperial Germany, 1890-1918," in *The State and Social Change in Germany, 1880-1980*, ed. W.R. Lee and Eve Rosenhaft (Oxford: Berg, 1990), 109; Klaus J. Bade, "Politik und Ökonomie der Ausländerbeschäftigung im preußischen Osten 1885-1910: Die Internationalisierung des Arbeitsmarkts im 'Rahmen der preußischen Abwehrpolitik,'" in *Preußen im Rückblick*, ed. Hans-Jürgen Puhle and Hans-Ulrich Wehler, 273-99 (Göttingen: Vandenhoeck and Ruprecht Verlag, 1980); Klaus J. Bade, "Immigration, Naturalization, and Ethno-National Traditions in Germany: From the Citizenship Law of 1913 to the Law of 1999," in *Crossing Boundaries: The Exclusion and Inclusion of Minorities in Germany and the United States*, ed. Larry Eugene Jones (New York: Berghahn Books, 2001), 34; Christiane Reinecke, "Governing Aliens in Times of Upheaval: Immigration Control and Modern State Practice in Early Twentieth-Century Britain, Compared with Prussia," *International Review of Social History* 54 (2009): 60; Wertheimer, *Unwelcome Strangers*, 20.

127 The period was subsequently lengthened.

128 Prussian Ministry of the Interior, cited in Klaus J. Bade, "'Preußengänger' und 'Abwehrpolitik': Ausländerbeschäftigung, Ausländerpolitik und Ausländerkontrolle auf dem Arbeitsmarkt in Preußen vor dem Erstem Weltkrieg," *Archiv für Sozialgeschichte* 24 (1984): 114.

129 Bade, "Politik und Ökonomie," 35-39.

130 Herbert, *History of Foreign Labor*, 28.

131 Ibid., 32-34.

132 Klaus J. Bade, "'Billig und willig' – die 'ausländischen Wanderarbeiter' im kaiserlichen Deutschland," in *Deutsche im Ausland – Fremde in Deutschland: Migration in Geschichte und Gegenwart*, ed. Klaus J. Bade (Munich: C.H. Beck, 1992), 315.

133 By-law of the German Farm Workers Agency, cited in Herbert, *History of Foreign Labor*, 35.

134 Herbert, *History of Foreign Labor*, 36.

135 Bade, "Labour," 75.

136 Forsberg, "Foreign Labour," 113.

137 Bade, "Labour," 64.

138 Bade, "'Preußengänger' und 'Abwehrpolitik,'" 146. For a detailed analysis of Prussian statistics, see Klaus J. Bade, ed., "Arbeiterstatistik zur Ausländerkontrolle: Die 'Nachweisungen' der preußischen Landräte über den 'Zugang, Abgang und Bestand der ausländischen Arbeiter im preußischen Staate' 1906-1914," *Archiv für Sozialgeschichte* 24 (1984): 163-283.

139 Ulrich Herbert, *Geschichte der Ausländerpolitik in Deutschland: Saisonarbeiter, Zwangsarbeiter, Gastarbeiter, Flüchtlinge* (Munich: C.H. Beck, 2001), 25. See also Reinecke, "Governing Aliens," 60.

140 Keith Tribe, "Introduction to Weber," *Economy and Society* 8, 2 (1979): 175; W.J. Mommsen, *The Age of Bureaucracy* (Oxford: Basil Blackwell, 1974), 25-33.

141 "Those who replace the Germans on the estates of the east are better able to submit to these conditions of existence: I mean the itinerant Polish workers, troops of nomads recruited by agents in Russia, who cross the frontier in tens of thousands in spring, and leave again in autumn." See Max Weber, "The National State and Economic Policy," in *Reading Weber*, ed. Keith Tribe, trans. Ben Faukes (London: Routledge, 1989), 193. See also Max Weber, "Developmental Tendencies in the Situation of East Elbian Rural Labourers," *Economy and Society* 8 (1979): 177-205.

142 Schönwälder, "Invited but Unwanted," 206.

143 Cited in Zolberg, "Wanted but Not Welcome," 67.

144 "Die Ausländergefahr im Deutschen Reich," *Alldeutscher Blätter* 45 (1907), cited in Herbert, *History of Foreign Labor*, 28-29.

145 Herbert, *History of Foreign Labor*, 29.

146 Forsberg, "Foreign Labour," 118.

147 Cited in Herbert, *History of Foreign Labor*, 49.

148 Salo Baron, *The Russian Jews under Tsars and Soviets*, rev. ed. (New York: Macmillan, 1976), 70-71.

149 Wertheimer, *Unwelcome Strangers*, 12.

150 Over 700,000 transmigrants embarked from German ports between 1905 and 1914. See Jack Wertheimer, "'The Unwanted Element': East European Jews in Imperial Germany," in *Migration in European History I*, ed. Colin Holmes (Brookfield: E. Elgar, 1996), 510.

151 See Ingo Blank, "'... nirgends eine Heimat, aber Gräber auf jedem Friedhof': Ostjuden in Kaiserreich und Weimarer Republik," in *Deutsche im Ausland – Fremde in Deutschland*, ed. Klaus J. Bade (Munich: C.H. Beck, 1992), 325-26. Approximately 78,000 East European Jews remained in Germany on the eve of the First World War. They constituted about 12 percent of the total Jewish population. See Bade, "Immigration," 34. See also Reinecke, "Governing Aliens," 62.

152 Dieter Gosewinkel, "Die Staatsangehörigkeit als Institution des Nationalstaats: Zur Enstehung des Reichs- und Staatsangehörigkeitsgesetzes von 1913," in *Offene Staatlichkeit: Festschrift für Ernst-Wolfgang Böckenförde zum 65 – Geburtstag*, ed. Rolf Grawert, Bernhard Schlink, Rainer Wahl, and Joachim Wieland (Berlin: Duncker and Humboldt, 1995), 369-70.

153 Wertheimer, *Unwelcome Strangers*, 33-41; Richard S. Levy, *The Downfall of the Anti-Semitic Political Parties in Imperial Germany* (New Haven, CT: Yale University Press, 1975).

154 Wertheimer, "Unwanted Element," 511. See also Katja Wüstenbecker, "Hamburg and the Transit of East European Emigrants," in *Migration Control in the North Atlantic World: The Evolution of State Practices in Europe and North America from the French Revolution to the Inter-War Period*, ed. Andreas Fahrmeir, Olivier Faron, and Patrick Weil, 223-36 (New York: Berghahn Books, 2003).

155 Reinecke, "Governing Aliens," 62.

156 Wertheimer, "Unwanted Element," 512.

157 Ibid.

158 Nathans, *Politics of Citizenship*, 146-48.

159 Wertheimer, "Unwanted Element," 512.

160 Fahrmeir, *Citizenship*, 92.

161 Prior to the 1913 law emigrants were stripped of their German citizenship "upon their departure from Germany or, at the latest, ten years after they left." See Nathans, *Politics of Citizenship*, 169.

162 Klaus J. Bade, "Transnationale Migration, ethnonationale Diskussion und Staatliche Migrationspolitik im Deutschland des 19. und 20. Jahrhunderts," in *Migration, Ethnizität, Konflikt*, ed. Klaus J. Bade (Osnabrück: Rasch, 1996), 415.

163 Dieter Gosewinkel, *Einbürgern und Ausschließen: Die Nationalisierung der Staatsangehörigkeit vom Deutschen Bund bis zur Bundesrepublik Deutschland* (Göttingen: Vandenhoek and Ruprecht, 2001), 324.

164 Gosewinkel, "Die Staatsangehörigkeit," 375-76; Fahrmeir, *Citizenship*, 92; Annemarie Sammartino, "Culture, Belonging, and the Law: Naturalization in the Weimar Republic," in *Citizenship and National Identity in Twentieth-Century Germany*, ed. Geoff Eley and Jan Palmowski (Stanford, CA: Stanford University Press, 2008), 60.

165 Andreas K. Fahrmeir, "Nineteenth-Century German Citizenships: A Reconsideration," *Historical Journal* 40, 3 (1997): 721-52; Gosewinkel, *Einbürgern und Ausschließen*.

166 Gosewinkel, *Einbürgern und Ausschließen*, 327.

167 Dieter Gosewinkel, "Citizenship and Naturalization Politics in Germany in the Nineteenth and Twentieth Centuries," in *Challenging Ethnic Citizenship: German and Israeli Perspectives on Immigration*, ed. Daniel Levy and Yfaat Weiss (New York: Berghahn Books, 2002), 65.

168 Gosewinkel, *Einbürgern und Ausschließen*, 321.

169 Proceedings of the German Reichstag, 23 (February 1912), 13, cited in Sebastian Edathy, *"Wo immer auch unsere Wiege gestanden hat": Parlamentarische Debatten über die deutsche Staatsbürgerschaft* (Frankfurt: IKO – Verlag für Interkulturelle Kommunikation, 2000), 58.

170 Edathy, *Parlamentarische Debatten über die deutsche Staatsbürgerschaft*, 70; Klaus J. Bade, *Migration in European History*, trans. Allison Brown (Oxford: Blackwell, 2003), 152-53.

171 Gerald D. Feldman, *Army, Industry, and Labor in Germany, 1914-1918* (Princeton: Princeton University Press, 1966).

172 Workers from captured territories (e.g., Belgium) were also "recruited" for the war effort by German authorities. See Herbert, *History of Foreign Labor*, 102-08.

173   Herbert, *History of Foreign Labor*, 119; Bade, *Migration in European History*, 172-73.
174   Germany was host to approximately 1 million civilian foreign workers at the end of the war. By 1924 this figure declined to 124,000. See Herbert, *History of Foreign Labor*, 121.
175   For a concise discussion of post-First World War emigration, see Jochen Oltmer, "Migration and Public Policy in Germany, 1918-1939," in *Crossing Boundaries: The Exclusion and Inclusion of Minorities in Germany and the United States*, ed. Larry Eugene Jones (New York: Berghahn Books, 2001), 51-54.
176   Reinecke, "Governing Aliens," 63.
177   Oltmer, "Migration and Public Policy," 56; Herbert, *History of Foreign Labor*, 123.
178   Oltmer, "Migration and Public Policy," 56; Herbert, *History of Foreign Labor*, 124.
179   See Sammartino, "Culture," 57-72.
180   Fahrmeir, *Citizenship*, 133; Nathans, *Politics of Citizenship*, 208.
181   Gosewinkel, *Einbürgern und Ausschließen*, 362-63. The notion that foreigners mimicked German ways to further their selfish economic interests had a long pedigree. See Wertheimer, *Unwelcome Strangers*, 30.
182   Cited in Gosewinkel, *Einbürgern und Ausschließen*, 363.
183   Nathans, *Politics of Citizenship*, 209. More generally, see Neil MacMaster, *Racism in Europe: 1870-2000* (Houndmills: Palgrave, 2001), 98-103; Paul Weindling, *Health, Race and German Politics between National Unification and Nazism, 1870-1945* (Cambridge: Cambridge University Press, 1989); Eric Kurlander, *The Price of Exclusion: Ethnicity, National Identity, and the Decline of German Liberalism, 1898-1933* (New York: Berghahn Books, 2006).
184   Zolberg, "Wanted but Not Welcome," 36-73.
185   See Barbara Roberts, "Shoveling Out the 'Mutinous': Political Deportation from Canada before 1936," *Labour/Le Travail* 18 (1986): 77-110.
186   Michael Burleigh and Wolfgang Wippermann, *The Racial State: Germany, 1933-1945* (Cambridge: Cambridge University Press, 1991); Peter C. Caldewell, "The Citizen and the Republic in Germany, 1918-1935," in *Citizenship and National Identity in Twentieth-Century Germany*, 54; Gosewinkel, *Einbürgern und Ausschließen*, 387; Fahrmeir, *Citizenship*, 135-36; Nathans, *Politics of Citizenship*, 217-34.
187   Cited in Naimark, *Fires of Hatred*, 67.
188   Irving Abella and Harold Troper, *None Is Too Many: Canada and the Jews of Europe, 1933-1948* (Toronto: Lester and Orpen Dennys, 1982), x.
189   Abella and Troper, *None Is Too Many*, 5.
190   Irving Abella and Harold Troper, "'The Line Must Be Drawn Somewhere': Canada and Jewish Refugees, 1933-1939," in *A Nation of Immigrants: Women, Workers, and Communities in Canadian History, 1840s-1960s*, ed. Franca Iacovetta, with Paula Draper and Robert Ventresca (Toronto: University of Toronto Press, 1998), 416.

CHAPTER 3: BETWEEN TWO WORLDS

1   Jürgen Habermas has noted that the Second World War marked the point where "the rug was pulled out from under *all* claims to legitimacy that did not at least rhetorically embrace the universalistic spirit of the political Enlightenment" (emphasis in

the original). Jürgen Habermas, "Aus Katastrophen lernen? Ein zeitdiagnostischer Rückblick auf das kurze 20. Jahrhundert," in his *Die postnationale Konstellation: Politische Essays* (Frankfurt am Main: Suhrkamp Verlag, 1998), 75; cited in John Torpey, "Making Whole What Has Been Smashed: Reflections on Reparations," *The Journal of Modern History* 73, 2 (2001): 343. See also Daniel Levy and Natan Sznaider, "The Institutionalization of Cosmopolitan Morality: The Holocaust and Human Rights," *Journal of Human Rights* 3, 2 (2004): 143-57.

2 In Robert Gordon Lauren's words, the Second World War "provided a mirror that forced countless numbers of people to look at themselves and to see the contradictions between their declared principles on the one hand and their actual practices on the other." See Robert Gordon Lauren, *Power and Prejudice: The Politics and Diplomacy of Racial Discrimination*, 2nd ed. (Boulder, CO: Westview Press, 1996), 146. The fragility of rights is a central theme in Hannah Arendt's seminal *The Origins of Totalitarianism* (New York: Harcourt Brace and Company, 1973).

3 Jack Donnelly, *International Human Rights*, 2nd ed. (Boulder, CO: Westview Press, 1998), 5; Sumner Welles, "New Hope for the Jewish People," *The Nation*, May 5, 1945, 511.

4 "Traditional international practice ... lacked even the language with which to condemn the horrors of the Holocaust. Realist diplomacy could find no material national interest that was threatened ... Traditional international law was as much at a loss: massacring one's own citizens simply was not an established international offense. The German government may have been legally liable for their treatment of citizens in occupied territories, but in gassing German nationals it was simply exercising its sovereign rights." See Jack Donnelly, "The Social Construction of International Human Rights," in *Human Rights in Global Politics*, ed. Tim Dunne and Nicholas J. Wheeler (Cambridge: Cambridge University Press, 1999), 72.

5 Michael R. Marrus, *The Nuremberg War Crimes Trial, 1945-46: A Documentary History* (Boston: Bedford Books, 1997).

6 Jack Donnelly, *Universal Human Rights in Theory and Practice* (Ithaca, NY: Cornell University Press, 1989), 210-11; James Avery Joyce, *The New Politics of Human Rights* (London: Macmillan, 1978), 45.

7 Anthony Padgen, "Human Rights, Natural Rights, and Europe's Imperial Legacy," *Political Theory* 21, 2 (2003): 191.

8 The Universal Declaration of Human Rights, available at http://www.un.org/.

9 Mark Mazower, "The End of Civilization and the Rise of Human Rights: The Mid-Twentieth Century Disjuncture," in *Human Rights in the Twentieth Century*, ed. Stefan-Ludwig Hoffmann, 29-44 (Cambridge: Cambridge University Press, 2011).

10 Elazar Barkan, *The Retreat of Scientific Racism: Changing Concepts of Race in Britain and the United States between the World Wars* (Cambridge: Cambridge University Press, 1993), 345.

11 Leo Kuper, ed., *Race, Science and Society* (Paris: UNESCO Press, 1950 [London: Allen and Unwin, 1975]), 343-47, cited in Marilyn Lake and Henry Reynolds, *Drawing the Global Colour Line: White Men's Countries and the International Challenge of Racial Equality* (Cambridge: Cambridge University Press, 2008), 351.

12 As reported in the *New York Times*, July 18, 1950, cited in Barkan, *Retreat of Scientific Racism*, 341. Referring to the American Civil Rights Movement, Barkan notes that reformers "expressed socio-political grievances and challenged the intellectual legitimacy of the racist tradition, among others by appealing to science, the only arbiter in a relativist world." See Barkan, *Retreat of Scientific Racism*, 343. See also Oscar Handlin, *Race and Nationality in American Life* (New York: Doubleday, 1957), 150.

13 Robert K.A. Gardiner, "Race and Color in International Relations," *Daedalus* 96, 2 (1967): 309. The rejection of racism did not necessarily lead to the rejection of race as a *classificatory* category. See Bruce Baum, *The Rise and Fall of the Caucasian Race: A Political History of Racial Identity* (New York: New York University Press, 2006), 187-91.

14 Robert H. Jackson, "The Weight of Ideas in Decolonization: Normative Change in International Relations," in *Ideas and Foreign Policy: Beliefs, Institutions, and Political Change*, ed. Judith Goldstein and Robert O. Keohane (Ithaca: Cornell University Press, 1993), 135. Alan Cairns, "Empire, Globalization, and the Fall and Rise of Diversity," in *Citizenship, Diversity and Pluralism*, ed. Alan Cairns, John C. Courtney, Peter MacKinnon, Hans J. Michelmann, and David E. Smith (Montreal and Kingston: McGill-Queen's University Press, 1999), 25.

15 R.J. Vincent, "Racial Equality," in *The Expansion of International Society*, ed. Hedley Bull and Adam Watson (Oxford: Clarendon Press, 1984), 252.

16 See Raymond F. Betts, *Decolonization* (London: Routledge, 1998), 5-18; Henri Grimal, *Decolonization: The British, French, Dutch and Belgian Empires, 1919-1963*, trans. Stephan De Vos (Boulder, CO: Westview Press, 1978); Rudolf von Albertini, "The Impact of the Two World Wars on the Decline of Colonialism," in *The End of European Empire: Decolonization after World War II*, ed. Tony Smith (Lexington, MA: D.C. Heath and Company, 1975), 3-22.

17 Geoffrey Barraclough, *An Introduction to Contemporary History* (New York: Basic Books, 1964), 148-49.

18 Cairns, "Empire," 32-33.

19 Roland Burke, *Decolonization and the Evolution of International Human Rights* (Philadelphia: University of Pennsylvania Press, 2010), 1-2.

20 Thomas Borstelmann, *The Cold War and the Color Line: American Race Relations in the Global Arena* (Cambridge, MA: Harvard University Press, 2001); Mary L. Dudziak, *Cold War Civil Rights: Race and the Image of American Democracy* (Princeton, NJ: Princeton University Press, 2000).

21 Mark Mazower, "The Strange Triumph of Human Rights, 1933-1950," *Historical Journal* 47, 2 (2004): 394.

22 Stefan-Ludwig Hoffmann, "Introduction: Genealogies of Human Rights," in *Human Rights in the Twentieth Century*, ed. Stefan-Ludwig Hoffmann (Cambridge: Cambridge University Press, 2011), 18.

23 Michael Banton, *The International Politics of Race* (Oxford: Polity, 2002), 43-44.

24 Robert Bothwell, *Alliance and Illusion: Canada and the World, 1945-1984* (Vancouver: UBC Press, 2007), 148-49.

25 Alan C. Cairns, *Citizens Plus: Aboriginal Peoples and the Canadian State* (Vancouver: UBC Press, 2000), 41.

26 Jennifer Clark, "'The Wind of Change' in Australia: Aborigines and the International Politics of Race, 1960-1972," *International History Review* 20, 1 (1998): 89-117; Alan Cairns, *Citizens Plus.*

27 Pagden, "Human Rights, Natural Rights," 171-99.

28 Aristide R. Zolberg, "Global Movements, Global Walls: Responses to Migration, 1885-1925," in *Global History and Migrations*, ed. Wang Gungwu, 279-303 (Boulder, CO: Westview Press, 1997); Ian Hany-López, *White by Law: The Legal Construction of Race* (New York: New York University Press, 1996); Angelo N. Ancheta, *Race, Rights, and the Asian American Experience* (New Brunswick, NJ: Rutgers University Press, 1998); James W. St. G. Walker, *"Race," Rights and the Law in the Supreme Court of Canada: Historical Case Studies* (Waterloo: Wilfrid Laurier University Press, 1997); Rogers Smith, *Civic Ideals: Conflicting Visions of Citizenship in US History* (New Haven: Yale University Press, 1997); Rogers Smith, "Beyond Tocqueville, Myrdal, and Hartz: The Multiple Traditions in America," *American Political Science Review* 87, 2 (1993): 549-66; Desmond King, *Making Americans: Immigration, Race, and the Origins of Diverse Democracy* (Cambridge: Harvard University Press, 2000); Desmond King, "Making Americans: Immigration Meets Race," in *E Pluribus Unum? Contemporary and Historical Perspectives on Immigrant Political Incorporation*, ed. Gary Gerstle and John Mollenkopf, 143-74 (New York: Russell Sage Foundation, 2001); Gary Gerstle, *American Crucible: Race and Nation in the Twentieth Century* (Princeton: Princeton University Press, 2001); Uday Mehta, "Liberal Strategies of Exclusion," *Politics and Society* 18 (1990): 427-54; Uday Mehta, *Liberalism and Empire: A Study in Nineteenth-Century British Liberal Thought* (Chicago: University of Chicago Press, 1999).

29 Margaret Keck and Katherine Sikkink, *Activists beyond Borders: Advocacy Networks in International Politics* (Ithaca, NY: Cornell University Press, 1998); Beth A. Simmons, *Mobilizing for Human Rights: International Law in Domestic Politics* (Cambridge: Cambridge University Press, 2009).

30 Gordon L. Weil, "The Evolution of the European Convention on Human Rights," *American Journal of International Law* 57, 4 (1963): 805. See also Andrew Moravcsik, "The Origins of Human Rights Regimes: Democratic Delegation in Postwar Europe," *International Organization* 54, 2 (2000): 217-52.

31 Mikael Rask Madsen, "'Legal Diplomacy': Law, Politics and the Genesis of Postwar European Human Rights," in *Human Rights in the Twentieth Century*, ed. Stefan-Ludwig Hoffmann (Cambridge: Cambridge University Press, 2011), 62.

32 Tony Judt, *Postwar: A History of Europe since 1945* (New York: Penguin, 2005), 156-57.

33 Ibid., 303-04; Willem Maas, *Creating European Citizens* (Lanham, MD: Rowman and Littlefield, 2007).

34 Madsen, "Legal Diplomacy," 62.

35 Ninette Kelley and Michael Trebilcock, *The Making of the Mosaic: A History of Canadian Immigration Policy* (Toronto: University of Toronto Press, 1998), 251.

36 Blair Fraser, *The Search for Identity: Canada, 1945-1967* (Toronto: Doubleday Canada, 1967), 114.

37 Alan G. Green, *Immigration and the Postwar Canadian Economy* (Toronto: Macmillan, 1976), 18.

38 Of the twenty-two thousand people of Japanese origin in Canada in 1941, seventeen thousand were Canadian born and 3,288 had been naturalized. See John Herd Thompson, *Ethnic Minorities during Two World Wars* (Ottawa: Canadian Historical Association, 1991), 15.

39 See Ann Gomer Sunahara, *The Politics of Racism: The Uprooting of Japanese Canadians during the Second World War* (Toronto: Lorimer, 1981).

40 Franca Iacovetta, "Ordering in Bulk: Canada's Postwar Immigration Policy and the Recruitment of Contract Workers from Italy," *Journal of American Ethnic History* 11, 1 (1991): 50-80.

41 Donald Creighton, *The Forked Road: Canada, 1939-1957* (Toronto: McClelland and Stewart, 1976), 118.

42 Ibid., 118-23.

43 Kelley and Trebilcock, *Making of the Mosaic*, 311; Kenneth McNaught, *The Penguin History of Canada*, new ed. (London: Penguin, 1988), 272.

44 Harold Troper, "Canada's Immigration Policy since 1945," *International Journal* 48 (1993): 257.

45 A 1946 Gallup Poll asked: "If Canada does allow more immigration, are there any of these nationalities which you would like to keep out?" Forty-nine percent of the respondents replied that Jewish immigrants ought to be barred from Canada, second only to Japanese. The poll results are cited in Nancy Tienhaara, *Canadian Views on Immigration and Population* (Ottawa: Department of Manpower and Immigration, 1974), 59.

46 Canada, House of Commons, *Debates*, May 1, 1947, 2644-46.

47 The same held for other non-preferred groups. In responding to a private citizen's criticism of discrimination against "natives of the West Indies," the director of the Immigration Branch of the Department of Mines and Resources noted: "Experience has taught that, generally speaking, coloured people in the present state of the white man's thinking are not a tangible community asset, and as a result are more or less ostracized. They do not assimilate readily and pretty much vegetate at a standard of living. Many cannot adapt themselves to our climatic conditions." See Letter from A.L. Jolliffe to J.G. Levy (Private Secretary to the Minister), Library and Archives Canada (hereafter LAC), RG 76, vol. 830, file 552-1-644, pt. 2.

48 Green, *Immigration*, 21.

49 Patricia Roy, *The Triumph of Citizenship: The Japanese and Chinese in Canada, 1941-1967* (Vancouver: UBC Press, 2007), 161.

50 Stephanie D. Bangarth, "'We Are Not Asking You to Open Wide the Gates for Chinese Immigration': The Committee for the Repeal of the Chinese Immigration Act and Early Human Rights Activism in Canada," *Canadian Historical Review* 84, 3 (2003): 1-16; Kelley and Trebilcock, *Making of the Mosaic*, 321-22; F.J. McEvoy, "'A Symbol of Racial Discrimination': The Chinese Immigration Act and Canada's Relations with China, 1942-1947," *Canadian Ethnic Studies* 14, 3 (1982): 24-42.

51 Carol Lee, "The Road to Enfranchisement: Chinese and Japanese in British Col-
    umbia," *BC Studies* 30 (1976): 44-76. Among the most important steps in this regard
    was the repeal of P.C. 1378. The order-in-council had made naturalization in Canada
    dependent on approval from the *Chinese* minister of the interior, "thus handing over
    to another power the right to say who should have Canadian citizenship." See
    "Obnoxious Regulation," *Globe and Mail*, March 23, 1948.
52 Roy, *Triumph of Citizenship*, 173.
53 Lee, "Road to Enfranchisement," 75.
54 Ibid.
55 Creighton, *Forked Road*, 129. Robert Craig Brown, "Full Partnership in the Fortunes
    and in the Future of the Nation," in *Ethnicity and Citizenship: The Canadian Case*,
    ed. Jean Laponce and William Safran, 9-25 (London: Frank Cass, 1996).
56 "Under the new act, immigrants could naturalize after attaining twenty-one years of
    age, five years of residence, demonstrating adequate knowledge of English or French,
    and showing understanding of the responsibilities and privileges of Canadian cit-
    izenship. Language requirements were waived for those with more than twenty
    years of residence ... Immigrants who were already British subjects enjoyed special
    rights in Canada: after a year of residence, they could vote in Canadian elections
    without naturalizing, and they could gain Canadian citizenship after five years of
    residence without seeing a citizenship judge." See Irene Bloemraad, *Becoming a
    Citizen: Incorporating Immigrants and Refugees in the United States and Canada*
    (Berkeley: University of California Press, 2006), 25.
57 William Kaplan, *The Evolution of Citizenship Legislation in Canada* (Ottawa: Multi-
    culturalism and Citizenship Canada, 1990), 20.
58 Bloemraad, *Becoming a Citizen*, 25.
59 Freda Hawkins, *Canada and Immigration: Public Policy and Public Concern*, 2nd ed.
    (Montreal and Kingston: McGill-Queen's University Press, 1988), 94-95.
60 Hawkins, *Canada and Immigration*, 99.
61 Green, *Immigration*, 22-23.
62 Irving Abella and Harold Troper, *None Is Too Many: Canada and the Jews of Europe,
    1933-1948* (Toronto: Lester and Orpen Dennys, 1982), chaps. 7, 8.
63 Howard Palmer, "Ethnicity and Politics in Canada: 1867-Present," in *From "Melting
    Pot" to Multiculturalism*, ed. Valeria Gennaro Lerda (Rome: Bulzoni, 1990), 192;
    William Peterson, *Planned Migration: The Social Determinants of the Dutch-
    Canadian Movement* (Berkeley: University of California Press, 1955); Hawkins,
    Canada and Immigration, 86. See also the statements of labour leaders as recorded
    in "Minutes of a meeting on Immigration matters between representatives of Federal
    and Provincial Governments, Labour, Management and Voluntary Organizations ...
    March 19, 1956," LAC, RG 26, vol. 116, file 3-24-24, pt. 3 "Labour Unions (Rep-
    resentations – Immigration)."
64 Senate, Standing Committee on Immigration and Labour, *Proceedings* (Ottawa:
    Queen's Printer, 1946-53).
65 See Hawkins, *Canada and Immigration*, 82-84.
66 David C. Corbett, *Canada's Immigration Policy: A Critique* (Toronto: University of
    Toronto Press, 1957), 4-8.

67 "Labour's Views on Immigration," submitted by the Canadian Congress of Labour to the Senate Committee on Immigration, Ottawa, July 25, 1946.

68 Hawkins, *Canada and Immigration*, 84.

69 The following draws from Richard J.F. Day, *Multiculturalism and the History of Canadian Diversity* (Toronto: University of Toronto Press, 2000), 158-65.

70 Watson Kirkconnell, *Canadians All: A Primer of Canadian National Unity* (Ottawa: Director of Public Information, 1941), 11, cited in Day, *Multiculturalism*, 161.

71 See Hawkins, *Canada and Immigration*, 85.

72 Senate, Standing Committee on Immigration and Labour, *Proceedings*, 17, cited in Hawkins *Canada and Immigration*, 85.

73 Kelley and Trebilcock, *Making of the Mosaic*, 323.

74 "Asiatic Immigration into Canada," LAC, RG 76, vol. 854, file 554-5, pt. 1.

75 A subsequent report arrived at a similar conclusion. See "Canadian Immigration Policy in regard to Asia, November 30, 1950," LAC, RG 76, vol. 854, file 554-5, pt. 1.

76 Opponents of quotas argued that they were not as flexible as Canada's existing system and would also be expensive to administer "as officers would require to be assigned to many countries throughout the world to examine prospective immigrants and grant visas to those found admissible." See "Memorandum Re Immigration," n.d., LAC, RG 76, vol. 948, file SF-C-1, pt. 1.

77 Minister of Citizenship and Immigration, J.W. Pickersgill, admitted: "we agreed upon this quota with India as a gesture for the improvement of commonwealth relations." See Canada, House of Commons, Special Committee on Estimates, *Minutes of Proceedings and Evidence*, 11, March 14, 1955, 301. The Indian high commissioner was also lobbying the Department of External Affairs; pressure by the Indian government helps to explain the timing of the decision. See Letter from Head of Consular Division, L.G. Chance, to Director of Citizenship and Immigration, September 25, 1950, LAC, RG 76, vol. 854, file 554-5, pt. 1.

78 "Memorandum to Cabinet: Admission of Restricted Classes of Immigrants, June 10, 1952," LAC, RG 26, vol. 125, file 3-33-7, pt. 2.

79 Hawkins, *Canada and Immigration*, 102.

80 According to section 39 of the act: "No court and no judge or officer thereof has jurisdiction to review, quash, reverse, restrain or otherwise interfere with any proceeding, decision or order of the Minister, Deputy Minister, Director, Immigration Appeal Board, Special Inquiry Officer or immigration officer had, made or given under the authority and in accordance with the provisions of this Act relating to the detention or deportation of any person, upon any ground whatsoever, unless such a person is a Canadian citizen or has Canadian domicile." The full text of the Immigration Act, 1952, is available at http://www.canadiana.org/.

81 Reg Whittaker, *Double Standard: The Secret History of Canadian Immigration* (Toronto: Letser and Orpen Dennys, 1987).

82 Immigration from the British West Indies, June 30, 1957, LAC, RG 76, vol. 830, file 552-1-644, pt. 2.

83 Memorandum for file, May 2, 1957, LAC, RG 76, box 266, vol. 830, file 552-1-644; Memorandum from Deputy Minister to Director of Immigration, January 27, 1958, LAC, RG 76, box, 266, vol. 830, file 552-1-644.

84 Confidential Letter from Director of Immigration, C.E.S. Smith, to Under-Secretary of State for External Affairs, G. McInnes, January 17, 1957, LAC, RG 76, vol. 830, file 552-1-644, pt. 2.

85 Linda Freeman, *The Ambiguous Champion: Canada and South Africa in the Trudeau and Mulroney Years* (Toronto: University of Toronto Press, 1997), 19.

86 On the development of multilateralism in postwar Canadian foreign policy, see Tom Keating, *Canada and World Order: The Multilateralist Tradition in Canadian Foreign Policy* (Toronto: McClelland and Stewart, 1993).

87 See "Meeting of Prime Ministers of the Commonwealth: Report by Prime Minister John G. Diefenbaker on the Commonwealth Prime Ministers' Conference, House of Commons, May 16, 1960," in *Canadian Foreign Policy 1955-1965: Selected Speeches and Documents*, ed. Arthur E. Blanchette (Toronto: McClelland and Stewart, 1977), 302-06; Freeman, *Ambiguous Champion*, 25; Bothwell, *Alliance and Illusion*, 143-44.

88 "South Africa Out of the Commonwealth," CBC Television News, December 27, 1961, available at http://archives.cbc/ca/.

89 Telegraph from Canadian Trade Commissioner in Port-of Spain to Department of External Affairs, Ottawa, March 20, 1961: "We think it highly probable that as West Indians credit CDA [Canada] with having played important role leading to South African decision they will, logically or not, begin to question degree to which this attitude will affect CDN immigration policy vis-à-vis coloured migrants including themselves."

90 New groups such as the Chinese Canadian Association (CCA) also organized to demand changes to governmental policy. The CCA consulted with other more established groups, such as the Canadian Council of Churches, the Jewish Labour Committee of Canada, and the Women's International League, for help in preparing its brief. The CCA also lobbied members of Parliament. See Chinese Canadian Association, constitution, minutes, reports and statements, 1951-1959, LAC, MG 28, vol. 145.

91 For example, a February 1958 statement prepared by the National Japanese Canadian Citizens Association declared that "the existence of ... inequalities still written into the Immigration Act is inconsistent with the rights of Canadian citizens, and also denies the principle contained in Article 16 of the UN Universal Declaration of Human Rights to which Canada is a subscribing party. (Article 16: 'The family is the natural and fundamental group unit of society and is entitled to protection by society and state.')" See LAC, MG 28, vol. 145, file 1957-59.

92 "Immigration by Discrimination," *The Black Worker*, March 1952, LAC, RG 26, vol. 123, file 3-32-24.

93 "Representations of the Joint Committee of Oriental Associations of Calgary," May 1, 1960, LAC, RG 26, vol. 123, file 3-32-21. The brief was endorsed by the city councils of Calgary and Winnipeg, the mayor of Hamilton, the United Church of Canada, and the junior and senior chambers of commerce of Calgary, among others.

94 David Corbett, "Canada's Immigration Policy, 1957-1962," *International Journal* 18, 2 (1963): 173; Vic Satzewich, "The Canadian State and the Racialization of Caribbean Migrant Farm Labour, 1957-1966," *Ethnic and Racial Studies* 11, 3 (1988): 289;

"Canada's Commonwealth Immigration Problems," March 24, 1960, LAC, RG 76, vol. 830, file 552-1-644, pt. 3.

95 Letter from Minister of Citizenship and Immigration Ellen Fairclough to Mrs. M.N. Jones, March 16, 1961, LAC, RG 76, vol. 778, file 537-7, pt. 12. See also see the letter from Minister Fairclough to Sydney Williams, Secretary, Canadian Association for the Advancement of Coloured People, August 25, 1959, LAC, RG 76, vol. 830, file 552-1-644, pt. 2.

96 Memorandum to Cabinet: Immigration Agreements with Pakistan and Ceylon, October 23, 1958, LAC, RG 76, vol. 948, file SF-C-1-1, pt. 2.

97 Memorandum to Cabinet: Immigration Policies and Procedures (Immigration from China and Japan), August 8, 1958, LAC, RG 76, vol. 948, file SF-C-1-1, pt. 2.

98 Memorandum to Cabinet, Royal Commission on Immigration, November 30, 1959, LAC, RG 26, vol. 164, file 3-15-8, cited in Nobuaki Suyama, "The Politics of Canada's Immigration and Refugee Policy-Making: From Consensus to Counter-Consensus (PhD diss., University of Alberta, 1994), 125.

99 Suyama, "Politics," 126.

100 Canada, House of Commons, *Debates*, June 9, 1960, 4713, cited in Suyama, "Politics," 127.

101 For background, see Norman M. Naimark, *Fires of Hatred: Ethnic Cleansing in Twentieth-Century Europe* (Cambridge, MA: Harvard University Press, 2001), 108-38.

102 Rainer Schulze, "Growing Discontent: Relations between Native and Refugee Populations in a Rural District in Western Germany after the Second World War," *German History* 7 (1989): 332-50.

103 Sigmund Neumann, "The New Crisis Strata in German Society," in *Germany and the Future of Europe*, ed. Hans J. Morgenthau (Chicago: University of Chicago Press, 1951), 25-39.

104 Ulrich Herbert, *A History of Foreign Labor in Germany, 1880-1990* (Ann Arbor: University of Michigan Press, 1990), 193.

105 Figures are drawn from the United States' *Strategic Bombing Survey: The Effects of Strategic Bombing on the German War Economy* (Washington, DC: Government Printing Office, 1945), 140, in Herbert, *History of Foreign Labor*, 193.

106 Herbert, *History of Foreign Labor*, chap. 4. See also Ulrich Herbert, *Hitler's Foreign Workers: Enforced Foreign Labour in Germany under the Third Reich* (Cambridge: Cambridge University Press, 1997).

107 A situation worsened by the decimation of working-age German males during the war and a long-standing decline in the German birth rate. See Klaus J. Bade, *Vom Auswanderungsland zum Einwanderungsland? Deutschland 1880-1980* (Berlin: Colloquium Verlag, 1983), 61. The active recruitment of skilled German workers by countries such as Canada further compounded problems. See BDA (*Bundesvereinigung der deutschen Arbeitgeberverbände*), *Jahresberichte* (Cologne: BDA, 1951), 138-39.

108 "Vollbeschäftigung ja ... aber mit Reserven," *Der Arbeitgeber*, September 5, 1955, 568, cited in John Bendix, *Importing Foreign Workers: A Comparison of German and American Policy* (New York: Peter Lang, 1990), 16-17.

109 Ulrich Herbert and Karin Hunn, "Guest Workers and Policy on Guest Workers in the Federal Republic: From the Beginning of Recruitment in 1955 until Its Halt in 1973," in *The Miracle Years: A Cultural History of West Germany, 1949-1968*, ed. Hanna Schissler, (Princeton: Princeton University Press, 2000), 189.

110 Ibid., 189.

111 Bendix, *Importing Foreign Workers*, 21-22.

112 Cord Pagenstecher, "Die ungewollte Einwanderung: Rotationsprinzip und Rück-kehrerwartung in der deutschen Ausländerpolitik," *Geschichte in Wissenschaft und Unterricht* 46, 12 (1995): 719; Rita Chin, *The Guest Worker Question in Postwar Germany* (Cambridge: Cambridge University Press, 2006), 38.

113 Herbert, *History of Foreign Labor*, 206.

114 Ibid., 205.

115 Bendix, *Importing Foreign Workers*, 24. The description of the selection process that follows draws on Bendix's detailed account.

116 Fritz Franz, "The Legal Status of Foreign Workers in the Federal Republic of West Germany," in *Manpower Mobility across Cultural Boundaries: Social, Economic and Legal Aspects*, ed. R.E. Krane (Leiden: E.J. Brill, 1975), 48.

117 Karen Schönwälder, "'Ist nur Liberalisierung Fortschritt?' Zur Entstehung des ersten Ausländergesetzes der Bundesrepublik," in *50 Jahre Bundesrepublik – 50 Jahre Einwanderung: Nachkriegsgeschichte als Migrationsgeschichte*, ed. Jan Motte, Rainer Ohliger, Anne von Oswald (Frankfurt: Campus Verlag, 1999), 127-30. See also Karen Schönwälder, *Einwanderung und ethnische Pluralität: Politische Entscheidungen und öffentliche Debatten in Großbritannien und der Bundesrepublik von den 1950er bis zu den 1970er Jahren* (Essen: Klartext, 2001), 222.

118 Fritz Franz, "Zur Reform des Ausländer-Polizeirechts," *Deutsches Verwaltungsblatt*, November 1, 1963, 797-803; Cord Pagenstecher, *Ausländerpolitik und Immigran-tenidentität: Zur Geschichte der 'Gastarbeit' in der Bundesrepublik* (Berlin: Dieter Bertz Verlag, 1994), 32. Indeed, in 1960 the law was characterized by Interior Minister Gerhard Schröder as being of Prussian, as opposed to National Socialist, provenance. See Schönwälder, "Ist nur Liberalisierung Fortschritt," 129-30.

119 Herbert, *History of Foreign Labor*, 208.

120 Daniel Kanstroom, "*Wer Sind Wir Wieder*? Laws of Asylum, Immigration, and Citizenship in the Struggle for the Soul of the New Germany," *Yale Journal of International Law* 18, 1 (1993): 177; Matthias Bös, "Ethnisierung des Rechts? Staats-bürgerschaft in Deutschland, Frankreich, Großbritannien und den USA," *Kölner Zeitschrift für Soziologie und Sozialpsychologie* 45, 4 (1993): 619-43; Andreas Fahrmeir, *Citizenship: The Rise and Fall of a Modern Concept* (New Haven: Yale University Press, 2007), 173.

121 Christhard Hoffmann, "Immigration and Nationhood in the Federal Republic of Germany," in *The Postwar Transformation of Germany: Democracy, Prosperity, and Nationhood*, ed. John S. Brady, Beverly Crawford, and Sarah Elise Willarty (Ann Arbor: University of Michigan Press, 1999), 360. See also Patricia Hogwood, "Citizenship Controversies in Germany: The Twin Legacies of Völkisch Nationalism and the Alleinvertretungsanspruch," *German Politics* 9, 3 (2000): 125-44; and

Amanda Klekowski von Koppenfels, "The Decline of Privilege: The Legal Background to the Migration of Ethnic Germans," in *Coming Home to Germany? The Integration of Ethnic Germans from Central and Eastern Europe in the Federal Republic*, ed. David Rock and Stefan Wolff (New York: Berghahn Books, 2002), 102-6.

122 Cited in Rogers Brubaker, *Citizenship and Nationhood in France and Germany* (Cambridge: Harvard University Press, 1992), 169.

123 Fahrmeir, *Citizenship*, 174.

124 Douglas B. Klusmeyer, "Aliens, Immigrants, and Citizens: The Politics of Inclusion in the Federal Republic of Germany," *Daedalus* 122, 3 (1993): 84-85; Daniel Levy, "The Transformation of Germany's Ethno-Cultural Idiom," in *Challenging Ethnic Citizenship: German and Israeli Perspectives on Immigration*, ed. Daniel Levy and Yfaat Weiss (New York: Berghahn Books, 2002), 224.

125 Stefan Senders, "Laws of Belonging: Legal Dimensions of National Inclusion in Germany," *New German Critique* 67 (1996): 162.

126 Judgment of February 25, 1975, 39 BVerfGE 1, 67, cited in Kanstroom, "*Wer Sind Wir Wieder*," 167-68. See also Eli Nathans, *The Politics of Citizenship in Germany: Ethnicity, Utility and Nationalism* (Oxford: Berg, 2004), 235; Douglas B. Klusmeyer and Demetrios G. Papademetriou, *Immigration Policy in the Federal Republic of Germany: Negotiating Membership and Remaking the Nation* (New York: Berghahn Books, 2009), 3-4.

127 Basic Law, Article 3. See Kanstroom, "*Wer Sind Wir Wieder*," 168.

128 Including the right to assemble peaceably (Article 8); the right to form partnerships, associations, and corporations (Article 9); freedom of movement throughout Germany (Article 11); the right to choose an occupation, place of work, study or training (Article 12); the right not to be extradited (Article 16); the right to resist overthrow of the constitutional order (Article 20); the right to uniform rights and duties in each state (Article 33[1]); and eligibility for public office (Article 33 [2]).

129 Herbert, *History of Foreign Labor*, 210.

130 The agreements with Turkey and Portugal had initially included provisions for rotation (maximum stay clauses) and limits on family reunification. As is noted below, these provisions, insisted upon by the Federal Ministry of the Interior, were subsequently dropped in response to complaints by the labour and economics ministries, the Foreign Ministry, and the Turkish government.

131 For commentary on reaction to the "one millionth guest-worker," see Horst Berger, "Großer Bahnhof für Armando sa Rodrigues: Der millionste Gastarbeiter in der Bundesrepublik empfangen," *Frankfurter Allgemeine Zeitung*, September 11, 1964; Bendix, *Importing Foreign Workers*, 31.

132 Anne von Oswald, Karen Schönwälder, and Barbara Sonnenberger, "Labour Migration, Immigration Policy, Integration: Reinterpreting West Germany's History?" Paper presented at conference entitled "Assimilation, Diasporization, and Representation: Historical Perspectives on Immigrants and Host Societies in Postwar Europe," Berlin, October 2000, p. 4.

133 "Bertreuung der ausländischen Arbeitnehmer," in *Amtliche Nachrichten der Bundesanstalt für Arbeitsvermittlung und Arbeitsversicherung* (Nuremberg: Bundes-

anstalt für Arbeitsvermittlung und Arbeitsversicherung, 1965), reprinted in English translation (by David Gramling) in *Germany in Transition: Nation and Migration, 1955-2005*, ed. Deniz Göktürk, David Gramling, and Anton Kaes (Berkeley, CA: University of California Press, 2005), 37.

134 Chin, *Guest Worker Question*, 47.

135 Theodor Blank, "Ein Schritt zur Völkerverständigung," *Der Arbeitgeber*, 17, Jg. 1965, 280, cited in Chin, *Guest Worker Question*, 47. See also Karin Hunn, "Nächstes Jahr kehren wir zurück ... " in *Die Geschichte der türkischen "Gastarbeiter" in der Bundesrepublik* (Göttingen: Wallstein Verlag, 2005), 58.

136 Heike Knortz argues that Germany's decision to pursue bilateral treaties for foreign labour recruitment in the 1960s was based on foreign policy considerations rather than on labour market needs. See *Diplomatische Tauschgeschichte: Gastarbeiter in der westdeutschen Diplomatie und Beschäftigungspolitik, 1953-1973* (Cologne: Böhlau Verlag, 2008). While there is some support for her claim in the broader literature (e.g., Hunn, *Die Geschichte*, 29), contending approaches would suggest that, while important and hitherto underappreciated, foreign policy considerations worked in combination with, rather than instead of, considerations based on perceived economic needs.

137 The term "guest worker" (*Gastarbeiter*) was used in place of "foreign worker" (*Fremdarbeiter*) in official discourse because of the latter's association with the Third Reich. See Karen Schönwälder, "West German Society and Foreigners in the 1960s," in *Coping with the Nazi Past: West German Debates on Nazism and Generational Conflict, 1955-1975*, ed. Philipp Gassert and Alan E. Steinweis (New York: Berghahn Books, 2006), 115.

138 Valentin Siebrecht, "Verdienen in Deutschland: Die zweite Phase der Ausländerbeschäftigung," *Die Zeit*, May 22, 1964, cited in Chin, *Guest Worker Question*, 54.

139 "Gastarbeiter oder Einwanderer?" *Kirchenzeitung für das Erzbistum Köln*, April 12, 1964.

140 Eberhard de Haan, "Integration, Assimilation oder was?" in *Arbeitsplatz Europa: Langfristige Perspektiven und europäische Aspekte zum Problem ausländischer Arbeitnehmer – Europäische Schriften des Bildungswerks Europäische Politik* (Cologne: Institut für Europäische Politik, 1966), 11-53.

141 The following draws on Schönwälder "Zukunftsblindheit oder Steuerungsversagen? Zur Ausländerpolitik der Bundesregierung der 1960er und frühen 1970er Jahre," in *Migration steuern und verwalten: Deutschland vom späten 19. Jahrhundert bis zur Gegenwart*, ed. Jochen Oltmer, 127-32 (Göttingen: IMIS-Schriften, Bd. 12, 2003). See also Anne von Oswald, Karen Schönwälder, and Barbara Sonnenberger, "*Einwanderungsland Deutschland*: A New Look at Its Post-War History," in *European Encounters*, 23; and Hunn, *Die Geschichte*, 47-70.

142 Hunn, *Die Geschichte*, 59.

143 Interior Minister Herman Höcherl, cited in Schönwälder, *Einwanderung und ethnische Pluralität*, 234.

144 Peter O'Brien, "Continuity and Change in Germany's Treatment of Non-Germans," *International Migration Review* 22, 3 (1988): 116. See also Helmut Rittstieg,

"Grundzüge des Aufenthaltsrechts," in *Einwanderungsland Bundesrepublik Deutschland?* ed. Gerhard Schult (Baden-Baden: Nomos Verlaggesellschaft, 1982), 32.

145 Chin, *Guest Worker Question*, 51. See also Günter Weißmann, *Ausländergesetz: Kommentar* (Berlin: De Gruyter, 1966), 34. Weißmann notes that the German government's emphasis on the liberality of its new foreigners law was in part for foreign consumption.

146 Schönwälder, "Zur Ausländerpolitik," 130-31.

147 Ibid., 132.

148 The Treaty of Rome, 25 March 1957, available at http://ec.europa.eu/.

149 Schönwälder, *Einwanderung und ethnische Pluralität*, 287.

150 The no non-Europeans stipulation is examined in detail in Karen Schönwälder, "Why Germany's Guest Workers Were Largely Europeans: The Selective Principles of Post-War Labour Recruitment Policy," *Ethnic and Racial Studies* 27, 2 (2003): 248-65.

151 "Zahl der Gastarbeiter ging um 24.5% zurück," *Bulletin der Bundesregierung*, March 21, 1968; Schönwälder, *Einwanderung und ethnische Pluralität*, 209.

152 Herbert, *History of Foreign Labor*, 224; Oswald et al., *"Einwanderungsland Deutschland,"* 25.

153 Karen Schönwälder, "The Difficult Task of Managing Migration: The 1973 Recruitment Stop," in *German History from the Margins*, ed. Neil Gregor, Nils Roemer, and Mark Roseman (Bloomington: Indiana University Press, 2006), 253.

154 See, for example, "Gastarbeiter – nützlich und gefragt, aber nicht beliebt," *Industriekurrier*, October 12, 1968; "Interview mit Walter Arendt," *Handelsblatt*, December 18, 1969; Walter Arendt, "Zum Geleit," *Das Parlament*, 21, 34-35, August 21, 1971, cited in Schönwälder, *Einwanderung und ethnische Pluralität*, 502.

155 Schönwälder, *Einwanderung und ethnische Pluralität*, 500.

156 Bundesanstalt für Arbeit, "Ergebnisse einer Repräsentativuntersuchung der Bundesanstalt: Ausländische Arbeitnehmer – Beschäftigung, Anwerbung, Vermittlung – Erfahrungsbericht 1969" (Nuremberg, 1970), 48-54, cited in Schönwälder, *Einwanderung und ethnische Pluralität*, 514.

157 These figures are based on yearly reports of the *Bundesanstalt für Arbeit*, cited in Herbert, *History of Foreign Labor*, 231.

158 Gunther Wollny, "Ausländer in der Bundesrepublik," *Bayern Kurier*, May 27, 1972.

159 Albert Müller, "Der Staat soll Gastarbeitern die Einbürgerung erleichtern," *Die Welt*, April 19, 1971; "In Zukunft deutsche Staatsangehörige?" *Rheinische Merkur*, April 30, 1971; "Sollen Gastarbeiter Deutsche werden?" *Quick*, April 28, 1971.

160 Presse- und Informationsamt der Bundesregierung, *Kommetarübersicht* (nach dem Gespräch BM Arendt-Stingl), March 30, 1971; "Nicht mehr Gäste, sondern Mitbürger," *Rheinische Post*, April 22, 1971; Wolfgang Borgmann, "Gast-Arbeiter?" *Stuttgarter Zeitung*, September 25, 1971; Franz Woschech, "Bald noch mehr Gastarbeiter," *Handelsblatt*, November 12-13, 1971; Rolf Weber, "Die BRD ist kein Einwanderungland," *Handelsblatt*, November 12-13, 1971; Gernot Römer, "Mitbürger aus der Fremde," *Augsburger Allgemeine*, January 29, 1972.

161 Schönwälder, "Zur Ausländerpolitik," 134.

162 See Rolf Weber, "Rotationsprinzip bei der Beschäftigung von Ausländern," *Auslandskurier* 11, 5 (1970): 10; "Rotation, Integration und Folgelasten," *Arbeit und Sozialpolitik* 27 (1973): 203-06.

163 Key L. Ulrich, "Was soll aus den Gastarbeitern werden?" *Frankfurter Allgemeine Zeitung*, May 25, 1973.

164 "Alternativentwurf 1970 zum Ausländergesetz 1965," *Studentische Politik* 1 (1970): 5-9.

165 "DGB kritisiert: Ausländergesetz verstößt gegen die Verfassung," *Westdeutsche Allgemeine Zeitung*, September 2, 1971.

166 Deutscher Gewerkschaftsbund, Bundesvorstand, *Forderung des DGBs zur Reform des Ausländerrechts*, February 8, 1973, cited in Bendix, *Importing Foreign Workers*, 57.

167 Herbert, *History of Foreign Labor*, 231.

168 "Politik der Bundesregierung gegenüber den ausländischen Arbeitnehmern in der Bundesrepublik Deutschland," Verhandlung des Deutschen Bundestags, 6, Wahlperiode, Anlagen, *Drucksache*, 3085, January 31, 1972, 4, cited in Schönwälder, "Zur Ausländerpolitik," 135.

169 Author's interview with Rosi-Wolf Almanasreh de C. Estevez, Frankfurt am Main, March 22, 2002. For details, see Schönwälder, *Einwanderung und ethnische Pluralität*, 547-63.

170 Nathans, *Politics of Citizenship*, 239.

171 Franz, "Legal Status of Foreign Workers," 57.

172 "Besuch in Rüsselsheim," *Bulletin des Presse- und Informationsamtes der Bundesregierung*, 2/3, January 4, 1974, 796-97.

173 Hans Dietrich Genscher, interview in the *Westdeutsche Allgemeine Zeitung*, October 5, 1972.

174 Hans Apel, "Vorurteil überwinden," *Neue Ruhr Zeitung*, June 12, 1971, cited in Schönwälder, *Einwanderung und ethnische Pluralität*, 549; "SPD fordert mehr Rechte für die Gastarbeiter," *SPD – Pressedienst*, July 27, 1973, cited in Schönwälder, *Einwanderung und ethnische Pluralität*, 549.

175 "Aktionsprogramm für Ausländerbeschäftigung" *Bulletin der Bundesregierung*, June 8, 1973, cited in Bendix, *Importing Foreign Workers*, 66.

176 "Rede vor dem Deutschen Städte- und Gemeindebund," October 5, 1973, cited in Schönwälder, *Einwanderung und ethnische Pluralität*, 562.

177 "Massnahmen zur Eindämmung der Ausländerbeschäftigung," *Bulletin der Bundesregierung*, November 27, 1973, cited in Bendix, *Importing Foreign Workers*, 68.

178 Cited in Schönwälder, "Zur Ausländerpolitik," 140.

179 Stephen Castles notes that the number of women over 16 years of age per 1,000 men rose from 585 in 1974 to 715 in 1984. See Stephen Castles, "The Guests Who Stayed: The Debate on 'Foreigners Policy' in the German Federal Republic," *International Migration Review* 19, 3 (1985): 520. See also *Report by the Federal Government's Commissioner for Foreigners' Affairs on the Situation of Foreigners in the Federal Republic of Germany in 1993* (Bonn: Beauftragte der Bundesregierung für Ausländerfragen, March 1994), 92-93.

180 Faruk Şen and Andreas Goldberg, *Türken in Deutschland: Leben zwischen zwei Kulturen* (Munich: C.H. Beck, 1994), 20-22. See also Martin Frey, "Ausländer in der Bundesrepublik Deutschland: Ein Statistischer Überblick," *Aus Politik und Zeitgeschichte,* June 26, 1982, 3-16; Jürgen Fijalkowski, "Nationale Identität versus multikulturelle Gesellschaft: Entwicklung der Problemlage und Alternativen der Orientierung in der politischen Kultur der Bundesrepublik in den 80er Jahren," in *Die Bundesrepublik in den achtziger Jahren: Innenpolitik, Politische Kultur, Außen-politik,* ed. Werner Süß (Opladen: Leske and Budrich, 1991), 237.

181 Stephen Castles, "Racism and Politics in Germany," *Race and Class* 25, 3 (1984): 40.

182 Herbert, *History of Foreign Labor*, 238.

CHAPTER 4: DISMANTLING WHITE CANADA

1 Brooke Jeffrey and Philip Rosen, "The Protection of Human Rights in Canada (1)," *Canadian Regional Review* 2, 3 (1979): 37-54; R. Brian Howe, "The Evolution of Human Rights Policy in Ontario," *Canadian Journal of Political Science* 24, 4 (1991): 783-802; Ross Lambertson, "'The Dresden Story': Racism, Human Rights, and the Jewish Labour Committee of Canada," *Labour/Le Travail* 47 (2001): 29-44; Ross Lambertson, *Repression and Resistance: Canadian Human Rights Activists, 1930-1960* (Toronto: University of Toronto Press, 2004); Ross Lambertson, "The Black, Brown, White and Red Blues: The Beating of Clarence Clemons," *Canadian Historical Review* 85, 4 (2004): 755-76; James W. St. G. Walker, "The 'Jewish Phase' in the Movement for Racial Equality in Canada," *Canadian Journal of Ethnic Studies* 34, 1 (2002): 1-29; James Walker, *"Race," Rights and the Law in the Supreme Court of Canada: Historical Case Studies* (Waterloo: University of Wilfrid Laurier Press, 1997); Carmela Patrias and Ruth A. Frager, "'This Is Our Country, These Are Our Rights': Minorities and the Origins of Ontario's Human Rights Campaigns," *Canadian Historical Review* 82 (2001): 1-35.

2 Alan G. Green, *Immigration and the Postwar Canadian Economy* (Toronto: Macmillan-Hunter Press, 1976), 34-35. See also Peter Li, *Destination Canada: Immigration Debates and Issues* (Toronto: Oxford University Press, 2003), 23. Freda Hawkins, along with Ninette Kelley and Michael Trebilcock, qualify the economic determinism of positions such as Green's by flagging the importance of foreign policy concerns and changing ideas. See Freda Hawkins, *Canada and Immigration: Public Policy and Public Concern,* 2nd ed. (Montreal and Kingston: McGill-Queen's University Press, 1988); Freda Hawkins, *Critical Years in Immigration: Canada and Australia Compared* (Kingston and Montreal: McGill-Queen's University Press, 1989); Ninette Kelley and Michael Trebilcock, *The Making of the Mosaic: A History of Canadian Immigration Policy* (Toronto: University of Toronto Press, 1998).

3 See Memorandum from Director of Immigration to Deputy Minister of Department of Citizenship and Immigration: Immigration Policy and Programming as Related to Economic and Employment Factors in Canada, December 9, 1960, Library and Archives Canada (hereafter LAC), RG 26, vol. 75, file 1-1-1, pt. 2.

4 Efforts were stepped up to generate increased immigration from traditional European sources through advertising and other means. It was felt that Canada's

passive approach to immigration was costing it in terms of attracting highly skilled Europeans. See materials in LAC, RG 26, vol. 75, file 1-1-8, pt. 3; LAC RG 76, vol. 909, file 572-15, pt. 2; and LAC, RG 76, vol. 778, file 537-7, pt. 14. At the same time, overall admissions were scaled back significantly as a consequence of the recession of February 1960-March 1961. See David M. Reimers and Harold Troper, "Canadian and American Immigration Policy since 1945," in *Immigration, Language, and Ethnicity: Canada and the United States*, ed. Barry R. Chiswick (Washington, DC: AEI Press, 1992), 32.

5 Hawkins notes that the 1961 Report of the Special Committee of the Senate on Manpower and Employment "reinforced the ideas of those who were preparing the new immigration regulations in the summer of 1961, in which the emphasis in admission was on skill." See Hawkins, *Canada and Immigration*, 139.

6 Memorandum from the Director of Immigration to the Deputy Minister, November 10, 1961, LAC, RG 26, vol. 100, file 3-15-1, pt. 8.

7 Memorandum to Cabinet Re: Immigration Regulations, October 16, 1961, LAC, RG 26, vol. 100, file 3-15-1, pt. 8.

8 Memorandum to Cabinet Re: Immigration Regulations, October 16, 1961, LAC, RG 26, vol. 100, file 3-15-1, pt. 8.

9 Ibid.

10 Ibid.

11 Ibid.

12 Canada, House of Commons, *Debates*, 24th Parliament, 5th Session, vol. 1, 1962, 10.

13 See LAC, RG 26, vol. 100, file 3-15-1, Canadian Immigration Act and Regulations – Amendments to.

14 Hawkins, *Canada and Immigration*, 31; Dominique Daniel, "The Debate on Family Reunification and Canada's Immigration Act of 1976," *American Review of Canadian Studies* 35, 4 (2005): 686-87.

15 Memorandum to Cabinet: Immigration Policies and Procedures (Immigration from China and Japan), August 8, 1958, LAC, RG 76, vol. 948, file SF-C-1-1, pt. 2.

16 Aide Memoire, Increasing Immigration to Canada, n.d., LAC, RG 76, vol. 816, file 551-10-1963, pt. 2. See also Draft Immigration Program – 1963-1964, LAC, RG 76, vol. 816, file 551-10-1963, pt. 1.

17 "In 1960 ... Canada maintained twenty-seven immigration offices outside North America. Twenty-four were in Europe and three in Asia (one of these being in Israel). None were in Africa or South America ... In 1963 a Canadian immigration office was opened in Egypt." See Reimers and Troper, "Canadian and American Immigration Policy," 33.

18 Memorandum to the Deputy Minister: Revision of Immigration Regulations, October 27, 1961, LAC, RG 26, vol. 1000, file 3-15-1, pt. 8.

19 Memorandum to the Deputy Minister: Revision of Immigration Regulations, October 27, 1961, LAC, RG 26, vol. 1000, file 3-15-1, pt. 8.

20 Langevin Cote, "Immigration Rule Change Starts Feb. 1," *Globe and Mail*, January 20, 1962.

21 "The Opening Door," *Globe and Mail*, January 22, 1962.

22 "Chinese See Ambiguity in Relaxed Entry Laws," *Globe and Mail*, January 22, 1962. See also Patricia Roy, *The Triumph of Citizenship: The Japanese and Chinese in Canada, 1941-1967* (Vancouver: UBC Press, 2007), 283.

23 Press reaction to the new immigration regulations, n.d., LAC, RG 26, vol. 100, file 3-15-1, pt. 4.

24 Memorandum to all posts abroad from Chief of Operations, Immigration Branch, regarding the Immigration Programme 1963, March 14, 1963, LAC, RG 76, vol. 816, file 551-10-1963, pt. 2; Memorandum from Attaché, Canadian Embassy Visa Office, Cologne, to Acting Chief of Operations [Department of Citizenship and Immigration], Ottawa, Annual Report for Germany for the Calendar Year 1962, LAC, RG 76, vol. 767, file 527-2-1962.

25 "I learned of the significance of administrative delay when I visited India. This was done at the request of Roland Michner, then our High Commissioner in New Delhi, who had told his friend the Prime Minister of his concern that our handling of immigration was giving us a bad name. I understood his concern when I went into a file room stacked to the ceiling with letters that had not even been opened." See Tom Kent, *A Public Purpose: An Experience of Liberal Opposition and Canadian Government* (Kingston and Montreal: McGill-Queen's University Press, 1988), 409.

26 Memorandum to the Minister from the Deputy Minister, January 21, 1963, LAC, RG 76, vol. 778, file 537-7, pt. 14.

27 Memorandum to the Minister, October 19, 1962, LAC, RG 76, vol. 778, file 537-7, pt. 14.

28 Letter from Immigration Attaché, New Delhi, India, to Acting Chief of Operations (Administrative Services), Department of Citizenship and Immigration, October 3, 1961, LAC, RG 76, vol. 823, file 552-1-567, pt. 2, Immigration from India General file.

29 "If we agree to relax our selection criteria, I am afraid areas of Montreal and Toronto would become inhabited by these people, mainly gaining entrance through the sponsored route, eventually producing a situation similar to that existing in London, England." See "Reviewing of applicants for immigration to Canada in Jamaica from January 10, 1963 to March 15, 1963," LAC, RG 76, vol. 824, box 200, file 552-1-577, Immigration from Jamaica: Policy and Instructions. On the British case, see Randall Hansen, *Citizenship and Immigration in Post-War Britain: The Institutional Origins of a Multicultural Nation* (Oxford: Oxford University Press, 2000), 80-99.

30 Confidential information for the prime minister: Canada and Commonwealth immigration, LAC, RG 26, vol. 145, file 3-33-6, Canada – West Indies Conference [1965].

31 David Corbett, "Canada's Immigration Policy, 1957-1962," *International Journal* 18, 2 (1962-63): 169.

32 Letter from Roy W. Blake, Canadian Government Trade Commissioner in Jamaica, to D.A. Reid, Chief of Operations, Immigration Branch, Department of Citizenship and Immigration, February 18, 1962, Subject: Revised Canadian Immigration Laws, LAC, RG 76, vol. 830, file 552-1-644, pt. 4. Blake noted that the response to the new regulations was overwhelming but that close to 90 percent of the applicants were likely to be rejected because they did not meet the government's skills requirement.

The lack of any clear standard for determining decisions heightened suspicions of racial discrimination. Blake requested some further clarification of what was meant by "skills" and "training." See also letter from G.C. McInnes, Office of the High Commissioner for Canada in Kingston Jamaica, to Under-Secretary of State for the Department of External Affairs, August 2, 1963, LAC, RG 76, vol. 830, file 552-1-644. On November 5, 1963, the *Globe and Mail* asked whether Canada was seeking "immigrants as actively in places such as the West Indies as in Western Europe."

33 Circular Document from Under-Secretary of State for External Affairs to the Heads of Posts Abroad: Effect of New Canadian Immigration Regulations, August 2, 1962, LAC, RG 25, vol. 5005, file 232-40, pt. 16.

34 Memo to Under-Secretary of State for External Affairs from Office of High Commissioner for Canada, Port-of-Spain, October 1, 1962, LAC, RG 25, vol. 5005, file 232-40, pts. 15, 16; Telegram from the Immigration Attaché in Delhi, India, to External Affairs regarding Canadian Immigration Procedures, March 19, 1963, LAC, RG 25, vol. 5006, box 232-40, file: Immigration to Canada (Regulations, Policy, Procedures). Similar complaints came in from throughout the "Third World." See letter from Canadian Consul General in the Philippines, T.G. Major, to Director of Immigration, Department of Citizenship and Immigration, W.R. Baskerville, September 21, 1962, LAC, RG 25, vol. 5005, file 232-40, pts.15, 16. Also consult materials in LAC, RG 19, acc. 87-88/011, 29, file 5945-00, pt. 2.

35 Hawkins, *Canada and Immigration*, 48-49.

36 Ibid.

37 The opposition Liberals did much to encourage Italian-Canadians' outrage. Former minister of citizenship and immigration Jack Pickersgill accused the Tories of implementing the policy because they "realized that more people of Italian origin than people from the United Kingdom came in last year ... They were afraid of many of their political supporters, and they felt they had to do something about it. Then they did this stupid, silly and inhumane thing." See Canada, House of Commons, *Debates, Official Report*, 24th Parliament, 2nd Session, no. 3, 1959, 2711. See also J. W. Pickersgill, *The Road Back: By a Liberal in Opposition* (Toronto: University of Toronto Press, 1986), 84-85.

38 The Diefenbaker Conservatives' interest in competing with the Liberal Party for the support of "ethnic voters" has not drawn the attention it deserves. For a notable exception, see C.P. Champion, *The Strange Demise of British Canada: The Liberals and Canadian Nationalism, 1964-1968* (Montreal and Kingston: McGill-Queen's University Press, 2010), 138-64. Champion persuasively argues that the Conservatives and Liberals actively courted the immigrant vote from the 1950s onward. Political incorporation therefore served as another means of expanding the scope of Canadian membership. See also Roy, *Triumph of Citizenship*, 284-87; Howard Palmer, "Ethnicity and Politics in Canada: 1867-Present," in *From "Melting Pot" to Multiculturalism: The Evolution of Ethnic Relations in the United States and Canada*, ed. Valeria Gennaro Lerda (Rome: Bulzoni Editore, 1990), 195-96.

39 J.L. Finlay and D.N. Sprague, *The Structure of Canadian History* (Toronto: Prentice-Hall, 1997), 441-44.

40 "Questions," *Globe and Mail*, November 5, 1963.

41 Brief from the Chinese Benevolent Association to Minister of Citizenship and Immigration Guy Favreau, December 1963, LAC, RG 76, vol. 819, file 552-1-526, pt. 4.

42 "Japan Wants Canada's Door Opened," *Toronto Telegram*, December 4, 1964. See also related materials in LAC, RG 76, vol. 1109, file 552-1-578, "Immigration from Japan Policy."

43 Comments on Liberal Party Resolution, September 20, 1962, LAC, RG 76, vol. 778, file 537-7, pt. 14. See also Champion, *Strange Demise*, 152-53; Roy, *Triumph of Citizenship*, 290; and Pickersgill, *Road Back*, 85-86.

44 In an effort to follow through on his predecessor's positions on South Africa, Pearson had signed the Declaration of Racial Equality at the Commonwealth Prime Ministers conference in 1964.

45 Daniel Tichenor, *Dividing Lines: The Politics of Immigration Control in America* (Princeton: Princeton University Press, 2002), 207-18; Aristide R. Zolberg: *A Nation by Design: Immigration Policy in the Fashioning of America* (New York/Cambridge, MA: Russell Sage Foundation/Harvard University Press, 2006), 325-36.

46 Prime Minister Lester B. Pearson's Press Conference, Jamaica, November 30, 1965, LAC, RG 76, vol. 824, file 552-1-577. A year later, Pearson called for the extension of the Assisted Passenger and Loans Scheme to the West Indies. See Memorandum to the Cabinet Committee on the Canada-West Indies Conference from the Prime Minister, May 30, 1966, LAC, RG 76, vol. 948, file SF-C-1.1, pt. 1.

47 Vic Satzewich, "The Canadian State and the Racialization of Caribbean Farm Labour: The Government's View of Caribbean Migration, 1962-1966," *Canadian Ethnic Studies* 21, 1 (1989): 295.

48 Given that temporary workers lacked sponsorship rights, the 1965 decision to accept farm workers from the Caribbean was deemed a low-cost means of deflecting "pressure to accept unskilled workers from the West Indies as immigrants." See memo from the Assistant Deputy Minister of Immigration to the Deputy Minister, Department of Citizenship and Immigration, January 13, 1965, LAC, RG 76, vol. 842, file 553-67, pt. 1, cited in Satzewich, "Canadian State," 295.

49 "Immigration to Canada from the Commonwealth Caribbean (Background Paper Prepared by Canada)," LAC, RG 26, vol. 125, file 3-33-6.

50 Memorandum to the Cabinet Committee on Immigration, October 15, 1964, LAC, RG 76, vol. 948, file SF-C-1-1, pt. 3.

51 Memorandum from Assistant Deputy Minister, E.P. Beasley, to Deputy Minister, Tom Kent, regarding Conference of Commonwealth Caribbean Countries in Canada, May 26, 1966, LAC, RG 26, vol. 125, file 3-33-6. See also memorandum to the Cabinet Committee on Immigration, October 15, 1964, LAC, RG 76, vol. 948, file SF-C-1-1, pt. 3: "In short, if sponsored immigration is to be more than a humanitarian program and become a real asset to our expanding economy in terms both of consumption and production, it must be placed on a more selective basis, especially considering that without a change of this sort there is serious danger of a substantial and largely uncontrollable sponsored movement in the future from many of the underdeveloped countries which are beginning to make a small but significant contribution to our total immigration."

52 Memorandum to the Cabinet on Immigration Policy, October 15, 1964, LAC, RG 76, vol. 777, file 536-52, pt. 1.

53 Hawkins, *Canada and Immigration*, 151-53; Louis Parai, "Canada's Immigration Policy, 1962-1974," *International Migration Review* 9, 4 (1975): 449-77. The Citizenship Branch of the old Department of Citizenship and Immigration was shifted to the Department of the Secretary of State. See Leslie A. Pal, *Interests of State: the Politics of Language, Multiculturalism, and Feminism in Canada* (Montreal and Kingston: McGill-Queen's University Press, 1993), 97.

54 Tom Kent, who served as Marchand's first deputy minister in the newly formed Department of Manpower, believed that Marchand was genuinely aggrieved by the persistence of discrimination in Canada's immigration policies. Tom Kent, interview with author, Kingston, Ontario, August 3, 2006.

55 Canada, Department of Manpower and Immigration, *White Paper on Immigration* (Ottawa: Queen's Printer and Controller of Stationery, October 1966). A White Paper is an "official document presented by Ministers of the Crown which state and explain the government's policy on a certain issue ...'[G]reen-papers' are issued by government to invite public comment and discussion on an issue prior to policy formulation." See Parliament of Canada, White Papers, http://www.parl.gc.ca/.

56 Canada, *White Paper on Immigration*, 17.

57 Ibid., 15.

58 Memorandum to Cabinet, Immigration White Paper – Sponsored Immigration to Canada, November 24, 1965, LAC, RG 76, vol. 948, file SF-C-1-1, pt. 3.

59 Canada, House of Commons, *Debates*, "Tabling of White Paper on Government Policy," October 14, 1966, 8652.

60 Memorandum to Cabinet, Admissible Classes and Security Screening of Immigrants, June 22, 1966, LAC RG 76, vol. 823, file 552-1-567, pt. 2; Memorandum to Cabinet, Immigration White Paper – Sponsored Immigration to Canada, November 24, 1965, LAC, RG 76, vol. 948, file SF-C-1-1, pt. 3.

61 "A compromise of this nature will not please the ethnic groups but it is hard for them to criticize effectively and probably is better than many of them expect. It should be seen as reasonable to public opinion generally, particularly as it can be applied on a non-discriminatory basis." See Memorandum to Cabinet: Admissible Classes and Security Screening of Immigrants, June 22, 1966, LAC, RG 19, vol. 5798, file 5945-00, pt. 2.

62 Canada, Special Joint Committee of the Senate and House of Commons on Immigration, *Minutes of the Proceedings and Evidence* (Ottawa: Queen's Printer and Controller of Stationery, 1967), 535-37, 565-66. For a useful summary of several of the briefs submitted by groups appearing before the Committee, see Kelley and Trebilcock, *Making of the Mosaic*, 354-58.

63 Canada, Special Joint Committee of the Senate and House of Commons on Immigration, *Minutes of the Proceedings and Evidence*, 4, December 13, 1966, 126-27.

64 Reimers and Troper, "Canadian and American Immigration Policy," 35.

65 "A statement in a White Paper, no matter how laudable, [is] no substitute for law and there is nowhere in the White Paper any suggestion that this policy of no discrimination, which is the mood of our times, should be incorporated into the substance of

law rather than remain merely a statement. The White Paper will be lost but a blue paper, being an immigration act, will take this place and that either will say something about it or will not say anything about it. If it says nothing about it, then it is left in a vague situation where some pious declarations were made." See Statement of Saul Hayes, Vice-President, Canadian Jewish Congress, February 22, 1967, in Canada, Special Joint Committee of the Senate and House of Commons on Immigration, *Minutes of the Proceedings and Evidence*, 9, 407.

66 Hawkins, *Canada and Immigration*, 159.
67 Kent, interview with author.
68 Hawkins, *Canada and Immigration*, 162.
69 Kent, *A Public Purpose*, 409.
70 Kent, *Public Purpose*, 409-10. In an interview with the author (Kingston, Ontario, August 3, 2006) Tom Kent also noted that the version of the White Paper that he was given after taking up the position of deputy minister amounted to little more than a defence of the status quo. While efforts were made to improve the text, some of the earlier draft's defensive tone remained in the penultimate version of the White Paper.
71 Kent, *Public Purpose*, 410.
72 Remarks to the Parliamentary Committee on Immigration by the Honourable Jean Marchand, Minister of Manpower and Immigration, April 18, 1967, LAC, RG 76, vol. 965, file 5000-14-2, pt. 13; Tom Kent, interview with author.
73 Memorandum to Cabinet re: a new immigration selection system – amendments to the immigration regulations, pt. 1, July 31, 1967, LAC, RG 76, vol. 948, file SF-C-1-1, pt. 3.
74 Memorandum from the Assistant Deputy Minister (Immigration) to the Deputy Minister on the Parliamentary Committee on Immigration, February 19, 1968, 6, LAC, RG 76 vol. 966, file 5000-14-2, pt. 14.
75 Remarks for Parliamentary Committee on Immigration, Minister of Manpower and Immigration, April 11, 1967, LAC, RG 76, vol. 823, file 552-1-567, pt. 2.
76 Memorandum to Cabinet re: a new immigration selection system – amendments to the immigration regulations, pt. 1, LAC, RG 76, vol. 948, file SF-C-1-1, pt. 3.
77 This paragraph draws on Department of Manpower and Immigration, Information Service Project Instructions, 10/67 (Draft), July 1967, LAC, RG76, vol. 965, file 5000-14-2, pt. 13.
78 Michael Gillan, "Point Count Will Assess Immigrants," *Globe and Mail*, September 14, 1967.
79 "Immigration: An End to Hit-and-Miss," *Toronto Star*, September 14, 1967.
80 Ibid.
81 Department of Manpower and Immigration Information Service Project Instruction, 10/67 (Draft), July 1967, LAC, RG 76, vol. 965, file 5000-14-2, pt. 13.
82 Kent, interview with author.
83 Gerald Dirks, *Canada's Refugee Policy: Indifference or Opportunism?* (Montreal and Kingston: McGill-Queen's University Press, 1977), 233-34; Michael Lanphier, "Canada's Response to Refugees," *International Migration Review* 15, 1-2 (1981): 114.

84 Aristide R. Zolberg (with the assistance of Ursula Levelt), "Response to Crisis: Refugee Policy in the United States and Canada," in *Immigration, Language, and Ethnicity: Canada and the United States*, ed. Barry R. Chiswick (Washington, DC: AEI Press, 1992), 66.

85 Reimers and Troper, "Canadian and American Immigration Policy," 38.

86 Zolberg, "Response to Crisis," 66.

87 Mass public opinion was less certain. A January 1965 Gallup Poll found that 44 percent of Canadians believed the present population level was "about right," 48.6 percent believed it should be "much larger," and 7.4 percent were undecided (see Table 6). Another poll conducted by Gallup in September 1965 asked whether Canadians approved or disapproved of the government's intention to "bring thousands of skilled workers" to Canada: 37.4 percent of respondents approved, 49.9 percent disapproved, 5.7 percent offered qualified approval, and 7 percent expressed no opinion. A 1966 Gallup Poll found that 36.5 percent of respondents disapproved of the government's immigration policy, while 36.2 percent approved and 27.3 remained undecided. The results of these polls suggest that the Canadian population as a whole did not share Canadian elites' interest in implementing decisive changes in immigration policy. For polling results, see Nancy Tienhaara, *Canadian Views on Immigration and Population* (Ottawa: Department of Manpower and Immigration, 1974), 71-72.

88 In responding to a journalist's query as to whether there was any way of justifying Canada's admissions policy short of racial discrimination, Pickersgill noted: "I don't know the difference between the word 'selective' and the word 'discrimination.' In my vocabulary they both mean the same thing. We say we have a selective immigration policy, that means we have a discriminatory immigration policy." See "Press Conference interviewing Jack Pickersgill," November 24, 1954, LAC, RG 26, vol. 92, file 3-5-6.

89 See Robert Bothwell, Ian Drummond, and John English, *Canada since 1945: Power, Politics, and Provincialism*, rev. ed. (Toronto: University of Toronto Press, 1989), 315; Kenneth McRoberts, *Misconceiving Canada: The Struggle for National Unity* (Toronto: Oxford University Press, 1997), 31-54; J.L. Granatstein, *Canada 1957-1967: The Years of Uncertainty and Innovation* (Toronto: McClelland and Stewart, 1986); Richard J.F. Day, *Multiculturalism and the History of Canadian Diversity* (Toronto: University of Toronto Press, 2000), 177-208.

90 Canada, *Royal Commission on Bilingualism and Biculturalism* (Ottawa: Queen's Printer, 1967), 1: 173-74.

91 Hugh Donald Forbes, "Trudeau as the First Theorist of Multiculturalism," in *Multiculturalism and the Canadian Constitution*, ed. Stephen Tierney (Vancouver: UBC Press, 2007), 30. For background, see also Sarah Wayland, "Immigration, Multiculturalism and National Identity in Canada," *International Journal on Minority and Group Rights* 5 (1997): 33-58; Freda Hawkins, "Multiculturalism," in *Critical Years in Immigration: Canada and Australia Compared*, 2nd ed. (Montreal and Kingston: McGill-Queen's University Press, 1991); Kenneth McRoberts, "Multiculturalism: Reining in Duality," in *Misconceiving Canada: The Struggle for National Unity* (Toronto: Oxford University Press, 1997); and Day, *Multiculturalism*.

92 This and the next paragraph draw from Canada, House of Commons, *Debates*, 28th Parliament, 3rd Session, October 8, 1971, 8580-81.

93 David Hagen, "So Many Agendas: Federal-Provincial Relations in the Ethnic Policy Field in Quebec" (MA thesis, McGill University, 1995), 47.

94 José Iguarta, *The Other Quiet Revolution: National Identities in English Canada, 1945-1971* (Vancouver: UBC Press, 2006); Champion, *Strange Death*.

95 Valerie Knowles, *Strangers at Our Gates: Canadian Immigration and Immigration Policy, 1540-1997*, rev. ed. (Toronto: Dundurn, 1997), 162.

96 Hawkins, *Critical Years*, 45; Knowles, *Strangers at Our Gates*, 163.

97 Hawkins, *Critical Years*, 45-46; Anthony H. Richmond, "The Green Paper: Reflections on the Canadian Immigration and Population Study," *Canadian Ethnic Studies* 7, 1 (1975): 7.

98 Norman Hartley, "Thousands Are Proving Immigration Points System Is Pointless," *Globe and Mail*, December 29, 1973; Parai, "Canada's Immigration Policy," 467.

99 Hawkins, *Critical Years*, 47. Although Minister of Manpower and Immigration Bryce Mackasey denied that the decision to suspend the right of visitors to apply for landed immigrant status from within Canada had anything to do with the federal Liberals' poor showing in the 1972 election, it is worth noting that he defended the policy during the campaign, stating that there was "nothing devious or underhanded about a person applying for landed immigrant status from within the country." See "Landed Immigrant Policy Suspended," *Globe and Mail*, November 4, 1972. Mackasey had also complained of a "redneck backlash" against immigration and bilingualism in the immediate wake of the Liberals' drubbing.

100 Hawkins, *Critical Years in Immigration*, 47; Kelley and Trebilcock, *Making of the Mosaic*, 360-61.

101 "Bryce Mackasey Takes a Stand: A New Deal for Our Immigrants," *Calgary Herald*, June 28, 1972; Parai, "Canada's Immigration Policy," 468; Hawkins, *Critical Years*, 47-50.

102 Kelley and Trebilcock, *Making of the Mosaic*, 361.

103 The following three paragraphs draw from Memorandum to Cabinet, "Subject: Controlling the Size and Composition of the Immigration Flow," August 2, 1974, LAC, RG 76, vol. 997, file 5881-2, pt. 6.

104 Canada, Privy Council Office, Record of Cabinet Decision, "Controlling the Size and Composition of the Immigration Flow," meeting of August 8, 1974, LAC, RG 76, vol. 997, file 5881-2, pt. 6.

105 Memorandum to Cabinet, "Subject: Controlling the Size and Composition of the Immigration Flow," September 25, 1974, LAC, RG 76, vol. 997, file 5881-2, pt. 6.

106 Canada, House of Commons, *Debates*, October 22, 1974, 591-94.

107 This paragraph draws from Robert Trumbull, "Canada Tightens Rules Covering Immigrant Flow," *New York Times*, October 23, 1974.

108 Freda Hawkins, "Immigration and Population: The Canadian Approach," *Canadian Public Policy* 1, 3 (1975): 289.

109 The Green Paper consisted of four separate volumes and was accompanied by eight supplementary studies.

110 "Touchy Race Question Delicately Handled," *Globe and Mail*, February 4, 1975. See also Mary Janigan, "Andras Cautions Race Should Not Dominate Immigration Debate," *Toronto Star*, February 4, 1975. *The Economist* was less circumspect, noting that "the government [had] moved quickly to keep Canada predominantly white." See "Do You Want to Let Them In?" *The Economist*, May 31, 1975, 42.

111 William Borders, "Canada Begins a Debate on Immigration," *New York Times*, March 15, 1975.

112 Canada, Department of Manpower and Immigration, *Green Paper on Immigration and Population*, vol. 1: *Immigration Policy Perspectives* (Ottawa: Department of Manpower and Immigration, 1974), 84.

113 Canada, *Immigration Policy Perspectives*, 86. See also John R. Wood, "East Indians and Canada's New Immigration Policy," *Canadian Public Policy* 4, 4 (1978): 551.

114 Canada, Department of Manpower and Immigration, Canadian Immigration and Population Study, *Highlights from the Green Paper* (Ottawa: Department of Manpower and Immigration, 1974), 9.

115 Canada, *Immigration Policy Perspectives*, 12.

116 Jean Burnet, "Multiculturalism, Immigration and Racism: A Comment on the Canadian Immigration and Population Study," *Canadian Ethnic Studies* 7, 1 (1975): 35-39.

117 Summaries of the four options are included in Canada, *Highlights from the Green Paper*, 13-14.

118 William Johnson, "Cabinet Warned about Effect of Non-European Immigrant Trend," *Globe and Mail*, October 29, 1974.

119 "Parliament," *Globe and Mail*, October 17, 1974.

120 Kelley and Trebilcock, *Making of the Mosaic*, 374.

121 William Johnson, "Ottawa's Mail on Immigration Has One Strong Theme: Stop It," *Globe and Mail*, September 19, 1975. The quotations from letters to the SJC that follow draw from this source.

122 Peter Dobell and Susan d'Aquino, *The Special Joint Committee on Immigration Policy 1975: An Exercise in Participatory Democracy* (Toronto: Canadian Institute of International Affairs, 1976), 13; Kelley and Trebilcock, *Making of the Mosaic*, 374; Daniel, "Debate on Family Reunification," 693.

123 Canada, Special Joint Committee of the Senate and the House of Commons on Immigration Policy, *Minutes and Proceeding of the Special Joint Committee of the Senate and the House of Commons on Immigration Policy*, issue 27, May 25 (Ottawa: House of Commons, 1975), 68.

124 Canada, *Minutes and Proceeding of the Special Joint Committee of the Senate and the House of Commons on Immigration Policy*, issue 16, 43-44.

125 Special Joint Committee of the Senate and the House of Commons on Immigration Policy, *Report to Parliament* (Ottawa: Queen's Printer, 1975), 15-16.

126 Daniel, "Debate on Family Reunification," 693.

127 Ibid., 694.

128 Ibid., 696.

129 As outlined in section 3, part 1 of the act. See Valerie Knowles, *Strangers at Our Gates*, 169.

130 Hawkins, *Canada and Immigration*, 377-78; Kelley and Trebilcock, *Making of the Mosaic*, 396.

131 Donald Galloway, "The Dilemmas of Canadian Citizenship Law," in *From Migrants to Citizens: Membership in a Changing World*, ed. T. Alexander Aleinikoff and Douglas Klusmeyer (Washington, DC: Carnegie Endowment for International Peace, 2000), 99; Irene Bloemraad, *Becoming a Citizen: Incorporating Immigrants and Refugees in the United States and Canada* (Berkeley: University of California Press, 2006), 49-50.

132 Wood, "East Indians," 558.

133 On the federal Liberal Party's fading popularity in 1976-77, see Stephen Clarkson, "The Defeat of the Government, the Decline of the Liberal Party, and the (Temporary) Fall of Pierre Trudeau," in *Canada at the Polls, 1979 and 1980: A Study of the General Elections*, ed. Howard R. Penniman, 152-89 (Washington, DC: The American Enterprise Institute for Public Policy Research, 1981). The Liberals lost 46 seats in the 1972 election, going from 155 in 1968 to 109; the party's percentage of the popular vote fell from 45 percent to 38 percent. In Ontario, the Liberals slipped from 64 to 36 seats. Defeated candidates, such as John Roberts, "urged more aggressive use of [multiculturalism] policy to garner ethnic support." See Pal, *Interests of State*, 118-19. See also John Jaworsky, "A Case Study of the Canadian Federal Government's Multicultural Policy" (MA thesis, Carleton University, 1979), 100-01.

134 Wood, "East Indians," 559.

135 Ibid.

136 Ibid.

137 John C. Courtney, "Campaign Strategy and Electoral Victory: The Progressive Conservatives and the 1979 Election," in Howard R. Penniman, *Canada at the Polls, 1979 and 1980: A Study of the General Elections* (Washington, DC: The American Enterprise Institute for Public Policy Research, 1981), 139.

138 The politics accompanying the passage of the Immigration Act, 1976, provide evidence in support of Gary Freeman's theory of immigration policy making in liberal-democratic countries: the "concentrated" interests of pro-immigration groups prevailed over "diffuse" support for restriction. In the Canadian case, the role of institutions was key to amplifying the voice of pro-immigrant groups. It was not simply that pro-immigration groups organized; politicians also recognized that they could effectively express their interests at the ballot box. See Gary Freeman, "Modes of Immigration Politics in Liberal Democratic Societies," *International Migration Review* 29, 4 (1995): 881-902.

139 Canada, Department of Justice, Canadian Charter of Rights and Freedoms, available at http://laws-lois.justice.gc.ca/. For a discussion of section 27, see Joan Small, "Multiculturalism, Equality, and Canadian Constitutionalism: Cohesion and Difference," in *Multiculturalism and the Canadian Constitution*, ed. Stephen Tierney, 196-211 (Vancouver: UBC Press, 2007); and Varun Uberoi, "Multiculturalism and the Canadian Charter of Rights and Freedoms," *Political Studies* 57, 4 (2008): 805-27.

140 Canada, Department of Justice, Canadian Multiculturalism Act, available at http://laws-lois.justice.gc.ca/.

141 Jack W.P. Veugelers, "State-Society Relations in the Making of Canadian Immigration Policy during the Mulroney Era," *Canadian Review of Sociology and Anthropology* 37, 1 (2000): 108. See also Hugh Winsor, "McDougall Wins Battle to Increase Immigration: Minister Sees New Source of Voters for the Conservatives," *Globe and Mail*, October 24, 1990.

142 Yasmeen Abu-Laban and Daiva Stasiulis, "Ethnic Pluralism under Siege: Popular and Partisan Opposition to Multiculturalism," *Canadian Public Policy* 18, 4 (1992): 365-86.

143 David Laycock, *The New Right and Democracy in Canada: Understanding Reform and the Canadian Alliance* (Don Mills: Oxford University Press, 2002); Neil Nevitte, André Blais, Elisabeth Gidengil, Richard Johnston, and Henry Brady, "The Populist Right in Canada: The Rise of the Reform Party of Canada," in *The New Politics of the Right: Neo-Populist Parties and Movements in Established Democracies*, ed. Hans-Georg Betz and Stefan Immerfall, 173-202 (New York: St. Martin's Press, 1998).

144 Lila Sarick, "Family Immigration Faces Change: Marchi under Pressure to Restrict Reunification of Relatives," *Globe and Mail*, October 24, 1994; Yasmeen Abu-Laban, "Welcome/STAY OUT: The Contradictions of Canadian Integration and Immigration Policies at the Millennium," *Canadian Ethnic Studies* 30, 3 (1998): 190-211.

145 Miro Cernetig, "Reform Party Sees Radicals as Problem: Image a Factor in National Drive," *Globe and Mail*, April 4, 1991; Tom Flanagan, *Waiting for the Wave: The Reform Party and the Conservative Movement* (Montreal and Kingston: McGill-Queen's University Press, 2009), 89-98.

146 Rod Mickleburgh, "Harper Defends Canadian Diversity: PM Rejects Calls to Curb Immigration, Calls Open Society 'Our Greatest Strength,'" *Globe and Mail*, June 20, 2006; Daniel Leblanc, "Tories Target Specific Ethnic Voters," *Globe and Mail*, October 16, 2007; John Ibbitson and Joe Friesen, "Conservative Immigrants Boost Tory Fortunes," *Globe and Mail*, October 4, 2010.

147 Haroon Siddiqui, "Siddiqui: On Multiculturalism, Harper's Got It Right," *Toronto Star*, April 16, 2011.

148 Kenyon Wallace, "Liberals Crushed in GTA," *Toronto Star*, May 3, 2011.

CHAPTER 5: GUEST WORKERS INTO GERMANS

1 Dorothee Soehlne, "Probleme schon auf dem Schulweg," *Der Tagesspiegel*, August 25, 1974; "Ausländerkinder sind stärker unfallgefährdet als deutsche," *Die Welt*, November 11, 1975.

2 Hartmut M. Griese, "Die Situation der Kinder von Wanderarbeitnehmern: Bundesrepublik Deutschland," in *Wanderarbeiter in der EG*, Band 2: *Länderberichte*, ed. Wolf-Dieter Just and Annette Groth (Mainz: Matthias-Grünewald-Verlag, 1985), 115.

3 The Caritas report is discussed in Karl-Heinz Meier-Braun, *Deutschland, Einwanderungsland* (Frankfurt am Main: Suhrkamp Verlag, 2002), 44-45. See also Herman Korte, "Guestworker Question or Immigration Issue? Social Sciences and Public Debate in the Federal Republic of Germany," in *Population, Labour and Migration in 19th- and 20th-Century Germany*, ed. Klaus J. Bade (Leamington Spa, UK: Berg, 1987), 169.

4 Simon Green, *The Politics of Exclusion: Institutions and Immigration Policy in Contemporary Germany* (Manchester: University of Manchester Press, 2004).

5 Peter O'Brien, "Continuity and Change in Germany's Treatment of Non-Germans," *International Migration Review* 22, 3 (1988): 119; Stephen Castles, "The Guests Who Stayed: The Debate on 'Foreigners Policy' in the German Federal Republic," *International Migration Review* 19, 3 (1985): 524; Ulrich Spies, *Ausländerpolitik und Integration* (Frankfurt am Main: Peter Lang, 1982), 27-28; Ingrid Drees, "Integration als Ziel der aktuellen Ausländerpolitik in der Bundesrepublik Deutschland" (PhD diss., University of Hannover, 1991), 70-71.

6 Ulrich Herbert, *A History of Foreign Labor in Germany, 1880-1980: Seasonal Workers, Forced Laborers, Guest Workers*, trans. William Templer (Ann Arbor: University of Michigan Press, 1990), 248.

7 Ibid.; Rita Chin, *The Guest Worker Question in Postwar Germany* (Cambridge: Cambridge University Press, 2007), 93-94.

8 This section draws on the analysis of the decision in Gerald L. Neuman, "Immigration and Judicial Review in the Federal Republic of Germany," *New York University Journal of International Law and Politics* 23, 1 (1990): 35-86; and Christian Joppke, *Immigration and the Nation-State: The United States, Germany, and Great Britain* (New York: Oxford University Press, 1999), 73.

9 Neuman, "Immigration and Judicial Review," 49-50. See also Christian Joppke, "The Legal-Domestic Sources of Immigrant Rights: The United States, Germany, and the European Union," *Comparative Politics* 34, 4 (2001): 349-50.

10 Joppke, *Immigration and the Nation-State*, 73.

11 Bundesministerium für Arbeit und Sozialordnung, *Vorschläge der Bund-Länder-Kommission zur Fortentwicklung einer umfassenden Konzeption der Ausländerbeschäftigungspolitik*, cited in Drees, "Integration als Ziel," 71; and Martin Frey, "Ausländerpolitik in der Bundesrepublik Deutschland," in *Ausländer bei uns – Fremde oder Mitbürger?* ed. Martin Frey and Ulf Müller (Bonn: Bundeszentrale für Politische Bildung, 1982), 92-94.

12 Simon Green, "The Politics of Exclusion: Immigration, Residence and Citizenship Policy in Germany, 1955-1998" (PhD diss., University of Birmingham, 1999), 94.

13 This section draws on Simon Green, "Citizenship Policy in Germany: The Case of Ethnicity over Residence," in *Towards a European Nationality: Citizenship, Immigration, and Nationality Law in the EU*, ed. Randall Hansen and Patrick Weil (London: Macmillan, 2000), 30-31; Hans Dieter Rauscher, "Deutsches Staatsangehörigkeitsrecht – Gesetzliche Grundlagen und Rechtsprechung zur Einbürgerung," in *Aufenthalt – Niederlassung – Einbürgerung*, ed. Klaus Barwig, Klaus Lörcher, and Christoph Schumacher, 129-43 (Baden-Baden: Nomos Verlagsgesellschaft, 1987); Gerald L. Neuman, "Nationality Law in the Federal Republic of Germany: Structure and Current Problems," in *Paths toward Inclusion: The Integration of Migrants in the United States and Germany*, ed. Peter Schuck and Rainer Münz (New York: Berghahn Books, 1997), 265.

14 Bernd Geiß, senior official, Office of the Federal Commissioner for Foreigners' Affairs, interview with author, 7 March 2002, Berlin. See also Karl-Heinz Meier-

Braun, *Integration und Rückkehr? Zur Ausländerpolitik des Bundes und Länder, insbesondere Baden-Württembergs* (Mainz: Grünewald-Kaiser, 1988), 15.

15 Heinz Kühn, *Stand und Weiterentwicklung der Integration der ausländischen Arbeitnehmer und ihrer Familien in der Bundesrepublik Deutschland. Memorandum des Beauftragten der Bundesregierung*, Bonn, 1979, 13-14. For discussion, see Bernd Geiß, "Die Ausländerbeauftragten der Bundesregierung in der ausländerpolitischen Diskussion," in *Deutschland – ein Einwanderungsland? Rückblick, Bilanz and neue Fragen* (Stuttgart: Lucias and Lucias, 2001); Klaus J. Bade, *Ausländer, Aussiedler, Asyl in der Bundesrepublik Deutschland*, 3rd ed. (Hannover: Niedersächsische Landeszentrale für Politische Bildung, 1994), 19; Green, "Politics of Exclusion," 96-97; Chin, *Guestworker Question*, 104-05.

16 Kühn, *Stand und Weiterentwicklung.*

17 Castles, "Guests Who Stayed," 525.

18 Meier-Braun, *Deutschland, Einwanderungsland*, 47.

19 In later years, Kühn confided that most of his Cabinet colleagues were, on the whole, less than enthusiastic. See Heinz Kühn, "Vorwort zur 1. Auflage," in *Zur Situation der ausländischen Arbeitnehmer und ihrer Familien – Bestandsaufnahme und Perspektiven für die 90er Jahre*, 2nd ed., ed. Beauftragte der Bundesregierung für die Integration der ausländischen Arbeitnehmer und ihrer Familienangehörigen (Bonn: Bundesministerium für Arbeit und Sozialordnung, 1990), 10. See also Ulrich Herbert, *Geschichte der Ausländerpolitik in Deutschland. Saisonarbeiter, Zwangsarbeiter, Gastarbeiter, Flüchtlinge* (Munich: C.H. Beck, 2001), 246.

20 Cited in Dietrich Thränhardt, "Ausländer als Objekt deutscher Interessen und Ideologien," in *Der gläserne Fremde*, ed. Hartmut M. Griese (Opladen: Leske and Budrich, 1984), 124.

21 "Weiterentwicklung der Ausländerpolitik: Beschlüsse der Bundesregierung vom 19. März 1980," Sozialdemokratische Partei Deutschland, Parteivorstand, Archiv, file X3 – Ausländer – I; Drees, "Integration als Ziel," 76.

22 "Material für die Presse. Bilanz der Legislaturperiode: Die Arbeit der Regierung Schmidt/Genscher seit 1976," Sozialdemokratische Partei Deutschland, Parteivorstand, Archiv, file X3 – Ausländer – I.

23 Unemployment stood at 3.8 percent in 1980 and rose to 5.5 percent in 1981, 7.5 percent in 1982, and 9.1 percent in 1983.

24 Karen Schönwälder, "Migration, Refugees and Ethnic Plurality as Issues of Public and Political Debates in (West) Germany," in *Citizenship, Nationality and Migration in Europe*, ed. David Cesarani and Mary Fulbrook (London: Routledge, 1996), 168-69; Karen Schönwälder, "Zu viele Ausländer in Deutschland? Zur Entwicklung ausländerfeindlicher Einstellungen in der Bundesrepublik," *Vorgänge* 4 (1991): 4-5; Dietrich Thränhardt, "Die Bundesrepublik Deutschland – ein unerklärtes Einwanderungsland," *Aus Politik und Zeitgeschichte* 24 (1988): 3-13; Meier-Braun, *Deutschland, Einwanderungsland*, 49-53.

25 For discussion, see Gerd Knischewski, "Post-War Identity in Germany," in *Nation and Identity in Contemporary Europe*, ed. Brian Jenkins and Spiros A. Sofos, 124-51 (London: Routledge, 1996); Chin, *Guest Worker Question*, 153-57.

26 Cited in Martin Greiffenhagen, "Die Bundesrepublik Deutschland 1945-1990," *Aus Politik und Zeitgeschichte* 1-2 (1991): 16. Strauß was minister president of Bavaria from 1978 to 1988 and the CDU/CSU's chancellor candidate in the 1980 general election (which he lost to the SPD's Helmut Schmidt).

27 Cited in Bodo Morshäuser, *Hauptsache Deutsche* (Frankfurt am Main: Suhrkamp, 1992), 129.

28 Cited in Stephen Castles, "Racism and Politics in Germany," *Race and Class* 25, 3 (1984): 48.

29 Schönwälder, "Zu viele Ausländer in Deutschland?" 5; Herbert, *Geschichte der Ausländerpolitik*, 258.

30 Christine Morgenstern, *Rassismus – Konturen einer Ideologie: Einwanderung im politischen Diskurs der Bundesrepublik Deutschland* (Hamburg: Argument Verlag, 2002), 263-69.

31 Thomas Faist, "How to Define a Foreigner? The Symbolic Politics of Immigration in German Partisan Discourse, 1978-1992," in *The Politics of Immigration in Western Europe*, ed. Martin Baldwin-Edwards and Martin Schain (London: Frank Cass, 1994), 63. For further discussion, see Michael Minkenberg, *Die neue radikale Rechte im Vergleich: USA, Frankreich, Deutschland* (Opladen: Westdeutscher Verlag, 1998); Chin, *Guestworker Question*, 150-53.

32 Bade, *Ausländer, Aussiedler*, 24.

33 Klaus Merten, *Das Bild der Ausländer in der deutschen Presse: Ergebnisse einer systematischen Inhaltsanalyse* (Frankfurt am Main: Dagyeli, 1986); Zentrum für Türkeistudium, ed., *Das Bild der Ausländer in der Öffentlichkeit: Eine theoretische und empirische Analyse zur Fremdenfeindlichkeit* (Opladen: Leske and Budrich, 1995); Ute Gerhard, "Wenn Flüchtlinge und Einwanderer zu 'Asylantenfluten' werden: Über den Diskurs des Rassismus in den Medien und im allgemeinen Bewusstsein," *Frankfurter Rundschau*, October 19, 1991; Rachel Tobey Greenwald, "The German Nation Is a Homogeneous Nation? Race, the Cold War, and German National Identity, 1970-1993" (PhD diss., University of California, Irvine, 2000).

34 Rita Chin, Heide Fehrenbach, Geoff Eley, and Atina Grossmann, "Guest Worker Migration and the Unexpected Return of Race," in *After the Nazi Racial State: Difference and Democracy in Germany and Europe* (Ann Arbor: University of Michigan Press, 2009), 93.

35 Chin, *Guest Worker Question*, 152-53.

36 Meier-Braun, *Deutschland, Einwanderungsland*, 51.

37 "Ein Rechtsanspruch auf Einbürgerung: Erleichterung für junge Ausländer," *Frankfurter Allgemeine Zeitung*, January 7, 1982.

38 "CSU will Ausländer bremsen," *Frankfurter Allgemeine Zeitung*, January 15, 1982; Karl Hugo Pruys, "Ausländerpolitik – Züundstoff für 1982," *Münchner Merkur*, January 20, 1982; CDU/CSU Fraktion im Deutschen Bundestag, "Entschliessungsantrag zur Ausländerpolitik," January 20, 1982, Archiv für Christlich-Demokratische Politik, file 0/07 – Ausländer – Asylgewährung.

39 "Bundesrat lehnt Einbürgerungsanspruch ab," *Frankfurter Allgemeine Zeitung*, February 13, 1982; Green, "Politics of Exclusion," 173.

40 Verhandlungen des Deutschen Bundestages, 9, Wahlperiode, 111, Sitzung, September 9, 1982, 6772, cited in Morgenstern, *Rassismus*, 308.

41 Drees, "Integration als Ziel," 83.

42 Bundesminister des Innern, *Kommission "Ausländerpolitik" aus Vertretern von Bund, Ländern und Gemeinden* (Bonn: Bundesministerium des Innern, 1983).

43 Jürgen Haberland, "Die Vorschläge der Kommission Ausländerpolitik," *Zeitschrift für Ausländerrecht* 2 (1983): 56; Green, "Politics of Exclusion," 132.

44 "Kohl will Behutsamkeit in der Ausländerpolitik," *Frankfurter Rundschau*, March 3, 1983; R.D. Groos, "Die Diskussion über die Novellierung des Ausländerrechts: Synoptische Darstellung," Deutscher Bundestag, Wissenschaftliche Dienste, August 31, 1988, Sozialdemokratische Partei Deutschland, Parteivorstand, Archiv, file X3 – Ausländer; Fritz Franz, "Zwischenbilanz des deutschen Ausländerrechts," *Zeitschrift für Ausländerrecht* 4 (1992): 158; Green, "Politics of Exclusion," 130; Castles, "Guests Who Stayed," 531.

45 Interview with Volker Roßocha, DGB Migration Section, Berlin, November 3, 2003. See also *Erklärung des DGB-Bundesvorstandes zur Ausländerpolitik*, September 28, 1983, Sozialdemokratische Partei Deutschland, Parteivorstand, Archiv, file X3 – Ausländer – F.

46 Alfons Pieper, "FDP warnt scharf vor Senkung des Nachzugs-Alters. Hirsch: Zimmermanns Plan unmenschlich," *Westdeutsche Allgemeine Zeitung*, January 3, 1983.

47 "Hirsch: Die FDP wird in der Ausländerpolitik nicht vom Vorrang der Integration und humanitären Grundsätzen abweichen," *FDK Tagesdienst*, June 9, 1983, Archiv für Christlich-Demokratische Politik, file 0/07 – Ausländer – Asylgewährung.

48 Herbert, *Geschichte der Ausländerpolitik*, 253.

49 CDU Pressedienst, Arbeitskreis Christlich-Demokratischer-Juristen der CDU Rheinland-Pfalz, June 13, 1983, Archiv für Christlich-Demokratische Politik, file 0/07 – Ausländer – Asylgewährung.

50 "Aus der Asche," *Der Spiegel*, 41, August 10, 1984; Herbert, *Geschichte der Ausländerpolitik*, 253.

51 The CDU/CSU won 48.8 percent of the popular vote; Chin, *Guest Worker Question*, 154.

52 Detlef Bischoff and Werner Teubner, *Zwischen Einbürgerung und Rückkehr: Ausländerpolitik und Ausländerrecht in der Bundesrepublik Deutschland* (Berlin: Hitit Verlag, 1992), 56-57; Castles, "Guests Who Stayed," 530.

53 Green, "Politics of Exclusion," 106.

54 "'Kölner Appell' Gegen eine menschfeindliche Ausländerpolitik," *Frankfurter Rundschau*, November 2, 1983; DGB, "Rückkehrprämie ist eine politische Fehlgeburt," *DGB Nachrichten Dienst*, June 22, 1983, Archiv für Christlich-Demokratische Politik, file 0/07 – Ausländer – Asylgewährung; Der Beauftragte der Bundesregierung für Ausländerfragen, *Informationen, Meinungen, Anregungen* (Bonn: Beauftragte der Bundesregierung für Ausländerfragen, 1984); "Kirchen zu einer Offensive für Wende in der Ausländerpolitik aufgefordert," *Evangelischer Pressedienst*, February 25, 1985, Archiv für Christlich-Demokratische Politik, file 0/07 – Ausländer – Asylgewährung.

55 Peter Katzenstein, *Policy and Politics in West Germany: The Growth of a Semi-Sovereign State* (Philadelphia: Temple University Press, 1987), 224-25.

56 "FDP will Ausländer nach fünf Jahren einbürgern," *Bonner Rundschau*, July 12, 1983; "Leitbild der Integration," *Sozialdemokratischer Pressedienst*, March 2, 1983, Archiv für Christlich-Demokratische Politik, file 0/07 – Ausländer – Asylgewährung.

57 For discussion, see Klaus Sieveking, ed., *Das Kommunalwahlrecht für Ausländer* (Baden-Baden: Nomos Verlag, 1989); William A. Barbieri, Jr., *Ethics of Citizenship: Immigration and Group Rights in Germany* (Durham, NC: Duke University Press, 1998), 58-65. On the democratic rights of guest workers, see Michael Walzer, *Spheres of Justice: A Defense of Pluralism and Equality* (New York: Basic Books, 1983), 52-62. It should be noted that in 1984 the CDU/CSU-FDP government explicitly acknowledged that the presence of a large number of disenfranchised residents in Germany did not conform to democratic norms and was therefore untenable in the long run. However, as is pointed out below, this proclamation was not followed by policy proposals until opposition pressure was brought to bear. The 1984 statement is cited in Heike Hagedorn, *Wer darf Mitglied werden? Einbürgerung in Deutschland und Frankreich im Vergleich* (Opladen: Leske and Budrich, 2001), 204.

58 "Leitbild der Integration," *Sozialdemokratischer Pressedienst*, March 2, 1983, Archiv für Christlich-Demokratische Politik, file 0/07 – Ausländer – Asylgewährung.

59 Manfred Zuleeg, "Entwicklung und Stand des Ausländerrechts in der Bundesrepublik Deutschland," *Zeitschrift für Ausländerrecht* 2 (1984): 80-87.

60 "Zimmermann will Ausländerrecht in diesem Jahr ändern," *Frankfurter Allgemeine Zeitung*, October 3, 1987.

61 "Zuwanderung von Ausländern abwehren," *Der Spiegel*, 16, April 18, 1988.

62 For discussion, see Green, "Politics of Exclusion," 135-36; and Heribert Prantl, *Deutschland – leicht entflammbar: Ermittlung gegen die Bonner Politik* (Munich: Carl Hanser Verlag, 1994), 69-70.

63 Green, "Politics of Exclusion," 136.

64 Bundesministerium des Innern, *Entwurf für ein Gesetz zur Neuregelung des Ausländerrechts*, February 1, 1988, 23, cited in Green, "Politics of Exclusion," 136.

65 Green, "Politics of Exclusion," 134.

66 "'Ausländerrecht in der Diskussion': Ein Diskussionsbeitrag des Diakonischen Werkes der EKD zur Novellierung des Ausländergesetzes," *Diakonie Korrespondenz*, January 23, 1989.

67 DGB, *"Der Deutsche Gewerkschaftsbund und die ausländischen Arbeitnehmer": Dokumentation über die Behandlung der Ausländerthematik auf dem 14. Ordentlichen Bundeskongress des DGB, vom 20–26, Mai 1990 in Hamburg* (Düsseldorf: DGB-Bundesvorstand, Abt. Ausländische Arbeitnehmer, 1990).

68 Verhandlungen des Deutschen Bundestages, 11. Wahlperiode, 88, Sitzung, June 24, 1988, 6041, cited in Morgenstern, *Rassismus*, 324-25.

69 Klaus Wedmeier, "Zimmermanns Ausländerpolitk mutet gespenstisch an: Unser Land muß Stärke und Humanität beweisen," *Sozialdemokratischer Pressedienst*, August 30, 1988, Archiv für Christlich-Demokratische Politik, file 0/07 – Ausländer – Asylgewährung.

70 CDA, "Partnerschaft und Integration: Thesen zur Novellierung des Ausländerrechts," Bonn, February 17, 1988, cited in Meier-Braun, *Integration und Rückkehr*, 63.

71 "'Zimmermann spielt Rechtsradikalen in die Hände,'" *Saarbrücker Zeitung*, March 1, 1989.

72 "Zuwanderung von Ausländern abwehren," 23.

73 Mitteilungen der Beauftragten der Bundesregierung für Ausländerfragen, Anregungen der Ausländerbeauftragten zur Novellierung des Ausländerrechts (Bonn: Beauftragte der Bundesregierung für Ausländerfragen, December 1987); "Recht absonderlich," *Der Spiegel*, 18, May 2, 1988.

74 Green, "Politics of Exclusion," 138.

75 Bade, *Ausländer, Aussiedler*, 21.

76 Joppke, *Immigration and the Nation-State*, 83. The *Republikaner* had gained 14.6 percent of the vote in Bavaria in the 1989 European election. See Green, "Politics of Exclusion," 140.

77 Roger Karapin, "Far-Right Parties and the Construction of Immigration Issues in Germany," in *Shadows over Europe: The Development and Impact of the Extreme Right in Western Europe*, ed. Martin Schain, Aristide Zolberg, and Patrick Hossay (New York: Palgrave, 2002), 203-04.

78 "Die 'Eckwerte' für ein neues Ausländerrecht," *Frankfurter Rundschau*, April 22, 1989.

79 The FDP's positions were presented in "Positionen einer liberalen Ausländerpolitik," *Freie demokratische Korrespondenz*, April 6, 1988, Archiv für Christlich-Demokratische Politik, file 0/07 – Ausländer – Asylgewährung.

80 For a concise review of the types of residence permits offered under the term of the 1990 Foreigners Law, see Green, "Politics of Exclusion," 63; and Douglas B. Klusmeyer and Demetrios G. Papademetriou, *Immigration Policy in the Federal Republic of Germany: Negotiating Membership and Remaking the Nation* (New York: Berghahn Books, 2009), 114-15.

81 Herbert, *Geschichte der Ausländerpolitik*, 284.

82 "Stoiber kritisiert Referentenentwurf zum Ausländerrecht," *Frankfurter Allgemeine Zeitung*, October 28, 1989.

83 "Koalition über Ausländergesetz einig," *Süddeutsche Zeitung*, December 6, 1989.

84 "DGB sieht Bundesrepublik als Einwanderungsland," *Deutsche Presse-Agentur*, April 7, 1990; Klaus Barwig, "Zur Diskussion um die Novellierung des Ausländerrechts," *Zeitschrift für Ausländerrecht* 4 (1989): 173-83.

85 "Über 20 000 Demonstranten gegen neues Ausländergesetz," *Deutsche Presse-Agentur*, April 1, 1990. A photo of a demonstrator with such a placard is featured on the cover of Jan Motte and Rainer Ohliger, eds., *Geschichte und Gedächtnis in der Einwanderungsgesellschaft: Migration zwischen historischer Rekonstruktion und Erinnerungspolitik* (Essen: Klartext, 2004).

86 Monika Bethscheider and Gabriele Köppe, eds., *Die Multikulturelle Gesellschaft: Für eine demokratische Umgestaltung in der Bundesrepublik – Positionen und Dokumentation* (Bonn: Die Grünen im Bundestag, 1990); Jürgen Fijalkowski, "Nationale Identität versus multikulturelle Gesellschaft: Entwicklung der Problemlage und

Alternativen der Orientierung in der politischen Kultur der Bundesrepublik in den 80er Jahren," in *Die Bundesrepublik in den achtziger Jahren*, ed. Werner Süß (Opladen: Leske and Budrich, 1991), 244-45.

87 Jürgen Micksch, Intercultural Council, interview with author, Darmstadt, March 21, 2001. See also Jürgen Micksch, ed., *Multikulturelles Zusammenleben: Theologische Erfahrungen* (Frankfurt am Main: O. Lembeck, 1983); Sabine von Dirke, "Multikulti: The German Debate on Multiculturalism," *German Studies Review* 17 (1994): 513-36; Konrad H. Jarausch, *After Hitler: Recivilizing Germans, 1945-1995* (Oxford: Oxford University Press, 2006), 245-46.

88 Ulf Fink, "Multikulturelle Gesellschaft – Realität heute," *Gewerkschaftliche Monatshefte*, 7/89 (1989): 443-47. Fink was the federal chairman of the CDU's Committee on Social Affairs. The CDU's general secretary, Heiner Geißler, also stood in favour of a "multicultural society." In Geißler's understanding, "[a] multicultural society means the readiness to live together with people from other countries and cultures, respectful of their customs, without wishing to assimilate or Germanize them." Cited in Günter Bannas, "Geißler fürchtet den 'Volksgeist,'" *Frankfurter Allgemeine Zeitung*, March 28, 1990.

89 Robert M. Daguillard, "The Idealists and the Noble Savages: The German Green Party and Immigration Politics, 1980-2000" (PhD diss., Georgetown University, 2000), 194-99.

90 Laura Murray, "Einwanderungsland Bundesrepublik Deutschland? Explaining the Evolving Positions of German Political Parties on Citizenship Policy," *German Politics and Society* 33 (1994): 23-56.

91 Christian Joppke, "Toward a New Sociology of the State: On Rogers Brubaker's *Citizenship and Nationhood in France and Germany*," *Archives Européennes de Sociologie* 36, 1 (1995): 176; Klusmeyer and Papademetriou, *Immigration Policy*, 153-54.

92 Karen Schönwälder, "'Persons Persecuted on Political Grounds Shall Enjoy the Right of Asylum – But Not in Our Country': Asylum Debates about Refugees in the Federal Republic of Germany," in *Refugees, Citizenship and Social Policy in Europe*, ed. Alice Bloch and Carl Levy, 76-90 (Houndmills: Macmillan Press, 1999).

93 "Asyl – 'Bis an die Grenze des Zulässigen,'" *Der Spiegel*, July 28, 1986.

94 Norman M. Naimark, *Fires of Hatred: Ethnic Cleansing in Twentieth-Century Europe* (Cambridge: Harvard University Press, 2001), 139-84.

95 Schönwälder, "Migration."

96 Daniel Kanstroom, "Wer Sind Wir Wieder? Laws of Asylum, Immigration, and Citizenship in the Struggle for the Soul of the New Germany," *Yale Journal of International Law* 18, 1 (1993): 194; Jeffrey K. Olick, "What Does It Mean to Normalize the Past? Official Memory in German Politics since 1989," *Social Science History* 22, 4 (1998): 547-71.

97 Alfons Söllner, "Die Änderung des Grundgesetzes wäre nichts als blanker Zynismus," *Frankfurter Rundschau*, August 6, 1986.

98 Ute Gerhard, "Wenn Flüchtlinge und Einwanderer zu 'Asylantenfluten' werden," *Frankfurter Rundschau*, October 19, 1991.

99 "Wettrennen in Schäbigkeit: Burkhard Hirsch (FDP) und Edmund Stoiber (CSU) über das Asylrecht," *Der Spiegel*, November 5, 1990; "FDP nennt Stoiber politischen Heuchler," *Süddeutsche Zeitung*, August 26, 1991.

100 See Prantl, *Deutschland*, 100-28; Herbert, *Geschichte der Ausländerpolitik*, 312; Klusmeyer and Papademetriou, *Immigration Policy*, 141-42; Edmund Stoiber, "Ohne Änderung kein Ausweg," *Bayernkurier*, December 21, 1991.

101 Ute Gerhard, "'Fluten,' 'Ströme,' 'Invasionen' – Mediendiskurs und Rassismus," in *Zwischen Nationalstaat und multikultureller Gesellschaft: Einwanderung und Fremdenfeindlichkeit in der Bundesrepublik Deutschland*, ed. M. Hessler, 239-53 (Freiburg: Hitit, 1993).

102 Herbert, *Geschichte der Ausländerpolitik*, 303; Horst Becker, "Einstellungen zu Ausländern in der Bevölkerung der Bundesrepublik Deutschland 1992," in *Zuwanderung und Asyl in der Konkurrenzgesellschaft*, ed. Bernhard Blanke, 141-49 (Opladen: Leske and Budrich, 1993).

103 "Frau Funcke kündigt ihren Rücktritt an: Enttäuscht von den Parteien und der Bundesregierung," *Frankfurter Allgemeine Zeitung*, June 20, 1991.

104 Klaus J. Bade, "Immigration and Social Peace in United Germany," *Daedalus* 123, 1 (1994): 94.

105 Herbert, *Geschichte der Ausländerpolitik*, 304; "Lieber sterben als nach Sachsen," *Der Spiegel*, September 30, 1991.

106 Beauftragte der Bundesregierung für Ausländerfragen, *Daten und Fakten zur Ausländersituation* (Bonn: Beauftragte der Bundesregierung für Ausländerfragen, 1988).

107 Cited in Herbert, *Geschichte der Ausländerpolitik*, 315.

108 Herbert, *Geschichte der Ausländerpolitik*, 316; Barbara Marshall, *The New Germany and Migration in Europe* (Manchester: Manchester University Press, 2000), 146.

109 "Koalition spricht vom drohenden Staatsnotstand," *Süddeutsche Zeitung*, November 5, 1992.

110 Tyler Marshall, "Anti-Foreigner Attack Kills 3 in Germany," *Los Angeles Times*, November 24, 1993.

111 Cited in Bade, *Ausländer, Aussiedler*, 26.

112 Stephen Kinzer, "Germany Ablaze: It's Candlelight, Not Firebombs," *New York Times*, January 13, 1993.

113 "DGB fordert Umkehr in der Ausländerpolitik," *Deutsche Presse-Agentur*, December 10, 1992; Leo Monz, "Reform des Staatsangehörigkeitsrechts: Chancen für eine gleichberechtigte Zukunft aller Kinder," in *Deutsche Türken – Türkische Deutsche? Die Diskussion um die doppelte Staatsbürgerschaft*, ed. Andreas Goldgerg and Faruk Şen (Münster: Lit Verlag, 1999), 47; "Rat der Evangelischen Kirche warnt vor Abschottung gegenüber Fremden," *Frankfurter Allgemeine Zeitung*, March 1, 1993.

114 "'Deutscher Paß für ausländische Jugendliche,'" *Süddeutsche Zeitung*, December 9, 1992; "SPD-Vorstoß zur Erleichterung der Einbürgerung," *Süddeutsche Zeitung*, February 3, 1993. Schmalz-Jacobsen and the SPD's deputy leader, Herta Däubler-Gmelin, proposed a draft law that would include automatic citizenship for children of legally resident migrants and the tolerance of dual citizenship. It was rejected out of hand by conservatives in the CSU. See CSU Landesgruppe im Deutschen

Bundestag, *Presse Mitteilungen*, 39/1993, Staatsangehörigkeit, February 5, 1993, Archiv für Christlich-Demokratische Politik, file 24 – Staatsangehörigkeit.

115 "Von Weizsaeker Calls for Easier Naturalization Laws," *Agence France Presse*, December 24, 1992.

116 "Aufmacher Weizsäcker Weihnachtsansprache: Wir und die Anderen," *Süddeutsche Zeitung*, December 24, 1992.

117 "SZ Interview mit dem Präsidenten des Bundesverfassungsgerichts," *Süddeutsche Zeitung*, March 30, 1993.

118 Inge Günther, "Doppelte Staatsbürgerschaft – das Millionending?" *Franfurther Rundschau*, February 27, 1993; Olaf Mack, "Aktion Doppelte Staatsangehörigkeit Unterschriften statt Lichterkette," *Süddeutsche Zeitung*, March 1, 1993; "Referendum rollt nach Bonn," *Frankfurter Rundschau*, July 2, 1993.

119 Referendum Doppelte Staatsbürgerschaft, ed., *Referendum Doppelte Staatsbürger-schaft*, Archiv Grünes Gedächtnis, Bibliothek, 2000/02.

120 "Eine Million Unterschriften für zweite Staatsbürgerschaft," *Süddeutsche Zeitung*, October 21, 1993.

121 *Independent on Sunday* (London), November 30, 1992, cited in Herbert, *Geschichte der Ausländerpolitik*, 316.

122 Helsinki Watch, *Foreigners Out: Xenophobia and Anti-Foreigner Violence in Germany* (New York: Helsinki Watch, 1992).

123 Karen Breslau, "Faultless to a Fault: After the Jewish Problem, the Polish Problem, and the Asylum Problem – What about the German Problem?" *Newsweek*, September 28, 1992.

124 "The Other Germans," *Times* (London), March 8, 1993. See also Judy Dempsey, "Germany's Citizenship Challenge: The Hurdles Placed in the Way of Those Seeking Naturalization," *Financial Times* (London), December 3, 1992.

125 "Kinkel: Rechtextremistische Gewalt gefährdet deutsches Ansehen," *Deutsche Presse-Agentur*, December 5, 1992.

126 The remainder of this paragraph draws from Thomas Wittke, "Das Auslandsbild der Deutschen ist nach Mölln verheerend," *Generalanzeiger* (Bonn), December 3, 1992. See also Fritz Wirth, "USA: Ende des Goodwill?" *Die Welt*, December 14, 1992; "Das Deutschlandbild droht in den Staaten Schaden zu nehmen," *Frankfurter Allgemeine Zeitung*, December 8, 1992; "Der gute Ruf ist schwer erschüttert," *Der Spiegel*, December 7, 1992.

127 Meier-Braun, *Deutschland, Einwanderungsland*, 85. On German firms' reactions to the Mölln murders and racist violence more generally, see Donald G. Phillips, *Post-National Patriotism and the Feasibility of Post-National Community in United Germany* (Westport, CT: Praeger, 2000), 157-67.

128 Riva Kastoryano, *Negotiating Identities: States and Immigrants in France and Germany* (Princeton, NJ: Princeton University Press, 2002), 159.

129 "Der Kompromiß soll ein versöhnendes Signal setzen," *Frankfurter Allgemeine Zei-tung*, December 8, 1992; Klusmeyer and Papademetriou, *Immigration Policy*, 169-87.

130 Daniel Levy, "The Transformation of Germany's Ethno-Cultural Idiom," in *Challenging Ethnic Citizenship: German and Israeli Perspectives on Immigration*, ed. Daniel Levy and Yfaat Weiss (New York: Berghahn Books, 2002), 229-30.

131 Deutscher Bundestag, *Die Grundrechte,* available at http://www.bundestag.de/.

132 Kay Hailbronner, "Asylum Law Reform in the German Constitution," *American University Journal of International Law and Policy* 9, 4 (1994): 161-62.

133 Schönwälder, "Persons Persecuted," 86; Dr. Cornelia Sonntag-Wolgast, member of the German Bundestag (SPD), interview with author, Berlin, April 2, 2004.

134 Klusmeyer and Papademetriou, *Immigration Policy,* 159-67; Adrian Favell and Randall Hansen, "Markets against Politics: Migration, EU Enlargement and the Idea of Europe," *Journal of Ethnic and Migration Studies* 28, 4 (2002): 581-602.

135 Sandra Lavenex, "Shifting Up and Out: The Foreign Policy of European Immigration Control," *West European Politics* 29, 2 (2006): 329-50; Virginie Giraudon and Gallya Lahav, "Actors and Venues in Immigration Control: Closing the Gap between Political Demands and Policy Outcomes," *West European Politics* 29, 2 (2006): 201-23.

136 Prantl, *Deutschland,* 122-23.

137 Arthur Allen, "Despite Crackdown, New Law, Germany Can't Stop Attacks on Foreigners," *Associated Press,* May 31, 1993; "Angst vor dem Krieg auf der Strasse," *Focus,* June 7, 1993.

138 "Neo-Nazis Hurting Economy, German Business Leaders Warn," *Globe and Mail,* June 9, 1993.

139 Stephen Kinzer, "Germans Feel Pressure to Do More to Protect Foreigners," *New York Times,* June 2, 1993.

140 Ibid.

141 Klaus-Peter Schmid, "Ungeliebte Moffen," *Die Zeit,* September 17, 1993.

142 Terrence Petty, "Kohl Accuses Countrymen of Coldness toward Foreigners," *Associated Press,* June 17, 1993.

143 Stephen Scheinberg and Ian J. Kagedan, "No Place to Call Homeland: Germany Should Amend Its Citizenship Law," *Toronto Star,* June 10, 1993. For a useful summary of foreign radio and television reactions to the Solingen murders see Presse- und Informationsamt der Bundesregierung, "Sonderdienst zum Echo von Rundfunk und Fernsehen des Auslands auf den Mordanschlag von Solingen," *Fernseh- und Hörfunkspiegel Ausland,* 101, June 1, 1993, Archiv für Christlich-Demokratische Politik, file 010715-8.

144 "Blood Laws," *Times* (London), June 2, 1993. See also Alan Watson, "Germany Needs a Passport to Peace," *Independent* (London), June 3, 1993; Andrew Nagorski and Theresa Waldrop, "The Laws of Blood," *Newsweek,* June 14, 1993.

145 Gwynne Dyer, "Germany's Citizenship Law is Insupportable," *Record* (Kitchener), June 21, 1993. This article was also carried in several other Canadian and British newspapers.

146 William Safire, "Blood and Irony," *New York Times,* June 17, 1993.

147 "German Citizen Law Has No Nazism Link," *New York Times,* July 2, 1993.

148 A point developed with great sophistication by Patrick Weil in *How to Be French: Nationality in the Making Since 1789,* trans. Catherine Porter (Durham, NC: Duke University Press, 2008), 173-93.

149 "Doppelte Staatsbürgerschaft: Koalition diskutiert über Lex Türkei," *Süddeutsche Zeitung,* June 3, 1993.

150 Christian Müller, "Trauerfeiern für die Mordopfer von Solingen," *Neue Zürcher Zeitung*, June 4, 1993; "Kohl Promises Tougher Fight against Racist Violence," *Inter Press Service*, June 17, 1993; "Europe's Foreigners – and Citizens," *Washington Post*, June 21, 1993.

151 Presse- und Informationsamt der Bundesregierung, "Trauer um die Opfer des Brandschlages von Solingen," *Bulletin* (Bonn), June 9, 1993.

152 Presse- und Informationsamt der Bundesregierung, "Erklärung der Bundesregierung zur aktuellen Lage der deutsche-türkischen Beziehungen, Bekämpfung von Gewalt und Extremismus sowie zu Maßnahmen für eine verbesserte Integration der Ausländer in Deutschland," *Bulletin* (Bonn), June 18, 1993.

153 According to the new regulations, immigrants between the ages of sixteen and twenty-three, along with those with fifteen or more years of residence, would be granted a "right" to naturalization, subject to certain conditions, including release from former citizenship. The change set further limits to officials' discretion in the conferring of citizenship to eligible applicants. For discussion, see Green, "Citizenship Policy," 33-34.

154 Green, "Politics of Exclusion," 178.

155 Green, "Politics of Exclusion," 179; Joppke, *Immigration and the Nation-State*, 207.

156 Green, *The Politics of Exclusion*, 91.

157 Gerald L. Neuman, "Nationality Law," 284-85; Heribert Prantl, "Juristische Zeugung deutschähnlicher Kinder," *Süddeutsche Zeitung*, November 14, 1994.

158 Elke Eckert, "Ein kleines bisschen Staatsbürgerschaft," *die tageszeitung*, November 15, 1994.

159 Eckert, "Ein kleines bisschen Staatsbürgerschaft."

160 Dan Fesperman, "Second-Class Germans? Bonn Ponders 'Trial Citizenship' in Shakeup of Immigration Law," *Baltimore Sun*, November 30, 1994.

161 See, for example, Klaus J. Bade, ed., *Das Manifest der 60: Deutschland und die Einwanderung* (Munich: C.H. Beck, 1994).

162 See SPD, Bundestagsfraktion, *Dokumentation: Einbürgerung erleichtern – Integration fördern* (Bonn, SPD-Bundestagsfraktion – Fraktionsservice: 1995); Sozialdemokratische Partei Deutschland, Parteivorstand, Archiv, file X3 – Ausländer – K; Deutscher Bundestag, Stenographischer Bericht, 13, Wahlperiode, 18, Sitzung, February 9, 1995, 1218.

163 See Bundestag Drucksache, 13/423, 13/3472, 13/3719.

164 Cem Özdemir, interior affairs spokesperson Green Party parliamentary group, interview with author, Berlin, March 15, 2002; Klaus Geiger, professor of political sociology, University of Kassel, interview with author, Kassel, March 22, 2002. See Bündnis 90/Die Grünen, *Fremd ist Fremde nur in der Fremde: Warum wir ein Einwanderungsgesetz brauchen. Diskussionspapier* (Berlin: Bündnis 90/Die Grünen, September 1991); Sozialdemokratische Partei Deutschland, Parteivorstand, Archiv, file X3 – Ausländer – September 1991.

165 Peter Altmaier, "Reform des Staatsangehörigkeitsrechts – Ist die Hinnahme mehrfacher Staatsbürgerschaft überfällig?" *Civis* 3-4 (1996), available at http://www.peteraltmaier.de/.

166 Peter Altmaier, member of the German *Bundestag* (CDU), interview with author, Berlin, May 3, 2004.

167 Barbara Marshall, *The New Germany and Migration in Europe* (Manchester: University of Manchester Press, 2000), 147; Green, *The Politics of Exclusion*, 94.

168 A reworked version of the child citizenship proposal that included a "guarantee of naturalization" for children of immigrants born in Germany was introduced in November 1997. This proposal did not satisfy either liberals in the CDU or the opposition parties. See Green, "Citizenship Policy in Germany," 41-42.

169 Green, "Politics of Exclusion."

170 An excerpt of the agreement with the relevant sections is included in Federal Ministry of the Interior, *Policy and Law Concerning Foreigners in Germany* (Berlin: Ministry of the Interior, Public Relations Sector, 2000), 166-67.

171 Ministry of the Interior, *Policy and Law*; Rainer Münz and Ralf Ulrich, "Deutschland: Rot-Grün bringt Reform des Staatsbürgerschaftsrechts, aber kein Einwanderungsgesetz," *Migration und Bevölkerung*, November 1998, 1.

172 Cited in Marc Morjé Howard, *The Politics of Citizenship in Europe* (Cambridge: Cambridge University Press, 2009), 133.

173 Dieter Wiefelspütz, interior affairs spokesperson SPD parliamentary group, interview with Kaoru Iriyama, Berlin, April 24, 2002; Cem Özdemir, interior affairs spokesperson Green Party parliamentary group, interview by author March 15, 2002, Berlin.

174 "Alle Schwarzen gegen die doppelte Staatsbürgerschaft," *die tageszeitung*, January 4, 1999.

175 Wolfgang Zeitlmann, "Wir bekommen zweierlei Deutsche," *Die Welt*, January 13, 1999.

176 Randall Hansen and Jobst Koehler, "Issue Definition, Political Discourse and the Politics of Nationality Reform in France and Germany," *European Journal of Political Research* 44, 5 (2005): 638.

177 Alice Holmes Cooper, "Party Sponsored Protest and the Movement Society: The CDU/CSU Mobilises against Citizenship Law Reform," *German Politics* 11, 2 (2002): 88-104.

178 Cooper, "Party Sponsored Protest," 96; Green, *The Politics of Exclusion*, 98-99.

179 For a good summary and discussion of the campaign, see the essays in Irene Götz, ed., *Zündstoff doppelte Staatsbürgerschaft: Zur Veralltäglichung des Nationalen* (Münster: Lit Verlag, 2000); Andreas Klärner, *Aufstand der Ressentiments: Einwanderungsdiskurs, völkischer Nationalismus und die Kampagne der CDU/CSU gegen die doppelte Staatsbürgerschaft* (Cologne: PapyRossa, 2000).

180 Heribert Prantl, "Wie Liechtenstein, San Marino und Luxemburg," *Süddeutsche Zeitung*, January 4, 1999.

181 A point emphasized in my interviews with Cem Özdemir, Sebastian Edathy and Cornelia Sonntag-Wolgast. In his memoires, Gerhard Schröder describes the behaviour of Union politicians during the debate over the citizensip law as recklessly narrow-minded. Given his indignant tone, one might reasonably assume that he too was caught unprepared by the Union parties' tactics. See Gerhard Schröder,

Entscheidungen: Mein Leben in der Politik (Hamburg: Hoffmann und Campe, 2006), 260.

182 "Der Stammtisch darf nicht entscheiden," *Süddeutsche Zeitung*, January 12, 1999; F. Weckbach-Mara, "Weizsäcker: Unterschriften-Aktion schürt Ausländer-raus-Instinkte," *Bild am Sonntag*, January 10, 1999.

183 Rüdiger Schmitt-Beck, "Die hessische Landtagswahl vom 7, Februar 1999: Der Wechsel nach dem Wechsel," *Zeitschrift für Parlamentsfragen* 31 (2000): 13.

184 Randall Hansen, "The Problems of Dual Nationality in Europe," *ECPR News* 11, 2 (2000): 5; Götz, *Zündstoff doppelte Staatsbürgerschaft*; Cooper, "Party-Sponsored Protest."

185 Martina Fietz, "Doppelpass: Schily strebt Kompromiss an," *Die Welt*, March 5, 1999.

186 Hakki Keskin, "Der Kampf für Bürgerrechte muß fortgesetzt werden," in *Deutsche Türken – Türkische Deutsche? Die Diskussion um die doppelte Staatsbürgerschaft*, ed. Andreas Goldberg and Faruk Sen (Münster: Lit Verlag, 2000), 30.

187 See Sozialdemokratische Partei Deutschland, *Zuwanderer als Zielgruppe: Einstellungen und politisches Verhalten von EU-Bürgern und anderen Zuwandern*, Bonn, April 1997, Sozialdemokratische Partei Deutschland, Parteivorstand, Archiv, file X3 – Ausländer – K.

188 Deutscher Bundestag, Stenographischer Bericht, 14, Wahlperiode, 40, Sitzung, May 7, 1999, 3413-3462.

189 Georgios Tsapanos, "Was heißt denn hier fremd? Staatsangehörigkeit zwischen Ethnizität – Identität – Nationalität," in *Staatsbürgerschaft in Europa: Historische Erfahrungen und aktuelle Debatten*, ed. Christoph Conrad and Jürgen Kocka (Hamburg: Edition Körber Stiftung, 2001), 321; Christian Joppke, "Mobilization of Culture and the Reform of Citizenship Law: Germany and the United States," in *Challenging Immigration and Ethnic Relations Politics: Comparative European Perspectives*, ed. Ruud Koopmans and Paul Statham (Albany: State University of New York Press, 1999), 156.

190 Steffen Angenendt, "Einwanderungspolitik und Einwanderungsgesetzgebung in Deutschland 2000-2001," in *Migrationsreport 2002: Fakten – Analysen – Perspektiven*, ed. Klaus J. Bade and Rainer Münz (Frankfurt: Campus Verlag, 2002), 34.

191 Dieter Wiefelspütz, interior affairs spokesperson SPD parliamentary group, interview with Kaoru Iriyama, Berlin, April 24, 2002; Cem Özdemir, interior affairs spokesperson Green Party parliamentary group, interview with author, Berlin, March 15, 2002.

192 Cem Özdemir, interior affairs spokesperson Green Party parliamentary group, interview with author, Berlin, March 15, 2002.

193 Antje Scheidler, "Deutschland/USA: Ausländische Arbeitskräfte für die Computer-branche," *Migration und Bevölkerung*, February/March 2000.

194 Cornelia Sonntag-Wolgast, member of the German Bundestag (SPD), interview with author, Berlin, April 4, 2004. The "Green Card" designation is inaccurate as the proposal entailed a loosening of visa requirements only for workers in the area of information technology. Its nearest American equivalent was the H1-B visa.

195 Jürgen Rüttgers, the CDU's nominee for minister-president in the *Land* election in North Rhine-Westphalia, campaigned on the slogan *Kinder statt Inder* ("children

instead of Indians"). The president of the Association of German Industries, Hans-Olaf Henkel, came out strongly against such tactics, noting that Germany could no longer afford such provincial behaviour. See "Foreign Workers Plan Criticized," *Associated Press*, April 1, 2000.

196 United Nations, *Replacement Migration* (New York: UN Population Division, Department of Economic and Social Affairs, 2000), cited in Douglas Klusmeyer, "A Guiding Culture for Immigrants? Integration and Diversity in Germany," *Journal of Ethnic and Migration Studies* 27, 3 (2001): 519-32.

197 Rainer Münz, Chair, Department of Demography, Humboldt University, and member of the Süssmuth Commission, interview with author, Berlin, November 2, 2000.

198 Christiane Schlötzer, "Einwanderungsgesetz gefordert: Ministerpräsident Müller – Arbeitsmarkt nicht abschotten," *Süddeutsche Zeitung*, September 8, 2000.

199 Christiane Schlötzer, "Merz: Deutschland braucht Einwanderung," *Süddeutsche Zeitung*, October 23, 2000; Annette Ramelsberger, "Mit Schily könnte man sich in drei Monaten einigen: Bayerns Innenminister Beckstein (CSU) geht auf Annäherungskurs zur Bundesregierung – und die CDU auch," *Süddeutsche Zeitung*, October 24, 2000.

200 Annette Ramelsberger, "Stoiber fordert Verschärfung des Asylrechts," *Süddeutsche Zeitung*, November 18-19, 2000; Nico Fried, "Streit über Ausländerpolitik flammt wieder auf," *Süddeutsche Zeitung*, November 20, 2000.

201 Ramelsberger, "Stoiber fordert Verschärfung des Asylrechts." On the *Leitkultur* debate, see Oliver Schmidtke, "From Taboo to Strategic Tool in Politics: Immigrants and Immigration Policies in German Party Politics," in *Germany on the Road to "Normalcy": Policies and Politics of the Red-Green Federal Government (1998-2002)*, ed. Werner Reutter (Basingstoke: Plagrave Macmillan, 2004), 171; Klusmeyer, "Guiding Culture for Immigrants"; Erhard Denninger, "Integration und Identität: Bitte um etwas Nachdenklichkeit," *Kritische Justiz* 34, 4 (2001): 442-52.

202 Federal Ministry of the Interior, *Structuring Immigration, Fostering Integration: Report by the Independent Commission on Migration to Germany* (Berlin: Federal Ministry of the Interior, July 2001), 11.

203 For a summary of the commission's recommendations, see Angenendt, "Einwanderungspolitik und Einwanderungsgesetzgebung," 38-42.

204 Peter Finn, "German Panel Moves to Boost Immigration," *Washington Post*, July 5, 2001.

205 Antje Scheidler, "Deutschland: Erster Entwurf eines Zuwanderungsgesetzes," *Migration und Bevölkerung*, September 2001, 1-2.

206 Antje Scheidler, "Deutschland: Kabinett verabschiedete Gesetzentwurf zu Zuwanderung und Integration," *Migration und Bevölkerung*, November 2001, 1-2.

207 Joachim Käppner and Jeanne Rubner, "Union und Zuwanderung: Edmund Stoiber bleibt bei seiner Ablehnung des Regierungsentwurfs," *Süddeutsche Zeitung*, March 1, 2002.

208 Marianne Heauwagen, "Schröder warnt vor Missbrauch des Bundesrats," *Süddeutsche Zeitung*, Mach 2-3, 2002.

209 Green, *The Politics of Exclusion*, 125.

210 Ibid., 126.

211 Imke Kruse, Henry Edward Orren, and Steffen Angenendt, "The Failure of Immigration Reform in Germany," *German Politics* 12, 3 (2003): 129-45.

212 Karen Schönwälder, "Kleine Schritte, verpasste Gelegenheiten, neue Konflikte: Zuwanderungsgesetz und Migrationspolitik," *Blätter für deutsche und internationale Politik* 10 (2004): 1205-15.

213 "Gesetz über den Aufenthalt, die Erwebstätigkeit und die Integration von Ausländern im Bundesgebiet (Aufenthaltsgesetz – AufenthG)," in *Deutsches Ausländerrecht*, 21. Auflage (Munich: Beck-Texte im dtv, 2008). For the English translation, see Bundesministerium der Justiz, http://www.gesetze-im-internet.de/.

214 It is estimated that 385,541 young Germans will be affected by the law up to the year 2026. See Die Beauftragte der Bundesregierung für Migration, Flüchtlinge und Integration, 8. *Bericht der Beauftragten der Bundesregierung für Migration, Flüchtlinge und Integration über die Lage der Ausländerinnen und Ausländer in Deutschland* (Berlin: Beauftragte der Bundesregierung für Migration, Flüchtlinge und Integration, 2010), 588.

215 Susanne Worbs, "Die Einbürgerung von Ausländern in Deutschland," BAMF Working Paper 17, Nürnberg, 2008, 28.

216 Triadafilos Triadafilopoulos, Anna Korteweg, and Paulina Garcia Del Moral, "The Benefits and Limits of Pragmatism: Immigrant Integration Policy and Social Cohesion in Germany," in *Diverse Nations, Diverse Responses: Approaches to Social Cohesion in Immigrant Societies*, ed. Paul Spoonley and Erin Tolley (Montreal and Kingston: McGill-Queen's University Press, forthcoming).

CHAPTER 6: CONCLUSION

1 See Martin Schain, Aristide R. Zolberg, and Patrick Hossay, eds., *Shadows over Europe: The Development and Impact of the Extreme Right in Western Europe* (Basingstoke: Palgrave, 2002); Mabel Berezin, *Illiberal Policies in Neoliberal Times: Culture, Security and Populism in the New Europe* (Cambridge: Cambridge University Press, 2009); Cas Mudde, *Populist Radical Right Parties in Europe* (Cambridge: Cambridge University Press, 2007).

2 J.A. Sandy Irvine, "Canadian Refugee Policy and the Role of International Bureaucratic Networks in Domestic Paradigm Change," in *Policy Paradigms, Transnationalism, and Domestic Politics*, ed. Grace Skogstad, 171-201 (Toronto: University of Toronto Press, 2011); Douglas Klusmeyer and Demetrios G. Papademetriou, *Immigration Policy in the Federal Republic of Germany: Negotiating Membership and Remaking the Nation* (New York: Berghahn Books, 2010), 168-80.

3 Randall Hansen and Patrick Weil, "Citizenship, Immigration and Nationality: Towards a Convergence in Europe?" in *Towards a European Nationality: Citizenship, Immigration and Nationality Law in the EU*, ed. Randall Hansen and Patrick Weil, 1-23 (Basingstoke: Palgrave, 2001); Marc Morjé Howard, *The Politics of Citizenship in Europe* (Cambridge: Cambridge University Press, 2009); Christian Joppke, *Citizenship and Immigration* (Oxford: Polity Press, 2010); Audrey Macklin, "The

Securitization of Dual Citizenship," in *Dual Citizenship in Global Perspective: From Unitary to Multiple Citizenship*, ed. Thomas Faist and Peter Kivisto, 42-68 (Basingstoke: Palgrave Macmillan, 2007); Dora Kostakopoulou, "Matters of Control: Integration Tests, Naturalization Reform and Probationary Citizenship in the United Kingdom," *Journal of Ethnic and Migration Studies* 36, 5 (2010): 829-46.

4 Steven Vertovec and Susanne Wessendorf, "Introduction: Assessing the Backlash against Multiculturalism in Europe," in *The Multiculturalism Backlash: European Discourses, Policies and Practices*, ed. Steven Vertovec and Susanne Wessendorf, 1-31 (New York: Routledge, 2010); Geoffrey Brahm Levey, "Review Article: What Is Living and What Is Dead in Multiculturalism," *Ethnicities* 9, 1 (2009): 75-93.

5 Christian Joppke, "Beyond National Models: Civic Integration Policies for Immigrants in Western Europe," *West European Politics* 30, 1 (2007): 1-22.

6 Adam Tebble, "Exclusion for Democracy," *Political Theory* 34, 4 (2006): 463-87.

7 Triadafilos Triadafilopoulos, "Illiberal Means to Liberal Ends: Understanding Recent Immigrant Integration Policies in Europe," *Journal of Ethnic and Migration Studies* 37, 6 (2011): 861-80.

8 Liz Fekete, *A Suitable Enemy: Racism, Migration and Islamophobia in Europe*, Foreword by A. Sivanandan (London: Pluto Press, 2009); Sherene H. Razack, *Casting Out: The Eviction of Muslims from Western Law and Politics* (Toronto: University of Toronto Press, 2008); David Theo Goldberg, "Racial Europeanization," *Ethnic and Racial Studies* 29, 2 (2006): 331-64.

9 For background, see Elisabeth Musch, *Integration durch Konsultation? Konsensbildung in der Migrations- und Integrationspolitik in Deutschland und den Niederlanden* (Münster: Waxman, 2011), 290-310; Gabrieele Hermani, *Die Deutsche Islamkonferenz 2006-2009: Der Dialogprozess mit den Muslimen in Deutschland im Öffentlichen Diskurs* (Berlin: Finckenstein and Salmuth, 2010); Werner Schiffauer and Manuela Bojadzijev, "Es geht nicht um einen Dialog: Integrationsgipfel, Islamkonferenz und Anti-Islamismus," in *No Integration? Kulturwissenschaftliche Beiträge zur Integrationsdebatte in Europa*, 171-86 (Bielefeld: Transcrip, 2009); Benjamin Bruce, "Promoting Belonging through Religious Institutionalization? The French Council of the Muslim Faith (CFCM) and the German Islamkonferenz," *Political Perspectives* 4, 2 (2010): 49-69.

10 This paragraph draws on ongoing field research by the author.

11 Sacha Kneip and Christian Henkes, "Das Kopftuch im Streit zwischen Parlamenten und Gerichten: Ein Drama in drei Akten," in *WZB Discussion Paper*, 1-51 (Berlin: Wissenschaftszentrum Berlin für Sozialforschung [WZB], 2008); Richard Moon, ed., *Law and Religious Pluralism in Canada* (Vancouver: UBC Press, 2008).

12 Micheline Milot, "Modus Co-vivendi: Religious Diversity in Canada," in *International Migration and the Governance of Religious Diversity*, ed. Paul Bramadat and Matthias Koenig, 105-30 (Montreal and Kingston: McGill-Queen's University Press, 2009).

13 The remainder of this and the next paragraph draw from Supreme Court of Canada, *Multani v. Commission scolaire Marguerite-Bourgeoys* (2006) 1 S.C.R. 256.

14 Anna Korteweg, "The Sharia Debate in Ontario: Gender, Islam and the Representations of Muslim Women's Agency," *Gender and Society* 22 (2008): 434-54;

Les Perreaux, "Quebec's View on Niqab Creates Fault Line," *Globe and Mail*, March 19, 2010; Kneip and Henkes, "Das Kopftuch im Streit zwischen Parlamenten und Gerichten"; Franz Sommerfeld, ed., *Der Moscheestreit: Eine examplarische Debatte über Einwanderung und Integration* (Cologne: Kiepenheuer and Witsch, 2008).

Bibliography

ARCHIVAL SOURCES
Archiv für Christlich-Demokratische Politik
    File 0/07 – Ausländer – Asylgewährung
    File 24 – Staatsangehörigkeit
    File 010715-8
Archiv Grünes Gedächtnis, Berlin
    Bestand B. II. 1
Library and Archives Canada, Ottawa
    Canadian Congress of Labour, MG 28
    Department of Finance, RG 19
    Department of External Affairs, RG 25
    Department of Citizenship and Immigration, RG 26
    Immigration Branch, RG 76
Sozialdemokratische Partei Deutschland, Parteivorstand, Archiv, Berlin
    File X3 – Ausländer

OTHER SOURCES CITED
Abella, Irving, and Harold Troper. "'The Line Must Be Drawn Somewhere': Canada and Jewish Refugees, 1933-1939." In *A Nation of Immigrants: Women, Workers, and Communities in Canadian History, 1840s-1960s*, ed. Franca Iacovetta, with Paula Draper and Robert Ventresca. Toronto: University of Toronto Press, 1998.
–. *None Is Too Many: Canada and the Jews of Europe, 1933-1948.* Toronto: Lester and Orpen Dennys, 1982.

Abu-Laban, Yasmeen. "Welcome/STAY OUT: The Contradictions of Canadian Integration and Immigration Policies at the Millennium." *Canadian Ethnic Studies* 30, 3 (1998): 190-211.

Abu-Laban, Yasmeen, and Christina Gabriel. *Selling Diversity: Immigration, Multiculturalism, Employment Equity, and Globalization*. Peterborough: Broadview Press, 2002.

Abu-Laban, Yasmeen, and Daiva Stasiulis. "Ethnic Pluralism under Siege: Popular and Partisan Opposition to Multiculturalism." *Canadian Public Policy* 18, 4 (1992): 365-86.

Adler, Emanuel. "Seizing the Middle Ground: Constructivism in World Politics." *European Journal of International Relations* 3, 3 (1997): 319-63.

Adorno, Theodor. *Negative Dialectics*. New York: Continuum, 1983.

Alba, Richard. "Connecting the Dots between Boundary Change and Large-Scale Assimilation with Zolbergian Clues." *Social Research* 77, 1 (2010): 163-80.

Albertini, Rudolf von. "The Impact of the Two World Wars on the Decline of Colonialism." In *The End of European Empire: Decolonization after World War II*, ed. Tony Smith. Lexington, MA: D.C. Heath and Company, 1975.

Alderson, Kai. "Making Sense of State Socialization." *Review of International Studies* 27, 3 (2001): 415-33.

Alexander, Jeffrey C. "On the Social Construction of Moral Universals: The 'Holocaust' from War Crimes to Trauma Drama." *European Journal of Social Theory* 5, 1 (2002): 5-85.

"Alle Schwarzen gegen die doppelte Staatsbürgerschaft." *die tageszeitung*, January 4, 1999.

Allemann, Fritz. "Der neue fünfte Stand." *Die Welt*, December 4, 1964.

Allen, Arthur. "Despite Crackdown, New Law, Germany Can't Stop Attacks on Foreigners." *AP*, May 31, 1993.

Almanasreh de C. Esteves, Rosi-Wolf. "Alternativentwurf 1970 zum Ausländergesetz 1965." *Studentische Politik* 1 (1970): 5-9.

Altmaier, Peter. "Reform des Staatsangehörigkeitsrechts – Ist die Hinnahme mehrfacher Staatsbürgerschaft überfällig?" *Civis* 3-4 (1996), available online at http://www.peteraltmaier.de/.

Altmaier, Peter, and Norbert Röttgen. "Die Uhr läuft." *Die Zeit*, August 15, 1997.

Ancheta, Angelo N. *Race, Rights, and the Asian American Experience*. New Brunswick, NJ: Rutgers University Press, 1998.

Anderson, Kay J. "The Idea of Chinatown: The Power of Place and Institutional Practice in the Making of a Racial Category." In *Immigration in Canada: Historical Perspectives*, ed., Gerald Tulchinsky. Toronto: Copp Clark Longman, 1994.

Andracki, Stanislaw. *Immigration of Orientals into Canada with Special Reference to Chinese*. New York: Arno Press, 1978.

Angenendt, Steffen. "Einwanderungspolitik und Einwanderungsgesetzgebung in Deutschland 2000-2001." In *Migrationsreport 2002: Fakten – Analysen – Perspektiven*, ed. Klaus J. Bade and Rainer Münz. Frankfurt: Campus Verlag, 2002.

"Angst vor dem Krieg auf der Strasse." *Focus,* June 7, 1993.

Angus, H.F. "The Legal Status in British Columbia of Residents of Oriental Race and Their Descendants." *Canadian Bar Review* 9, 1 (1931): 1-12.

"Arbeiter, keine Sklaven." *Kölnische Rundschau,* May 2, 1971.

Arendt, Hannah. *The Origins of Totalitarianism.* New edition with added prefaces. New York: Harcourt Brace and Company, 1973.

"Asyl – 'Bis an die Grenze des Zulässigen.'" *Der Spiegel,* July 28, 1986.

"Aufmacher Weizsäcker Weihnachtsansprache: Wir und die Anderen." *Süddeutsche Zeitung,* December 24, 1992.

"Aus der Asche." *Der Spiegel,* August 10, 1984.

"'Ausländerrecht in der Diskussion': Ein Diskussionsbeitrag des Diakonischen Werkes der EKD zur Novellierung des Ausländergesetzes." *Diakonie Korrespondenz,* January 23, 1989.

Avery, Donald. *Reluctant Host: Canada's Response to Immigrant Workers, 1896-1994.* Toronto: McClelland and Stewart, 1995.

Backhouse, Constance. "The White Women's Labor Laws: Anti-Chinese Racism in Early Twentieth-Century Canada." *Law and History Review* 14, 2 (1996): 315-68.

Bade, Klaus J. *Ausländer, Aussiedler, Asyl in der Bundesrepublik Deutschland.* Bonn: Bundeszentrale für politische Bildung, 1992.

–. *Ausländer, Aussiedler, Asyl in der Bundesrepublik Deutschland.* 3rd ed. Hannover: Niedersächsische Landeszentrale für Politische Bildung, 1994.

–. "'Billig und willig' – die 'ausländischen Wanderarbeiter' im kaiserlichen Deutschland." In *Deutsche im Ausland – Fremde in Deutschland: Migration in Geschichte und Gegenwart,* ed. Klaus J. Bade. Munich: C.H. Beck, 1992.

–. "German Emigration to the United States and Continental Immigration to Germany in the Late Nineteenth and Early Twentieth Centuries." *Central European History* 13 (1980): 348-77.

–. "Immigration and Social Peace in United Germany." *Daedalus* 123, 1 (1994): 85-106.

–. "Immigration, Naturalization, and Ethno-National Traditions in Germany: From the Citizenship Law of 1913 to the Law of 1999." In *Crossing Boundaries: The Exclusion and Inclusion of Minorities in Germany and the United States,* ed. Larry Eugene Jones. New York: Berghahn Books, 2001.

–. "Kulturkampf auf dem Arbeitsmarkt: Bismarcks Polenpolitik 1885-1890." In *Innenpolitische Probleme des Bismarck-Reiches,* ed. Otto Pflanze. Munich: R. Oldenbourg, 1983.

–. "Labour, Migration, and the State: Germany from the Late 19th Century to the Onset of the Great Depression." In *Population, Labour and Migration in 19th- and 20th-Century Germany,* ed. Klaus J. Bade. New York: St. Martin's Press, 1987.

–. *Migration in European History,* trans. Allison Brown. Oxford: Blackwell, 2003.

–. "Politik und Ökonomie der Ausländerbeschäftigung im preußischen Osten 1885-1910: Die Internationalisierung des Arbeitsmarkts im 'Rahmen der preußischen Abwehrpolitik.'" In *Preußen im Rückblick,* ed. Hans-Jürgen Puhle and Hans-Ulrich Wehler. Göttingen: Vandenhoeck and Ruprecht Verlag, 1980.

–. "'Preußengänger' und 'Abwehrpolitik': Ausländerbeschäftigung, Ausländerpolitik und Ausländerkontrolle auf dem Arbeitsmarkt in Preußen vor dem Erstem Weltkrieg." *Archiv für Sozialgeschichte* 24 (1984): 91-162.

–. "Transnationale Migration, ethnonationale Diskussion und staatliche Migrationspolitik im Deutschland des 19. und 20. Jahrhunderts." In *Migration, Ethnizität, Konflikt*, ed. Klaus J. Bade. Osnabrück: Rasch, 1996.

–. *Vom Auswanderungsland zum Einwanderungsland? Deutschland, 1880-1980.* Berlin: Colloquium Verlag, 1983.

–, ed. "Arbeiterstatistik zur Ausländerkontrolle: Die 'Nachweisungen' der preußischen Landräte über den 'Zugang, Abgang und Bestand der ausländischen Arbeiter im preußischen Staate' 1906-1914." *Archiv für Sozialgeschichte* 24 (1984): 163-283.

–, ed. *Das Manifest der 60: Deutschland und die Einwanderung.* Munich: C.H. Beck, 1994.

–, ed. *Deutsche im Ausland – Fremde in Deutschland: Migration in Geschichte und Gegenwart.* Munich: C.H. Beck, 1992.

Baines, Dudley. "European Labor Markets, Emigration and Internal Migration, 1850-1913." In *Migration and the International Labor Market, 1850-1939*, ed. Timothy J. Hatton and Jeffrey G. Williamson. New York: Routledge, 1994.

BAMF (Bundesamt für Migration und Flüchtlinge). *Muslimisches Leben in Deutschland.* Im Auftrag der Deutschen Islam Konferenz, Nürnberg, 2009.

Bangarth, Stephanie D. "'We Are Not Asking You to Open Wide the Gates for Chinese Immigration': The Committee for the Repeal of the Chinese Immigration Act and Early Human Rights Activism in Canada." *Canadian Historical Review* 84, 3 (2003): 1-16.

Bannas, Günter. "Geißler fürchtet den 'Volksgeist.'" *Frankfurter Allgemeine Zeitung,* March 28, 1990.

Banton, Michael. *The International Politics of Race.* Oxford: Polity, 2002.

Banton, Michael, and Jonathan Harwood. *The Race Concept.* London: David and Charles, 1975.

Barbieri, William A., Jr. *Ethics of Citizenship: Immigration and Group Rights in Germany.* Durham, NC: Duke University Press, 1998.

Barkan, Elazar. *The Retreat of Scientific Racism: Changing Concepts of Race in Britain and the United States between the World Wars.* Cambridge: Cambridge University Press, 1992.

Barkin, J. Samuel, and Bruce Cronin. "The State and the Nation: Changing Norms and the Rules of Sovereignty in International Relations." *International Organization* 48, 1 (1994): 107-30.

Baron, Salo W. *The Russian Jews under Tsars and Soviets.* Rev. ed. New York: Macmillan, 1976.

Barraclough, Geoffrey. *An Introduction to Contemporary History.* New York: Basic Books, 1964.

Barwig, Klaus. "Zur Diskussion um die Novellierung des Ausländerrechts." *Zeitschrift für Ausländerrecht* 4 (1989): 173-83.

Bauböck, Rainer. "Integration in a Pluralistic Society: Strategies for the Future." Working Paper, Institute for Advanced Studies, Vienna, May 1993.

Baum, Bruce. *The Rise and Fall of the Caucasian Race: A Political History of Racial Identity*. New York: New York University Press, 2006.

BDA (*Bundesvereinigung der deutschen Arbeitgeberverbände*). *Jahresberichte*. Cologne: BDA, 1951.

Becker, Horst. "Einstellungen zu Ausländern in der Bevölkerung der Bundesrepublik Deutschland 1992." In *Zuwanderung und Asyl in der Konkurrenzgesellschaft*, ed. Bernhard Blanke. Opladen: Leske and Budrich, 1993.

Bélanger, Alain, and Éric Caron Malenfant. "Ethnocultural Diversity in Canada: Prospects for 2017." *Canadian Social Trends* 79 (2005), Statistics Canada – Catalogue 11-008.

Bendix, John. *Importing Foreign Workers: A Comparison of German and American Policy*. New York: Peter Lang, 1990.

Bendix, Reinhard. "Concepts and Generalizations in Comparative Sociological Studies." *American Sociological Review* 28, 4 (1963): 532-39.

Benhabib, Seyla. "Claiming Rights across Borders: International Human Rights and Democratic Sovereignty." *American Political Science Review* 103, 4 (2009): 698-99.

Berezin, Mabel. *Illiberal Policies in Neoliberal Times: Culture, Security and Populism in the New Europe*. Cambridge: Cambridge University Press, 2009.

"Bertreuung der ausländischen Arbeitnehmer." In *Amtliche Nachrichten der Bundesanstalt für Arbeitsvermittlung und Arbeitsversicherung*. Nuremberg: Bundesanstalt für Arbeitsvermittlung und Arbeitsversicherung, 1965). Reprinted in English translation (by David Gramling) in *Germany in Transition: Nation and Migration, 1955-2005*, ed. Deniz Göktürk, David Gramling, and Anton Kaes. Berkeley: University of California Press, 2005.

Bethscheider, Monika, and Gabriele Köppe, eds. *Die Multikulturelle Gesellschaft: Für eine demokratische Umgestaltung in der Bundesrepublik – Positionen und Dokumentation*. Bonn: Die Grünen im Bundestag, 1990.

Betts, Raymond F. *Decolonization*. London: Routledge, 1998.

Birnbaum, R., H. Monath, and J. Müller-Neuhof. "Karlsruhe kippt Zuwanderungsgesetz." *Der Tagesspiegel*, December 19, 2002.

Bischoff, Detlef, and Werner Teubner. *Zwischen Einbürgerung und Rückkehr: Ausländerpolitik und Ausländerrecht in der Bundesrepublik Deutschland*. Berlin: Hitit Verlag, 1992.

Blanchette, Arthur E., ed. *Canadian Foreign Policy, 1955-1965: Selected Speeches and Documents*. Toronto: McClelland and Stewart, 1977.

Blank, Ingo. "'... nirgends eine Heimat, aber Gräber auf jedem Friedhof': Ostjuden in Kaiserreich und Weimarer Republik." In *Deutsche im Ausland – Fremde in Deutschland: Migration in Geschichte und Gegenwart*, ed. Klaus J. Bade. Munich: C.H. Beck, 1992.

Bleich, Erik. "From International Ideas to Domestic Politics: Educational Multiculturalism in England and France." *Comparative Politics* 31, 1 (1998): 81-100.

Bloemraad, Irene. *Becoming a Citizen: Incorporating Immigrants and Refugees in the United States and Canada*. Berkeley: University of California Press, 2006.

"Blood Laws." *Times* (London), June 2, 1993.

Boli, John, and George M. Thomas. "World Culture in the World Polity: A Century of International Non-Governmental Organization." *American Sociological Review* 62, 2 (1997): 171-90.

Borders, William. "Canada Begins a Debate on Immigration." *New York Times*, March 15, 1975.

Borgmann, Wolfgang. "Gast-Arbeiter?" *Stuttgarter Zeitung*, September 25, 1971.

Borstelmann, Thomas. *The Cold War and the Color Line: American Race Relations in the Global Arena*. Cambridge, MA: Harvard University Press, 2001.

Bös, Matthias. "Ethnisierung des Rechts? Staatsbürgerschaft in Deutschland, Frankreich, Großbritannien und den USA." *Kölner Zeitschrift für Soziologie und Sozialpsychologie* 45, 4 (1993): 619-43.

Bosniak, Linda. *The Citizen and the Alien: Dilemmas of Contemporary Membership*. Princeton: Princeton University Press, 2006.

–. "Multiple Nationality and the Postnational Transformation of Citizenship." *Virginia Journal of International Law* 42 (2001-02): 1002-03.

Bothwell, Robert. *Alliance and Illusion: Canada and the World, 1945-1984*. Vancouver: UBC Press, 2007.

Bothwell, Robert, Ian Drummond, and John English. *Canada since 1945: Power, Politics, and Provincialism*, rev. ed. Toronto: University of Toronto Press, 1989.

Boustan, Leah Platt. "Were Jews Political Refugees or Economic Migrants? Assessing the Persecution Theory of Jewish Emigration, 1881-1914." In *The New Economic History: Essays in Honor of Jeffrey G. Williamson*, ed. Timothy J. Hatton, Kevin H. O'Rourke, and Alan M. Taylor. Cambridge: MIT Press, 2007.

Boyko, John. *Last Steps to Freedom: The Evolution of Canadian Racism*. Winnipeg: Witton and Dwyer, 1995.

Bradford, Neil. *Commissioning Ideas: Canadian National Policy Innovation in Comparative Perspective*. Toronto: Oxford University Press, 1998.

–. "Public-Private Partnership? Shifting Paradigms of Economic Governance in Ontario." *Canadian Journal of Political Science* 36, 5 (2003): 1005-34.

Breslau, Karen. "Faultless to a Fault: After the Jewish Problem, the Polish Problem, and the Asylum Problem – What about the German Problem?" *Newsweek*, September 28, 1992.

Breton, Raymond. "From Ethnic to Civic Nationalism: English Canada and Quebec." *Ethnic and Racial Studies* 11, 1 (1988): 85-102.

Brown, Michael. "From Stereotype to Scapegoat: Anti-Jewish Sentiment in French Canada from Confederation to World War I." In *Antisemitism in Canada: History and Interpretation*, ed. Alan Davies. Waterloo, ON: Wilfrid Laurier University Press, 1992.

Brown, Robert Craig. "Full Partnership in the Fortunes and in the Future of the Nation." In *Ethnicity and Citizenship: The Canadian Case*, ed. J.A. Laponce and William Safran. London: Frank Cass, 1996.

Brubaker, Rogers. *Citizenship and Nationhood in France and Germany.* Cambridge, MA: Harvard University Press, 1992.

–. "Comment on 'Modes of Immigration Politics in Liberal Democratic States.'" *International Migration Review* 29, 4 (1995): 909-13.

–. "The Return of Assimilation? Changing Perspectives on Immigration and Its Sequels in France, Germany, and the United States." *Ethnic and Racial Studies* 24, 4 (2001): 531-48.

Bruce, Benjamin. "Promoting Belonging through Religious Institutionalization? The French Council of the Muslim Faith (CFCM) and the German Islamkonferenz." *Political Perspectives* 4, 2 (2010): 49-69.

"Bryce Mackasey Takes a Stand: A New Deal for Our Immigrants." *Calgary Herald,* June 28, 1972.

Bundesamt für die Anerkennung ausländischer Flüchtlinge. *Migration und Asyl in Zahlen.* Nuremberg: Bundesamt für die Anerkennung ausländischer Flüchtlinge, 2003.

Bundesminister des Innern. *Kommission "Ausländerpolitik" aus Vertretern von Bund, Ländern und Gemeinden.* Bonn: Bundesministerium des Innern, 1983.

"Bundesrat lehnt Einbürgerungsanspruch ab." *Frankfurter Allgemeine Zeitung,* February 13, 1982.

Bundestag Drucksache, 13/423, 13/3472, 13/3719.

Bündnis 90/Die Grünen. *Fremd ist der Fremde nur in der Fremde: Warum wir ein Einwanderungsgesetz brauchen.* Berlin: Bündnis 90/Die Grünen, September 1991.

Burleigh, Michael, and Wolfgang Wippermann. *The Racial State: Germany, 1933-1945.* Cambridge: Cambridge University Press, 1991.

Burnet, Jean. "Multiculturalism, Immigration and Racism: A Comment on the Canadian Immigration and Population Study." *Canadian Ethnic Studies* 7, 1 (1975): 35-39.

Burrow, J.W. *The Crisis of Reason: European Thought, 1848-1914.* New Haven: Yale University Press, 2000.

Cairns, Alan C. *Citizens Plus: Aboriginal Peoples and the Canadian State.* Vancouver: UBC Press, 2000.

–. "Empire, Globalization, and the Fall and Rise of Diversity." In *Citizenship, Diversity, and Pluralism: Canadian and Comparative Perspectives,* ed. Alan C. Cairns, John C. Courtney, Peter MacKinnon, Hans J. Michelmann, and David E. Smith. Montreal and Kingston: McGill-Queen's University Press, 1999.

Caldewell, Peter C. "The Citizen and the Republic in Germany, 1918-1935." In *Citizenship and National Identity in Twentieth-Century Germany,* ed. Geoff Eley and Jan Palmowski. Stanford: Stanford University Press, 2007.

Campbell, P.C. *Chinese Coolie Emigration.* London: King and Son, 1923.

Canada. Department of Justice. Canadian Charter of Rights and Freedoms, http://laws-lois.justice.gc.ca/.

–. Department of Justice. Canadian Multiculturalism Act, http://laws-lois.justice.gc.ca/.

–. Department of Manpower and Immigration. *Green Paper on Immigration and Population*. Ottawa: Department of Manpower and Immigration, 1974.

–. Department of Manpower and Immigration. Canadian Immigration and Population Study, *Highlights from the Green Paper*. Ottawa: Department of Manpower and Immigration, 1974.

–. Department of Manpower and Immigration. *The Immigration Program*. Ottawa: Information Canada, 1974.

–. Department of Manpower and Immigration. *1972 Immigration Statistics*. Ottawa: Information Canada, 1974.

–. Department of Manpower and Immigration. *White Paper on Immigration*. Ottawa: Queen's Printer and Controller of Stationery, October 1966.

–. House of Commons *Debates*, 1947-75.

–. House of Commons. Special Committee on Estimates. *Minutes of Proceedings and Evidence*, 11, March 14, 1955.

–. *Report of the Royal Commission on Chinese and Japanese Immigration*. Ottawa: S.E. Dawson, 1902.

–. *Royal Commission on Bilingualism and Biculturalism*. Vol. 1. Ottawa: Queen's Printer, 1967.

–. Senate. Standing Committee on Immigration and Labour. *Proceedings*. Ottawa: Queen's Printer, 1946-53.

–. Special Joint Committee of the Senate and House of Commons on Immigration. *Minutes of the Proceedings and Evidence*. Ottawa: Queen's Printer and Controller of Stationery, 1967.

–. Special Joint Committee of the Senate and the House of Commons on Immigration Policy. *Minutes and Proceeding of the Special Joint Committee of the Senate and the House of Commons on Immigration Policy*. Ottawa: House of Commons, 1975.

–. Special Joint Committee of the Senate and the House of Commons on Immigration Policy. *Report to Parliament*. Ottawa: Queen's Printer, 1975.

Capoccia, Giovanni, and Daniel Kelemen. "The Study of Critical Junctures: Theory, Narrative, and Counterfactuals in Historical Institutionalism." *World Politics* 59 (2007): 341-69.

Careless, J.M.S. *Canada: A Story of Challenge*. New York: St. Martin's Press, 1965.

Carrothers, W.A. "The Immigration Problem in Canada." *Queen's Quarterly* 36 (1929): 516-31.

Carter, David J. *Behind Canadian Barbed Wire: Alien, Refugee and Prisoner of War Camps in Canada, 1914-1916*. Calgary: Tumbleweed, 1980.

Castles, Stephen. "The Guests Who Stayed: The Debate on 'Foreigners Policy' in the German Federal Republic." *International Migration Review* 19, 3 (1985): 517-34.

–. "How Nation-States Respond to Immigration and Ethnic Diversity." *New Community* 21, 3 (1995): 293-308.

–. "Racism and Politics in Germany." *Race and Class* 25, 3 (1984): 37-51.

Cernetig, Miro. "Reform Party Sees Radicals as Problem: Image a Factor in National Drive." *Globe and Mail*, April 4, 1991.

Champion, C.P. *The Strange Demise of British Canada: The Liberals and Canadian Nationalism, 1964-1968.* Montreal and Kingston: McGill-Queen's University Press, 2010.

Char, Tin-Yuke. "Legal Restrictions on Chinese in English-Speaking Countries in the Pacific." *Chinese Social and Political Science Review* 16, 3 (1932): 474-86.

Checkel, Jeffrey T. "The Constructivist Turn in International Relations Theory." *World Politics* 50 (1998): 324-48.

–. "Norms, Institutions, and National Identity in Contemporary Europe." *International Studies Quarterly* 43 (1999): 84-114.

Chin, Rita, Heide Fehrenbach, Geoff Eley, and Atina Grossman. "Guest Worker Migration and the Unexpected Return of Race." In *After the Nazi Racial State: Difference and Democracy in Germany and Europe.* Ann Arbor: University of Michigan Press, 2009.

–. *The Guest Worker Question in Postwar Germany.* Cambridge: Cambridge University Press, 2007.

"Chinese See Ambiguity in Relaxed Entry Laws." *Globe and Mail,* January 22, 1962.

Cholewinski, Ryszard. "Family Reunification and Conditions Placed on Family Members: Dismantling a Fundamental Human Right." *European Journal of Migration and Law* 4 (2002): 271-90.

Chrysler, K.M. "Canada Has Second Thoughts about Its Open Door to Immigrants." *US News and World Report,* October 3, 1977.

Church Office of the Evangelical Church in Germany, Secretariat of the German Bishop's Conference and Council of Christian Churches in Germany. *Joint Statement of the Churches Regarding the Challenges of Migration and Displacement.* Hanover: Evangelical Church in Germany, 1997.

Clark, Jennifer. "'The Wind of Change' in Australia: Aborigines and the International Politics of Race, 1960-1972." *International History Review* 20, 1 (1998): 89-117.

Clarkson, Stephen. "The Defeat of the Government, the Decline of the Liberal Party, and the (Temporary) Fall of Pierre Trudeau." In *Canada at the Polls, 1979 and 1980: A Study of the General Elections,* ed. Howard R. Penniman. Washington, DC: The American Enterprise Institute for Public Policy Research, 1981.

Cohen, Robin. "East-West and European Migration in a Global Context." *New Community* 18, 1 (1991): 9-26.

Cooper, Alice Holmes. "Party Sponsored Protest and the Movement Society: The CDU/CSU Mobilises against Citizenship Law Reform." *German Politics* 11, 2 (2002): 88-104.

Corbett, David C. *Canada's Immigration Policy: A Critique.* Toronto: University of Toronto Press, 1957.

–. "Canada's Immigration Policy, 1957-1962." *International Journal* 18, 2 (1962-63): 166-80.

Cornelius, Wayne A., Phillip L. Martin, and James F. Hollifield. "Introduction: The Ambivalent Quest for Immigration Control." In *Controlling Immigration: A Global Perspective,* ed. Wayne A. Cornelius, Phillip L. Martin, and James F. Hollifield. Stanford: Stanford University Press, 1994.

Cote, Langevin. "Immigration Rule Change Starts Feb. 1." *Globe and Mail*, January 20, 1962.

Courtney, John C. "Campaign Strategy and Electoral Victory: The Progressive Conservatives and the 1979 Election." In *Canada at the Polls, 1979 and 1980: A Study of the General Elections*, ed. Howard R. Penniman. Washington, DC: The American Enterprise Institute for Public Policy Research, 1981.

Creighton, Donald. *Dominion of the North: A History of Canada*. Rev ed. Toronto: Macmillan, 1957.

–. *The Forked Road: Canada, 1939-1957*. Toronto: McClelland and Stewart, 1976.

"CSU will Ausländer bremsen." *Frankfurter Allgemeine Zeitung*, 15 January, 1982.

Daguillard, Robert M. "The Idealists and the Noble Savages: The German Green Party and Immigration Politics, 1980-2000." PhD diss., Georgetown University, 2000.

Daniel, Dominique. "The Debate on Family Reunification and Canada's Immigration Act of 1976." *American Review of Canadian Studies* 35, 4 (2005): 686-87.

"Das Deutschlandbild droht in den Staaten Schaden zu nehmen." *Frankfurter Allgemeine Zeitung*, December 8, 1992.

Day, Richard J.F. *Multiculturalism and the History of Canadian Diversity*. Toronto: University of Toronto Press, 2000.

de Haan, Eberhard, ed. *Arbeitsplatz Europa: Langfristige Perspektiven und europäische Aspekte zum Problem ausländischer Arbeitnehmer – Europäische Schriften des Bildungswerks Europäische Politik. Band* 11. Cologne: Institut für Europäische Politik, 1966.

DeLaet, Debra L. *US Immigration Policy in an Age of Rights*. Westport, CT: Praeger, 2000.

Dempsey, Judy. "Germany's Citizenship Challenge: The Hurdles Placed in the Way of Those Seeking Naturalization." *Financial Times* (London), December 3, 1992.

Denninger, Erhard. "Integration und Identität: Bitte um etwas Nachdenklichkeit." *Kritische Justiz* 34, 4 (2001): 442-52.

Der Beauftragte der Bundesregierung für Ausländerfragen. In *Informationen, Meinungen, Anregungen*. Bonn: Beauftragte der Bundesregierung für Ausländerfragen, September 1984.

"Der gute Ruf ist schwer erschüttert." *Der Spiegel*, December 7, 1992.

"Der Kompromiß soll ein versöhnendes Signal setzen." *Frankfurter Allgemeine Zeitung*, December 8, 1992.

"Der Stammtisch darf nicht entscheiden." *Süddeutsche Zeitung*, January 12, 1999.

Deutscher Bundestag. Referat Öffentlichkeitsarbeit. *Reform des Staatsangehörigkeitsrechts – Die parlamentarische Beratung*. Bonn: Deutscher Bundestag, Referat Öffentlichkeitsarbeit, 1999.

–. Stenographischer Bericht, 13. Wahlperiode, 18. Sitzung, February 9, 1995, 1218.

–. Stenographischer Bericht, 14. Wahlperiode, 40. Sitzung, May 7, 1999, 3413-462.

Deutscher Gewerkschaftsbund. Bundesvorstand. Abteilung Ausländische Arbeitnehmer. *Aktion Aufenthaltsberechtigung. Für ein humanes Aufenthaltsrecht*. Düsseldorf: DGB-Bundesvorstand, Abt. Ausländ. Arbeitnehmer, July 1989.

–. Bundesvorstand. Abteilung Ausländische Arbeitnehmer. *Argumentationshilfe für ein humanes und partnerschaftliches Ausländerrecht: Gewerkschaftliche*

Bewertung der Vorstellung des Bundesinnenministeriums im Februar 1989.
Düsseldorf, 1989.

–. Bundesvorstand. *Forderung des DGBs zur Reform des Ausländerrechts,* February
8, 1973.

–. Bundesvorstand. Referat Migration, Internationale Abteilung. *Erleichterte Einbürgerung – ius soli – Doppelstaatsbürgerschaft.* Düsseldorf: Deutscher
Gewerkschaftsbund, Internationale Abteilung, 1999.

–. *"Der Deutsche Gewerkschaftsbund und die ausländischen Arbeitnehmer":
Dokumentation über die Behandlung der Ausländerthematik auf dem 14.
Ordentlichen Bundeskongress des DGB vom 20.-26, Mai 1990 in Hamburg.*
Düsseldorf: DGB-Bundesvorstand, Abt. Ausländische Arbeitnehmer, 1990.

–. Referat Migration, Internationale Abteilung. *Von der Ausländerbeschäftigung zur
Einwanderungspolitik: Beschlüsse, Stellungnahmen und Forderungen des DGB,
1990-1993.* Düsseldorf, 1996.

"'Deutscher Paß für ausländische Jugendliche.'" *Süddeutsche Zeitung,* December 9,
1992.

"DGB fordert Umkehr in der Ausländerpolitik." *Deutsche Presse-Agentur,* December
10, 1992.

"DGB Kritisiert: Ausländergesetz verstößt gegen die Verfassung." *Westdeutsche
Allgemeine Zeitung,* September 2, 1971.

"DGB sieht Bundesrepublik als Einwanderungsland." *Deutsche Presse-Agentur,* April
7, 1990.

Die Beauftragte der Bundesregierung für Ausländerfragen. *Bericht der Beauftragten
der Bundesregierung für Ausländerfragen über die Lage der Ausländer in der
Bundesrepublik Deutschland.* Bonn and Berlin: Die Beauftragte der Bundesregierung für Ausländerfragen, November 2001.

–. *Bericht der Beauftragten der Bundesregierung für Ausländerfragen über die Lage
der Ausländer in der Bundesrepublik Deutschland.* Berlin: Beauftragte der
Bundesregierung für Ausländerfragen, September 2002.

–. *Daten und Fakten zur Ausländersituation.* Bonn: Die Beauftragte der Bundesregierung für Ausländerfragen, 1988.

–. *Daten und Fakten zur Ausländersituation.* Berlin: Beauftragte der Bundesregierung
für Ausländerfragen, 2002.

–. *Mitteilungen der Beauftragten der Bundesregierung für Ausländerfragen, Anregungen der Ausländerbeauftragten zur Novellierung des Ausländerrechts.* Bonn:
Die Beauftragte der Bundesregierung für Ausländerfragen, December 1987.

Die Beauftragte der Bundesregierung für die Belange der Ausländer. *Das Ein-
bürgerungs- und Staatsangehörigkeitsrecht der Bundesrepublik Deutschland.*
Bonn: Die Beauftragte der Bundesregierung für die Belange der Ausländer, 1993.

Die Beauftragte der Bundesregierung für Migration, Flüchtlinge und Integration.
*Bericht der Beauftragten der Bundesregierung für Migration, Flüchtlinge und
Integration über die Lage der Ausländerinnen und Ausländer in Deutschland.
Band 8.* Berlin: Beauftragte der Bundesregierung für Migration, Flüchtlinge und
Integration, 2010.

"Die 'Eckwerte' für ein neues Ausländerrecht." *Frankfurter Rundschau,* April 22,
1989.

"Die geborgte Arbeitskraft: Die Ausländer in der Bundesrepublik haben nicht nur Pflichten." *Die Zeit,* May 5, 1965.

Dikötter, Frank. "Race and Culture: Recent Perspectives on the History of Eugenics." *American Historical Review* 103, 2 (1998): 467-78.

Dirks, Gerald. *Canada's Refugee Policy: Indifference or Opportunism?* Montreal and Kingston: McGill-Queen's University Press, 1977.

"Do You Want to Let Them In?" *The Economist,* May 31, 1975.

Dobell, Peter, and Susan d'Aquino. *The Special Joint Committee on Immigration Policy 1975: An Exercise in Participatory Democracy.* Toronto: Canadian Institute of International Affairs, 1976.

Dohse, Knuth. *Ausländische Arbeiter und bürgerlicher Staat: Genese und Funktion von staatlicher Ausländerpolitik und Ausländerrecht – Vom Kaiserreich bis zur Bundesrepublik Deutschland.* Königstein: Verlag Anton Hain, 1981.

Dolezal, Martin, Marc Helbling, and Swen Hutter. "Debating Islam in Austria, Germany and Switzerland: Ethnic Citizenship, Church-State Relations and Right-Wing Populism." *West European Politics* 33, 2 (2010): 171-90.

Donnelly, Jack. *International Human Rights.* 2nd ed. Boulder, CO: Westview Press, 1998.

–. "The Social Construction of International Human Rights." In *Human Rights in Global Politics,* ed. Tim Dunne and Nicholas J. Wheeler. Cambridge: Cambridge University Press, 1999.

–. *Universal Human Rights in Theory and Practice.* Ithaca: Cornell University Press, 1989.

"Doppelte Staatsbürgerschaft: Koalition diskutiert über Lex Türkei." *Süddeutsche Zeitung,* June 3, 1993.

Dornis, Christian. "Zwei Jahre nach der Reform des Staatsangehörigkeitsrechts – Bilanz und Ausblick." In *Migration Report 2002: Fakten-Analysen-Perspektiven,* ed. Klaus J. Bade and Rainer Münz. Frankfurt: Campus Verlag, 2002.

Drees, Ingrid. "Integration als Ziel der Aktuellen Ausländerpolitik in der Bundesrepublik Deutschland." PhD diss., University of Hannover, 1991.

Drohan, Madelaine. "Neo-Nazi Threat Crystal Clear." *Globe and Mail,* November 10, 1992.

Dudziak, Mary L. *Cold War Civil Rights: Race and the Image of American Democracy.* Princeton, NJ: Princeton University Press, 2002.

Dyer, Gwynne. "Germany's Citizenship Law Is Insupportable." *Record* (Kitchener), June 21, 1993.

Eckert, Elke. "Ein kleines bisschen Staatsbürgerschaft." *die tageszeitung,* November 15, 1994.

Economic Council of Canada. *Economic and Social Impacts of Immigration: A Research Report.* Ottawa: Economic Council of Canada Council, 1991.

Edathy, Sebastian. *"Wo immer auch unsere Wiege gestanden hat": Parlamentarische Debatten über die deutsche Staatsbürgerschaft.* Frankfurt: IKO – Verlag für Interkulturelle Kommunikation, 2000.

"Ein Rechtsanspruch auf Einbürgerung: Erleichterung für junge Ausländer." *Frankfurter Allgemeine Zeitung,* January 7, 1982.

"Ein 'Subproletariat' von Gastarbeitern? Ghettobildung, Geburtenhäufigkeit, Berufs-schwierigkeiten." *Frankfurter Allgemeine Zeitung,* November 20, 1976.

"Eine Million Unterschriften für zweite Staatsbürgerschaft." *Süddeutsche Zeitung,* October 21, 1993.

Eley, Geoff, ed. *From Unification to Nazism: Reinterpreting the German Past.* London: Routledge, 1986.

Elliot, Jean Leonard, and Augie Fleras. "Immigration and the Canadian Ethnic Mosaic." In *Race and Ethnic Relations in Canada,* ed. Peter S. Li. Toronto: Oxford University Press, 1990.

Elliot, Michael. "Human Rights and the Triumph of the Individual in World Culture." *Cultural Sociology* 1, 3 (2007): 343-63.

"Erste Einbürgerung nach neuem Staatsbürgerschaftsrecht." *Handelsblatt,* January 3, 2000.

"Erste Vorschläge für langfristige Ausländerpolitik." *Stuttgarter Zeitung,* October 17, 1972.

"Europe's Foreigners – and Citizens." *Washington Post,* June 21, 1993.

Eze, Emmanuel Chukwudi. "The Color of Reason: The Idea of 'Race' in Kant's Anthropology." In *Postcolonial African Philosophy: A Critical Reader,* ed. Emmanuel Chukwudi Eze. Oxford: Blackwell, 1997.

Fahrmeir, Andreas K. *Citizenship: The Rise and Fall of a Modern Concept.* New Haven: Yale University Press, 2007.

–. "Nineteenth-Century German Citizenships: A Reconsideration." *Historical Journal* 40, 3 (1997): 721-52.

Faist, Thomas. "How to Define a Foreigner? The Symbolic Politics of Immigration in German Partisan Discourse, 1978-1992." In *The Politics of Immigration in Western Europe,* ed. Martin Baldwin-Edwards and Martin Schain. London: Fran Cass, 1994.

Falleti, Tulia G., and Julia F. Lynch. "Context and Causal Mechanisms in Political Analysis." *Comparative Political Studies* 42, 9 (2009): 1143-66.

Favell, Adrian. *Philosophies of Integration: Immigration and the Idea of Citizenship in France and Britain.* London: Macmillan, 1997.

Favell, Adrian, and Randall Hansen. "Markets against Politics: Migration, EU Enlargement and the Idea of Europe." *Journal of Ethnic and Migration Studies* 28, 4 (2002): 581-602.

"FDP nennt Stoiber politischen Heuchler." *Süddeutsche Zeitung,* August 26, 1991.

"FDP will Ausländer nach fünf Jahren einbürgern." *Bonner Rundschau,* July 12, 1983.

Federal Ministry of the Interior (Germany). *Structuring Immigration, Fostering Integration: Report of the Independent Commission on Migration to Germany,* trans. Linda Fagan-Hos. Berlin: Federal Ministry of the Interior, 2001.

–. *Policy and Law Concerning Foreigners in Germany.* Berlin: Federal Ministry of the Interior, Public Relations Sector, 2000.

Fekete, Liz. *A Suitable Enemy: Racism, Migration and Islamophobia in Europe.* Foreword by A. Sivanandan. London: Pluto Press, 2009.

Feldman, Gerald D. *Army, Industry, and Labor in Germany, 1914-1918.* Princeton: Princeton University Press, 1966.

Fesperman, Dan. "Second-Class Germans? Bonn Ponders 'Trial Citizenship' in Shakeup of Immigration Law." *Baltimore Sun,* November 30, 1994.

Fetzer, Joel, and J. Christopher Soper. *Muslims and the State in Britain, France, and Germany.* Cambridge: Cambridge University Press, 2005.

Fietz, Martina. "Doppelpass: Schily strebt Kompromiss an." *Die Welt,* March 5, 1999.

"Figgen: Gastarbeiter dürfen nicht unsere 'Neger' werden." *Westdeutsche Allgemeine Zeitung,* November 17, 1972.

–. "Sie wollen bleiben." *Westdeutsche Allgemeine Zeitung,* November 17, 1972.

Fijalkowski, Jürgen. "Nationale Identität versus multikulturelle Gesellschaft: Entwicklung der Problemlage und Alternativen der Orientierung in der politischen Kultur der Bundesrepublik in den 80er Jahren." In *Die Bundesrepublik in den achtziger Jahren: Innenpolitik, Politische Kultur, Außenpolitik,* ed. Werner Süß. Opladen: Leske and Budrich, 1991.

Filla, Gerhard. "Gleichwertiges Mitglied der Gesellschaft: Eingliederung ausländischer Arbeitnehmer – eine wichtige Aufgabe." *Das Parlament,* August 21, 1971.

Fink, Ulf. "Multikulturelle Gesellschaft – Realität heute." *Gewerkschaftliche Monatshefte* 7, 89 (1989): 443-47.

Finlay, J.L., and D. N. Sprague. *The Structure of Canadian History.* Toronto: Prentice-Hall, 1997.

Finn, Peter. "German Panel Moves to Boost Immigration." *Washington Post,* July 5, 2001.

Finnemore, Martha. "Norms, Culture, and World Politics: Insights from Sociology's Institutionalism." *International Organization* 50, 2 (1996): 325-47.

Finnemore, Martha, and Kathryn Sikkink. "International Norm Dynamics and Political Change." *International Organization* 52, 4 (1998): 887-917.

–. "Taking Stock: The Constructivist Research Program in International Relations and Comparative Politics." *Annual Review of Political Science* 4 (2001): 391-416.

Flanagan, Tom. *Waiting for the Wave: The Reform Party and the Conservative Movement.* Montreal and Kingston: McGill-Queen's University Press, 2009.

Forbes, Hugh Donald. "Trudeau as the First Theorist of Multiculturalism." In *Multiculturalism and the Canadian Constitution,* ed. Stephen Tierney. Vancouver: UBC Press, 2007.

"Foreign Workers Plan Criticized." *Associated Press,* April 1, 2000.

Forester, John. "Bounded Rationality and the Politics of Muddling Through." *Public Administration Review* 44, 1 (1984): 23-31.

Forsberg, Martin. "Foreign Labour, the State and Trade Unions in Imperial Germany, 1890-1918." In *The State and Social Change in Germany, 1880-1980,* ed. W.R. Lee and Eve Rosenhaft. Oxford: Berg, 1990.

Franz, Fritz. "The Legal Status of Foreign Workers in the Federal Republic of West Germany." In *Manpower Mobility across Cultural Boundaries: Social, Economic and Legal Aspects,* ed. R.E. Krane. Leiden: E.J. Brill, 1975.

–. "Niederlassungsrecht: Juristische Bewertungen." In *Aufenthalt – Niederlassung – Einbürgerung,* ed. Klaus Barwig, Klaus Lörcher, and Christoph Schumacher. Baden-Baden: Nomos Verlagsgesellschaft, 1987.

–. "Zur Reform des Ausländer-Polizeirechts." *Deutsches Verwaltungsblatt*, November 1, 1963.

–. "Zwischenbilanz des deutschen Ausländerrechts." *Zeitschrift für Ausländerrecht* 4 (1992): 154-61.

Fraser, Blair. *The Search for Identity: Canada, 1945-1967*. Toronto: Doubleday Canada, 1967.

"Frau Funcke kündigt ihren Rücktritt an: Enttäuscht von den Parteien und der Bundesregierung." *Frankfurter Allgemeine Zeitung*, June 20, 1991.

Fredrickson, George M. *Racism: A Short History*. Princeton, NJ: Princeton University Press, 2002.

Freeman, Gary P. *Immigrant Labor and Racial Conflict in Industrial Societies: The French and British Experience, 1945-1975*. Princeton, NJ: Princeton University Press, 1979.

–. "Modes of Immigration Politics in Liberal Democratic Societies." *International Migration Review* 29, 4 (1995): 881-902.

Freeman, Linda. *The Ambiguous Champion: Canada and South Africa in the Trudeau and Mulroney Years*. Toronto: University of Toronto Press, 1997.

Frey, Martin. "Ausländer in der Bundesrepublik Deutschland: Ein Statistischer Überblick." *Aus Politik und Zeitgeschichte*, June 26, 1982.

–. "Ausländerpolitik in der Bundesrepublik Deutschland." In *Ausländer bei uns – Fremde oder Mitbürger?* ed. Martin Frey and Ulf Müller. Bonn: Bundeszentrale für Politische Bildung, 1982.

Fried, Nico. "Streit über Ausländerpolitik flammt wieder auf." *Süddeutsche Zeitung*, November 20, 2000.

Galloway, Donald. "The Dilemmas of Canadian Citizenship Law." In *From Migrants to Citizens: Membership in a Changing World*, ed. T. Alexander Aleinikoff and Douglas Klusmeyer. Washington, DC: Carnegie Endowment for International Peace, 2000.

Gardiner, Robert K.A. "Race and Color in International Relations." *Daedalus* 96, 2 (1967): 296-311.

Gaserow, Vera. "Das Symbol trägt Baby-Strampler." *Frankfurter Rundschau*, January 4, 2000.

"Gastarbeiter: Die große Völkerwanderung." *Bayern Kurier*, January 20, 1973.

"Gastarbeiter fleißiger als deutsche Arbeiter?" *Bild-Zeitung*, March 31, 1966.

"Gastarbeiter – nützlich und gefragt, aber nicht beliebt." *Industriekurrier*, October 12, 1968.

"Gastarbeiter oder Einwanderer?" *Kirchenzeitung für das Erzbistum Köln*, April 12, 1964.

"Gastarbeiter sind auch Menschen." *Hamburger Echo*, August 9, 1966.

Gates, Paul W. "Official Encouragement to Immigration by the Province of Canada." *Canadian Historical Review* 15, 1 (1934): 24-38.

Geiß, Bernd. "Die Ausländerbeauftragten der Bundesregierung in der ausländerpolitischen Diskussion." In *Deutschland – ein Einwanderungsland? Rückblick, Bilanz and neue Fragen*. Stuttgart: Lucias and Lucias, 2001.

Geißler, Rainer. "Multikulturalismus in Kanada – Modell für Deutschland?" *Aus Politik und Zeitgeschichte*, June 23, 2003.

Gerdes, Jürgen, Thomas Faist, and Beate Rieple. "We Are All 'Republican' Now: The Politics of Dual Citizenship in Germany." In *Dual Citizenship in Europe: From Nationhood to Societal Integration*, ed. Thomas Faist. Aldershot: Ashgate, 2007.

Gerhard, Ute. "'Fluten,' 'Ströme,' 'Invasionen' – Mediendiskurs und Rassismus." In *Zwischen Nationalstaat und multikultureller Gesellschaft: Einwanderung und Fremdenfeindlichkeit in der Bundesrepublik Deutschland*, ed. M. Hessler. Freiburg: Hitit, 1993.

–. "Wenn Flüchtlinge und Einwanderer zu 'Asylantenfluten' werden: Über den Diskurs des Rassismus in den Medien und im allgemeinen Bewusstsein." *Frankfurter Rundschau*, October 19, 1991.

"German Citizen Law Has No Nazism Link." *New York Times*, July 2, 1993.

"Germans Unite against Racism." *Globe and Mail*, November 9, 1992.

Gerring, John. "Case Selection Techniques for Case-Study Analysis: Qualitative and Quantitative Techniques." In *The Oxford Handbook of Political Methodology*, ed. Janet M. Box-Steffenmeier, Henry E. Brady, and David Collier. Oxford: Oxford University Press, 2008.

Gerstle, Gary. *American Crucible: Race and Nation in the Twentieth Century*. Princeton: Princeton University Press, 2001.

"Gesetz über den Auftenthalt, die Erwebstätigkeit und die Integration von Ausländern im Bundesgebiet (Aufenthaltsgesetz – AufenthG)." In *Deutsches Ausländerrecht*, 21. Auflage. Munich: Beck-Texte im dtv, 2008.

Geyer, Michael, and Charles Bright. "World History in a Global Age." *American Historical Review* 100 (1995): 1034-60.

Gillan, Michael. "Point Count Will Assess Immigrants." *Globe and Mail*, September 14, 1967.

Giraudon, Virginie. "Citizenship Rights for Non-Citizens: France, Germany, and the Netherlands." In *Challenge to the Nation-State: Immigration in Western Europe and the United States*, ed. Christian Joppke. New York: Oxford University Press, 1998.

Giraudon, Virginie, and Gallya Lahav. "Actors and Venues in Immigration Control: Closing the Gap between Political Demands and Policy Outcomes." *West European Politics* 29, 2 (2006): 201-23.

Goertz, Gary. *Contexts in International Politics*. Cambridge: Cambridge University Press, 1994.

Golberg, Andreas. "Islam in Germany." In *Islam: Europe's Second Religion*, ed. Shireen T. Hunter. Westport, CT: Praeger, 2002.

Goldberg, David Theo. "Racial Europeanization." *Ethnic and Racial Studies* 29, 2 (2006): 331-64.

Goldstein, Judith. "The Impact of Ideas on Trade Policy: The Origins of US Agricultural and Manufacturing Policies." *International Organization* 43, 1 (1989): 31-71.

Goodhart, David. "The Discomfort of Strangers." *Guardian*, February 24, 2004.

Gosewinkel, Dieter. "Citizenship and Naturalization Politics in Germany in the Nineteenth and Twentieth Centuries." In *Challenging Ethnic Citizenship: German and Israeli Perspectives on Immigration*, ed. Daniel Levy and Yfaat Weiss. New York: Berghahn Books, 2002.

–. "Die Staatsangehörigkeit als Institution des Nationalstaats: Zur Enstehung des Reichs- und Staatsangehörigkeitsgesetzes von 1913." In *Offene Staatlichkeit: Festschrift für Ernst-Wolfgang Böckenförde zum 65. Geburtstag*, ed. Rolf Grawer, Bernhard Schlink, Rainer Wahl, Joachim Wieland. Berlin: Duncker and Humboldt, 1995.

–. *Einbürgern und Ausschließen: Die Nationalisierung der Staatsangehörigkeit vom Deutschen Bund bis zur Bundesrepublik Deutschland*. Göttingen: Vandenhoeck und Ruprecht, 2001.

Götz, Irene, ed. *Zündstoff doppelte Staatsbürgerschaft: Zur Veralltäglichung des Nationalen*. Münster: Lit Verlag, 2000.

Gourevitch, Peter. "The Second Image Reversed: The International Sources of Domestic Politics." *International Organization* 32, 4 (1978): 881-912.

Goutor, David. *Guarding the Gates: The Canadian Labour Movement and Immigration, 1872-1934*. Vancouver: UBC Press, 2007.

Granatstein, J.L. *Canada 1957-1967: The Years of Uncertainty and Innovation*. Toronto: McClelland and Stewart, 1986.

Green, Alan G. "A Comparison of Canadian and US Immigration Policy in the Twentieth Century." In *Diminishing Returns: The Economics of Canada's Recent Immigration Policy*, ed. Don J. DeVoretz. Ottawa: C.D. Howe Institute, 1995.

–. *Immigration and the Postwar Canadian Economy*. Toronto: Macmillan-Hunter Press, 1976.

Green, Simon. "Between Ideology and Pragmatism: The Politics of Dual Nationality in Germany." *International Migration Review* 39, 4 (2005): 921-52.

–. "Beyond Ethnoculturalism? German Citizenship in the New Millennium." *German Politics* 9, 3 (2000): 105-24.

–. "Citizenship Policy in Germany: The Case of Ethnicity over Residence." In *Towards a European Nationality: Citizenship, Immigration, and Nationality Law in the EU*, ed. Randall Hansen and Patrick Weil. London: Macmillan, 2000.

–. "Immigration, Asylum and Citizenship in Germany: The Impact of Unification and the Berlin Republic." *West European Politics* 24, 4 (2001): 82-104.

–. "The Politics of Exclusion: Immigration, Residence and Citizenship Policy in Germany, 1955-1998." PhD diss., University of Birmingham, 1999.

–. *The Politics of Exclusion: Institutions and Immigration Policy in Contemporary Germany*. Manchester: Manchester University Press, 2004.

Greenwald, Rachel Tobey. "The German Nation Is a Homogeneous Nation? Race, the Cold War, and German National Identity, 1970-1993." Ph. diss., University of California, Irvine, 2000.

Greiffenhagen, Martin. "Die Bundesrepublik Deutschland 1945-1990." *Aus Politik und Zeitgeschichte* 1-2 (1991): 16-26.

Grekul, Jana, Harvey Krahn, and Dave Odynak. "Sterilizing the 'Feeble-Minded': Eugenics in Alberta, Canada, 1929-1972." *Journal of Historical Sociology* 17, 4 (2004): 358-84.

Griese, Hartmut M. "Die Situation der Kinder von Wanderarbeitnehmern: Bundesrepublik Deutschland." In *Wanderarbeiter in der EG, Band 2: Länderberichte*, ed. Wolf-Dieter Just and Annette Groth. Mainz: Matthias-Grünewald-Verlag, 1985.

"Großer Bahnhof für Armando sa Rodrigues: Der millionste Gastarbeiter in der Bundesrepublik empfangen." *Frankfurter Allgemeine Zeitung,* September 11, 1964.

"Grüne wandern aus." *die tageszeitung.* May 4, 2004.

Günther, Inge. "Doppelte Staatsbürgerschaft – das Millionending?" *Frankfurter Rundschau,* February 27, 1993.

Gurowitz, Amy. "Mobilizing International Norms: Domestic Actors, Immigrants, and the Japanese State." *World Politics* 51 (1999): 413-45.

Guzzini, Stefano. "A Reconstruction of Constructivism in International Relations." *European Journal of International Relations* 6, 2 (2000): 147-82.

Haberland, Jürgen. "Die Vorschläge der Kommission Ausländerpolitik." *Zeitschrift für Ausländerrecht* 2 (1983): 55-61.

Habermas, Jürgen. "Aus Katastrophen lernen? Ein zeitdiagnostischer Rückblick auf das Kurze 20. Jahrhundert." In *Die postnationale Konstellation: Politische Essays.* Frankfurt am Main: Suhrkamp, 1998.

Hagedorn, Heike. "Einbürgerungspolitik in Deutschland und Frankreich." *Leviathan* 29, 1 (2001): 36-57.

–. *Wer darf Mitglied werden? Einbürgerung in Deutschland und Frankreich im Vergleich.* Opladen: Leske and Budrich, 2001.

Hagen, David. "So Many Agendas: Federal-Provincial Relations in the Ethnic Policy Field in Quebec." MA thesis, McGill University, 1995.

Hagen, William H. *Germans, Poles, and Jews: The Nationality Conflict in the Prussian East, 1772-1914.* Chicago: University of Chicago Press, 1980.

Hailbronner, Kay. "Asylum Law Reform in the German Constitution." *American University Journal of International Law and Policy* 9, 4 (1994): 159-79.

–. "Citizenship Rights for Aliens in Germany." In *Citizenship in a Global World: Comparing Citizenship Rights for Aliens,* ed. Atsushi Kondo. Basingstoke, Hampshire: Palgrave, 2001.

Hall, Peter A. "Aligning Ontology and Methodology in Comparative Politics." In *Comparative Historical Analysis in the Social Sciences,* ed. James Mahoney and Dietrich Rueschemeyer. Cambridge: Cambridge University Press, 2003.

–. "Policy Paradigms, Experts, and the State: The Case of Macroeconomic Policy-Making in Britain." In *Social Scientists, Policy, and the State,* ed. Stephen Brooks and Alain-G. Gagnon. Westport, CT: Praeger, 1990.

–. "Policy Paradigms, Social Learning and the State: The Case of Economic Policymaking in Britain." *Comparative Politics* 25, 3 (1993): 275-96.

Hallett, Mary E. "A Governor General's Views on Oriental Immigration to British Columbia, 1904-1911." *BC Studies* 14 (1972): 51-72.

Handlin, Oscar. *Race and Nationality in American Life.* New York: Doubleday, 1957.

Haney-López, Ian. *White by Law: The Legal Construction of Race.* New York: New York University Press, 1996.

Hansen, Randall. *Citizenship and Immigration in Post-War Britain: The Institutional Origins of a Multicultural Nation.* Oxford: Oxford University Press, 2000.

–. "The Poverty of Postnationalism: Citizenship, Immigration, and the New Europe." *Theory and Society* 38, 1 (2009): 1-24.

–. "The Problems of Dual Nationality in Europe." *ECPR News* 11, 2 (2000): 19-20.

Hansen, Randall, and Desmond King. "Eugenic Ideas, Political Interests, and Policy Variance: Immigration and Sterilization Policy in Britain and the US." *World Politics* 53, 2 (2001): 237-63.

Hansen, Randall, and Jobst Koehler. "Issue Definition, Political Discourse and the Politics of Nationality Reform in France and Germany." *European Journal of Political Research* 44 (2005): 623-44.

Hansen, Randall, and Patrick Weil. "Citizenship, Immigration and Nationality: Towards a Convergence in Europe?" In *Towards a European Nationality: Citizenship, Immigration and Nationality Law in the EU*, ed. Randall Hansen and Patrick Weil. Basingstoke: Palgrave, 2001.

Harles, John. "Multiculturalism, National Identity, and National Integration: The Canadian Case." *International Journal for Canadian Studies* 17 (1998): 217-48.

Harney, Robert F. "The Padrone System and the Sojourner in the Canadian North, 1885-1920." In *Immigration in Canada: Historical Perspectives*, ed. Gerald Tulchinsky. Toronto: Copp Longman, 1994.

Hartley, Norman. "Thousands Are Proving Immigration Points System Is Pointless." *Globe and Mail*, December 29, 1973.

Hawkins, Freda. *Canada and Immigration: Public Policy and Public Concern.* 2nd ed. Montreal and Kingston: McGill-Queen's University Press, 1988.

–. *Critical Years in Immigration: Canada and Australia Compared.* Kingston and Montreal: McGill-Queen's University Press, 1989.

–. "Immigration and Population: The Canadian Approach." *Canadian Public Policy* 1, 3 (1975): 285-95.

Hay, Colin. *Political Analysis: A Critical Introduction.* New York: Palgrave, 2002.

Haydu, Jeffrey. "Making Use of the Past: Time Periods as Cases to Compare and as Sequences of Problem Solving." *American Journal of Sociology* 104, 2 (1998): 339-71.

Heauwagen, Marianne. "Schröder warnt vor Missbrauch des Bundesrats." *Süddeutsche Zeitung*, March 2-3, 2002.

Heclo, Hugh. *Modern Social Politics in Britain and Sweden.* New Haven: Yale University Press, 1974.

Held, David. *Democracy and the Global Order: From the Modern State to Cosmopolitan Governance.* Stanford: Stanford University Press, 1995.

Held, David, Anthony McGrew, David Goldblatt, and Jonathan Perraton. *Global Transformations: Politics, Economics and Culture.* Stanford: Stanford University Press, 1999.

Helsinki Watch. *"Foreigners Out": Xenophobia and Right-Wing Violence in Germany.* New York: Human Rights Watch, 1992.

Herbert, Ulrich. *Geschichte der Ausländerpolitik in Deutschland: Saisonarbeiter, Zwangsarbeiter, Gastarbeiter, Flüchtlinge.* Munich: C.H. Beck, 2001.

–. *A History of Foreign Labor in Germany, 1880-1980: Seasonal Workers, Forced Laborers, Guest Workers*, trans. William Templer. Ann Arbor: University of Michigan Press, 1990.

–. *Hitler's Foreign Workers: Enforced Foreign Labor in Germany under the Third Reich.* Cambridge: Cambridge University Press, 1997.

Herbert, Ulrich, and Karin Hunn. "Guest Workers and Policy on Guest Workers in the Federal Republic: From the Beginning of Recruitment in 1955 until Its Halt in 1973." In *The Miracle Years: A Cultural History of West Germany, 1949-1968,* ed. Hanna Schissler. Princeton: Princeton University Press, 2001.

Hermani, Gabriele. *Die Deutsche Islamkonferenz 2006-2009: Der Dialogprozess mit den Muslimen in Deutschland im Öffentlichen Diskurs.* Berlin: Finckenstein and Salmuth, 2010.

Hirschman, Albert O. "The Search for Paradigms as a Hindrance to Understanding." *World Politics* 22, 3 (1970): 329-43.

Hobsbawm, E.J. *The Age of Empire, 1875-1914.* New York: Vintage Books, 1989.

–. *Nations and Nationalism since 1870: Programme, Myth, Reality.* 2nd ed. Cambridge: Cambridge University Press, 1993.

Hoerder, Dirk. *Cultures in Contact: World Migrations in the Second Millennium.* Durham, NC: Duke University Press, 2002.

Hoffmann, Christhard. "Immigration and Nationhood in the Federal Republic of Germany." In *The Postwar Transformation of Germany: Democracy, Prosperity, and Nationhood,* ed. John S. Brady, Beverly Crawford, and Sarah Elise Willarty. Ann Arbor: University of Michigan Press, 1999.

Hoffmann, Stefan-Ludwig. "Introduction: Genealogies of Human Rights." In *Human Rights in the Twentieth Century,* ed. Stefan-Ludwig Hoffmann. Cambridge: Cambridge University Press, 2011.

Hogwood, Patricia. "Citizenship Controversies in Germany: The Twin Legacies of völkisch Nationalism and the Alleinvertretungsanspruch." *German Politics* 9, 3 (2000): 125-44.

Hollifield, James F. *Immigrants, Markets, and States: The Political Economy of Post-War Europe.* Cambridge: Harvard University Press, 1992.

–. "The Politics of International Migration: How Can We 'Bring the State Back In'?" In *Migration Theory: Talking across Disciplines,* ed. Caroline Brettell and James F. Hollifield. New York and London: Routledge, 2000.

Hossay, Patrick, and Aristide Zolberg. "Democracy in Peril?" In *Shadows over Europe: The Development and Impact of the Extreme Right in Western Europe,* ed. Martin Schain, Aristide Zolberg, and Patrick Hossay. New York: Palgrave, 2002.

Howard, Marc Morjé. *The Politics of Citizenship in Europe.* Cambridge: Cambridge University Press, 2009.

Howe, R. Brian. "The Evolution of Human Rights Policy in Ontario." *Canadian Journal of Political Science* 24, 4 (1991): 783-802.

Hugill, Peter J. *World Trade since 1431: Geography, Technology, and Capitalism.* Baltimore: Johns Hopkins University Press, 1993.

Human Rights Watch. *"Deutschland den Deutschen": Fremdenhaß und rassistische Gewalt in Deutschland.* New York: Human Rights Watch, 1995.

Hunn, Katrin. *"Nächstes Jahr kehren wir zurück ... ": Die Geschichte der türkischen "Gastarbeiter" in der Bundesrepublik.* Göttingen: Wallstein Verlag, 2005.

Hurd, Burton. "The Case for a Quota." *Queen's Quarterly* 36 (1929): 145-59.

Huttenback, R.A. "The British Empire as a 'White Man's Country': Racial Attitudes and Immigration Legislation in the Colonies of White Settlement." *Journal of British Studies* 13, 1 (1973): 108-37.

−. *Racism and Empire: White Settlers and Colored Immigrants in the British Self-Governing Colonies, 1830-1910.* Ithaca: Cornell University Press, 1976.

Huysmans, Jeff. "Migrants as a Security Problem: Dangers of 'Securitizing' Societal Issues." In *Migration and European Integration: The Dynamics of Inclusion and Exclusion*, ed. Robert Miles and Dietrich Thränhardt. London: Pinter, 1995.

Iacovetta, Franca. "Ordering in Bulk: Canada's Postwar Immigration Policy and the Recruitment of Contract Workers from Italy." *Journal of American Ethnic History* 11, 1 (1991): 50-80.

Ibbitson, John, and Joe Friesen. "Conservative Immigrants Boost Tory Fortunes." *Globe and Mail*, October 4, 2010.

Igartua, José E. *The Other Quiet Revolution: National Identities in English Canada, 1945-1971.* Vancouver: UBC Press, 2006.

Immergut, Ellen M. *Health Politics: Interests and Institutions in Western Europe.* New York: Cambridge University Press, 1992.

−. "The Rules of the Game: The Logic of Health Policy-Making in France, Switzerland, and Sweden." In *Structuring Politics: Historical Institutionalism in Comparative Analysis*, ed. Sven Steinmo, Kathleen Thelen, and Frank Longstreth. Cambridge: Cambridge University Press, 1992.

"Immigration: An End to Hit-and-Miss." *Toronto Star,* September 14, 1967.

"In Zukunft deutsche Staatsangehörige?" *Rheinischer Merkur,* April 30, 1971.

Indra, Doreen M. "Changes in Canadian Immigration Patterns over the Past Decade with a Special Reference to Asia." In *Visible Minorities and Multiculturalism: Asians in Canada*, ed. K. Victor Ujimoto and Gordon Hirabayashi. Toronto: Butterworths, 1980.

"Interview mit Walter Arendt." *Handelsblatt*, December 18, 1969.

Iriyama, Kaoru. "Konflikt und Koordination der gesellschaftlichen Interessen im Politikfeld Zuwanderung: Eine politische Prozessanalyse zur Zuwanderungsgesetzgebung in der Bundesrepublik Deutschland." MA thesis, Humboldt University, 2002.

Irvine, J.A. Sandy. "Canadian Refugee Policy and the Role of International Bureaucratic Networks in Domestic Paradigm Change." In *Policy Paradigms, Transnationalism, and Domestic Politics*, ed. Grace Skogstad. Toronto: University of Toronto Press, 2011.

Jackson, Robert H. "The Weight of Ideas in Decolonization: Normative Change in International Relations." In *Ideas and Foreign Policy: Beliefs, Institutions, and Political Change*, ed. Judith Goldstein and Robert O. Keohane. Ithaca: Cornell University Press, 1993.

Jacobson, David. "New Border Customs: Migration and the Changing Role of the State." *UCLA Journal of International Law and Foreign Affairs* 3 (1998-99): 443-62.

−. *Rights across Borders: Immigration and the Decline of Citizenship.* Baltimore: Johns Hopkins University Press, 1996.

–. "State and Society in a World Unbound." In *Public Rights and Public Rules: Constituting Citizens in the World Polity and National Policy*, ed. Connie L. McNeely. New York: Garland, 1998.

Jacobson, David, and Galya Benraieh Ruffer. "Social Relations on a Global Scale: The Implications for Human Rights for Democracy." In *Dialogues on Migration Policy*, ed. Marco Giugni and Florence Passy. Lanham: Lexington Books, 2006.

Jacobson, Matthew Frye. *Whiteness of a Different Color: European Immigrants and the Alchemy of Race*. Cambridge: Harvard University Press, 1998.

Janigan, Mary. "Andras Cautions Race Should Not Dominate Immigration Debate." *Toronto Star*, February 4, 1975.

"Japan Wants Canada's Door Opened." *Toronto Telegram*, December 4, 1964.

Jarausch, Konrad H. *After Hitler: Recivilizing Germans, 1945-1995*. Oxford: Oxford University Press, 2006.

Jaworsky, John. "A Case Study of the Canadian Federal Government's Multicultural Policy." MA thesis, Carleton University, 1979.

Jeffrey, Brooke, and Philip Rosen. "The Protection of Human Rights in Canada (1)." *Canadian Regional Review* 2, 3 (1979): 37-54.

Johnson, William. "Cabinet Warned about Effect of Non-European Immigrant Trend." *Globe and Mail*, October 29, 1974.

Johnston, Alastair Iain. "Treating International Institutions as Social Environments." *International Studies Quarterly* 45 (2001): 487-515.

Johnston, Hugh J.M. *British Emigration Policy, 1815-1830: "Shovelling Out Paupers."* Oxford: Clarendon, 1972.

Joppke, Christian. "Beyond National Models: Civic Integration Policies for Immigrants in Western Europe." *West European Politics* 30, 1 (2007): 1-22.

–. "Citizenship between De- and Re-Ethnicization." New York: Russell Sage Foundation, Working Paper 204, March 2003.

–. *Citizenship and Immigration*. Oxford: Polity Press, 2010.

–. "Immigration Challenges the Nation-State." In *Challenge to the Nation-State: Immigration in Western Europe and the United States*, ed. Christian Joppke. New York: Oxford University Press, 1998.

–. *Immigration and the Nation-State: The United States, Germany, and Great Britain*. Oxford: Oxford University Press, 1999.

–. "The Legal-Domestic Sources of Immigrant Rights: The United States, Germany, and the European Union." *Comparative Political Studies* 34, 4 (2001): 339-36.

–. "Mobilization of Culture and the Reform of Citizenship Law: Germany and the United States." In *Challenging Immigration and Ethnic Relations Politics: Comparative European Perspectives*, ed. Ruud Koopmans and Paul Strathearn. Albany: State University of New York Press, 1999.

–. *Selecting by Origin: Ethnic Migration in the Liberal State*. Cambridge: Harvard University Press, 2005.

–. "Toward a New Sociology of the State: On Rogers Brubaker's *Citizenship and Nationhood in France and Germany*," *Archives Européennes de Sociologie* 36, 1 (1995): 168-78.

–. "Why Liberal States Accept Unwanted Immigration." *World Politics* 50 (1998): 268-69.

Joyce, James Avery. *The New Politics of Human Rights*. London: Macmillan, 1978.

Judt, Tony. *Postwar: A History of Europe since 1945*. New York: Penguin, 2005.

Kalbach, Warren E. "A Demographic Overview of Racial and Ethnic Groups in Canada." In *Race and Ethnic Relations in Canada*, ed. Peter S. Li. Toronto: Oxford University Press, 1990.

−. "Growth and Distribution of Canada's Ethnic Populations, 1871-1981." In *Ethnic Canada: Identities and Inequalities*, ed. Leo Driedger. Toronto: Copp Clark Pitman, 1987.

Kanstroom, Daniel. "*Wer Sind Wir Wieder*? Laws of Asylum, Immigration, and Citizenship in the Struggle for the Soul of the New Germany." *Yale Journal of International Law* 18, 1 (1993): 155-214.

Kaplan, William. *The Evolution of Citizenship Legislation in Canada*. Ottawa: Multiculturalism and Citizenship Canada, 1990.

Käppner, Joachim, and Jeanne Rubner. "Union und Zuwanderung: Edmund Stoiber bleibt bei seiner Ablehnung des Regierungsentwurfs." *Süddeutsche Zeitung*, March 1, 2002.

Karapin, Roger. "Far-Right Parties and the Construction of Immigration Issues in Germany." In *Shadows over Europe: The Development and Impact of the Extreme Right in Western Europe*, ed. Martin Schain, Aristide Zolberg, and Patrick Hossay. New York: Palgrave, 2002.

Kastoryano, Riva. *Negotiating Identities: States and Immigrants in France and Germany*. Princeton, NJ: Princeton University Press, 2002.

Kattenstroth, Ludwig. "Grußwort der Bundesregierung." In *"Magnet Bundesrepublik" – Probleme der Ausländerbeschäftigung: Informationstag der Bundesvereinigung der Deutschen Arbeitgeberverbände*. Cologne, 1966.

Katzenstein, Peter. "Introduction: Alternative Perspectives on National Security." In *Cultural Norms and National Security*, ed. Peter J. Katzenstein. Ithaca: Cornell University Press, 1996.

−. *Policy and Politics in West Germany: The Growth of a Semisovereign State*. Philadelphia: Temple University Press, 1987.

Katznelson, Ira. "Structure and Configuration in Comparative Politics." In *Comparative Politics: Rationality, Culture, and Structure*, ed. Mark Irving Lichbach and Alan S. Zuckerman. Cambridge: Cambridge University Press, 1997.

Keating, Tom. *Canada and World Order: The Multilateralist Tradition in Canadian Foreign Policy*. Toronto: McClelland and Stewart, 1993.

Keck, Margaret, and Katherine Sikkink. *Activists beyond Borders: Advocacy Networks in International Politics*. Ithaca, NY: Cornell University Press, 1998.

Kelley, Ninette, and Michael Trebilcock. *The Making of the Mosaic: A History of Canadian Immigration Policy*. Toronto: University of Toronto Press, 1998.

Kent, Tom. *A Public Purpose: An Experience of Liberal Opposition and Canadian Government*. Kingston and Montreal: McGill-Queen's University Pres, 1988.

Kertzer, David I., and Dominique Arel. "Censuses, Identity Formation, and the Struggle for Political Power." In *Census and Identity: The Politics of Race, Ethnicity, and Language in National Censuses*, ed. David I. Kertzer and Dominique Arel. Cambridge: Cambridge University Press, 2002.

Keskin, Hakki. "Der Kampf für Bürgerrechte muß fortgesetzt werden." In *Deutsche Türken – Türkische Deutsche? Die Diskussion um die doppelte Staatsbürgerschaft*, ed. Andreas Goldberg and Faruk Şen. Münster: Lit Verlag, 2000.

Keyserlingk, Robert H., ed. *Breaking Ground: The 1956 Hungarian Refugee Movement to Canada*. Toronto: York Lanes Press, 1993.

Kim, Hyung-Chan, ed. *Asian Americans and the Supreme Court: A Documentary History*. Westport, CT: Greenwood, 1992.

Kindleberger, Charles P. *Europe's Postwar Growth: The Role of Labor Supply*. Cambridge, MA: Harvard University Press, 1967.

King, Desmond. *Making Americans: Immigration, Race, and the Origins of Diverse Democracy*. Cambridge, MA: Harvard University Press, 2000.

–. "Making Americans: Immigration Meets Race." In *E Pluribus Unum? Contemporary and Historical Perspectives on Immigrant Political Incorporation*, ed. Gary Gerstle and John Mollenkopf. New York: Russell Sage Foundation, 2001.

"Kinkel: Rechtextremistiche Gewalt gefährdet deutsches Ansehen." *Deutsche Presse-Agentur*, December 5, 1992.

Kinzer, Stephen. "Germany Ablaze: It's Candlelight, Not Firebombs." *New York Times*, January 13, 1993.

–. "Germans Feel Pressure to Do More to Protect Foreigners." *New York Times*, June 2, 1993.

Kirchenamt der Evangelischen Kirche in Deutschland. Kommission für Ausländerfragen und ethnische Minderheiten der EKD. *Gesichtspunkte zur Neufassung des Ausländerrechts*. Hanover: EKD, 1985.

–. *Flüchtlinge und Asylsuchende in unserem Land*. Hanover: EKD, 1986.

Klärner, Andreas. *Aufstand der Ressentiments: Einwanderungsdiskurs, völkischer Nationalismus und die Kampagne der CDU/CSU gegen die doppelte Staatsbürgerschaft*. Cologne: Papyrossa, 2000.

Klekowski von Koppenfels, Amanda. "The Decline of Privilege: The Legal Background to the Migration of Ethnic Germans." In *Coming Home to Germany? The Integration of Ethnic Germans from Central and Eastern Europe in the Federal Republic*, ed. David Rock and Stefan Wolff. New York: Berghahn Books, 2002.

Klinkner, Philip A., and Rogers M. Smith. *The Unsteady March: The Rise and Decline of Racial Equality in America*. Chicago: Chicago University Press, 1999.

Klotz, Audie. "Norms Reconstituting Interests: Global Racial Equality and US Sanctions against South Africa." *International Organization* 49, 3 (1995): 451-78.

Klusmeyer, Douglas B. "A Guiding Culture for Immigrants? Integration and Diversity in Germany." *Journal of Ethnic and Migration Studies* 27, 3 (2001): 519-32.

–. "Aliens, Immigrants, and Citizens: The Politics of Inclusion in the Federal Republic of Germany." *Daedalus* 122, 3 (1993): 81-114.

Klusmeyer, Douglas B., and Demetrios G. Papademetriou. *Immigration Policy in the Federal Republic of Germany: Negotiating Membership and Remaking the Nation*. New York: Berghahn Books, 2009.

Kneip, Sacha, and Christian Henkes. "Das Kopftuch im Streit zwischen Parlamenten und Gerichten: Ein Drama in drei Akten." WZB Discussion Paper, Berlin, Wissenschaftszentrum Berlin für Sozialforschung (WZB), 2008.

Knischewski, Gerd. "Post-War Identity in Germany." In *Nation and Identity in Contemporary Europe*, ed. Brian Jenkins and Spiros A. Sofos. London: Routledge, 1996.

Knortz, Heike. *Diplomatische Tauschgeschichte: "Gastarbeiter" in der westdeutschen Diplomatie und Beschäftigungspolitik 1953-1973*. Cologne: Böhlau Verlag, 2008.

Knowles, Valerie. *Strangers at Our Gates: Canadian Immigration and Immigration Policy, 1540-1990*. Toronto: Dundurn, 1992.

–. *Strangers at Our Gates: Canadian Immigration and Immigration Policy, 1540-1997*. Rev. ed. Toronto: Dundurn, 1997.

"Koalition spricht vom drohenden Staatsnotstand." *Süddeutsche Zeitung*, November 5, 1992.

"Koalition über Ausländergesetz einig." *Süddeutsche Zeitung*, December 6, 1989.

Koehl, Robert Lewis. "Colonialism Inside Germany: 1886-1918." *Journal of Modern History* 25, 3 (1953): 255-72.

Koenig, Matthias. "Incorporating Muslim Migrants in Western Nation-States: A Comparison of the United Kingdom, France, and Germany." *Journal of International Migration and Integration* 6, 2 (2005): 219-34.

–. "Institutional Change in the World Polity: International Human Rights and the Construction of Collective Identities." *International Sociology* 23, 1 (2008): 95-114.

"Kohl Promises Tougher Fight against Racist Violence." *Inter Press Service*, June 17, 1993.

"Kohl will Behutsamkeit in der Ausländerpolitik." *Frankfurter Rundschau*, March 3, 1983.

"'Kölner Appell' gegen eine menschfeindliche Ausländerpolitik." *Frankfurter Rundschau*, November 2, 1983.

Koopmans, Ruud, and Paul Strathearn. "Migration and Ethnic Relations as a Field of Political Contention: An Opportunity Structure Approach." In *Challenging Immigration and Ethnic Relations Politics: Comparative European Perspectives*, ed. Ruud Koopmans and Paul Strathearn. New York: Oxford University Press, 2000.

Koopmans, Ruud, Paul Statham, Marco Giugni, and Florence Passy. *Contested Citizenship: Immigration and Cultural Diversity in Europe*. Minneapolis: University of Minnesota Press, 2005.

Korte, Herman. "Guestworker Question or Immigration Issue? Social Sciences and Public Debate in the Federal Republic of Germany." In *Population, Labour and Migration in 19th- and 20th-Century Germany*, ed. Klaus J. Bade. Leamington Spa: Berg, 1987.

Korteweg, Anna. "The Sharia Debate in Ontario: Gender, Islam and the Representations of Muslim Women's Agency." *Gender and Society* 22 (2008): 434-54.

Kostakopoulou, Dora. "Matters of Control: Integration Tests, Naturalization Reform and Probationary Citizenship in the United Kingdom." *Journal of Ethnic and Migration Studies* 36, 5 (2010): 829-46.

Krasner, Stephen. "Sovereignty: An Institutional Perspective." *Comparative Political Studies* 21, 1 (1988): 66-94.

Kröter, Thomas, and Iris Hilberth. "Zuwanderungsstreit beginnt von Neuem." *Frankfurter Rundschau,* December 19, 2002.

Kruse, Imke, Henry Edward Orren, and Steffen Angenendt. "The Failure of Immigration Reform in Germany." *German Politics* 12, 3 (2003): 129-45.

Kühn, Heinz. *Stand und Weiterwicklung der Integration der ausländischen Arbeitnehmer und ihrer Familien in der Bundesrepublik Deutschland. Memorandum des Beauftragten der Bundesregierung.* Bonn, 1979.

–. "Vorwort zur 1. Auflage." In *Zur Situation der ausländischen Arbeitnehmer und ihrer Familien – Bestandsaufnahme und Perspektiven für die 90er Jahre.* 2nd ed., ed. Beauftragte der Bundesregierung für die Integration der ausländischen Arbeitnehmer und ihrer Familienangehörigen. Bonn, 1990.

Kurlander, Eric. *The Price of Exclusion: Ethnicity, National Identity, and the Decline of German Liberalism, 1898-1933.* New York: Berghahn Books, 2006.

Kurthen, Herman. "Germany at the Crossroads: National Identity and the Challenges of Immigration." *International Migration Review* 29, 4 (1995): 914-38.

Lake, Marilyn, and Henry Reynolds. *Drawing the Global Colour Line: White Men's Countries and the International Challenge of Racial Equality.* Cambridge: Cambridge University Press, 2008.

Lam, Fiona Tinwei. "The Pursuit of Cultural Homogeneity and Social Cohesion in Immigration and Naturalization Policy: The Example of the Chinese in Canada." LLM thesis, University of Toronto, 1994.

Lambertson, Ross. "The Black, Brown, White and Red Blues: The Beating of Clarence Clemons." *Canadian Historical Review* 85, 4 (2004): 755-76.

–. "'The Dresden Story': Racism, Human Rights, and the Jewish Labour Committee of Canada." *Labour/Le Travail* 47 (2001): 29-44.

–. *Repression and Resistance: Canadian Human Rights Activists, 1930-1960.* Toronto: University of Toronto Press, 2004.

"Landed Immigrant Policy Suspended." *Globe and Mail,* November 4, 1972.

Lanphier, Michael. "Canada's Response to Refugees." *International Migration Review* 15, 1-2 (1981): 113-30.

Lauren, Paul Gordon. *Power and Prejudice: The Politics and Diplomacy of Racial Discrimination.* Boulder, CO: Westview Press, 1996.

Lavenex, Sandra. "Shifting Up and Out: The Foreign Policy of European Immigration Control." *West European Politics* 29, 2 (2006): 329-50.

Laycock, David. *The New Right and Democracy in Canada: Understanding Reform and the Canadian Alliance.* Don Mills: Oxford University Press, 2002.

Leblanc, Daniel. "Tories Target Specific Ethnic Voters." *Globe and Mail,* October 16, 2007.

Lee, Carol. "The Road to Enfranchisement: Chinese and Japanese in British Columbia." *BC Studies* 30 (1976): 44-76.

Leggewie, Claus. "Neigung gegen Null." *Frankfurter Rundschau,* May 6, 2004.

Levey, Geoffrey Brahm. "Review Article: What Is Living and What Is Dead in Multiculturalism." *Ethnicities* 9, 1 (2009): 75-93.

Levitt, Joseph. "Race and Nation in Canadian Anglophone Historiography." *Canadian Review of Studies on Nationalism* 8 (1981): 1-16.

Levy, Daniel. "The Transformation of Germany's Ethno-Cultural Idiom." In *Challenging Ethnic Citizenship: German and Israeli Perspectives on Immigration*, ed. Daniel Levy and Yfaat Weiss. New York: Berghahn Books, 2002.

Levy, Daniel, and Natan Sznaider. "The Institutionalization of Cosmopolitan Morality: The Holocaust and Human Rights." *Journal of Human Rights* 3, 2 (2004): 143-57.

Levy, Richard S. *The Downfall of the Anti-Semitic Political Parties in Imperial Germany*. New Haven: Yale University Press, 1975.

Li, Peter. *Destination Canada: Immigration Debates and Issues*. Toronto: Oxford University Press, 2003.

"Lieber sterben als nach Sachsen." *Der Spiegel*, September 30, 1991.

Lieberman, Evan S. "Casual Inference in Historical Institutional Analysis: A Specification of Periodization Strategies." *Comparative Political Studies* 34, 9 (2001): 1011-35.

Lieberman, Robert C. "Ideas, Institutions, and Political Order: Explaining Political Change." *American Political Science Review* 96, 4 (2002): 697-712.

Lindblom, Charles. "Still Muddling, Not Yet Through." *Public Administration Review* 39, 6 (1979): 517-26.

–. "The Science of Muddling Through." *Public Administration Review* 19, 2 (1959): 79-88.

Maas, Willem. *Creating European Citizens*. Lanham, MD: Rowman and Littlefield, 2007.

Mack, Olaf. "Aktion Doppelte Staatsangehörigkeit. Unterschriften statt Lichterkette." *Süddeutsche Zeitung*, March 1, 1993.

Macklin, Audrey. "Historicizing Narratives of Arrival: The Other Indian Other." In *Storied Communities: Narratives of Contact and Arrival in Constituting Political Community*, ed. Hester Lessard, Rebecca Johnson, and Jeremy Webber. Vancouver: UBC Press, 2010.

–. "The Securitization of Dual Citizenship." In *Dual Citizenship in Global Perspective: From Unitary to Multiple Citizenship*, ed. Thomas Faist and Peter Kivisto. Basingstoke: Palgrave Macmillan, 2007.

MacMaster, Neil. *Racism in Europe 1870-2000*. Houndmills: Palgrave, 2001.

Madsen, Mikael Rask. "'Legal Diplomacy': Law, Politics and the Genesis of Postwar European Human Rights." In *Human Rights in the Twentieth Century*, ed. Stefan-Ludwig Hoffmann. Cambridge: Cambridge University Press, 2011.

Mahoney, James. "Analyzing Path Dependence: Lessons from the Social Sciences." In *Understanding Change: Models, Methodologies, and Metaphors*, ed. Andreas Wimmer and Reinhart Kössler. New York: Palgrave Macmillan, 2006.

–. "Path Dependence in Historical Sociology." *Theory and Society* 28, 4 (2000): 507-48.

Maier, Charles S. "Consigning the Twentieth Century to History: Alternative Narratives for the Modern Era." *American Historical Review* 105, 3 (2000): 807-31.

Mann, Michael. *The Sources of Social Power*. Vol. 2: *The Rise of Classes and Nation-States, 1760-1914*. Cambridge: Cambridge University Press, 1993.

Marrus, Michael. *The Nuremberg War Crimes Trial, 1945-46: A Documentary History*. Boston: Bedford Books, 1997.

–. *The Unwanted: European Refugees in the Twentieth Century*. New York: Oxford University Press, 1985.

Marshall, Barbara. *The New Germany and Migration in Europe*. Manchester: University of Manchester Press, 2000.

Marshall, Tyler. "Anti-Foreigner Attack Kills 3 in Germany." *Los Angeles Times*, November 24, 1993.

Maurer, Trude. *Ostjuden in Deutschland, 1918-1933*. Hamburg: Hamburger Beiträge zur Geschichte der deutschen Juden 12, 1986.

Mazower, Mark. *Dark Continent: Europe's Twentieth Century*. New York: Alfred A. Knopf, 1999.

–. "An International Civilization? Empire, Internationalism and the Crisis of the Mid-Twentieth Century." *International Affairs* 82, 3 (2006): 553-66.

–. "Paved Intentions: Civilization and Imperialism." *World Affairs* 171, 2 (2008): 72-85.

–. "The Strange Triumph of Human Rights, 1933-1950." *Historical Journal* 47, 2 (2004): 379-98.

McCarthy, Thomas. *Race, Empire and the Idea of Human Development*. New York: Cambridge University Press, 2009.

McEvoy, F.J. "'A Symbol of Racial Discrimination': The Chinese Immigration Act and Canada's Relation with China, 1942-1947." *Canadian Ethnic Studies* 14, 3 (1982): 24-42.

McInnis, Marvin. "Immigration and Emigration: Canada in the Late Nineteenth Century." In *Migration and the International Labor Market: 1850-1939*, ed. Timothy J. Hattan and Jeffrey G. Williamson. London: Routledge, 1994.

McMichael, Philip. "Incorporating Comparison within a World-Historical Perspective: An Alternative Comparative Method." *American Sociological Review* 55 (1990): 385-97.

McNaught, Kenneth. *The Penguin History of Canada*. New ed. London: Penguin, 1988.

McRoberts, Kenneth. *Misconceiving Canada: The Struggle for National Unity*. Toronto: Oxford University Press, 1997.

"Meeting of Prime Ministers of the Commonwealth: Report by Prime Minister John G. Diefenbaker on the Commonwealth Prime Ministers' Conference, House of Commons, May 16, 1960." In *Canadian Foreign Policy 1955-1965: Selected Speeches and Documents*, ed. Arthur E. Blanchette. Toronto: McClelland and Stewart, 1977.

Mehta, Uday. "Liberal Strategies of Exclusion." *Politics and Society* 18 (1990): 427-54.

–. *Liberalism and Empire: A Study in Nineteenth-Century British Liberal Thought*. Chicago: University of Chicago Press, 1999.

Meier-Braun, Karl-Heinz. *Deutschland, Einwanderungsland*. Frankfurt am Main: Suhrkamp, 2002.

–. *Integration und Rückkehr? Zur Ausländerpolitik des Bundes und Länder, insbesondere Baden-Württembergs*. Mainz: Grünewald-Kaiser, 1988.

Merten, Klaus. *Das Bild der Ausländer in der Deutschen Presse: Ergebnisse einer systematischen Inhaltsanalyse.* Frankfurt am Main: Dagyeli, 1986.

Messina, Anthony. *The Logics and Politics of Post-WWII Migration to Europe.* Cambridge: Cambridge University Press, 2007.

Meyer, John W., John Boli, George M. Thomas, and Francisco O. Ramirez. "World Society and the Nation-State." *American Journal of Sociology* 103, 1 (1997): 144-81.

Meyers, Eytan. "Theories of International Immigration Policy: A Comparative Analysis." *International Migration Review* 34, 4 (2000): 1245-82.

Mickleburgh, Rod. "Harper Defends Canadian Diversity: PM Rejects Calls to Curb Immigration, Calls Open Society 'Our Greatest Strength.'" *Globe and Mail,* June 20, 2006.

Micksch, Jürgen, ed. *Multikulturelles Zusammenleben: Theologische Erfahrungen.* Frankfurt am Main: Lembeck, 1983.

Mill, J.S. *A System of Logic.* London: Longman, 1843.

Miller, Mark J. *Foreign Workers in Western Europe: An Emerging Political Force.* New York: Praeger, 1981.

Milot, Micheline. "Modus Co-vivendi: Religious Diversity in Canada." In *International Migration and the Governance of Religious Diversity,* ed. Paul Bramadat and Matthias Koenig. Montreal and Kingston: McGill-Queen's University Press, 2009.

Minkenberg, Michael. *Die neue radikale Rechte im Vergleich: USA, Frankreich, Deutschland.* Opladen: Westdeutscher Verlag, 1998.

Moch, Leslie Page. "The European Perspective: Changing Conditions and Multiple Migrations, 1750-1914." In *European Migrations: Global and Local Perspectives,* ed. Dirk Hoerder and Leslie Page Moch. Boston: Northwestern University Press, 1996.

–. "Migration and the Social History of Modern Europe." *Historical Methods* 22, 1 (1989): 27-35.

Molik, Witold. "Die preußische Polenpolitik im 19. und zu Beginn des 20. Jahrhunderts: Überlegungen zu Forschungsstand und – Perspektiven." In *Nationale Minderheiten und staatliche Minderheitenpolitik in Deutschland im 19. Jahrhundert,* ed. Hans Hennig Hahn and Peter Kunze. Berlin: Akademie Verlag, 1999.

Mommsen, Wolfgang J. *The Age of Bureaucracy.* Oxford: Basil Blackwell, 1974.

Monz, Leo. "Reform des Staatsangehörigkeitsrechts: Chancen für eine gleichberechtigte Zukunft aller Kinder." In *Deutsche Türken – Türkische Deutsche? Die Diskussion um die doppelte Staatsbürgerschaft,* ed. Andreas Goldberg and Faruk Şen. Münster: Lit Verlag, 1999.

Moon, Richard ed. *Law and Religious Pluralism in Canada.* Vancouver: UBC Press, 2008.

Moravcsik, Andrew. "The Origins of Human Rights Regimes: Democratic Delegation in Postwar Europe." *International Organization* 54, 2 (2000): 217-52.

Morgenstern, Christine. *Rassismus – Konturen einer Ideologie: Einwanderung im politischen Diskurs der Bundesrepublik Deutschland.* Hamburg: Argument Verlag, 2002.

Morshäuser, Bodo. *Hauptsache Deutsche*. Frankfurt am Main: Suhrkamp, 1992.

Morton, W.L. *The Canadian Identity*. Toronto: University of Toronto Press, 1965.

Mosse, George L. *Toward the Final Solution: A History of European Racism*. New York: Howard Fertig, 1978.

Motte, Jan, and Rainer Ohliger, eds. *Geschichte und Gedächtnis in der Einwanderungsgesellschaft: Migration zwischen historischer Rekonstruktion und Erinnerungspolitik*. Essen: Klartext, 2004.

Motte, Jan, Rainer Ohliger, Anne von Oswald, eds. *50 Jahre Bundesrepublik – 50 Jahre Einwanderung: Nachkriegsgeschichte als Migrationsgeschichte*. Frankfurt: Campus Verlag, 1999.

Mudde, Cas. *Populist Radical Right Parties in Europe*. Cambridge: Cambridge University Press, 2007.

Müller, Albert. "Der Staat soll Gastarbeitern die Einbürgerung erleichtern." *Die Welt*, April 19, 1971.

Müller, Christian. "Trauerfeiern für die Mordopfer von Solingen." *Neue Zürcher Zeitung*, June 4, 1993.

Münz, Rainer, and Ralf Ulrich. "Changing Patterns of Immigration to Germany, 1945-1995." In *Migration Past, Migration Future: Germany and the United States*, ed. Klaus J. Bade and Myron Weiner. New York: Berghahn Books, 1997.

–. "Deutschland: Rot-Grün bringt Reform des Staatsbürgerschaftsrechts, aber kein Einwanderungsgesetz." *Migration und Bevölkerung*, November 1998, 1.

Murray, Laura. "Einwanderungsland Bundesrepublik Deutschland? Explaining the Evolving Positions of German Political Parties on Citizenship Policy." *German Politics and Society* 33 (1994): 23-56.

Musch, Elisabeth. *Integration durch Konsultation? Konsensbildung in der Migrations- und Integrationspolitik in Deutschland und den Niederlanden*. Münster: Waxman, 2011.

Nagorski, Andrew, and Theresa Waldrop. "The Laws of Blood." *Newsweek*, June 14, 1993.

Naimark, Norman. *Fires of Hatred: Ethnic Cleansing in Twentieth-Century Europe*. Cambridge: Harvard University Press, 2001.

Nathans, Eli. *The Politics of Citizenship in Germany: Ethnicity, Utility and Nationalism*. Oxford: Berg, 2004.

"Neo-Nazis Hurting Economy, German Business Leaders Warn." *Globe and Mail*, June 9, 1993.

Neubach, Helmut. *Die Ausweisungen von Polen und Juden aus Preußen 1885/86*. Wiesbaden: Harrassowitz, 1967.

Neuman, Gerald L. "Immigration and Judicial Review in the Federal Republic of Germany." *New York University Journal of International Law and Politics* 23, 1 (1990): 35-86.

–. "Nationality Law in the United States and the Federal Republic of Germany: Structure and Current Problems." In *Paths toward Inclusion: The Integration of Migrants in the United States and Germany*, ed. Peter Schuck and Rainer Münz. New York: Berghahn Books, 1997.

Neumann, Sigmund. "The New Crisis Strata in German Society." In *Germany and the Future of Europe*, ed. Hans J. Morgenthau. Chicago: University of Chicago Press, 1951.

Nevitte, Neil, André Blais, Elisabeth Gidengil, Richard Johnston, and Henry Brady. "The Populist Right in Canada: The Rise of the Reform Party of Canada." In *The New Politics of the Right: Neo-Populist Parties and Movements in Established Democracies*, ed. Hans-Georg Betz and Stefan Immerfall. New York: St. Martin's Press, 1998.

Ngai, Mae M. "The Architecture of Race in American Immigration Law: A Re-examination of the Immigration Act of 1924." *Journal of American History* 86 (1999): 67-92.

"Nicht mehr Gäste, sondern Mitbürger." *Rheinische Post*, April 22, 1971.

Nock, David. "Patriotism and Patriarchs: Anglican Archbishops and Canadianization." *Canadian Ethnic Studies* 14 (1982): 85-100.

Norrie, Kenneth, and Douglas Owram. *A History of the Canadian Economy*. Toronto: Harcourt Brace Jovanovich, 1991.

Nugent, Walter. *Crossings: The Great Transatlantic Migrations, 1870-1914*. Bloomington: Indiana University Press, 1992.

O'Brien, Peter. *Beyond the Swastika*. London: Routledge, 1996.

–. "Continuity and Change in Germany's Treatment of Non-Germans." *International Migration Review* 22, 3 (1988): 109-34.

Olick, Jeffrey K. "What Does It Mean to Normalize the Past? Official Memory in German Politics since 1989." *Social Science History* 22, 4 (1998): 547-71.

"Obnoxious Regulation." *Globe and Mail*, March 23, 1948.

Oltmer, Jochen. "Migration and Public Policy in Germany, 1918-1939." In *Crossing Boundaries: The Exclusion and Inclusion of Minorities in Germany and the United States*, ed. Larry Eugene Jones. New York: Berghahn Books, 2001.

–, ed. *Migration steuern und verwalten: Deutschland vom späten 19. Jahrhundert bis zur Gegenwart*. Göttingen: V&R Unipress, 2003.

"The Opening Door." *Globe and Mail*, January 22, 1962.

O'Rourke, Kevin H., and Jeffrey G. Williamson. *Globalization and History: The Evolution of the Nineteenth-Century Atlantic Economy*. Cambridge: MIT Press, 2001.

Orren, Karen, and Stephen Skowronek. "Beyond the Iconography of Order: Notes for a New Institutionalism." In *The Dynamics of American Politics: Approaches and Interpretations*, ed. L. Dodd and C. Jillson. Boulder, CO: Westview Press, 1994.

"The Other Germans." *Times* (London), March 8, 1993.

Özcan, Veysel. "Deutschland: Einbürgerungszahlen 2002." *Migration und Bevölkerung* 6 (July/August 2003): 1-2.

Padgen, Anthony. "Human Rights, Natural Rights, and Europe's Imperial Legacy." *Political Theory* 21, 2 (2003): 171-99.

–. *Peoples and Empires: Europeans and the Rest of the World, from Antiquity to the Present*. London: Weidenfeld and Nicholson, 2001.

Pagenstecher, Cord. *Ausländerpolitik und Immigrantenidentität: Zur Geschichte der "Gastarbeit" in der Bundesrepublik.* Berlin: Dieter Bertz Verlag, 1994.

–. "Die ungewollte Einwanderung: Rotationsprinzip und Rückkehrerwartung in der deutschen Ausländerpolitik." *Geschichte in Wissenschaft und Unterricht* 46, 12 (1995): 718-37.

Pal, Leslie A. *Interests of State: The Politics of Language, Multiculturalism, and Feminism in Canada.* Montreal and Kingston: McGill-Queen's University Press, 1993.

Palmer, Howard. "Ethnicity and Politics in Canada: 1867-Present." In *From "Melting Pot" to Multiculturalism: The Evolution of Ethnic Relations in the United States and Canada,* ed. Valeria Gennaro Lerda. Rome: Bulzoni Editore, 1990.

–. *Patterns of Prejudice: A History of Nativism in Alberta.* Toronto: McClelland and Stewart, 1982.

–. "Reluctant Hosts: Anglo-Canadian Views of Multiculturalism in the Twentieth Century." In *Immigration in Canada: Historical Perspectives,* ed. Gerald Tulchinsky. Toronto: Copp Longman, 1994.

Parai, Louis. "Canada's Immigration Policy, 1962-1974." *International Migration Review* 9, 4 (1975): 449-77.

"Parliament," *Globe and Mail,* October 17, 1974.

Parliament of Canada, *White Papers,* available at http://www.parl.gc.ca/.

Patrias, Carmela, and Ruth A. Frager. "'This Is Our Country, These Are Our Rights': Minorities and the Origins of Ontario's Human Rights Campaigns." *Canadian Historical Review* 82 (2001): 1-35.

Peng, Ito, and Joseph Wong. "Institutions and Institutional Purpose: Continuity and Change in East Asian Social Policy." *Politics and Society* 36, 1 (2008): 61-88.

Penniman, Howard R. *Canada at the Polls, 1979 and 1980: A Study of the General Elections.* Washington, DC: The American Enterprise Institute for Public Policy Research, 1981.

Penninx, Rinus, and Judith Roosblad. "Conclusion." In *Trade Unions, Immigration and Immigrants in Europe 1960-1993: A Comparative Study of the Actions of Trade Unions in Seven West European Countries,* ed. Rinus Penninx and Judith Roosblad. New York: Berghahn Books, 2000.

Perkins, J.A. "The Agricultural Revolution in Germany, 1850-1914." *Journal of European Economic History* 10 (1981): 71-118.

Perreaux, Les. "Quebec's View on Niqab Creates Fault Line." *Globe and Mail,* March 19, 2010.

Peterson, William. *Planned Migration.* Berkeley: University of California Press, 1955.

Petras, Elizabeth. "The Role of National Boundaries in a Cross-National Labour Market." *International Journal of Urban and Regional Research* 4, 2 (1980): 157-94.

Petty, Terrence. "Kohl Accuses Countrymen of Coldness toward Foreigners." *Associated Press,* June 17, 1993.

Phillips, Donald G. *Post-National Patriotism and the Feasibility of Post-National Community in United Germany.* Westport, CT: Praeger, 2000.

Pickersgill, J.W. *The Road Back: By a Liberal in Opposition.* Toronto: University of Toronto Press, 1986.

Pieper, Alfons. "FDP warnt scharf vor Senkung des Nachzugs-Alters. Hirsch: Zimmermanns Plan unmenschlich." *Westdeutsche Allgemeine Zeitung,* January 3, 1988.

Pierson, Paul. "Increasing Returns, Path Dependence, and the Study of Politics." *American Political Science Review* 94, 2 (2000): 251-67.

–. "Not Just What, But *When*: Timing and Sequence in Political Processes." *Studies in American Political Development* 14 (2000): 72-92.

–. "Public Policies as Institutions." In *Rethinking Political Institutions: The Art of the State,* ed. Ian Shapiro, Stephen Skowronek, and Daniel Galvin. New York: New York University Press, 2006.

–. "When Effect Becomes Cause: Policy Feedback and Political Change." *World Politics* 45, 4 (1993): 595-628.

Polanyi, Karl. *The Great Transformation: The Political and Economic Origins of Our Time.* Boston: Beacon Press, 1957.

Prantl, Heribert. *Deutschland – leicht entflammbar: Ermittlung gegen die Bonner Politik.* Munich: Carl Hanser Verlag, 1994.

–. "Juristische Zeugung deutschähnlicher Kinder." *Süddeutsche Zeitung,* November 14, 1994.

–. "Wie Liechtenstein, San Marino und Luxemburg." *Süddeutsche Zeitung,* January 4, 1999.

Presse- und Informationsamt der Bundesregierung. "Erklärung der Bundesregierung zur aktuellen Lage der deutsch-türkischen Beziehungen, Bekämpfung von Gewalt und Extremismus sowie zu Maßnahmen für eine verbesserte Integration der Ausländer in Deutschland." *Bulletin* (Bonn), June 18, 1993.

–. "Trauer um die Opfer des Brandschlages von Solingen." *Bulletin* (Bonn), June 9, 1993.

Price, Charles A. *The Great White Walls Are Built: Restrictive Immigration to North America and Australia.* Canberra: Australian National University Press, 1972.

Pruys, Karl Hugo. "Ausländerpolitik – Züundstoff für 1982." *Münchner Merkur,* January 20, 1982.

Przeworski, Adam. "Methods of Cross-National Research, 1970-1983: An Overview." In *Comparative Policy Research: Learning from Experience,* ed. Meinolf Dierkes, Hans N. Weiler, and Ariane Berthoin Antal. Brookfield, VT: Gower, 1987.

"Questions." *Globe and Mail,* November 5, 1963.

Ramelsberger, Annette. "Mit Schily könnte man sich in drei Monaten einigen: Bayerns Innenminister Beckstein (CSU) geht auf Annäherungskurs zur Bundesregierung – und die CDU auch." *Süddeutsche Zeitung,* October 24, 2000.

–. "Stoiber fordert Verschärfung des Asylrechts." *Süddeutsche Zeitung,* November 18-19, 2000.

"Rat der Evangelischen Kirche warnt vor Abschottung gegenüber Fremden." *Frankfurter Allgemeine Zeitung,* March 1, 1993.

Räthzel, Nora. "Germany: One Race, One Nation." *Race and Class* 32, 3 (1991): 31-48.

Rauscher, Hans Dieter. "Deutsches Staatsangehörigkeitsrecht – Gesetzliche Grundlagen und Rechtsprechung zur Einbürgerung." In *Aufenthalt – Niederlassung – Einbürgerung*, ed. Klaus Barwig, Klaus Lörcher, and Christoph Schumacher. Baden-Baden: Nomos Verlagsgesellschaft, 1987.

Rawls, John. *The Law of Peoples*. Cambridge: Harvard University Press, 1999.

Razack, Sherene H. *Casting Out: The Eviction of Muslims from Western Law and Politics*. Toronto: University of Toronto Press, 2008.

Rea, J.E. "My Main Line Is the Kiddies ... Make Them Good Christians and Good Canadians, Which Is the Same Thing." In *Identities: The Impact of Ethnicity on Canadian Society*, ed. Wsevolod Isajiw. Toronto: Peter Martin Associates, 1977.

"Recht absonderlich." *Der Spiegel*, May 2, 1988.

"Referendum rollt nach Bonn." *Frankfurter Rundschau*, July 2, 1993.

Reimers, David M., and Harold Troper. "Canadian and American Immigration Policy since 1945." In *Immigration, Language and Ethnicity: Canada and the United States*, ed. Barry R. Chiswick. Washington, DC: AEI Press, 1992.

Reinecke, Christiane. "Governing Aliens in Times of Upheaval: Immigration Control and Modern State Practice in Early Twentieth-Century Britain, Compared with Prussia." *International Review of Social History* 54 (2009): 39-65.

Renner, Günter. "Was ist neu am neuen Staatsangehörigkeitsrecht?" *Zeitschrift für Ausländerrecht und Ausländerpolitik* 19, 4 (1999): 154-63.

Report by the Federal Government's Commissioner for Foreigners' Affairs on the Situation of Foreigners in the Federal Republic of Germany in 1993. Bonn: Federal Government Commissioner for Foreigners' Affairs, March 1994.

Richmond, Anthony H. "The Green Paper: Reflections on the Canadian Immigration and Population Study." *Canadian Ethnic Studies* 7, 1 (1975): 5-21.

Risse, Thomas. "International Norms and Domestic Change: Arguing and Communicative Behavior in the Human Rights Arena." *Politics and Society* 27, 4 (1999): 529-59.

–. "'Let's Argue!': Communicative Action in World Politics." *International Organization* 54, 1 (2000): 1-39.

Risse, Thomas, and Kathryn Sikkink. "The Socialization of International Human Rights Norms into Domestic Practices: Introduction." In *The Power of Human Rights: International Norms and Domestic Change*, ed. Thomas Risse, Stephen C. Ropp, and Kathryn Sikkink. Cambridge and York: Cambridge University Press, 1999.

Risse, Thomas, Stephen C. Ropp, and Kathryn Sikkink, eds. *The Power of Human Rights: International Norms and Domestic Change*. Cambridge: Cambridge University Press, 1999.

Rittstieg, Helmut. "Grundzüge des Aufenthaltsrechts." In *Einwanderungsland Bundesrepublik Deutschland?* ed. Gerhard Schult. Baden-Baden: Nomos Verlaggesellschaft, 1982.

Roberts, Barbara. "Shoveling Out the 'Mutinous': Political Deportation from Canada before 1936." *Labour/Le Travail* 18 (1986): 77-110.

Römer, Gernot. "Mitbürger aus der Fremde." *Augsburger Allgemeine,* January 29, 1972.

"Rot-Grün verlagert Zuwanderungsstreit." *Frankfurter Rundschau,* May 8, 2004.

Roy, Patricia E. "Educating the 'East': British Columbia and the Oriental Question in the Interwar Years." *BC Studies* 18 (1973): 50-69.

–. *The Oriental Question: Consolidating a White Man's Province, 1914-1941.* Vancouver and Toronto: UBC Press 2003.

–. *The Triumph of Citizenship: The Japanese and Chinese in Canada, 1941-1967.* Vancouver: UBC Press, 2007.

–. *A White Man's Province: British Columbia Politicians and Chinese and Japanese Immigrants, 1858-1914.* Vancouver: UBC Press, 1989.

Rueschemeyer, Dietrich, and John D. Stephens. "Comparing Historical Sequences: A Powerful Tool for Causal Analysis." *Comparative Social Research* 17 (1997): 55-72.

Ryder, Bruce. "Racism and the Constitution: The Constitutional Fate of British Columbia Anti-Asian Immigration Legislation, 1884-1909." *Osgoode Hall Law Journal* 29 (1991): 619-76.

Safire, William. "Blood and Irony." *New York Times.* June 17, 1993.

Sammartino, Annemarie. "Culture, Belonging, and the Law: Naturalization in the Weimar Republic." In *Citizenship and National Identity in Twentieth-Century Germany,* ed. Geoff Eley and Jan Palmowski. Stanford, CA: Stanford University Press, 2008.

Sarick, Lila. "Family Immigration Faces Change: Marchi under Pressure to Restrict Reunification of Relatives." *Globe and Mail,* October 24, 1994.

Sassen, Saskia. "Commentary: The De-Nationalizing of the State and the Re-Nationalizing of Political Discourse over Immigration." In *Dialogues on Migration Policy,* ed. Marco Giugni and Florence Passy. Lanham: Lexington Books, 2006.

–. "The *de facto* Transnationalizing of Immigration Policy." In *Challenge to the Nation-State: Immigration in Western Europe and the United States,* ed. Christian Joppke. New York: Oxford University Press, 1998.

–. *Guests and Aliens.* New York: The New Press, 1999.

Satzewich, Vic. "The Canadian State and the Racialization of Caribbean Farm Labour." *Ethnic and Racial Studies* 11, 3 (1988): 282-304.

–. "Racism and Canadian Immigration Policy: The Government's View of Caribbean Migration, 1962-1966." *Canadian Ethnic Studies* 21, 1 (1989): 77-97.

–. "Racisms: The Reactions to Chinese Migrants in Canada at the Turn of the Century." *International Sociology* 4, 3 (1989): 311-27.

Schain, Martin, Aristide R. Zolberg, and Patrick Hossay, eds. *Shadows over Europe: The Development and Impact of the Extreme Right in Western Europe.* Basingstoke: Palgrave, 2002.

Scheidler, Antje. "Deutschland: Erster Entwurf eines Zuwanderungsgesetzes." *Migration und Bevölkerung* 6 (2001): 1-2.

–. "Deutschland: Kabinett verabschiedete Gesetzentwurf zu Zuwanderung und Integration." *Migration und Bevölkerung* 8 (2001): 1-2.

–. "Deutschland/USA: Ausländische Arbeitskräfte für die Computerbranche." *Migration und Bevölkerung* 2 (2000): 1.

Scheinberg, Stephen, and Ian J. Kagedan. "No Place to Call Homeland: Germany Should Amend Its Citizenship Law." *Toronto Star,* June 10, 1993.

Schiffauer, Werner, and Manuela Bojadzijev. "Es geht nicht um einen Dialog: Integrationsgipfel, Islamkonferenz und Anti-Islamismus." In *No Integration? Kulturwissenschaftliche Beiträge zur Integrationsdebatte in Europa.* Bielefeld: Transcript, 2009.

Schlötzer, Christiane. "Einwanderungsgesetz gefordert. Ministerpräsident Müller: Arbeitsmarkt nicht abschotten." *Süddeutsche Zeitung,* September 8, 2000.

–. "Merz: Deutschland braucht Einwanderung." *Süddeutsche Zeitung,* October 23, 2000.

Schmid, Klaus-Peter. "Ungeliebte Moffen." *Die Zeit,* September 17, 1993.

Schmidt, Vivian. "Discursive Institutionalism: The Explanatory Power of Ideas and Discourse." *Annual Review of Politics* 11 (2008): 303-26.

Schmidtke, Oliver. "From Taboo to Strategic Tool in Politics: Immigrants and Immigration Policies in German Party Politics." In *Germany on the Road to "Normalcy": Policies and Politics of the Red-Green Federal Government (1998-2002),* ed. Werner Reutter. Basingstoke: Plagrave Macmillan, 2004.

Schmitt-Beck, Rüdiger. "Die hessische Landtagswahl vom 7. Februar 1999: Der Wechsel nach dem Wechsel." *Zeitschrift für Parlamentsfragen* 31 (2000): 3-17.

Schönwälder, Karen. *Einwanderung und ethnische Pluralität: Politische Entscheidungen und öffentliche Debatten in Großbritannien und der Bundesrepublik von den 1950er bis zu den 1970er Jahren.* Essen: Klartext Verlag, 2001.

–. "Invited but Not Wanted? Migrants from the East in Germany, 1890-1990." In *The German Lands and Eastern Europe: Essays on the History of Their Social, Cultural and Political Relations,* ed. Roger Bartlett and Karen Schönwälder. Houndmills: Macmillan, 1999.

–. " 'Ist nur Liberalisierung Fortschritt?' Zur Entstehung des ersten Ausländergesetzes der Bundesrepublik." In *50 Jahre Bundesrepublik – 50 Jahre Einwanderung: Nachkriegsgeschichte als Migrationsgeschichte,* ed. Jan Motte, Rainer Ohliger, and Anne von Oswald. Frankfurt: Campus Verlag, 1999.

–. "Kleine Schritte, verpasste Gelegenheiten, neue Konflikte: Zuwanderungsgesetz und Migrationspolitik." *Blätter für deutsche und internationale Politik* 10 (2004): 1205-15.

–. "Migration, Refugees and Ethnic Plurality as Issues of Public and Political Debates in (West) Germany." In *Nationality and Migration in Europe,* ed. David Cesarini and Mary Fulbrook. London: Routledge, 1997.

–. " 'Persons Persecuted on Political Grounds Shall Enjoy the Right of Asylum – But Not in Our Country': Asylum Debates about Refugees in the Federal Republic of Germany." In *Refugees, Citizenship and Social Policy in Europe,* ed. Alice Bloch and Carl Levy. Houndmills: Macmillan, 1999.

–. "West German Society and Foreigners in the 1960s." In *Coping with the Nazi Past: West German Debates on Nazism and Generational Conflict, 1955-1975,* ed. Philipp Gassert and Alan E. Steinweis. New York: Berghahn Books, 2006.

–. "Why Germany's Guest Workers Were Largely Europeans: The Selective Principles of Post-War Labour Recruitment Policy." *Ethnic and Racial Studies* 27, 2 (2004): 248-65.

–. "Zu viele Ausländer in Deutschland? Zur Entwicklung ausländerfeindlicher Einstellungen in der Bundesrepublik." *Vorgänge* 4 (1991): 1-11.

–. "Zukunftsblindheit oder Steuerungsversagen? Zur Ausländerpolitik der Bundesregierung der 1960er und frühen 1970er Jahre." In *Migration steuern und verwalten*, ed. Jochen Oltmer. Göttingen: V and R Unipress, 2003.

Schröder, Gerhard. *Entscheidungen: Mein Leben in der Politik*. Hamburg: Hoffmann und Campe, 2006.

Schubert, Dirk. "Wohlstandkulis oder Mitbürger?" *Deutsche Zeitung, Christ und Welt*, October 13, 1972.

Schuck, Peter. "Immigration Law and the Problem of Community." In *Clamor at the Gates: The New American Immigration*, ed. Nathan Glazer. San Francisco: ICS Press, 1985.

Schulze, Rainer. "Growing Discontent: Relations between Native and Refugee Populations in a Rural District in Western Germany after the Second World War." *German History* 7 (1989): 332-50.

Şen, Faruk, and Andreas Goldberg. *Türken in Deutschland: Leben zwischen zwei Kulturen*. Munich: C.H. Beck, 1994.

Senders, Stefan. "Laws of Belonging: Legal Dimensions of National Inclusion in Germany." *New German Critique* 67 (1996): 147-76.

Sewell, Jr., William H. "Marc Bloch and the Logic of Comparative History." *History and Theory* 6, 2 (1967): 208-18.

Sherwell, Philip. "Kohl Continues Ambivalent Approach to Racist Surge." *Globe and Mail*, June 17, 1993.

Siddiqui, Haroon. "Siddiqui: On Multiculturalism, Harper's Got It Right." *Toronto Star*, April 16, 2011.

Siebrecht, Valentin. "Die Gastarbeiter zum Problem." *Süddeutsche Zeitung*, August 12, 1965.

Sieveking, Klaus, ed. *Das Kommunalwahlrecht für Ausländer*. Baden-Baden: Nomos Verlag, 1989.

Sikkink, Kathryn. "The Power of Principled Ideas: Human Rights Policies in the United States and Western Europe." In *Ideas and Foreign Policy: Beliefs, Institutions, and Political Change*, ed. Judith Goldstein and Robert O. Keohane. Ithaca: Cornell University Press, 1993.

Simeon, Richard. "Studying Public Policy." *Canadian Journal of Political Science* 9, 4 (1976): 548-80.

Simmons, Beth A. *Mobilizing for Human Rights: International Law in Domestic Politics*. Cambridge: Cambridge University Press, 2009.

Skocpol, Theda, and Margaret Somers. "The Uses of Comparative History in Macrosocial Inquiry." *Comparative Studies in Society and History* 22, 2 (1980): 174-97.

Skrentny, John D. *The Minority Rights Revolution*. Cambridge: Harvard University Press, 2002.

Small, Joan. "Multiculturalism, Equality, and Canadian Constitutionalism: Cohesion and Difference." In *Multiculturalism and the Canadian Constitution*, ed. Stephen Tierney. Vancouver: UBC Press, 2007.

Smedley, Audrey. *Race in North America: Origin and Evolution of a Worldview.* Boulder: Westview Press, 1993.

Smiley, Donald V. "Canada and the Quest for a National Policy." *Canadian Journal of Political Science* 3, 1 (1975): 40-62.

Smith, Miriam. "Diversity and Canadian Political Development: Presidential Address to the Canadian Political Science Association, May 27, 2009." *Canadian Journal of Political Science*, 42, 4 (2009): 847-49.

Smith, Rogers. *Civic Ideals: Conflicting Visions of Citizenship in US History.* New Haven: Yale University Press, 1997.

–. "Beyond Tocqueville, Myrdal, and Hartz: The Multiple Traditions in America." *American Political Science Review* 87, 2 (1993): 549-66.

Soehlne, Dorothee. "Probleme schon auf dem Schulweg." *Der Tagesspiegel,* August 25, 1974.

"Sollen Gastarbeiter Deutsche werden?" *Quick,* April 28, 1971.

Söllner, Alfons. "Die Änderung des Grundgesetzes wäre nichts als blanker Zynismus." *Frankfurter Rundschau,* August 6, 1986.

Solomos, John, and Les Black. *Racism and Society.* Houndmills: Macmillan, 1996.

Sommerfeld, Franz ed. *Der Moscheestreit: Eine examplarische Debatte über Einwanderung und Integration.* Cologne: Kiepenheuer and Witsch, 2008.

"South Africa Out of the Commonwealth." CBC Television News. December 27, 1961, available at http://archives.cbc.ca/.

Soysal, Yasemin Nuhoğlu. "Changing Citizenship in Europe: Remarks on Postnational Membership and the National State." In *Citizenship, Nationality and Migration in Europe*, ed. David Ceasarini and Mary Fulbrook. London and New York: Routledge, 1996.

–. *Limits of Citizenship: Migrants and Postnational Membership in Europe.* Chicago: University of Chicago Press, 1994.

"SPD-Vorstoß zur Erleichterung der Einbürgerung." *Süddeutsche Zeitung,* February 3, 1993.

Spies, Ulrich. *Ausländerpolitik und Integration.* Frankfurt am Main: Peter Lang, 1982.

Staeck, Klaus, and Inge Karst, eds. *Macht Ali deutsches Volk kaputt?* Göttingen: Steidl Verlag, 1982.

Steinert, Johannes-Dieter. *Migration und Politik: Westdeutschland – Europa – Übersee 1945-1961.* Osnabrück: Secolo Verlag, 1995.

Steinmo, Sven. *Taxation and Democracy.* New Haven: Yale University Press, 1993.

Stepan, Nancy. *The Idea of Race in Science.* Hamden, CT: Archon Books, 1982.

Stinchcombe, Arthur. *Constructing Social Theories.* New York: Harcourt, Brace and World, 1968.

Stoiber, Edmund. "Ohne Änderung kein Ausweg." *Bayernkurier,* December 21, 1991.

"Stoiber kritisiert Referententwurf zum Ausländerrecht." *Frankfurter Allgemeine Zeitung,* October 28, 1989.

Stone, Lawrence. *The Past and Present Revisited*. London: Routledge and Kegan Paul, 1981.

Strong-Boag, Veronica. "'The Citizenship Debates': The 1885 Franchise Act." In *Contesting Canadian Citizenship: Historical Readings*, ed. Robert Adamoski, Dorothy E. Chunn, and Robert Menzies. Peterborough: Broadview Press, 2002.

Sunahara, Ann Gomer. *The Politics of Racism. The Uprooting of Japanese Canadians during the Second World War*. Toronto: Lorimer, 1981.

Supreme Court of Canada. *Multani v. Commission scolaire Marguerite-Bourgeoys* (2006) 1 S.C.R. 256.

Swidler, Ann. "Culture in Action." *American Sociological Review* 51, 2 (1986): 273-86.

"SZ Interview mit dem Präsidenten des Bundesverfassungsgerichts." *Süddeutsche Zeitung*, March 30, 1993.

Tebble, Adam. "Exclusion for Democracy." *Political Theory* 34, 4 (2006): 463-87.

Tichenor, Daniel. *Dividing Lines: The Politics of Immigration Control in America*. Princeton: Princeton University Press, 2002.

Thelen, Kathleen. "How Institutions Evolve." In *Comparative Historical Analysis in the Social Sciences*, ed. James Mahoney and Dietrich Rueschemeyer. Cambridge: Cambridge University Press, 2003.

Thelen, Kathleen, and Sven Steinmo. "Historical Institutionalism in Comparative Politics." In *Structuring Politics: Historical Institutionalism in Comparative Analysis*, ed. Sven Steinmo, Kathleen Thelen, and Frank Longstreth. Cambridge: Cambridge University Press, 1992.

Thompson, Debra. "Seeing Like a Racial State: The Census and the Politics of Race in the United States, Great Britain and Canada." PhD diss., University of Toronto, 2010.

Thompson, John Herd. *Ethnic Minorities during Two World Wars*. Ottawa: Canadian Historical Association, 1991.

Thompson, John Herd, and Stephen J. Randall. *Canada and the United States: Ambivalent Allies*. Athens, GA: University of Georgia Press, 1994.

Thompson, John Herd, and Morton Weinfeld. "Entry and Exit: Canadian Immigration Policy in Context." *The Annals of the American Academy of Political and Social Science* 538 (March 1995): 185-98.

Thränhardt, Dietrich. "Ausländer als Objekt deutscher Interessen und Ideologien." In *Der gläserne Fremde*, ed. Hartmut M. Griese. Opladen: Leske and Budrich, 1984.

–. "Die Bundesrepublik Deutschland – ein unerklärtes Einwanderungsland." *Aus Politik und Zeitgeschichte* 24 (1988): 3-13.

–. "Germany: An Undeclared Immigration Country." In *Europe: A New Immigration Continent – Policies and Politics in Comparative Perspective*, ed. Dietrich Thränhardt. Münster: Lit Verlag, 1992.

Tienhaara, Nancy. *Canadian Views on Immigration and Population*. Ottawa: Department of Manpower and Immigration, 1974.

Tilly, Charles. *Big Structures, Large Processes, Huge Comparisons*. New York: Russell Sage Foundation, 1984.

–. "Why and How History Matters." In *The Oxford Handbook of Contextual Political Analysis*, ed. Robert Goodin and Charles Tilly. Oxford: Oxford University Press, 2006.

Timlin, Mabel. "Canada's Immigration Policy, 1896-1910." *Canadian Journal of Economics and Political Science* 26, 4 (1960): 517-32.

Torpey, John. *The Invention of the Passport*. New York: Cambridge University Press, 2000.

–. "Making Whole What Has Been Smashed: Reflections on Reparations." *Journal of Modern History* 73, 2 (2001): 333-58.

–. "States and the Regulation of Migration in the Twentieth-Century North Atlantic World." In *The Wall around the West: State Borders and Immigration Controls in North America and Europe*, ed. Peter Andreas and Timothy Snyder. Lanham: Rowman and Littlefield, 2000.

"Touchy Race Question Delicately Handled." *Globe and Mail*, February 4, 1975.

Triadafilopoulos, Triadafilos. "Illiberal Means to Liberal Ends? Understanding Recent Immigrant Integration Policies in Europe." *Journal of Ethnic and Migration Studies* 37, 6 (2011): 861-80.

Triadafilopoulos, Triadafilos, Anna Korteweg, and Paulina Garcia Del Moral. "The Benefits and Limits of Pragmatism: Immigrant Integration Policy and Social Cohesion in Germany." In *Diverse Nations, Diverse Responses: Approaches to Social Cohesion in Immigrant Societies*, ed. Paul Spoonley and Erin Tolley. Montreal and Kingston: McGill-Queen's University Press, forthcoming.

Tribe, Keith. "Introduction to Weber." *Economy and Society* 8, 2 (1979): 172-76.

Troper, Harold. "Canada's Immigration Policy since 1945." *International Journal* 48 (1993): 255-81.

–. "The Creek-Negroes of Oklahoma and Canadian Immigration, 1909-1911." *Canadian Historical Review* 53, 3 (1972): 272-88.

–. "The Historical Context for Citizenship Education in Urban Canada." In *Citizenship in Transformation in Canada*, ed. Yvonne M. Hébert. Toronto: University of Toronto Press, 2002.

–. *Only Farmers Need Apply: Official Canadian Government Encouragement of Immigration from the United States, 1896-1911*. Toronto: Griffin House, 1972.

Truesdell, Leon E. *The Canadian-Born in the United States, 1865-1930*. New Haven, CT: Yale University Press, 1943.

Trumbull, Robert. "Canada Tightens Rules Covering Immigrant Flow." *New York Times*, October 23, 1974.

Tsapanos, Georgios. "Was heißt denn hier Fremd? Staatsangehörigkeit zwischen Ethnizität – Identität – Nationalität." In *Staatsbürgerschaft in Europa: Historische Erfahrungen und aktuelle Debatten*, ed. Christoph Conrad and Jürgen Kocka. Hamburg: Edition Körber Stiftung, 2001.

Tsebelis, George. "Decision Making in Political Systems: Veto Players in Presidentialism, Parliamentarism, Multicameralism, and Multipartyism." *British Journal of Political Science* 25 (1995): 289-325.

Tyner, James A. "The Geopolitics of Eugenics and the Exclusion of Phillipine Immigrants from the United States." *Geographical Review* 89, 1 (1999): 54-73.

"Über 20 000 Demonstraten gegen neues Ausländergesetz." *Deutsche Presse-Agentur*, April 1, 1990.

Uberoi, Varun. "Multiculturalism and the Canadian Charter of Rights and Freedoms." *Political Studies* 57, 4 (2008): 805-27.

Ulrich, Key L. "Was soll aus den Gastarbeitern werden?" *Frankfurter Allgemeine Zeitung*, May 25, 1973.

"Unfairness to Chinese." *Ottawa Citizen*, February 17, 1948.

"Unsere Meinung: Ausländer-Polizeiverordnung." *Der Tagesspiegel*, January 7, 1960.

"Verbesserung des Aufenthaltsrechts zum Schutz ausländischer Mitbürger." *EPD Dokumentation*, March 6, 1978.

Vertovec, Steven, and Susanne Wessendorf. "Introduction: Assessing the Backlash against Multiculturalism in Europe." In *The Multiculturalism Backlash: European Discourses, Policies and Practices*, ed. Steven Vertovec and Susanne Wessendorf. New York: Routledge, 2010.

Vetter, Ernst Günter. "Der Arbeitsmarkt vor einer neuen Zerreißprobe." *Frankfurter Allgemeine Zeitung*, April 13, 1962.

Veugelers, Jack W.P. "State-Society Relations in the Making of Canadian Immigration Policy during the Mulroney Era." *Canadian Review of Sociology and Anthropology* 37, 1 (2000): 95-110.

Vincent, R.J. "Racial Equality." In *The Expansion of International Society*, ed. Hedley Bull and Adam Watson. Oxford: Clarendon Press, 1984.

"Vom Gastarbeiter zum Stammarbeiter." *Frankfurter Allgemeine Zeitung*, September 5, 1966.

von Dirke, Sabine. "Multikulti: The German Debate on Multiculturalism." *German Studies Review* 17 (1994): 513-36.

von Oswald, Anne, Karen Schönwälder, and Barbara Sonnenberger. "*Einwanderungsland Deutschland*: A New Look at Its Post-War History." In *European Encounters: Migrants, Migration and European Societies since 1945*, ed. Rainer Ohliger, Karen Schönwälder, and Triadafilos Triadafilopoulos. Aldershot: Ashgate, 2003.

–. "Labour Migration, Immigration Policy, Integration: Reinterpreting West Germany's History?" Paper presented at conference entitled "Assimilation, Diasporization, and Representation: Historical Perspectives on Immigrants and Host Societies in Postwar Europe, Berlin, October, 2000.

"Von Weizsaecker Calls for Easier Naturalization Laws." *Agence France Presse*, December 24, 1992.

Walker, James W. St. G. "The 'Jewish Phase' in the Movement for Racial Equality in Canada." *Canadian Journal of Ethnic Studies* 34, 1 (2002): 1-29.

–. *"Race," Rights and the Law in the Supreme Court of Canada: Historical Case Studies*. Waterloo: Wilfrid Laurier University Press, 1997.

Wallace, Kenyon. "Liberals Crushed in GTA." *Toronto Star*, May 3, 2011.

Walzer, Michael. "The Distribution of Membership." In *Boundaries: National Autonomy and Its Limits*, ed. Peter G. Brown and Henry Shue. Totowa, NJ: Rowman and Littlefield, 1981.

–. *Spheres of Justice: A Defense of Pluralism and Equality*. New York: Basic Books, 1983.

Ward, Peter. *White Canada Forever: Popular Attitudes and Public Policy toward Orientals in British Columbia*. Montreal and Kingston: McGill-Queen's University Press, 1978.

Watson, Alan. "Germany Needs a Passport to Peace." *Independent* (London), June 3, 1993.

Wayland, Sarah. "Immigration, Multiculturalism and National Identity in Canada." *International Journal on Minority and Group Rights* 5 (1997): 33-58.

Weber, Max. "Developmental Tendencies in the Situation of East Elbian Rural Labourers." *Economy and Society* 8 (1979): 177-205.

−. "The National State and Economic Policy." In *Reading Weber*, ed. Keith Tribe, trans. Ben Faukes. London: Routledge, 1989.

Weber, Rolf. "Die BRD ist kein Einwanderungland." *Handelsblatt*, November 12-13, 1971.

−. "Einwanderungsland?" *Der Arbeitgeber*, August 1965.

−. "Rotation, Integration und Folgelasten." *Arbeit und Sozialpolitik* 27 (1973): 203-6.

−. "Rotationsprinzip bei der Beschäftigung von Ausländern." *Auslandskurier* 11, 5 (1970): 10.

Weckbach-Mara, F. "Weizsäcker: Unterschriften-Aktion schürt Ausländer-raus-Instinkte." *Bild am Sonntag*, January 10, 1999.

Wehler, Hans-Ulrich. *Krisenherde des Kaiserreichs 1871-1918*. Göttingen: Vandenhoeck & Ruprecht, 1979.

Weil, Gordon L. "The Evolution of the European Convention on Human Rights." *American Journal of International Law* 57, 4 (1963): 804-27.

Weil, Patrick. *How to Be French: Nationality in the Making since 1789*, trans. Catherine Porter. Durham, NC: Duke University Press, 2008.

Weindling, Paul. *Health, Race and German Politics between National Unification and Nazism, 1870-1945*. Cambridge: Cambridge University Press, 1989.

Weiner, Myron. *The Global Migration Crisis*. New York: Harper Collins, 1995.

Weißmann, Günter. *Ausländergesetz: Kommentar*. Berlin: De Gruyter, 1966.

"Welche Gefahr droht uns von den Gastarbeitern?" *Quick*, September 20, 1973.

Welles, Sumner. "New Hope for the Jewish People." *The Nation*, May 5, 1945.

Wertheimer, Jack. "'The Unwanted Element': East European Jews in Imperial Germany." In *Migrations in European History I*, ed. Colin Holmes. Brookfield, VT: E. Elgar, 1996.

−. *Unwelcome Strangers: East European Jews in Imperial Germany*. New York: Oxford University Press, 1987.

"Wettrennen in Schäbigkeit. Burkhard Hirsch (FDP) und Edmund Stoiber (CSU) über das Asylrecht." *Der Spiegel*, November 5, 1990.

Whitaker, Reg. *Canadian Immigration Policy since Confederation*. Ottawa: Canadian Historical Association, 1991.

−. *Double Standard: The Secret History of Canadian Immigration*. Toronto: Letser and Orpen Dennys, 1987.

Wiener, Antje. "Contested Compliance: Interventions on the Normative Structure of World Politics." *European Journal of International Relations* 10, 2 (2004): 189-234.

Williamson, Jeffrey G. *Globalization and the Poor Periphery before 1950*. Cambridge: MIT Press, 2006.

Willinsky, John. *Learning to Divide the World: Education at Empire's End*. Minneapolis: University of Minnesota Press, 1998.

Wilsford, David. "Path Dependency, or Why History Makes It Difficult but Not Impossible to Reform Health Care Systems in a Big Way." *Journal of Public Policy* 14, 3 (1994): 251-83.

Wimmer, Andreas, and Nina Glick Schiller. "Methodological Nationalism, the Social Sciences, and the Study of Migration: An Essay in Historical Epistemology." *International Migration Review* 37, 3 (2003): 576-610.

Winsor, Hugh. "McDougall Wins Battle to Increase Immigration: Minister Sees New Source of Voters for the Conservatives." *Globe and Mail*, October 24, 1990.

Wirth, Fritz. "USA: Ende des Goodwill?" *Die Welt*, December 14, 1992.

Wittke, Thomas. "Das Auslandsbild der Deutschen is nach Mölln verheerend." *Generalanzeiger* (Bonn), December 3, 1992.

Wollny, Gunther. "Ausländer in der Bundesrepublik." *Bayern Kurier*, May 27, 1972.

Wood, John R. "East Indians and Canada's New Immigration Policy." *Canadian Public Policy* 4, 4 (1978): 547-67.

Woodsworth, Charles J. *Canada and the Orient: A Study in International Relations*. Toronto: Macmillan, 1941.

Woodsworth, J.S. *Strangers within Our Gates: Or, Coming Canadians*. Toronto: University of Toronto Press, 1972.

Worbs, Susanne. "Die Einbürgerung von Ausländern in Deutschland." BAMF Working Paper 17, Nürnberg, 2008.

Woschech, Franz. "Bald noch mehr Gastarbeiter." *Handelsblatt*, November 12, 1971.

Wüst, Andreas M. *Wie wählen Neubürger? Politische Einstellungen und Wahlverhalten eingebürgerter Personen in Deutschland*. Opladen: Leske and Budrich, 2002.

Wüstenbecker, Katja. "Hamburg and the Transit of East European Emigrants." In *Migration Control in the North Atlantic World: The Evolution of State Practices in Europe and North America from the French Revolution to the Inter-War Period*, ed. Andreas Fahrmeir, Olivier Faron, and Patrick Weil. New York: Berghahn Books, 2003.

Xenos, Nicholas. "Nation, State and Economy: Max Weber's Freiburg Inaugural Lecture." In *Reimagining the Nation*, ed. Marjorie Ringrose and Adam J. Lerner. Buckingham: Open University Press, 1993.

"Zahl der Gastarbeiter ging um 24.5% zurück." *Bulletin der Bundesregierung*, March 21, 1968.

Zeitlmann, Wolfgang. "Wir bekommen zweierlei Deutsche." *Die Welt*, January 13, 1999.

Zentrum für Türkeistudien, ed. *Das Bild der Ausländer in der Öffentlichkeit: eine theoretische und empirische Analyse zur Fremdenfeindlichkeit*. Opladen: Leske and Budrich, 1995.

"'Zimmermann gefährdet Bonns Ansehen': Die FDP will in der Ausländerpolitik nicht zurückweichen." *Frankfurter Allgemeine Zeitung*, September 5, 1984.

"'Zimmermann spielt Rechtsradikalen in die Hände.'" *Saarbrücker Zeitung*, March 1, 1989.

"Zimmermann will Ausländerrecht in diesem Jahr ändern." *Frankfurter Allgemeine Zeitung*, October 3, 1987.

Zlotnik, Hania. "International Migration 1965-96: An Overview." *Population and Development Review* 24 (1998): 429-68.

Zolberg, Arisitde R. "Are the Industrial Countries under Siege?" In *Migration Policies in Europe and the United States*, ed. Giacomo Luciani. Dordrecht: Kluwer Academic Publishers, 1993.

–. "Beyond the Nation-State: Comparative Politics in a Global Perspective." In *Beyond Progress and Development*, ed. J. Berting and W. Blockmans. Aldershot: Gower Publishing, 1987.

–. "Bounded States in a Global Market: The Uses of International Labor Migrations." In *Social Theory for a Changing Society*, ed. Pierre Bourdieu and James S. Coleman. New York/Boulder: Russell Sage Foundation/Westview Press, 1991.

–. "Contemporary Transnational Migrations in Historical Perspective: Patterns and Dilemmas." In *US Immigration and Refugee Policy: Domestic and Global Issues*, ed. Mary M. Kritz. Lexington, MA: Lexington Books, 1983.

–. "The Dawn of Cosmopolitan Denizenship." *Indiana Journal of Global Legal Studies* 7, 2 (2000): 511-18.

–. "Dilemmas at the Gate: The Politics of Immigration in Advanced Industrial Societies." Paper presented at the 1982 meeting of the American Political Science Association.

–. "The Exit Revolution." In *Citizenship and Those Who Leave: The Politics of Emigration and Expatriation*, ed. Nancy L. Green and François Weil. Urbana and Chicago: Illinois University Press, 2007.

–. "Global Movements, Global Walls: Responses to Migration, 1885-1925." In *Global History and Migrations*, ed. Wang Gungwu. Boulder, CO: Westview Press, 1997.

–. "International Migration Policies in a Changing World System." In *Human Migration: Patterns and Policies*, ed. William H. McNeill and Ruth S. Adams. Bloomington: Indiana University Press, 1978.

–. "International Migrations in Political Perspective." In *Global Trends in Migration: Theory and Research on International Population Movements*, ed. Mary M. Kritz, Charles B. Keely, and Silvano M. Tomasi. New York: Center for Migration Studies, 1981.

–. "The Main Gate and the Back Door: The Politics of American Immigration Policy, 1950-1976." Unpublished manuscript, Council on Foreign Relations, 1978.

–. "A Nation by Design: Immigration Policy in the Fashioning of America." Paper presented at the 2002 meeting of the American Political Science Association.

–. *A Nation by Design: Immigration Policy in the Fashioning of America*. New York/ Cambridge, MA: Russell Sage Foundation/Harvard University Press, 2006.

–. "The Politics of Immigration Policy: An Externalist Perspective." In *Immigration Research for a New Century*, ed. Nancy Foner, Rubén G. Rumbaut, and Steven J. Gold. New York: Russell Sage Foundation, 2000.

–. "Wanted but Not Welcome: Alien Labor in Western Development." In *Population in an Interacting World*, ed. William Alonso. Cambridge: Harvard University Press, 1987.

Zolberg, Aristide, R., with the assistance of Ursula Levelt. "Response to Crisis: Refugee Policy in the United States and Canada." In *Immigration, Language, and Ethnicity: Canada and the United States*, ed. Barry R. Chiswick. Washington, DC: AEI Press, 1992.

Zolf, Larry. "Boil Me No Melting Pots." In *Canada: A Guide to the Peaceable Kingdom*, 2nd ed., ed. William Kilbourn. Toronto: Macmillan, 1975.

Zuleeg, Manfred. "Entwicklung und Stand des Ausländerrechts in der Bundesrepublik Deutschland." *Zeitschrift für Ausländerrecht* 2 (1984): 80-87.

"Zuwanderung von Ausländern abwehren." *Der Spiegel*, April 18, 1988.

Index

Printed and bound in Canada by Friesens

Set in Futura Condensed and Warnock by Artegraphica Design Co. Ltd.

Copy editor: Joanne Richardson

Proofreader: Dianne Tiefensee

Indexer: Annette Lorek